The First Week in August

Fifty Years of the Sidmouth Festival

The First Week in August

Fifty Years of the Sidmouth Festival

Derek Schofield

Sidmouth International Festival

Published by
Sidmouth International Festival Ltd
PO Box 296
Matlock
Derbyshire
DE4 3XU
UK

Tel: 01629 827012
Fax: 01629 821874
Email: info@sidmouthfestival.com

Website: www.sidmouthfestival.com

ISBN 0-9547502-0-9

British Library Cataloguing in Publication Data
A catalogue record for this book is available from the British Library.

Design by Rockford Graphics
Littledown Lane
Newton Poppleford
Devon EX10 0BG
Tel: 01395 567466
jd@rockfordgraphics.co.uk

Printed by BemroseBooth (Derby) Ltd. Tel: 01332 294242

For continuing information about the Sidmouth International Festival contact
Leisure and Lifestyles Department
East Devon District Council
The Knowle
Sidmouth
Devon EX10 8HL

Front cover photograph: Gordon Read
Back cover photographs from top:
1 Jason Locke, 2 & 3 Derek Schofield, 4 Yolande Kortlever,
5 Ron Hill, 6 Andrea Holland

Contents

Acknowledgements

I am grateful to Malcolm Taylor of the Vaughan Williams Memorial Library of the English Folk Dance and Song Society for allowing me access to the archives of the Sidmouth International Festival held by the Library, and for other assistance; to the staff of Sidmouth Museum for allowing me access to back copies of the *Sidmouth Herald;* and to the staff of Mrs Casey Music.

In listing all the people whose letters, emails, phone calls, messages and conversations have been used in writing the book, I am bound to miss someone out, so my apologies if your name is not mentioned here, but should be.

John Adams, Ian Anderson, Ian Ankers, Erica Archer, Frankie Armstrong, Gavin Atkin, Mike Bailey, Roy Bailey, Alan Barber, Les and Janet Barclay, Michael Barraclough, Alvin Barrett, Gerry Bates, Alan Bearman, Brian Bell, Mike Bettison, Bob Blair, Peter Boyce, Jim and Georgina Boyes, John Braithwaite, Richard and Pat Brecknock, Jane Brenner, Jon Brenner, Gill Brice, John and Mary Brock, Duncan Broomhead, Dave and Jenifer Broughton, Tom Brown, Antony Brunt, Iain Bryden, John Burgess, Paul Burgess, Sue Burgess, Sue Burnett, Simon Care, Val Carman, Eliza Carthy, Martin Carthy, Richard Carver, Alan and Iris Casey, Steve Cates, Keith Chandler, Bernie Cherry, Pete Civico, Bert Cleaver, Chris Coe, Pete Coe, Mike Coleman, Shirley Collins, Bob and Pam Common, John Conolly, Trevor and Chris Cook, Muriel Cope, Kirsty Cotter, Rosie Cross, Jeff Dando, Janet Dashwood, Louisa Davies, Phil Davies,

Tony Day, Jim Dewar, Roy Dommett, John and Mandy Dowell, Janet Dowling, Maurice Dunsford, Roger Edwards, Alison Ellacott, Martin Ellison, Mark Emerson, Molly Evans, Margaret Evis, Tim van Eyken, Bob and Margaret Fagan, James Fagan, Ian Ferguson, Mark 'Gaffer' Ferris, Kerry Fletcher, John Foreman, John Forrest, Ricky Forster, Tony Foxworthy, George Frampton, Fi Fraser, Ruth Fraser, Jo Freya, Vin Garbutt, Keith Glover, Marianne Glover, Tristan Glover, John Goddard, Sean Goddard, Pamela Gold, Great Western Morris, Margaret Guest, Sheila Guest, Jack Hamilton, Johnny Handle, Jeannie Harris, Rolf Harris, Roy Harris, Sue Harris, Derek Harrison, Jennie Hawes, Bob Hawkes, Alistair Hay, Colin Healey, Steve Heap, Lawrence Heath, Seamus Heffernan, John Heydon, John Hill, Nicholas Hill, Rhona Hitchcock, Pat Hoban, Andrea Holland, Helen Holt, Jenny Howard, John and Katie Howson, Dave Hunt, Geoff Hughes, Ashley Hutchings, Paul Hutchinson, Mike Jackson, Chris Jaycott, Bill Jones, Brian Jones, Cyril Jones, Griff Jones, Robin Jowett, Beryl Jukes, Keith Kendrick, Nancy Kerr, Sandra Kerr, Bill and Barbara Kinsman, Sid Kipper, John Kirkpatrick, Mandy Lang, Sandra Lang, Ken Langsbury, Ray and Bev Langton, Peter and Lyn Law, Tim Laycock, Barry Lister, Sid Long, Dave Longly, Sheila Mainwaring, Denis Manners, Nibs Matthews, Roger and Beryl Marriott, Paul Marsh, Colin and Mary Mayfield, Mel McClellan, Mac McCulloch, John McDonald, Alison McMorland, Mary Meeks, Ann Mettam, David Mills, Pat Mitchell, Jim

Moray, Clive Morgan, Becky Morris, Nita Mulford, Martin Nail, Roger and Daphne Nicholls, Jane Oates, Gary and Carolyn O'Mahoney, Baz Parkes, John Parsons, Jacquie Patten, Derek Pearce, Marion Percy, Bob Perry, Martyn and Penny Perryman, Eileen Phelan, Nick Pilley, Chris Pitt, Ted and Ivy Poole, Gordon Potts, Mike Price, Abigail Reid, Derek and Pippa Reid, Rachel Reid, Dan Quinn, Kat Radford, Mikey Radford, Lynne Render, Tubby and Betty Reynolds, Hugh Rippon, Kath Roberts, Tony and Pauline Roberts, Chris and Tracey Rose, Dave Rose, Kate Rose, Megan Rose, Ron Rudd, Keith Rusby, Terry Rutter, Patrick Ryan, Bonny Sartin, Mary-Jo Searle, Paddy Searle, Jean Seymour, Tim Shardlow, David and Eva Sharp, Jenny Shotliff, Kevin Sheils, Pete Shutler, Lester Simpson, David and Kirsten Slater, Greg and Kay Smallbone, Josh, Todd, Willow and Zach Smallbone, Ron Smedley, Viv Smith, Chris Sugden, Pel and Lyn Squance, Dick Stanger, Ted Stevens, Brian Stone, Rod and Danny Stradling, George Stuart, Douglas Swift, Laurel Swift, Sue and John Swift, June Tabor, John Tams, Taz Tarry, Cyril and Rosemary Tawney, Malcolm Taylor, Ian Telfer, Taffy and Chrissie Thomas, Sam Thomas, Pippa Todd, Andy Turner, Jean Turner, Eddie Upton, Kitty Vernon, Margaret and Peter Vipond, Norma Waterson, Roger Watson, Frances Watt, Sally Wearing, Peta Webb, Paul Weir, Rees Wesson, Alex West, Bob West, Alan White, Tony Wiggins, Christine Williams, Julie Williams, Aileen Wills, Heather Wood, Rollo Woods.

Foreword
Martin Carthy MBE
Festival Patron

On the fiftieth anniversary of the oldest and longest running Festival in the country it really is most appropriate to take a look back over the years to show just how and by how much this Festival has changed as it has grown.

From its beginnings as a small, mostly voluntary and largely dance-orientated West Country affair, it has grown into an enormous and truly international undertaking featuring dance and song, amateur and professional in pretty equal measure. There have been memorable performances over the years when audience and artists alike have been privileged to see and hear some of the very greatest performers of traditional dance and song from all over the world on large stages and on small.

I suppose I have my own stories to tell as (I'm sure) has everyone else who has ever worked there for the week. Mine include the 'gunslinger' who in 1969 inveigled his way on to the stage at the Beach Store to try to outpace Dave Swarbrick in public and humiliate him. And who was by Swarb dispatched with an efficiency and an aplomb which took my breath away. To say nothing of the other bloke's.

Then in the 1990s, and on the much more positive side, there was the sheer pleasure of reminding the great Packie Byrne of a tune which he had taught Swarb and myself in the 1960s and which had slipped his mind in the intervening thirty years. The look of delight on his face will live with me.

For our family the week is topped and tailed by the excitement of heading South knowing that what we are going to see and hear will include some examples of just how beautiful the dance and song of ordinary people(s) can be, and of standing on the last night with a lump in our collective throat as the torches are doused in the sea signalling again that the Festival is done for another year.

The dynamic of which the present Festival itself is possessed has not appeared as if by magic but was sought out by Alan Bearman and Steve Heap, the current Festival organisers, and is nurtured by them assiduously. It's a dynamic which has clearly prevented it from standing still for long enough ever to become stuck in the cultural mud. The legendary Beach Store may be long gone but The Volunteer and divers other sessions live. Plus ça change mais plus c'est la meme chose? Perhaps yes, but only because what endures does so because the Festival organisers have seen to it that there exists an environment where the individual may prosper in the middle of the highly organised week which is Sidmouth. A Sidmouth which now consists of at least half a dozen Festivals all running at the same time mixing dance with song, small with large and amateur with professional in a way Bill Rutter could only have dreamed of.

And perhaps he did.

Sponsors and Supporters

The publisher is grateful to the following individuals and organisations for their financial support of this publication:

Angela Ball, Swansea
Shirley Beck, Taunton
John, Sheila and Sarah Bentham, Loughborough
City Clickers, Bristol
Trevor Coucill, Southampton
Jenepher J. Parry Davies, Southampton
Sandra Derrick, Portishead, Avon
Roger Edwards, Whittle-le-Woods, Lancashire
Chris Foren, Bedford
John Heydon, Aylesbury
Colin Healey, Sidmouth
Peter and Chris Knight, Reading
Ray and Bev Langton, Wem, Shropshire
Peter and Lyn Law, Chester
Musicians' Union
Marion Percy, Malvern, Worcestershire
Bob Perry, Eastbourne
Anna Philpott, Bath
Janet Purdy, Bedford
David and Sheila Rabson, Wellington, Somerset
John Richardson-Dawes, Exeter
Chris Rothwell, Sutton Coldfield, West Midlands
Ron Rudd, Bridgwater, Somerset
Terry Rutter, Clyst Hydon, Devon
Sidmouth Steppers North-West Morris
Peter Simpson, London
Rosemary Sowden, Sidmouth
Jean Turner and Andy Turner, Ashford, Kent
Aukje van Heerdt, The Netherlands
Christine Williams, Ringwood, Hampshire in
    memory of Dave Williams

Introduction
Derek Schofield

When I wrote an article about the Sidmouth International Festival in its fortieth year, I little thought that ten years later I would be writing the history of the Festival in a book-length format.

It has been my considerable pleasure, not only to have attended and contributed to the Sidmouth International Festival most years since 1971, but also to have shared the memories and impressions of dozens and dozens of fellow festival-goers in the preparation of this book.

The Sidmouth International Festival is, I believe, unique, certainly within the world of folk and roots music, but also within the wider arts community.

It was Nibs Matthews and his early colleagues who identified the potential of the location. But it was Bill Rutter who took the small-scale dance festival and truly made it the international event that it has now become. It was his liberal attitude, his desire to encourage young people – to give them their head and develop their interest – his concern for the beginner as much as, if not more than, the 'expert'. And above all, his humanity, his passionate belief in promoting love for his fellow human beings, respect for their traditions, peace and co-operation. He was a great enthusiast, and had a great ability to enthuse others and to help them develop, and they responded by offering to help others in return.

These values so underlined the basis of the Festival that they had become the natural way of doing things by the time Bill retired in 1979, and his successor John Dowell became Festival Director.

When a different organisation took over the Festival in 1987, those principles were maintained and they have been the basis of Steve Heap's strategic development and Alan Bearman's artistic direction.

There is another reason why the Festival is unique, and that lies in the town of Sidmouth itself. There is no doubt that Sidmouth is one of the most beautiful towns in Devon. The rich, red sandstone cliffs that 'hug you in', giving an 'intimacy not found elsewhere', as Mary Mayfield remarked to me. The unspoilt nature of the town has engendered a passionate defence amongst its residents to resist dramatic modern development, and it is a cause that finds ready support from visitors to the town, the festival-goers amongst them. Arguably, the Festival has allowed the town to maintain its unique identity – without the Festival's financial boost, truly commercial interests might have imposed unwelcome changes to the town.

The festival-goers journey from all over the country – indeed from different parts of the world. For most of us, I suspect, the town of Sidmouth has, over the years, changed visually far less than our own home towns, and most of the changes that have taken place have been in response to the natural power of the sea. The visual stability must be one of the reasons why so many festival-goers refer to Sidmouth as a 'second home'. How many of us, I wonder, indulge in the same arrival ritual each year: driving past the camp-site, past the Arena, straight down to the Esplanade and then turning left to look at the red sandstone cliffs of Salcombe Hill. I thought I was the only one, but I've found out that I'm not!

The location is important, but the Festival gives us more. It is a place where friendships have been made and are renewed each year, it is a place where people have met their life partners, where they have brought their families and watched them grow. It is a place where teenagers are happy to accompany their parents and grandparents: it appears to be a truly multi-generational event.

And all of that happens against a backdrop of traditional music, dance and song, not only of our own country, but also of many different cultures and countries of the world.

The Festival gives the opportunity, not only to watch and to listen, but also to join in. As the Festival's Artistic Director Alan Bearman recognises, the distinction between performer and audience is considerably blurred – everyone wants to contribute. And this is what makes the Festival unique in the wider arts world: it is not a collection of individual events with a separation between audience and performer. It is integrated and overlapping, participatory and developmental. And it's huge fun!

For the residents of East Devon, and particularly of the town itself, the Festival is the most significant arts event of the year: it is an accessible and enriching experience. The town can now boast its own Morris dance group, the Sidmouth Steppers, as well as Scottish, American and English folk dance clubs. The Friends of Sidmouth Festival, a charitable organisation, has been able to support a number of artistic projects in the town.

The values that the Festival imparts; the quality of life afforded by the physical location; the international peace, goodwill and understanding promoted by the event; the promotion of our own traditional folk culture for the present and future and the appreciation of the music and dance of other cultures and communities. All of these are very powerful and are the reasons why the Sidmouth Festival should never be lost.

Elsewhere, I acknowledge the many people who have given me assistance in writing this book. Here I should like to thank some of the people who have most closely shared the process of research and writing.

Firstly, I should like to thank Steve Heap for giving me the opportunity to write this book. I am sure that neither of us knew what we were letting ourselves in for late in the last century, when he asked and I accepted the challenge.

The task of turning written text into this finished publication could not have been accomplished without the assistance of the designer, John Dowell. As a former Festival Director, still living just outside Sidmouth, John's considerable knowledge of the event and the town, as well as his professional expertise have been invaluable. I am also grateful to John, and his wife Mandy, for their kind and generous hospitality.

Several people have read and commented on drafts of the book, and have tirelessly answered my questions. In particular, I should like to mention Alan Bearman, Richard Brecknock, Gill Brice, Ray and Bev Langton, Taffy Thomas and John Kirkpatrick, as well as Steve Heap and John Dowell. Georgina Boyes proof-read the whole book. Thanks also to Tony Day and Alan White whose own publication *Where they Laugh, Drink and Sing* chronicles 25 years of the Middle Bar Singers. My thanks to them all. Any errors and omissions are, of course, mine alone.

I list the photographic credits elsewhere in this book, but I am most grateful to Elizabeth Read for giving me access to her late husband Gordon Read's collection of negatives of the first ten years of the Festival. My thanks also to Alan Gentle who loaned me a set of photographs taken of the Festival in the years 1966-1971, and to Ron Hill for photographs taken in the last few years.

Finally then, my thanks to all the people who have contributed stories and memories. I hope that you find your own stories here, but if not, then I hope you will recognise your own experiences in someone else's story.

The Folk Dance Revival

Folk Dancers at Burford – Cecil Sharp (centre), Douglas Kennedy (sitting on grass)

In the late nineteenth and early twentieth centuries, there was a determination to improve the musical life of England through the creation of a distinctly English classical music, and by changing the type of songs being sung in schools. As in other European countries, inspiration was found in traditional folk music.

Some early collections of folk music had been published by the time the Folk-Song Society was founded in 1898, but when Cecil Sharp started collecting in 1903, he popularised the use of folk songs in schools. Earlier, in 1899, Sharp had seen the Headington Quarry Morris Dancers and noted their tunes, but it was not until 1905 that the dances were performed in a new context, by the young working-class female members of the Esperance Club in London, led by Mary Neal.

By the time the English Folk Dance Society was founded in 1911, Sharp was promoting the fruits of his collecting: Morris dances from the South Midlands, sword dances from Yorkshire and the North-East, traditional social dances, and folk songs. He also re-constructed historical dances from the Playford collections, which Sharp interpreted as the original form of the social dances. So, in addition to the use of folk songs as inspiration for classical music by composers such as Ralph Vaughan Williams and George Butterworth, there was this 'first revival' of folk songs, dances and music in education, and to a new, largely middle-class, group of enthusiasts.

After Cecil Sharp's death in 1924, there was some resistance to varying Sharp's interpretations and repertoire. The Morris dance revival was in its early days, and very little Morris dancing took place outdoors, but in 1934 The Morris Ring was formed to bring together the increasing number of men's Morris

clubs. Folk song performance still owed more to classical music both in terms of context and style. Folk dance parties were held, but it was assumed that the dancers would already have learnt the dances at classes or vacation schools where dancers could extend their repertoire and thence acquire the appropriate folk dance certificates.

But by the mid-1930s, the movement was ready for change. There was an increasing interest in traditional social dances (as opposed to the historical Playford repertoire) as a way of encouraging

> **The aim was to allow people to walk in off the street and take part straight away**

more people. Douglas Kennedy was crucial in encouraging this new approach: he was Sharp's successor as Director of the English Folk Dance Society, which became the English Folk Dance and Song Society (EFDSS) in 1932 when the two societies merged, but there was still some resistance to change.

The Second World War gave Douglas Kennedy the opportunity to force the pace of change. He reorganised the EFDSS to give him central control over the staff and what they taught. In order to make folk dance more accessible, he introduced the concept of the 'caller' from America to explain the dances

and he promoted folk dance bands based on his own Square Dance Band in London. He also changed the repertoire from the Playford dances, which required prior tuition, to the traditional dances, including American square dances, which could be learned by watching and copying. The aim was to allow people to walk in off the street and take part straight away. The new popularity of folk dancing was greatly helped by the Square Dance boom, which was prompted when the Queen, then Princess Elizabeth, and Prince Philip took part in a square dance in Canada in 1951.

The focus for the new approach was the Stratford-upon-Avon Festival, where folk dancers spent the mornings rehearsing for the daily performances in the Bancroft Gardens, with social gatherings in the evenings. The emphasis was on enjoyment, and on encouraging the audience members to join in. Morris and sword dance displays were given by the men: at the time, there was a common repertoire and each individual dance was performed in the same way, so that Morris men from different parts of the country could perform together. The Festival lasted two weeks and was led by EFDSS staff, although most of the dancers attended for just one week.

Folk songs were included in the activities of the EFDSS and of the Morris sides, but the 'second' folk song revival was only just starting in the early fifties.

Folk Dance in Devon in the 1950s

The Devon District was part of the South-West Area of the EFDSS, with Mrs Margaret Grant as the Area Organiser. In the ten years following the Second World War, the EFDSS staff in the Area had included at one time or another Jean Forsyth, Nibs Matthews, Ron Smedley, Peter Kennedy, Eileen Brading, Tony Foxworthy, Edith Humphreys, Eileen Gunnell and Irene Harcourt. The main aim of the staff was to promote folk dancing to the general public, including schoolchildren, and local education authorities made grants to the EFDSS for the latter. By the early 1950s, Nibs Matthews and Jean Forsyth had married and they moved to the Midland Area of the EFDSS, living in Cheltenham.

One of the events used to promote folk dance was the Whit Monday tour of Devon, led by Nibs Matthews and first held in 1949. Morris men, musicians and dancers performed in towns and villages including Branscombe, Salcombe Regis, Honiton, Beer, Seaton, Sidbury and Sidmouth.

Sidmouth was one of the stops on that first tour when an audience of hundreds watched the show and joined in the social dances. The following year there was reported to be an audience of over 1,000 holiday-makers. The performers included Nibs and Jean, Bob Rundle, Peter Fox (a vicar in nearby Exmouth), Dick Witt and Wyn Humphreys. In 1952 there was Morris and country dancing in the Connaught Gardens in Sidmouth on Whit Saturday, with Ron Smedley as MC. In 1953 there was a Country Dance Party at Brownlands in Sid Road, and then in February 1955 there was a Day of Singing and Dancing held at the Manor Pavilion in Sidmouth. There was already a folk dance club at Salcombe Regis, founded in 1947 by Doris Moore, wife of the vicar; and children from Sidmouth Secondary Modern School at Woolbrook gave folk dance displays in the Connaught Gardens during the summer for the holiday-makers. The Sidmouth Valley Townswomen's Guild also folk danced in the Connaught Gardens.

> **Children gave folk dance displays in the Connaught Gardens for the holiday-makers**

The Humphreys family from Sidbury were local folk dance enthusiasts. Fiddle player Wyn Humphreys was the headteacher of Sidbury primary school, and his wife Doris and daughter Edith were dancers: Edith worked for the EFDSS. In the village of Sidbury, the Humphreys family discovered a local tradition of music-making and dancing which Peter Kennedy recorded. Son of Douglas, Peter Kennedy was employed by the EFDSS before being seconded to the BBC to work as a fieldworker on their Folk Music and Dialect Recording Scheme. Tunes and songs were collected from William Rew, and a collection of local dances was published by the EFDSS in 1957 as *Dances for a Party*. Music and songs from the village were broadcast on radio by the BBC. A mummers' play from Sidmouth was also discovered.

Eileen Brading worked for the EFDSS in Somerset and Cornwall before her marriage in 1953. Husband Peter Phelan was by then working at W.H.Smith in Sidmouth and they made their home in the town, with Eileen working part-time for the EFDSS. Amongst her regular events were the dances she led in Tedbury's Cafe in the Winter Gardens, now Carinas Night Club.

Dance Display in Connaught Gardens, Whitsun 1951

Sidmouth is an Ideal Place for a Seaside Holiday with Dancing

1955 At the EFDSS Staff Conference in July 1954, Douglas Kennedy suggested that they should look beyond the Stratford-upon-Avon Festival, and asked for ideas for new venues. Half in jest, Eileen Phelan suggested Sidmouth. Margaret Grant was fearful that the summer traffic in Devon would prevent the dancers travelling to the town, but other staff members re-assured Douglas Kennedy, who then asked Eileen to speak to the local council.

Eileen did talk to the local council – at that time Sidmouth Urban District Council – but because Eileen was pregnant, Margaret Grant soon took over the arrangements. Aileen Wills (then Aileen Gubb) was Mrs Grant's secretary and a folk dance enthusiast, and remembers accompanying Mrs Grant to the meetings with the council and also touring the town's hotels and block-booking accommodation. Discussions with the council were made easier because one of the councillors, Alan Gibberd, was an EFDSS member. Ted Pinney and Frank Lock were two other councillors who supported the Festival then, and for the rest of their lives.

FOLK DANCE FESTIVAL
SIDMOUTH
AUGUST 1st - 5th, 1955
(by permission of Sidmouth Urban District Council)

English Morris, Sword and Country Dance Displays
with
Community Dancing in which all may join

Monday, August 1st	-	3 and 8 p.m.
Tuesday, August 2nd	-	3 p.m. only
Wednesday, August 3rd	-	8 p.m. only
Thursday, August 4th	-	3 p.m. only
Friday, August 5th	-	3 and 8 p.m.

OUTDOOR PERFORMANCES FREE
Collection taken
DO COME AND JOIN IN THE DANCING

Afternoon Performances in the Connaught Gardens.
Evening Dancing on the Ham or in Blackmore Gardens.
If wet dancing will be at the Manor Pavilion. Limited admission at 2/-

Friday, August 5th — Final Square Dance 8 - 11 p.m.
at the Manor Pavilion.   Admission 2s. 6d.

The English Folk Dance & Song Society
Cecil Sharp House, 2 Regent's Park Road, London, N.W.1

Printed in England by F. J. Milner & Sons Ltd., of Brentford. STI/700/15/8232

The first announcement for the Festival appeared in the EFDSS's magazine *English Dance and Song* in February 1955. The two Festivals, Stratford and Sidmouth, had a similar style, but with different extra attractions. 'Each festival will provide a combination of dance instruction and public displays in holiday surroundings: Sidmouth with the attraction of the sea and Devon countryside, Stratford with the theatre and the river. Sidmouth is an ideal place for a seaside holiday with dancing.'

The dates of the first Festival in Sidmouth were Saturday 30 July to Saturday 6 August. As now, the Festival week was fixed so that it included the first Monday in August, which at that time was the August Bank Holiday.

The first Festival was directed by Nibs Matthews and Margaret Grant, with Nibs in charge of the artistic aspects. The fees for the whole Festival were £4 double, and £2-10s (£2.50) for a single man and £2 for a

Dancing in Connaught Gardens

Dance Display in Connaught Gardens

single 'girl': separate tickets were available for the Bank Holiday weekend. The Festival arranged hotel and boarding house accommodation and also 'hoped to arrange camping facilities'. The price difference for single men and women perhaps reflected the higher wages of men and the fact that men had the added attraction of Morris dancing.

There was a need to balance the sexes so that there was an equal number of men and women for the dance displays. If single dancers were coming to the Festival without a partner, they were paired up with another dancer. No doubt some romantic attachments resulted from this pairing, but as Aileen Wills recalls, 'for some people it could be hell'. Dancers who were not really good enough for public displays were put in a hobby horse costume or given other roles, such as collecting the donations.

The first Festival attracted about a hundred people. The Saturday evening get-together was held in the Girl Guide Hut 'with shaky floor and walls too close together', but this did not deter the dancers. The dancing and singing on that first evening made the event a truly social occasion with people meeting old friends and making new. Many of the festival-goers were in their

twenties, and the format ensured that there was a festive atmosphere.

On the Sunday morning, the dancers and musicians met in the Manor Pavilion (this was before it was turned into a theatre) ready to start rehearsing for the public performances. Following the social dance rehearsal, the men practised Morris and sword dances under the direction of Nibs Matthews, helped by Tony Foxworthy, who had just joined the EFDSS staff, and Jack Hamilton. The dancers included five members of Jockey Morris Men from Birmingham, as well as dancers from White Horse Morris Men from Wiltshire. Colin Mayfield remembers the Morris

practices taking place on the Manor Pavilion car park. The rehearsals continued on Monday before the first public display.

Ernie and Hilda Hales wrote about the Festival in *English Dance and Song* magazine. 'After gathering on the Ham on Monday afternoon we walked and danced along the Promenade, a most spectacular procession with colour made more brilliant by the absence of the gaudy disfigurements which characterise many of our sea-side fronts today. The public travelled with us on either side and traffic did not object to the short hold-up. Here Mrs Grant, who led the procession, nobly held up the forbidding hand to all on-coming cars, etc. So smooth was our progress that we found ourselves at the Connaught Gardens 15 minutes ahead of time.'

Alan Barber remembers that he and his girlfriend Joyce, later his wife, led the dancers in the procession with the 'Gisburn Processional Dance'. John Goddard recalls that amongst the dances performed in the displays were 'The Rifleman' and the 'Abram Circle Dance'. He also remembers rehearsing a suite of dances of different formations, tempos and rhythms, inspired no doubt by the displays at the EFDSS's Royal Albert Hall Festival then held in January each year. Beryl Jukes (née Vivian) remembers that they included the 'good show dances' such as 'Dorset Four-Hand Reel',

Wyn Humphreys, Ioan Jenkins, Jean Forsyth, unknown, Gordon Fredericks, Bill Brown

'Pins and Needles', 'Nottingham Swing' and 'Morpeth Rant'.

'The afternoon's performance went without a hitch, in full party spirit and it seemed that the feet of many of the public were tapping long before Nibs's invitation came for them to join in. Children and adults lost no time in getting on to the green. So began the week, blessed throughout with brilliant sunshine,' wrote the Hales. The dancers and audience were welcomed to the Connaught Gardens by the Chairman of Sidmouth Urban District Council, Brigadier C.C. Crick, who had been

> **Mrs Grant, who led the procession, nobly held up the forbidding hand to all on-coming cars**

an acquaintance of Cecil Sharp. The *Sidmouth Herald* carried a brief report of the Festival, commenting that the Monday procession attracted, 'one of the largest concourses of people seen in the town, even on a Bank Holiday'.

The displays in the Connaught Gardens were held at 3.00pm on Monday, Tuesday, Thursday and Friday, as well as on the Ham on Monday, Wednesday and Friday at 8.00pm: this was in the days before the Ham Marquee, and the performances took place in the open air. The audiences contributed to the collections which were taken at each display, and Aileen Wills and Beryl Jukes remember counting the money every day in the hotel room they shared.

The musicians at the first few Festivals were led by Jean Forsyth, and some members of the Moonrakers Band from Wiltshire: Ioan Jenkins, Jack Kempster and Bill Brown, plus Gordon Fredericks and Wyn Humphreys. During the week there was a demonstration of a broom dance collected in Bradninch a few miles from Sidmouth, by the Humphreys family.

Who attended that first Festival? Pat Mitchell recalls that many of the young people at the Festival had been children during the war: they had a great desire to express their freedom. There were no motorways and few people had cars, so that many of the dancers travelled by train – Sidmouth had its own railway station then. Alan Barber recalls that for many people, a festival by the sea seemed to be an attractive alternative to Stratford. He was living in London, and a regular dancer at Cecil Sharp House, the EFDSS's headquarters in Camden Town. Some of the dancers at 'The House' were university students who lived in the South-West and they no doubt extolled the virtues of the Devon resort. The folk dance movement had a fair number of teachers, such as Beryl Jukes who was able to attend both Sidmouth and the second week of Stratford in that first year. For others, including Alan Barber, the typical holiday entitlement at the time was just two weeks. Alan had already spent a week at an EFDSS holiday course at Easter, and so he and Joyce came for just the Bank Holiday weekend, travelling down by train overnight on the Friday and back to London on the 3.00am Tuesday morning train, arriving in London at 6.00am, before a Lyon's

• Churchill replaced by Eden as Prime Minister
• ITV starts transmission
• Teddy Boys
• University College of the South-West becomes University of Exeter
• Duke of Edinburgh Award started
• Rose Marie by Slim Whitman top of the hit parade in early August
• Bill Haley's 'Rock Around the Clock', Dicky Valentine and Jimmy Young all at Number 1

1955

Corner House breakfast and straight to work.

John Goddard worked for a building firm in Sussex, and used up a week of his precious two weeks' holiday to come down to Sidmouth: at the age of almost 30, it was his first ever holiday away from home. With his friend Bill Horton and their dancing partners Mary Davis-Winstone and Shirley Goring, they met up with other dancers on the train journey from London.

The staff stayed in the Kingswood Hotel on the Esplanade, and although some of the dancers did camp, there were no 'facilities'. The location of the site in that first year is uncertain, but was either in the field at Bulverton that is still used by the Festival, or at Stowford on the A3052 on the field that is now Sidmouth Garden Centre. In 1994, Pearl White recalled that

Dancers and Musicians in the Manor Pavilion

The first camp-site

she was one of a group of dancers who camped in that first year. Each morning, one couple stayed behind to cook the lunch, and the costumes were kept fresh using flat irons which were heated on a Primus stove. A Sidmouth resident was overheard to say that she wished the campers were staying longer, as she lived near the field and enjoyed their singing.

Some of the dancers had attended the Stratford Festival in previous years and undoubtedly knew what to expect, but for others, it was a first time experience. Morning rehearsals and afternoon displays were a surprise to John Goddard, but it was a pleasant experience. No doubt the dancers got a tremendous buzz from the performance and the applause of the audience, and John Goddard returned to his local folk dance clubs with renewed enthusiasm. Les Barclay had a similar experience, but he also remembers that by the middle of the week, his legs were aching with all the dancing.

Beryl Jukes went straight from Sidmouth to Stratford, and certainly preferred Sidmouth. She felt that Stratford was much more formal and too spread out without a real focus, whereas in Sidmouth, the Esplanade was a natural focus for the town, and the activity was concentrated in a smaller area. Sidmouth also had the attraction of the beach – 'you felt you were on holiday,' recalls Aileen Wills.

The greater informality of Sidmouth must have appealed to the young dancers who came into the folk dance movement in the 1950s. Students, single twenty-somethings, looking for fun and romance at the seaside: it is a description of generations of Sidmouth festival-goers.

> ### The costumes were kept fresh using flat irons heated on a Primus stove

In addition to the public displays, there were evening folk dances in the Manor Pavilion, and the Wednesday evening Square Dance Party was broadcast on BBC Radio. This was the period before universal television ownership, when radio was the dominant broadcast medium. Square and barn dances were a regular and popular feature on the radio, and Nibs Matthews was a nationally-known radio personality, through his square-dance calling broadcasts. John Goddard remembers rehearsing the chorus of 'The Derby Ram' which was sung by Pat Shaw for the broadcast. One of the dance displays during the week was filmed for a regional television feature. The garden of the Volunteer Inn and especially the Marine Bar on the Esplanade were two venues where informal music, singing and dancing took place. Sometime during the week, Exeter Morris Men

gave a performance at the Festival, although Colin Mayfield was the only member of the team who attended for the full week. Although he only lived in Exeter, the journey took over an hour by public transport and he stayed in Sidmouth during the week.

The aim of involving and interesting the local people and the holiday-makers in folk dancing obviously worked. The Hales wrote, 'The enthusiasm of the spectators was shown at the Public Party held at the Pavilion on Friday evening, by a large queue which was forming half an hour before time. By then they were accomplished and happy to dance without the support of the main force of Festival dancers who were engaged in the Final Performance on The Ham.'
A surprise item on the final evening was a performance of the Sidmouth Mummers' Play, arranged by Wyn Humphreys. After this final dance, the campers invited everyone back to a party – there was a barrel of beer and glasses from the Volunteer Inn and food, which included mushrooms picked on the camp-site field.

The *Express and Echo* quoted Margaret Grant as saying that the Festival had been 'successful beyond all expectations', and on the Friday morning the councillors invited the dancers for coffee, telling them 'how much Sidmouth had enjoyed our visit and hoped we would be returning next year'.

Nibs Matthews

It is Thought that Sidmouth will Continue to Dance

1956 With the words, 'It is thought that Sidmouth will continue to dance', Ernie and Hilda Hales ended their report of the first Festival in Sidmouth. They also hoped that 'its inhabitants may be convinced that dancing is the "magic" which rules rain or sunshine as desired'. The EFDSS was also pleased that the 'magic' had earned a surplus of £238-18-8d (about £238.93), which was almost as much as Stratford had raised in three weeks. As soon as the 1955 Festival ended, plans were started for a second Festival the following year.

The reputation of the Festival was spread by word of mouth as well as by the report in *English Dance and Song*, and a photograph from the Festival published in the EFDSS's Royal Albert Hall Festival programme in January 1956 also helped the publicity. The number of people attending the 1956 Festival was 130 – a slight increase on the previous year and there must have been an upper limit on tickets because by July the Festival was sold out.

For those who had attended in 1955 there was some trepidation

about returning. 'Travelling down to Sidmouth for the second time to the Folk Dance Festival we wondered if we would be disappointed. Could it be as good as last year? But on arrival our doubts were soon dispelled,' wrote Molly Barnard in *English Dance and Song*.

The programme of dance displays in the Connaught Gardens and on the Ham, as well as square dances in the Manor Pavilion, was repeated in 1956. With the exception of the Bank Holiday Monday, when rain forced the afternoon show to be transferred to the Manor Pavilion, the Festival was again blessed with fine weather.

The dancers were involved in a performance, and therefore there had to be some sort of costume. Men who were also Morris dancers were expected to come with their Morris kit, which meant white trousers or black breeches, white shirts and baldricks and a decorated hat. Many Morris men at the time

had an embroidered waistcoat. The women were expected to wear 'festival dress', which comprised a white blouse, black waistcoat and coloured skirt, made of felt. The skirts were made from a plain circle of cloth. Late 1950s fashion included layers and layers of net petticoats so that the festival skirt stuck out, and the swirling skirts looked very dramatic in the displays. They lent themselves to excellent action photographs, and the town photographer, Gordon Read, was there to capture them on film.

Amongst the festival-goers was Kenneth Loveless, vicar of Hoxton in

- *First Aldermaston March against nuclear weapons*
- *Premium Bonds started*
- *Suez Crisis*
- *Melbourne Olympics*
- *Osborne's Look Back in Anger premiere*
- *Skiffle and Elvis Presley are in the hit parade.*

Jack Hamilton with his famous hat

Kenneth Loveless leads the singing

London, a member of the EFDSS's National Executive, a singer, anglo-concertina player, Morris dance musician and, some years later, Squire of The Morris Ring. Kenneth provided the music for one of the display items, the Flamborough Sword Dance, performed by the men in blue jerseys and white trousers. This item was preceded by a group of men singing a sea shanty, probably led by Kenneth who contributed further songs to the outdoor performances. Kenneth created quite an impression, 'his energy untiring, he was eager to accompany any Morris side "busking" round the villages'.

Another personality at the Festival was Jack Hamilton, described as 'Nibs' right-hand man, MC, solo jig performer, filler-in of any Morris side and general "king-pin" of the dancing arena'. A trade-mark of Jack was his hat. In 1955, he had been asked the origin and meaning of his 'animal hat', which was similar to that used by the captain of the Grenoside Traditional Sword Dancers from Sheffield. By 1956, the American Western character Davy Crockett was well-known through films, TV and a hit record and Jack's hat needed no further explanation!

Apart from a second appearance by the Exeter Morris Men, no other Morris teams were booked to appear at the Festival, although several dancers from the same side all came to the Festival. Several members of Jockey

> ## 'Sidmouth Festival has become a "must" in the folk dancers' calendar'

Morris Men attended the Festival and, with the addition of one or two dancers from other teams, they were able to perform together in the displays. Muriel Cope remembers that the Jockey men and their women partners danced in the road outside Pebblestone Cottage on the corner of Seafield Road and Station Road for a bed-ridden man who wanted to see the dancing. Their ability to dance in the road says something about traffic in the 1950s! Les Barclay returned to the Festival in 1956 with his brother Mike and several other members of the Benfleet Hoymen Morris side from Essex, including their fiddler, Brian Connor. Colin Mayfield from Exeter was invited to become the sixth dancer so that they could dance as a complete side. For Les, this was a tremendous opportunity for a local team from Essex to dance at a prestige event.

Wyn Humphreys, Ioan Jenkins, Jack Kempster, Bill Brown, unknown, Gordon Fredericks, Jean Forsyth

Colin Mayfield's future wife Mary attended the 1956 Festival and remembers that the young dancers made the atmosphere 'almost like an extension of university or training college'. Ernie and Hilda Hales attended the Festival again, and Colin recalls that Ernie was in his early fifties: the fact that he was a grandfather and still dancing was celebrated as something unusual!

Molly Barnard's report on the Festival in *English Dance and Song* magazine suggested the reasons for the enthusiasm of the dancers and the success of the event. There was the acceptance of the Festival by the town – 'The people of Sidmouth really seemed pleased to see us again; from the Mayor, who welcomed us so sincerely on the first night, to the shopkeepers and waitresses in the restaurants where, when we entered in Festival dress, we were greeted with, "How nice to see you again!" … Sidmouth really accepted us'. Secondly, there was the good weather. Another reason was the setting – the 'lovely' Connaught Gardens and the Ham with its 'natural cliffside grandstand'. Then there was the artistic direction of the Festival under Nibs Matthews 'whose vital personality put us all on our toes to give a good show worthy of the EFDSS and at the same time to enjoy ourselves'. The organisation

Morris Dancers

£7 each per week, full board, including afternoon tea, at the Royal York

of the Festival was seen to be excellent in the hands of 'that wizard of organisation, Margaret Grant … and her cheerful band of willing helpers'. Finally, there was the hard work and commitment of all the Festival staff. 'Thank you, Staff; and thank you, Sidmouth!'

The views in this report were reinforced by a letter from folk dancer Grahame Trapp from London to the Council's Entertainments and Publicity Committee, 'What I want to say is how much we all love Sidmouth and we want to come back year after year to enjoy dancing for you and your visitors. … The Sidmouth Festival has become a "must" in the folk dancers' calendar.'

- Macmillan becomes Prime Minister – 'Most of our people have never had it so good'
- Sputnik – first spacecraft
- Treaty of Rome creates Common Market
- Tommy Steele, and 'Cumberland Gap' by Lonnie Donegan at No 1 in charts.

1957

1957

The 1957 Festival was affected by unsettled weather, but nevertheless it was voted a great success by festival-goers and the audiences. The Manor Pavilion was used for rained-off displays, with an admission price of two shillings (10p). One of the square dances was again recorded by BBC Radio for their *Country Dancing* broadcasts. By this time, Alan Barber had married his girlfriend Joyce, and when they met Margaret Grant at the EFDSS's Royal Albert Hall Festival in January, they told her that they wanted to come to the Festival, but extend their holiday for a further week. Mrs Grant booked them into the Faulkner Hotel (now the Royal York and Faulkner on the Esplanade) for £7 each per week full board, including afternoon tea. When Alan and Joyce returned to the Festival for the Silver Jubilee in 1979, their stay at the Royal York and Faulkner cost them £7 each … per day. In 2004, the rates at similar hotels were quoted at about £60 per person per day.

On the Bank Holiday Monday in 1958, the procession was greeted at the Connaught Gardens by Council members who told the dancers, 'it never rains in Sidmouth, but we do get a heavy sea mist!'

Beryl Vivian dancing on the Ham

Connaught Gardens

The afternoon's proceedings were cut short by a very heavy downpour, and Alan Barber swears that Joyce's skirt shrunk by two inches: certainly the paper flowers in his hat striped his face with many colours. Alan also remembers the Humphreys family teaching the Sidbury dances and launching the dance book *Dances for a Party* at the Festival.

The Festival was fully-booked by the time that the May-June issue of *English Dance and Song* magazine was published, and when the 1958 Festival was announced in November 1957, 'early application' was advised.

1958

Although there was some bad weather in 1958, the *Sidmouth Herald* stated that 'outdoor performances which it has been possible to hold, have attracted large and appreciative audiences'. The newspaper also reported that one of the Sidbury dances, 'Hunt the Squirrel', was performed in the opening display, before the rain started.

A photograph shows Nibs Matthews holding an umbrella over Pat Shaw's head to keep him and his guitar dry whilst singing.

By this time, the Festival dancers were giving informal displays in the outlying villages. Pat Mitchell, who had been to every festival, was a member of the 'C Company' whose members included Kenneth Loveless. Amongst the neighbouring towns and villages visited were Budleigh Salterton and Exmouth.

- *CND launched*
- *Vaughan Williams dies*
- *Munich air crash kills 8 Manchester United players*
- *Jerry Lee Lewis's 'Great Balls of Fire' and Elvis's 'Jailhouse Rock' at No 1.*

Flamborough Sword Dance

The Exmouth Years

Sea Front Lawns in Exmouth

1959

After the 1958 Festival, it was decided to have a change of venue. The EFDSS did not want to outstay its welcome in Sidmouth, and the number of people taking part and watching was growing so a larger venue was needed. So the Festival moved for two years to Exmouth – a larger holiday resort further along the coast from Sidmouth, enjoying views across the estuary of the River Exe. The hoteliers were enthusiastic about the Festival, and they responded to a newspaper request for their support and their hotel rooms.

Early in 1959 Margaret Grant retired as the EFDSS's Area Organiser, leaving Irene Harcourt and Eileen Gunnell as the staff based in Exeter. The tune that Pat Shaw wrote to mark her retirement, 'Margaret's Waltz', has since been played from the Shetlands to Cape Breton. Nibs Matthews once again led the artistic direction of the Festival with his wife Jean in charge of the music, whilst Eileen dealt with the administration.

The open-air displays followed the pattern established in Sidmouth, and were held on the Sea Front Lawns, opposite the Pavilion Theatre. The local council in Exmouth did not know what to expect, but the Chairman told the Festival organisers that he had no idea the performances would be so skilful and professional: he was suitably impressed. The Repertory Company complained to the council that the folk dance displays were depriving them of their audiences!

By this stage, a regular event was a meeting of the dancers on the

- *First section of M1 opened*
- *Mini car launched*
- *Castro takes over Cuba*
- *Cliff Richard's 'Living Doll' at No 1*

The Repertory Company complained that the folk dance displays were depriving them of their audiences!

Saturday morning after the Festival had finished – an opportunity to say goodbye to friends and give some feedback on the Festival. At the 1959 meeting, the dancers clearly wanted to return to Exmouth for another year although Les and Janet Barclay remember that there was 'not the same kind of welcome' at Exmouth, compared with Sidmouth.

1960

And so seventy-four dancers, plus a further six dancers for the weekend, gathered in Exmouth for the 1960 Festival. This was about half the number that had attended in 1959, which was seen to be an advantage in terms of arranging and rehearsing the displays, but a disadvantage financially. In her report, Eileen Gunnell wrote, 'We felt there was a good case for not allowing the numbers to get much larger than

this', which must be the first recorded comment about not letting the size of the Festival increase. It has been a recurring theme!

Although the Exmouth Urban District Council had enthusiastically welcomed the Festival, they wanted to alter the 1960 displays. The EFDSS was adamant that the only suitable site was the Sea Front Lawns, but some changes were made to the timing to avoid clashing with Pavilion Theatre shows. The Wednesday afternoon show was switched from 3.00pm to 5.00pm, and there were just two evening performances, on Monday and Friday.

The 1960 Festival started on the Saturday evening with a get-together and dancing in the Church Hall in Rolle Street, which was used for rehearsals on the Sunday from 10.00am until noon, and again at 8.00pm, followed by general dancing. Each subsequent morning, the rehearsals continued with Morris and sword dancing from 9.30 to 10.45am, and social dance rehearsals from 11.15am until 12.30. Monday 1 August was the Bank Holiday and a procession from the car park behind the boating lake to the Sea Front Gardens preceded the 3.00pm

A hot afternoon in 1960!

English Folk Dance & Song Society Festival

EXMOUTH
(By kind permission of Exmouth Urban District Council)

DAILY DISPLAYS
of English, Country,
Morris and Sword Dances
followed by
GENERAL DANCING
in which the public may join

Wednesday:
SQUARE DANCE
Church Hall
M.C.—NIBS MATTHEWS
(Radio and T.V. Caller)
Admission — 2s. 6d.
9 p.m.

ADMISSION FREE — COLLECTION
Monday, 1st August — Friday, 5th August — 1960

show which was opened by the Chairman of Exmouth Urban District Council. Alas, the heavens opened and a deluge of rain descended just before the collection, severely denting the finances.

The weather for the rest of the week was perfect, and the audience for the Friday evening show was the largest of the week. On Wednesday evening, a Square Dance was held in the Church Hall, with Nibs as MC and Tony Foxworthy (by now employed at the EFDSS's North-East office) and Jack Hamilton as guest callers. 'During the evening David Butson, a young man from Essex, sang some delightful English and American songs', reported the *Exmouth Chronicle*.

A list of all the Festival participants survives, indicating that there were complete teams of Morris dancers from the Benfleet Hoymen, and from the Greensleeves side in London, plus several dancers from Offley Morris from Hitchin in Hertfordshire, and from the Coventry, St Helens and Jockey teams. Fred Hamer, a former Squire of The Morris Ring and member of the EFDSS National Executive was the principal Morris musician and Geoff Mendham recalls 'learning the craft of Morris musicianship' from him: 'The Festival has always been a great place to learn – if that's what you want to do!'

Nibs Matthews continued to plan the displays and act as master of ceremonies: the *Exmouth Chronicle* wrote that he was 'known on radio and TV as the foremost caller in England'. Accommodation was

provided for the staff and musicians, and expenses were paid to the musicians who were not EFDSS employees – the five musicians received a total of £14-15s-0d (£14.75). The income from fees from the participants was £160, the collections brought in £130, busking £45 and the Square Dance raised £45. Out of a turnover of £360, just over £127 profit was declared, although the staff time for organisation was not included in the expenditure.

In addition to a Festival flyer which advertised the displays, a general leaflet 'Do you want to Dance?' was produced to encourage holiday-makers to search out their local folk dance club when they returned home. This emphasis on publicity was due to a new member of staff at the EFDSS – the newly-appointed Area Organiser for the South-West, Bill Rutter.

Back in 1956, a Romanian dance group visiting Britain was keen to come to the Festival, but there was no accommodation for the twenty-five dancers. The same problem prevented Swedish folk dance groups coming to the 1959 and 1960 Festivals. No doubt this sowed some seeds in Bill Rutter's imagination for future years.

- *Macmillan's 'Wind of Change' speech*
- *Lady Chatterley's Lover court case*
- *Kennedy wins US Presidential election*
- *'My Old Man's A Dustman' at No 1*

1960

After two years in Exmouth, the Festival returned to Sidmouth. The EFDSS was approached by the Sidmouth Council towards the end of the 1960 Festival with a view to returning to the town. Nibs Matthews wrote to Eileen Gunnell in the week after the Festival, 'I'm sure Sidmouth is the place – we would be most welcome and the dancers would love it – so restful after Exmouth though I'm sure we were right to venture into the "outside world" – good for us!'

For Colin and Mary Mayfield, Exmouth did not have the same atmosphere as Sidmouth. 'At Sidmouth the hills tend to hug you in, but Exmouth was flat and didn't have the same atmosphere. Sidmouth had an intimacy that Exmouth did not have'.

By mid-August, Bill Rutter had made an appointment to see the Town Clerk of Sidmouth Council. The matter was urgent because a repertory company was trying to hire the Manor Pavilion, which had been the Festival's venue for rehearsals and public dances.

Years later Bill Rutter, in a letter to Eileen Phelan, wrote, 'We prefer to forget those two years at Exmouth which is always referred to as "when Sidmouth went to Exmouth!"'. This was perhaps a little unfair. If nothing else, it made Sidmouth realise what it had missed, and confirmed to the festival-goers that 'location' was an important consideration.

Back to Sidmouth

Bill Rutter

1961 Bill's background was quite different to that of Margaret Grant. Aged forty-six when he started working for the EFDSS, Bill had been a farmer in Kent, a pacifist during the war, Entertainments Manager at a holiday camp in Corton in Norfolk and Liberal Agent for the Yeovil constituency. He became interested in folk dance after the Second World War and learnt to be a dance caller. When he was first appointed to the EFDSS staff, he worked part-time and continued as Liberal Agent. Bill's widow, Terry, remembers that his whole attitude was 'dancing is for fun', and he was more concerned with encouraging participation than in promoting precision, or the 'right' way of doing things. He had a great knack of enthusing people, and always encouraged involvement amongst young people. Like his predecessor, he was a great organiser, and Margaret and Bill became great friends.

After concentrating on publicity at Exmouth, Bill oversaw the return of the Festival to Sidmouth. By the time of the 1961 Festival, he was working for the EFDSS full-time, and the event followed the earlier pattern. Bill was able to take stock and consider the options for future development. Repeating the existing format was not an option: Bill was intent on putting his own mark on the Festival. He could see the potential of the Festival, and had a vision for the future. It is doubtful, however, that he could have articulated the details of that vision in 1961. He responded to the changing nature of the folk dance, and emerging folk song, scenes during the 1960s. He had an ability to see what was needed in the future, and to respond quickly to the changing conditions.

In the decade from 1961 to 1971, the Festival changed enormously. Something new was introduced every year, and by 1971 the pattern of the modern Festival was largely established. All the ingredients that we now take for granted were established during that decade – the separate song events, a programme of workshops, invitations to teams of dancers (rather than putting together the displays from festival-goers), international dance groups, the children's events, the torchlight procession, a camp-site, a published programme, a daily newsletter, the Arena at the Knowle, an out-of-town Late Night Extra. All of these features were developed by Bill during the 1960s.

The 1961 Festival saw a change in its artistic personnel, with Tony Foxworthy and Beryl Marriott replacing Nibs Matthews and Jean Forsyth. Tony had attended all the previous Festivals, whilst Beryl was highly regarded as one of the EFDSS's leading young musicians. Living near Birmingham with her husband Roger, Beryl was heavily involved with the local, and national, English folk dance scene.

It was the responsibility of the leader of the musicians to invite other musicians to play for the dance displays and for the social dances. Beryl's main instrument was the piano, although it was increasingly difficult to find pianos in the venues used for folk dancing, and she often shifted to the piano-accordion. Her first choice as fellow musician was her friend, fiddle-player Kate Graham, and other musicians included Mike Harnett on guitar, Alan Robertson on accordion and Tom Woodward on accordion and flute. She also invited a young fiddle player from Birmingham who she had been teaching and encouraging. This was Dave Swarbrick.

Dave Swarbrick was still learning his trade as a fiddle player, and although only just out of his teens, he was already playing in the Ian Campbell Folk Group; and the Ewan MacColl, Peggy Seeger and Charles Parker Radio Ballad, *The Big Hewer*, on which Dave played, was first broadcast on the radio the week after the 1961 Festival. Later, of course, came the duo with Martin Carthy, membership of Fairport Convention, and many other memorable musical partnerships.

The Ham could not be used for displays because of essential work on the water treatment unit located on the site, so that all the displays were scheduled for the Connaught Gardens. The Festival was not the only entertainment in the Gardens during the summer: the Sidmouth Town Silver Band had their concerts, and there was a weekly variety show. In addition, there were Friday evening open-air folk dances throughout the high summer – these took place while the Festival was in Exmouth and indeed, on Bank Holiday Monday in 1959, there had been two open-air dances in the afternoon and evening to fill the gap caused by the Festival's absence. These folk dances and the Festival

were supported by two local folk dance clubs, the established Salcombe Regis club and Sidmouth's Two Valley Eights which had started with a largely teenage membership in 1961.

Sidmouth resident Gordon Read had continued to photograph the Festival in Exmouth, but he was no doubt relieved when the Festival moved back to Sidmouth. His widow, Elizabeth Read, remembers him spending hours processing and printing films ready for the display board each morning and then taking the orders for copies. His collection is an amazing visual archive of the Festival's early years.

A repertory company had leased the Manor Pavilion, leaving the

Festival without its usual centre for practices, public dances and a wet-weather venue. Bill's response was to make use of the Festival's first marquee, fortunately with a wooden floor, which was erected on the north end of the Coburg Field, near the hospital, and next to the Blackmore Gardens.

The Festival was not blessed with fine weather, and displays could only take place in the Connaught Gardens on three occasions. A national bus strike also restricted visitors to the town. Nevertheless, the Festival was a financial and artistic success, and Bill was keen to invite Tony and Beryl to direct the Festival again in 1962.

- *New English Bible published*
- *Berlin Wall*
- *Off-course betting shops legalised*
- *Russia puts first man in space – Yuri Gagarin*
- *Helen Shapiro's 'Walking Back to Happiness' at No 1*

1961

The Seventh Festival – Saturday 5th -Saturday 12th August 1961

The Folk Song Revival

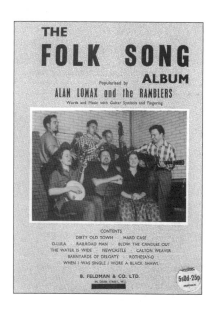

Before the Second World War, there was no folk song revival as we would recognise it today. The EFDSS did include folk song in its events, but this was a mixture of community singing from the books with piano accompaniment or solo singing which stylistically owed more to the standards of the classical music concert hall. Recitals of English folk songs by professional singers were a frequent feature of evenings at Cecil Sharp House and BBC music programmes, whilst folk songs were the staple diet of school music lessons.

By the end of the war, programmes of American blues and folk songs could occasionally be heard on BBC Radio, and news filtered through of the American revival, led by such people as Pete Seeger, The Almanac Singers, Woody Guthrie and Alan Lomax.

Lomax was based in Britain from 1950 and was one of the catalysts of the British folk song revival. He was instrumental in persuading the BBC to embark on its Folk Music and Dialect Recording Scheme, which started in 1952 to record traditional singers and musicians, and Peter Kennedy and Seamus Ennis were employed as the fieldworkers. The resulting radio programmes, entitled *As I Roved Out*, were broadcast from 1953. Lomax introduced Ewan MacColl to A.L.Lloyd, and these two men had the greatest impact on the emerging folk song revival. In 1953, MacColl and Lloyd, plus Isla Cameron, sang British folk songs on Humphrey Lyttelton's radio programme *Ballads and Blues*, and the same title was used for concerts and eventually, in about 1956, for a folk club – one of the first in England. By then, Shirley Collins, John Hasted and Bob Davenport were all making a mark through their singing, and in 1954 Eric Winter started *Sing* magazine.

Skiffle hit the headlines in 1956, although the Ken Collyer Skiffle Group had already shared the Royal Festival Hall stage with MacColl, Lloyd, Cameron and others in a Ballads and Blues concert in 1954. Skiffle Clubs, often held in the new coffee bars, sprang up all over the country and music making became accessible to a whole generation of young people. The American folk songs that formed the basis of the skiffle repertoire led some of the singers back to British folk songs, giving a great impetus to the embryonic folk revival.

The EFDSS had organised a folk song club in Cecil Sharp House as early as 1950, and the Copper family had sung at the Royal Albert Hall Festival in 1952. Folk song events were held at Cecil Sharp House,

By 1959, there were estimated to be nine folk clubs in the whole of England

including a couple of concerts featuring American Burl Ives, and Peter Kennedy hosted events at which he played recordings from the BBC scheme. Appalachian singer Jean Ritchie spent a year in Britain and Ireland, and often sang at EFDSS events. From 1954 the monthly Ceilidhe Club at Cecil Sharp House provided an opportunity for traditional and revival singers and musicians to gather informally.

The EFDSS launched the first English Folk Music Festival (its first festival without any dance events) at Cecil Sharp House in 1957, and although its format provoked fierce debate amongst the various elements of the then-small folk song revival, it was a focus. 1958 saw the founding of the two influential folk groups, The Spinners and The Ian Campbell Folk Group, and the first of the Radio Ballads was broadcast. By 1959, there were estimated to be nine folk clubs in the whole of England, six of them in London, whilst over in the USA, the Newport Folk Festival followed the style of the better-known jazz festival. Penguin published *The Penguin Book of English Folk Songs*, whilst in 1961

A.L.Lloyd and Ewan MacColl

Martin Carthy received his first folk club booking outside central London and MacColl's club was renamed The Singers' Club. The Troubadour had already become a meeting place for emerging singers living in, and visiting, London, whilst in the provinces, singers such as Louis Killen, Johnny Handle and Harry Boardman were making an impression. By 1962 there were approximately seventy-eight folk clubs.

This post-war folk song revival was based on a more 'natural' style of singing, which drew more inspiration from the style of traditional singers. In terms of repertoire, the collections of the EFDSS Library were invaluable for singers who wanted to sing British material. There was a left-wing political element in this early revival, with left-wing choirs such as the London Youth Choir, and a strong connection with the Campaign for Nuclear Disarmament (CND). Topic Records were already issuing a small number of records of folk music. MacColl and Lloyd were spearheading the inclusion of industrial songs in the folk singer's repertoire – songs of coalminers, textile workers and railwaymen – to place alongside the songs of rural England collected by Cecil Sharp and

Ian Campbell Folk Group

others. Members of Morris teams sang folk songs as part of their post-dancing relaxation.

At the first Festival in Sidmouth, John Burgess, a Morris man and country dancer from Bath, had the honour of singing the first folk song at the Festival, when he sang at the Saturday evening get-together. The song was 'Jimmy Crackcorn' or 'The Blue Tailed Fly', from the singing of Burl Ives. Bill Astley also sang that evening. Other singers at the first few Festivals included Kenneth Loveless, Pat Shaw and David Butson, who all

sang at the open-air dance displays. John came into folk song through his Morris dancing and EFDSS events, Kenneth's style tended towards the classical, Pat Shaw had collected folk songs and David Butson was a young revival singer – many of the elements of the post-war song revival were therefore on display at the Festival.

For the first seven years of the Festival, dance was, not surprisingly, the major focus and folk song was only a minor part of the activities. But by 1962, the situation was beginning to change.

The Sidmouth Folk Festival

1962

'I am billing the event this year as "The Sidmouth Folk Festival"', Bill Rutter wrote prior to the 1962 Festival. Not dance, or music, or song – just 'folk'. Today, we take this term for granted, but then it was the first festival in England to have such a title. The main reason for the change in title was the inclusion of a separate folk song event.

Bill set out his intentions in a letter to Ron Smedley in November 1961, 'We shall try for a shop, stable or basement, which we will convert into a coffee bar for the public and a club for the Festival dancers. We want to invite someone, such as

> '... a shop, stable or basement, which we will convert into a coffee bar for the public and a club for the Festival dancers'

John Burgess, to act as a singing compere, who will bear the brunt of the work with the help of local singers of some standing. In addition we should like to put on a "star" or "stars" who are names to the public and yet are acceptable to the Society.' At the time, coffee bars were new and very fashionable amongst the young, and a frequent venue for music making, especially folk and blues. It was felt that a song event in one of the pubs might not be so attractive to festival-goers and the general public and, in any case, Bill had already visited all the pubs in the town, and they were too busy to be involved. It appears that Fred Hamer suggested the idea of the 'coffee club'.

Ron Smedley was, by then, working for the BBC and Bill enlisted his help to invite his chosen 'stars' – Robin Hall and Jimmie

MacGregor, who were then household names through their regular appearances on the BBC television programme *Tonight*. Their agent wanted a fee for the weekend of £130, but both the Finance Committee of the EFDSS and the Sidmouth Council rejected Bill's request to spend the money. Bill wrote, 'We are failing to capture the public because we are shy of modern methods', but given that the Festival's total income was only £500, the rejection was not so surprising. Instead, the 'star' singer was Cyril Tawney. Even before he left the Royal Navy in 1959, Cyril Tawney had established a reputation as a singer, making regular radio and television appearances. Cyril had already sung at the open-air displays in 1961, when he performed some of the songs with his friend Norman May. He returned in 1962 to sing at the song events, plus occasional performances at the dance displays.

John Burgess was the 'singing compere' and ran the event like a folk club. He was supported by singers such as David Rye, Pat Montgomery, Andrew Bryden, John

Marks and especially Bob Blair. Bob is now highly regarded as a singer of Scottish traditional songs, and later in the sixties became a member of MacColl's influential, yet controversial group, The Critics. In the early sixties, he was living in Weston-super-Mare and was a casual visitor to the Festival. As a member of Mendip Morris Men and a country dancer, Bob took part in the dance displays but was also a mainstay of the song event. At the time he was singing some West Country songs, but Cyril Tawney encouraged him to sing more Scottish songs and played him recordings of traditional singers.

Cyril Tawney sings in the marquee

Bob Blair leads the singing in the Song Loft

Bill Rutter leads the procession

Bob remembers, 'We were all desperate for material to sing, and there was a lot of informal discussion about where people got songs and why they sang them in a particular way'.

The venue was the upstairs room of The Sidmouth Pottery in Cross Lane – also known as Trumps Lane, which is a narrow foot-path between Fore Street and Old Fore Street. It was, as Bill declared, 'a bit of a dump' but he decorated the walls with record sleeves. The events were extensively publicised with posters and a thousand flyers, with the slogan 'Have a Coffee and a Song at the Folk Song Loft'. As with the dance events, the 'target audience' was the general public. There were three sessions a day, at 11.00am, 4.30 and 9.30pm, programmed to start at about the same time that the dance displays were finishing, and they lasted for about one hour. The venue only held about thirty or forty people. At the time, there was no festival season ticket, and the admission price was one shilling per session (5p) which also included a cup of coffee. The total expenditure was £45 and Bill expected to make a loss, although he hoped that the sale of records would offset this: 'In any case, if you have full sessions of the public, who cares.'

The event was an undoubted success, although the attendances may have benefited from the awful weather. Les and Mike Barclay and their partners attended the Festival primarily as dancers, but the two brothers sang as a duo, and the two couples also sang as a foursome. Les and Janet remember that they sang a version of 'Seven Drunken Nights' (this was several years before The Dubliners took the song into the charts), 'Rosebud in June' and 'Bushes and Briars'. The atmosphere was very good and informal, the small room very crowded and everyone joined in the choruses, they recall.

For Bill, the increased attendance (about 110) was evidence that the Festival had recovered from the absence of Nibs Matthews. He also observed a younger generation of dancers coming to the Festival. 'What we wish to avoid at all costs is that we are involved in "Ye Olde Englishe" – we are up-to-date, alive. These young people are just as likely to "rock and roll" as they are to "balance and swing"'. Festival goers were asked for their age on the booking forms, the only year for which the forms have survived, and these indicate that about 45 percent were under 25 years old, 45 percent were aged 25 to 35, and the other 10 percent were over 35.

Kate Graham, Tom Woodward, Wyn Humphreys, Dave Swarbrick, Mike Harnett, Beryl Marriott, Alan Robertson

The established pattern of rehearsing the dances in the mornings followed by displays in the Connaught Gardens continued: the Ham was still out of use. There were seven displays during the week, repeating the pattern of the 1955 Festival almost exactly. As in 1961 the weather was dreadful, with only two of the shows taking place out of doors, but there was no dampening of spirits, indeed the adversity seemed to engender an atmosphere of great camaraderie. Tony Foxworthy had been much influenced by the dances of the North-East and his love for dances with rant steps was a source of much joking during the week. Bob Blair remembers a fifteen-minute rant sequence which exhausted the dancers. Beryl Marriott was again in charge of the music.

In 1962, complete sides of Morris dancers came from the established Morris Ring sides, Bedford and Offley, as well as from Chanctonbury Ring in Sussex – five of the six dancers were under the age of thirty. Even younger were the Sheffield University Morris Men and the Cutlers sword team. Joss Mellor from Sheffield taught the University team, one of whose members was John Parsons, who was able to persuade his fellow dancers to come to Sidmouth based on personal experience. John came from Sidford, and had been introduced to folk dancing at the Salcombe Regis Folk Dance Club before he went to university. John remembers that there were just four male dancers for the rapper sword team so they found an extra dancer at the Festival, and Johnny Burke from Staffordshire and Bill Astley from Birmingham were the 'fool' characters, Tommy and Betty. Music came from Dave Swarbrick, who was obviously captivated by the rapper sword tradition. A small

Sheffield Cutlers with Johnny Burke (Tommy), Dave Swarbrick (musician), Bill Astley (Betty), Joss Mellor (holding swords)

group of festival-goers, including Dave and Cyril Tawney, spent the last night drinking a keg of beer on the campsite. The night ended with Dave and Cyril disastrously trying their hand at rapper dancing, using wooden long swords which did not have the flexibility of the rapper: in

> **The night ended with Dave and Cyril disastrously trying their hand at rapper dancing ...**

the chaos that resulted, they only succeeded in tumbling through a field of newly-mown hay.

Conscription had recently ended, but some young men were still completing their National Service in one of the armed forces, and some of the letters in the Festival archives are from men in the forces hoping that they could get leave. Ian Paul was in the RAF and coming to the Festival without a partner. In response to Bill's letter assuring him that a woman dancer would be found for him, Ian wrote, 'I am sure that all the young ladies are most charming, but can you guarantee that they can dance?'

The 1961 location of the marquee had been too near the hospital, so

Sidmouth Urban District Council gave permission for a marquee on the hard tennis courts at the Coburg Field, between Amyatts Terrace and Coburg Terrace, with changing facilities for the dancers in Church House. The local residents were concerned about the potential noise, but Bill reassured the Council that if it rained in the evening, the display in the marquee would be finished by 10.30pm, and the Council placed an 11.00pm curfew on Wednesday evening for the public square dance. The last night party was held at Woolcombe Hall, ending at 1.00am. But generally, the Council was very supportive, and the Town Clerk, Mr Eric Howarth, wrote to the residents near Coburg Fields, 'The National Folk Dance Festival is widely welcomed in the town, not only for the trade it brings, but for the entertainment which it provides for visitors and residents alike. The Council are very anxious that the dancers should have, in Sidmouth, at least as good facilities as they would obtain elsewhere.'

The problem of travelling to Sidmouth in the year's busiest holiday week was illustrated by Angela McNamara who wrote to cancel her Festival visit because she could not get a train seat from Manchester. Bill tried to get her a lift, but she solved the problem herself, by booking a flight to Exeter – costing £6 one way.

- *New Coventry Cathedral opened*
- *The film Lawrence of Arabia released*
- *Nelson Mandela imprisoned*
- *Marilyn Monroe dies*
- *Cuban Missile Crisis*
- *The Beatles release first single: 'Love me Do'*

1962

The Irish Arrive

1963 Just as significant as the Festival's expansion into song, was the international music and dance which first became a feature in 1963.

Establishing connections with the folk dance movements in other countries started early in the twentieth-century revival. By the 1920s the EFDSS was sending its main dance demonstration group to appear at festivals and concerts in Europe as well as in Canada and the USA. In return, groups of dancers from overseas visited the EFDSS's Royal Albert Hall Festival, a practice which continued after the war. A significant event was the 1935 International Folk Dance Festival held in London, organised by Maud Karpeles and the EFDSS. In Wales the Llangollen International Eisteddfod included a folk dance competition from 1948. It was therefore not so surprising that an EFDSS festival in the 1960s should seek to invite dance groups from abroad.

The first international dance group came from Ireland. The EFDSS and the Irish Folk Dance Society had already organised an Anglo-Irish folk dance course near Dublin and Margaret Grant had retired to Ireland to be near her brother. These two factors led to an invitation to Lily Comerford of the Irish Folk Dance Society to send a group of dancers to the 1963 Festival, but at the last minute the group cancelled its visit. A replacement group was sent – The Rory O'Connor Dancers. Rory was the best-known figure in Irish dancing and had already danced at the Royal Albert Hall Festival, although he did not personally accompany his dancers on this first Sidmouth visit. He sent his 'Special Figure Dance Team', all young teenagers who had been undefeated in competition for the previous three years and who included the All-Ireland solo champion. Just eight dancers – but they set the Festival alight. Bob Common remembers that they created as much excitement as *Riverdance* many years later.

Bill decided that the people directing the dance and the music would change every two years because he believed that it was the Festival and the place that were important, rather than the personalities. After Tony Foxworthy, he turned to Jack Hamilton from Kent who had been Nibs's assistant in the 1950s, and Jack directed the dance in 1963 and 1964. The musicians in 1963 were

Just eight dancers – but they set the Festival alight

led by Denis Smith. Processions along the Esplanade preceded most of the displays and when they arrived in the Gardens, the dancers paraded round the dance area. For the first time, the Blackmore Gardens were also used for the evening displays on Monday, Wednesday and Friday. There was a distinct improvement in the weather, and no displays were moved to the marquee, which was now located on its more permanent site on the Ham, where it was used exclusively for rehearsals and the square dance. Bill described the final evening display in the Blackmore Gardens as a 'carnival atmosphere of controlled English fun', but the ensuing late-night party in the marquee until 1.00am drew complaints from the residents. Bill's response was to ensure that all the councillors were invited in future!

Bill had already observed that the Festival was attracting 'newer, younger dancers' but, of course, they were less experienced and some of them were not really good enough to take part in the shows. Some people thought that Jack Hamilton did not pursue high enough standards, but Bill defended him, describing Jack's approach as 'more informal; we have taken ourselves too seriously for years'.

The Rory O'Connor Irish Dancers

The procession makes its way to the Connaught Gardens

dancing. This was several years before women's Morris in public, although there were instances of mixed couples dancing a few Morris dances. Bert wrote to Bill: 'Can we avoid all forms of female Morris (eg Winster, Abram)? Tell the girls to leave their sensible hankies at home.'

After the success of the folk song event in 1962, a larger venue was needed, but Bill struggled to find one. The Winter Gardens was suggested for a late evening event, but finally, just weeks before the Festival started, Bill secured the use of All Saints Church Hall on All Saints Road, although it failed to generate the right atmosphere. John Burgess was again in charge, and Cyril Tawney was the official guest, performing for about ten minutes at every session, plus a spot in the Monday afternoon dance display.

In addition to the three song sessions a day, the Manor Pavilion was hired for a Sunday evening concert. The running order still exists on a scrap of paper in Bill's characteristic green ink. The performers included The Rivermen from Bideford, The King Pins from The King's School Ottery St Mary led by teacher Tony Frank from Seaton, John Burgess, Cyril Tawney and Bob Cann. A late addition was a young singer from a new folk song club in Exeter: Bill wrote, 'Tony Rose, whom I am assured is good …

But the participants enjoyed it all enormously. 'I ended the festival week in a positive haze of excitement, sleeplessness and rough cider,' wrote one young woman. Another dancer, Jenifer Barlow (now Broughton), wrote, 'I have not been on a week's holiday festival before, but it was the best holiday I've ever had, and I shall book for next year as soon as I can!' Indeed, Jenifer came to the Festival each year until 1966, and then again in 1970 and 1971. In her diaries, she kept a note of the dances that were performed in the displays, and in 1963 they included suites from the North Country ('La Russe', 'Circassian Circle', 'Cheviot Rant' and 'Cumberland Square Eight'), the West Country ('Dorset Ring Dance', 'Wiltshire Six-Hand Reel', 'Wiltshire Tempest' and 'Bonny Breast Knot') and Sidbury ('Double Scottische', 'Sidbury Reel', 'A-Hunting We Will Go' and 'Danish Waltz') as well as American and Midlands suites.

Many of these dances were included in the *Community Dance Manuals*, published by the EFDSS.

Both Chanctonbury Ring and the Cutlers from Sheffield University returned in 1963. Bill Horton, who had attended the first Festival and who had subsequently joined Chanctonbury Ring Morris, no doubt encouraged the side to go, although John Beeston organised the trip. Amongst the dancers were Paul Setford and Derek Lockwood, who were also singers. Bert Cleaver acted as Jack Hamilton's deputy and directed the Morris and sword

- *Profumo scandal*
- *Beeching Report on the Railways*
- *Great Train Robbery*
- *Kennedy assassinated*
- *The Beatles and Gerry and the Pacemakers have No 1 hits*
- *Cliff Richard's 'Bachelor Boy' and 'Summer Holiday' at No 1*

Anne Chandler and Bob Common

Sheffield Cutlers with Bill Astley (Betty) and Bert Cleaver (Tommy), Joss Mellor, Brian Mason, John Graham, John Parsons, Graham Cole and Brian Hayden (musician)

own home. Cooks from the secondary school provided the meals. The Irish dancers stayed in the hostel, looked after by Terry Yells, who later became Bill's wife.

An innovation at the Festival was the showing of films about folk music and dance from the EFDSS Library. Financially, the venture was not a great success, but it was indicative of Bill's attempts to introduce something different. The BBC regional television news programme *South West at Six* included a feature on the Festival, but its depiction of the festival-goers as eccentric was not appreciated, and several people wrote to the BBC to complain.

has promised to come down on Saturday ... and I have said we will include him on the programme Sunday evening.' A surprise visitor later in the week was the traditional singer, melodeon player and bargeman, Bob Roberts from Suffolk, who happened to be on holiday in the town. 'I should like to attract more like him', wrote Bill.

There was spontaneous singing on the Esplanade late in the evenings, and the young singers in The King Pins brought great energy to the singing. Bill suggested that the singers should congregate at different places along the Esplanade each evening, but on one occasion he had to intervene to stop them when it 'degenerated into rugby-club singing'. There was also comment on the singers' 'festival dress' – 'that scruffy, unwashed and unemployed look' as one festival-goer jokingly described it.

The Festival was continuing to arrange hotel accommodation for festival-goers, if they so wished it. As Bill put it, 'It is worse than a jig-saw puzzle fitting up everyone', but as the numbers increased, so did the problems. There was also a demand for camping, which was satisfied informally by Edwin Hill, a farmer and local councillor, who made a field available at his farm, Bulverton Well, the same site that is used today. Archie Bryden from South Petherton in Somerset camped with a group of twelve family members and friends: 'It will mean bicycles down to the town,' wrote Bill. The facilities were probably rather primitive, possibly non-existent.

In between the hotels and campsite, there was a need for some sort of hostel accommodation – something cheap without the rigours of camping. The visit by the young Irish dancers led Bill to set up a hostel in the Infants' School on Manstone Avenue, a couple of miles from the Esplanade. Three dozen people stayed there, for a fee of £5.00 for the week – all meals included. Camp beds came from the army, blankets from the Red Cross, and a variety of items including carpets, pans, kettles and curtains from Bill's

> *Camp beds came from the army, blankets from the Red Cross and a variety of items, including carpets, pans, kettles and curtains from Bill's own home*

After the Festival, Ivy Lock from London wrote to thank Bill 'for making such a marvellous week possible. There seems to be so much good-will for us in Sidmouth that I feel we owe them the best possible show.'

Song Spot, All Saints Church Hall. John Burgess on guitar, Andrew Bryden on his right, then Anne Chandler, Bob Common, Helen and Bob Blair

Trefusis, Storrow and Israel

1964 After the success of the Irish dancers, Bill Rutter was determined to invite more from abroad. A team of English dancers from the South-West had performed at the 1963 Confolens Festival in France, where they had seen a group dancers from Israel, whom they recommended to Bill. An invitation was issued and accepted, and Sidmouth Urban District Council was said to be 'all agog' at the prospect of such an 'exotic' addition to the Festival. The twenty-seven dancers came from Haifa and were all in their late teens or early twenties, offering a two-hour performance of Israeli dances and songs.

The correspondence between Bill and the group leader, Zeev Sternberg, illustrates most of the issues which arose in negotiations with overseas dance groups over the following forty years. Groups arriving by air or ferry generally needed to be collected from one of the London airports or from Dover or Harwich and they often arrived a day or two before the Festival – therefore requiring accommodation for extra days. Then there was the issue of finding and funding accommodation and meals for these groups, and transport around the Festival, at a time when the displays were free, and income was still very largely dependent on voluntary contributions from the audiences, and on the weather.

The Israeli group arrived on Tuesday and were accommodated in 'Hostel D', which was a tin hut behind the church in All Saints Road. On Wednesday and Thursday evenings before the Festival started, the dancers performed outdoors in Exmouth, splitting the collection with the Festival. Appearances in Sidmouth started on Friday evening and continued all week.

Israeli dancers

The group created a tremendous impression. The lines of dancers weaving in and out of the audience seated on the grass, dancing barefoot, in modern clothes in a more choreographed style was all very different to what the audiences had been accustomed to. They also gave an evening dance concert in the Methodist Church Hall. Some of the English dancers somewhat disparagingly referred to them as 'ballet dancers', but the audiences loved them. Peter Dashwood had just joined the staff of the EFDSS and one of his first tasks was to stop the Israeli dancers rehearsing in their hostel at 2.00am!

The Irish Folk Dance Society sent an adult group in 1964: ten dancers performing ceili and step dances, aged between 18 and 28 years, and therefore 'the same age as most of our dancers,' wrote Bill. But he preferred the Rory O'Connor Dancers, who were invited year after year until 1968 when their popularity was recognised in their award of the Freedom of the Festival.

In response to the comments of the previous year, the English dancers were split into two companies. Rather than calling them Company A and Company B (Bill wrote, 'this suggests one is superior over the other. Whilst this will be true, we do not wish to suggest it') they were called Trefusis and Storrow. These were the surnames of two benefactors of the EFDSS who had had rooms at Cecil Sharp House named after them. Lady Mary Trefusis had been the President of the English Folk Dance Society, whilst Helen Storrow from Boston, USA had been a supporter of Sharp and his work since before the First World War. The idea was that one company would rehearse suites of dances with different formations, whilst the other group would simply perform a dance, then stop, re-form and perform another dance.

Jack Hamilton felt that the general dancing at the end of the display was an anticlimax to the show, and he reduced this aspect of the event. But public participation had always been a feature of the Festival and

The Beach Store

somersault early in the week, then a double somersault a few days later. At the end of the week, they had nine dancers, with a four somersault finale. They dressed one of their men as an Israeli dancer and dragged him out of the audience to complete the nine dancers and it brought the house down as the audience really thought he was an Israeli.

The 1964 Festival coincided with a large folk dance event in Stratford-upon-Avon as part of Shakespeare's four-hundredth birthday celebrations. There was a fear that there would not be enough dancers for both events, although suggestions that Sidmouth should not go ahead were quickly over-ruled. In fact, Sidmouth attracted even more dancers than in 1963. Bill was afraid of the impact of cancellation on the growing, and potentially independent, folk song movement: 'My chief worry is that having alerted the folk song world, they will try to fill the vacuum if we do nothing in 1964.'

The song venue moved again – this time to the Beach Store, which was where the council kept the deck-

> *... suggestions that Sidmouth should not go ahead were quickly over-ruled*

chairs in the winter (not, as suggested by generations of parents to their children, where they stored the beach in the winter!). It was located on the corner of Ham Lane and York Street behind Ted Andrews's garage on the Esplanade, on a site now occupied by flats. It was hardly a sophisticated venue. The *Sidmouth Herald* reported that it was decorated to represent a beach setting at night. The open roof was replaced with blue polythene, underlain with fish net. Subdued lighting came from hurricane and ships' lanterns, and the blue ceiling was floodlit. 'Tables with coloured umbrellas, seats from casks, lobster pots, fish netting and a boat

there was therefore less opportunity for the audience to take part. For the first time, a list of display dances was sent out in advance so that the dancers could make sure that they knew them. Alas, the standard of display dancing did not improve. Bill was not satisfied with the display dancing and wrote, 'I was ashamed of the English at Sidmouth and on one occasion ran and hid myself behind a tree!' Perhaps there were also too many dancers involved in the displays – some people thought that the massed dancing looked formless, and that two or three sets would be more effective.

Instead of the usual Monday afternoon start to the displays, Bill arranged the opening for Friday night and a further display the following evening, even though most of the Festival dancers did not arrive until Saturday. Bill directed these shows, and invited local dancers to put on displays on these two evenings. Friday evening was billed as 'Devon Night' and Saturday

as 'Somerset Night', with the addition of the Irish and the Israelis. He introduced an element of informal competition to see which county could produce the best show. Bill expected country dance and Morris, and each county was expected to fill about thirty-five minutes, with ten minutes from the Irish dancers, and twenty minutes from the Israelis. That left almost an hour for dancing by the public. The Devon Night display included pupils from Honiton Secondary School, led by EFDSS member Miss Margaret Roach of Colyton. Jim Dewar was one of the pupils – in fact he was the school dance captain that year and he remembers Bill Rutter and then Dick Witt teaching Morris dancing as part of the curriculum. Jim remembers the pleasure that he got from Margaret Roach's dancing classes, plus 'introductions to lots of girls!' Jim went on to dance with Bath University Morris.

1964 saw Morris teams from Chanctonbury Ring, The Cutlers from Sheffield University, Rumford and Headington Quarry at the Festival, as well as a boys' team from Lutterworth, made up of pupils from the grammar school, taught by one of their teachers, Griff Jones, a Morris dancer, musician and EFDSS activist. The Cutlers built up their rapper over the week, starting with a single

- *Mods and Rockers clash at Clacton*
- *Harold Wilson wins election for Labour*
- *Post Office Tower opens*
- *BBC 2 starts*
- *No 1 hits for The Searchers, Dave Clark 5, Cilla Black, The Rolling Stones, The Kinks and … The Beatles*

1964

complete the sea-shore scene', the newspaper reported. Admission to the Song Spot was two shillings (10p) including coffee. For the first time, all festival-goers were issued with a 'season ticket' costing only £1, which contrasted with the 'festival fee' of £2-5s (£2.25) in 1963.

The three song sessions a day of previous years were increased to four during the Festival because of the popularity of the event. After the Festival, Bill described the four events in a letter, '11am a few public but worth this contact to invite them to other sessions. 4.30pm more regular folk singers attend. 8.30pm crowded with public and many folk singers. 10.30pm packed tight with singers and dancers – really "The Company". The dancers pour in. It is hard work at 11am, 4.30pm it becomes interesting and at 8.30pm onwards exciting.'

Bill saw no reason to change the winning formula and John Burgess and Cyril Tawney again appeared. Bill tried unsuccessfully to book The Spinners and The Ian Campbell Folk Group, but Cyril Tawney persuaded the young singer Frankie Armstrong to come and Bill gave her a fee of two guineas (£2.10). Frankie remembers her first visit to the Festival as full of excitement. 'We were pioneers – I remember the warm, friendly atmosphere, and Cyril was marvellous – he knew everybody!'

By this time, Bob Blair was stationed with the RAF in Grimsby and he and his wife Helen were singing at the local folk club with the resident group, The Meggies. He persuaded his fellow group members, John Conolly and Bill Meek, to come to the Festival. Later, after Bob and Helen left, the group became The Broadside and John's song 'Fiddler's Green' became a folk club standard.

In 1964 a quartet of young men – Bob Common, Pete Shutler, Mac McCulloch and Bonny Sartin – made their singing debut at the Festival. Known as The Yetties, the Festival was very important in establishing the group's national reputation – but equally, The Yetties helped spread the fame of the Festival before and after they turned professional in 1967. They had first visited the Festival on a day trip in 1962 as The Yetminster and Ryme Intrinseca Junior Folk Dance Display Team, and had given displays along the Esplanade. They saw Cyril Tawney and heard the song 'The Barley Mow' for the first time. In 1963 Bonny was on a folk dance trip to France, but the other three 'men' (Pete and Mac were still too young to drink in pubs) tape-recorded everything that Cyril sang, and they also danced in the displays. They slept in one of the hostels, without permission, and hid under the beds whenever Bill Rutter paid a visit.

Pete was already playing the accordion, and when the musician with the Irish dance group had stage fright, Pete stepped in to play for them. But most of the time that year, The Yetties sang at the song events in the Beach Store. 'It was all Cyril Tawney songs then', they now recall. The Yetties were an excellent example of Bill Rutter's persuasive powers, especially when it came to enthusing young people: in addition

> They had first visited the Festival on a day trip in 1962 as The Yetminster and Ryme Intrinseca Junior Folk Dance Display Team

to dancing, singing and playing, they were also general managers of the Beach Store song spot – they took the money at the door, sold the records, and helped if the coffee rota broke down.

The Sunday evening Manor Pavilion concert featured John, Cyril, Frankie and others, including Andy and Lynden Tunmer, son and daughter of the local bank manager, and the Journeymen, a resident group at the Jolly Porter Folk Club in Exeter, whose members included Ken Penney and Dave Robins. The singers were involved in other parts of the Festival – they carried their guitars in the Monday afternoon procession and opened the Friday display with some massed singing. Not everyone was impressed with the singing, however. A Sidmouth resident attended the concert, but wrote, 'the singing – is it right to encourage young people to be pleased with such low standards? However a young man beside me screamed and whistled in his ecstasy – so some enjoyed it.' Bill replied diplomatically that the young singers were trying to sing in a more authentic style, rather than in a 'refined' classical style.

The offer of hostel accommodation was very popular, and six halls were

Lutterworth Boys' Morris

The Yetties: Bob, Mac, Bonny and Pete

The Meggies in the Beach Store, 1964

turned into hostels – St Francis Hall, the Guide and Scout Huts, Woolcombe Hall, All Saints School and the Drill Hall, in total accommodating eighty-five people. All the Israelis were in All Saints School, fourteen women were in the Drill Hall, and the other hostels housed the men, mainly Morris dancers. Halse's Yard, one of the buildings on what is now the west side of the Ham car park, was used for cooking and serving the meals. Three meals a day and a camp-bed still cost only £5.00 for the week, in contrast to about £12 to £14 a week for hotels (full board, three meals a day) and £10 for guest houses. The Festival was still desperate for accommodation, and a plea in the *Sidmouth Herald* led to several offers of bed and breakfast from home owners. Meanwhile, Bill

and many of the Festival staff stayed in the Wyndham Hotel on the Esplanade, owned by Tom and Gladys Foyle. Their daughter Penny and her husband Martyn Perryman helped her parents, and for over forty years the hotel, later converted into apartments, was filled with Festival performers and staff.

Bill borrowed exhibits and photographs from the EFDSS's Vaughan Williams Memorial Library for an exhibition, which Geoff Rye from Weston-super-Mare, a professional librarian, supervised with EFDSS library assistant Jenny Barton, who also ran the legendary Troubadour Folk Club in London.

1964 saw a big push to publicise the Festival, and Sidmouth Urban District Council's Publicity Officer Mrs Eileen Allen, and committee chairman Frank Lock, were of great assistance. To attract different audiences each day, Bill wrote to all the coach companies in Devon, Cornwall and Somerset and to 340 Women's Institutes in Devon: over thirty of them agreed to run village trips to the Festival. Letters from the Council were franked with 'Sidmouth Folk Festival August Week', AA signs were ordered, the *Express and Echo* carried a full page of Festival publicity with the full programme, shops were encouraged

to mount window displays, posters were given to all the pubs, car stickers were printed, the Esplanade lamp-posts were decorated with ribbons and the EFDSS sword-lock logo, an Information Bureau was established near the Drill Hall (in a specially-purchased garden shed), and BBC television and radio covered the Festival.

Some of these ideas for publicity came from the Town-Festival Liaison Committee, which drew upon the Chamber of Commerce, the Council (Frank Lock, Ted Pinney and Alan Gibberd), hoteliers and the Ratepayers' Association, as well as local folk dance supporters such as Alison Rice. This was all evidence of greater town and Council commitment to the Festival, and the desire to create a joyous, festive atmosphere. The result was that the Festival 'broke on to a new level for public relations'. Bill recognised that the townspeople were far more conscious of the Festival, giving it their overwhelming support. The Chairman of the Council, Councillor A.G.Skinner, said that, 'Nothing could be more appropriate for Sidmouth than a folk festival'.

'It was the best holiday we have had for a long time – it was great fun from beginning to end and we thoroughly enjoyed every minute of the day', one festival-goer wrote.

'You Must Come to Sidmouth at Least Once in Your Life'

1965

The 1965 Festival exploded with innovations – the first Torchlight Procession, the first children's event (the Hobby Horse Club), the first souvenir programme, and square dances in the surrounding villages.

There were still no other summer folk festivals that lasted more than a day, but in 1965 two important weekend festivals made their debut. The Keele Folk Festival was held in mid-July in the North Midlands as a major gathering of traditional and revival singers and musicians from all over Britain and Ireland. And coinciding with the first weekend of Sidmouth was the Cambridge Folk Festival: just a two-day event that first year, but with The Clancy Brothers and Tommy Makem as headline guests, and Paul Simon as the newcomer. In fact, there is an unconfirmed report that Paul Simon came on from Cambridge to spend a couple of days in Sidmouth. Any fears that these two festivals would draw audiences away from Sidmouth were totally unfounded. The folk song scene was growing so fast that there were more than enough enthusiasts for all three festivals, and Sidmouth attracted its largest audiences yet for the folk song events.

In 1965 Tony Foxworthy became Director of Folk Song and the number of song enthusiasts who bought season tickets grew to over a hundred people. Louis Killen was the resident song guest, whilst other singers included Cyril Tawney, Roy Harris and Clive Bennett from Sussex. Louis introduced a new teenage singer to the Festival: Maddy Prior. The previous year, Rosemary Radmore, who later married Cyril Tawney, had organised a coach trip for three dozen people from Plymouth for the Sunday evening concert and, although she reserved the same number of seats again, she found that there was not enough demand for the coach – most of the club members were coming to the Festival for the full week.

The main song venue was once again the Beach Store. The Yetties had developed considerably over the year, and they sang a great deal at the Song Spot, bringing the final session on Friday evening to a close. Pete was also in demand as a musician for the dancing. Bill Rutter wrote of 'a wizard on the accordion 19-year-old handsome and dark, untutored Pete Shutler'.

Following an appearance at Cambridge Folk Festival, four young singers from Hull arrived at the Festival without tickets or beds. Although they were fast gaining a national reputation, Bill Rutter would not let them into the late-night Festival events without the coveted green season tickets – even if they were The Watersons! Norma Waterson remembers that a group of festival-goers performed an impromptu Morris dance at the late-night event, holding green tickets instead of handkerchiefs.

Louis Killen in the Beach Store

Bill got the message, and Norma, Lal and Mike Waterson and John Harrison, plus their friend the singer Anne Briggs, were let in. Accommodation was no problem – they slept on the beach!

Sue Burgess, the first of many singers from the folk club in Cheltenham, travelled to Sidmouth on her scooter, and one morning cooked breakfast on the camp-site for Norma Waterson and Anne Briggs. Megan Grimshaw (later Megan Rose) had visited the Festival with her folk dancer parents but now sixteen-years-old, they let her come to the Festival alone, although she knew The Yetties and was already a member of their folk club. Another first-time visitor was singer and Kingston Fighting Cocks song club organiser Rod Stradling. Rod remembers the excitement at hearing new songs and singers, and after each Song Spot many of the singers stayed on in the Beach Store for an informal singaround, such was the enthusiasm for sharing their favourite songs with others. Rod and members of The Watersons became life-long friends that week.

> *... four young singers from Hull arrived at the Festival without tickets or beds*

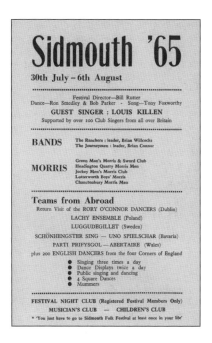

Sidmouth '65

30th July – 6th August

Festival Director—Bill Rutter
Dance—Ron Smedley & Bob Parker - Song—Tony Foxworthy

GUEST SINGER : LOUIS KILLEN
Supported by over 100 Club Singers from all over Britain

BANDS — The Ranchers : leader, Brian Willcocks
The Journeymen : leader, Brian Connor

MORRIS — Green Man's Morris & Sword Club
Headington Quarry Morris Men
Jockey Men's Morris Club
Lutterworth Boys' Morris
Chanctonbury Morris Men

Teams from Abroad
Return Visit of the RORY O'CONNOR DANCERS (Dublin)
LACHY ENSEMBLE (Poland)
LUGGUDEGILLET (Sweden)
SCHÖNHENGSTER SING — UNO SPIELSCHAR (Bavaria)
PARTI PRIFYSGOL — ABERTAIRE (Wales)
plus 200 ENGLISH DANCERS from the four corners of England
● Singing three times a day
● Dance Displays twice a day
● Public singing and dancing
● 4 Square Dances
● Mummers

FESTIVAL NIGHT CLUB (Registered Festival Members Only)
MUSICIAN'S CLUB — CHILDREN'S CLUB
* 'You just have to go to Sidmouth Folk Festival at least once in your life'

Connaught Gardens

Ron Smedley became Dance Director with a clear brief from Bill: 'He well knows what his job is – to bring the standards up.' More and more experienced dancers and teams were going abroad to festivals and on exchanges, some of which Bill organised, leaving Sidmouth with the less knowledgeable and less experienced. Bill had already started using the marketing slogan 'You must come to Sidmouth at least once in your life', but he acknowledged that this 'makes Sidmouth a starting point whereas in the early days it was a culmination'. The two companies, Trefusis and Storrow, were retained and they performed the same programme of dances, rehearsing in the marquee on the Ham, and on the grass outside. Instead of trying to be too clever with the dances, Bill told Ron 'I recommend the slogan "the simpler the better" '. He also insisted that each display must be followed by general dancing for the public.

Ron had worked for the EFDSS, but he then pursued a career in the BBC, eventually becoming Deputy Head of Department of BBC Schools TV, producer of *Grange Hill* and the recipient of several awards including, in 2002, a BAFTA Silver Mask for lifetime achievement in

broadcasting. He produced several of the EFDSS's Royal Albert Hall shows, was director of the Sunday Practice Club which became the London Festival Dancers and eventually London Folk.

The downside of Ron's brief to drive up standards was the impact this had on the dancers who were not up to it, or who thought they knew it anyway, or who just wanted to have a holiday. He expected his dancers to work hard and be committed, to have confidence, project and make a connection with

the audience. One dancer wrote that, 'after taking the trouble and expense to do what I like doing, dancing, it was very disappointing' to be left out of the display team. Another regular attender wrote that at the first rehearsal, 'Ron had to drive us very hard (unnecessarily for most of us) in order to bring these few poor or inexperienced dancers up to public performance standard. (No mention of the word "holiday" was made during the whole week!!)'.

Nevertheless, Ron's strategy attracted more dancers to the Festival, and larger audiences to the displays. Bill was relieved when Ron agreed to direct the dance displays again the following year – in fact Ron was bubbling with enthusiasm – 'try and keep us away'.

Bill tried to hold the balance between the need to improve the standard of the displays, and the dancers who just wanted to dance

Schönhengster Sing und Spielschar from Germany and Austria

for fun. But for the dancers not selected for displays, and for those dancers who did not want to dance in the displays anyway, not to mention the singers who wanted to dance, there needed to be more to do.

Before 1965 the only opportunities to dance socially were at the end of the displays, and informally along the Esplanade, plus the mid-week dance in the marquee. Brian Hayden, who had come to the Festival with the Sheffield Cutlers, wrote to Bill with suggestions for public dancing in the 'turnaround' at Port Royal and in the Market Square, greater use of the marquee for evening dances and square dances in the halls of neighbouring villages. As a result, Brian was put in charge of village square dances in 1965 – Sidford on Monday evening, Newton Poppleford on Tuesday and Otterton on Wednesday (Thursday was the dance in the marquee). MCs or callers were arranged but securing bands was more difficult, and Pete Shutler of The Yetties provided the music.

By 1965, it was accepted that the Morris men need not dance in the country dancing unless they really wanted to. That year, the Midlands provided the bulk of the Morris men, with both the Green Man's and Jockey sides. On Thursday evening in the Market Square they jointly recreated the 'Princess Royal Suite' that had been a feature of the Royal Albert Hall Festival earlier in the year – a combination of the versions of the song, tune and dance, 'Princess Royal'. The Market Square had already been the venue for a mummers' play performed by members of Chanctonbury Ring Morris in 1964, and this was repeated on Tuesday evening the following year. Both events were followed by dancing for the general public. Police permission was needed because the Market Square was not yet traffic-free. On Monday and Wednesday evening at 9.00pm there was public dancing at Port Royal.

Bill Rutter leads the first children's event, 1965

Luggudegillet dance group from Helsingborg in Sweden visited the Festival as one leg of an exchange visit and English dancers from the South-West led by Geoff Rye travelled to Sweden later in the month. The appearance of the Schönhengster Sing und Spielschar Ensemble was a timely reminder of the upheavals resulting from war-ravaged Europe. The group was made up of German speakers from Bohemia and Moravia (then in Czechoslovakia) who moved as refugees to Germany and Austria after 1945.

As in 1964, there were displays on Friday and Saturday evenings. Friday was an All Britain night, with England represented by Honiton Secondary School. Bill had problems finding some Scottish dancers, but the Welsh dancers came from Swansea University, called Parti Prifysgol, Abertawe. They included a couple of regular festival-goers – Roger Luckwill whose father Leonard was an EFDSS National Executive member, and Iain Bryden, son of Archie. Neither of them were Welsh, they just happened to be

Luggudegillet from Sweden

students in Swansea. Saturday included the international groups and a team of dancers from the South-West.

Alongside Ron Smedley's new approach, Bill was also anxious to take a different direction with the music that accompanied the display and general dancing. Hitherto, one person had put together a collection of musicians, but something more formal was needed. 'We need something with a punch and the newer beat,' Bill wrote. Complete bands were booked instead – The Ranchers, led by Brian Willcocks, and The Journeymen – not the song group from Exeter but Brian Connor's band from Essex: Brian was an early Festival visitor and had played for Benfleet Hoymen.

In addition to the last-night party, there was also a demand for a late-night event every night of the week. In 1964, an additional song spot had been included at 10.30pm, but with Tony Foxworthy in charge of folk song, there was a change in focus in 1965. 'Tony's idea of turning the night spot into a ceilidhe was marvellous and I shall never forget the Welsh man dancing on the wagon or the Sheffield Cutlers or the sight of all the singers dancing. It was really great,' wrote Mary Goyle from Norwich. The wagon

was part of the Council's decoration in the Beach Store. 'Magical' was the word Bill used in his report. 'The singers danced (and the dancers sang?). Hardly, but famous names are now convinced that "Virginia Reel" ranks with "Barley Mow",' Bill wrote. How anybody managed to dance in the Beach Store is a bit of a puzzle, as it only had a tiny wooden floor surrounded by sand. Something different would be needed for 1966.

> *The locals told Bob Common the crowd was bigger than for the victory celebrations after the war*

With a more complex programme of events, and a greater variety of dance groups and singers to see and hear, a souvenir programme was needed to sell to the general public. 3,000 programmes were printed, selling at one shilling (5p) each. The front cover was illustrated with a 1964 photograph of a decorated lamp-post on the Esplanade.

The Festival was attracting more people and a slightly wider age range which inevitably meant that some people brought their children

to the Festival. Bill decided that the continuing mission of the Festival to appeal to the general public and to the local residents, should be extended to children. The result was a daily event in the morning for children, to include dancing and singing games, and Bill decided to call it the Hobby Horse Club. Bill's first attempts to find someone to lead this event were unsuccessful – the people he asked were teachers who preferred to have a holiday – so Bill took the sessions himself. Admission was by six-penny Hobby Horse Club badge (2.5 pence). The families of the Jockey Morris Men helped to make the Hobby Horse Club a real success in that first year.

The Festival came to a dramatic climax on Friday evening with a Torchlight Procession. When it was first suggested by Bill Rutter, Sidmouth Urban District Council thought it 'an excellent idea'. The final night display was in the Blackmore Gardens, and the procession came through the town centre and onto the Esplanade. Bill's report on the Festival described it as 'fantastic – hundreds were expected; thousands turned up'. The locals told Bob Common that the crowd was bigger than for the victory celebrations after the war.

The first Torchlight Procession, 1965

Singing in Harmony

Sidmouth Folk Festival

Pageant of Dance & Song
August 1966

Souvenir Programme

1966 By 1966 the folk song revival had really taken off. From seventy-eight clubs in 1962, there were now estimated to be over 300. The EFDSS set up the Western Federation of Folk Song Clubs and Ken Penney from the Jolly Porter Folk Club in Exeter became Tony Foxworthy's assistant in running the folk song events.

The increased popularity of song was reflected at the Festival – Joss Mellor from Sheffield wrote that 'some of our folk song people are crying out for the Sidmouth leaflet. Please supply 50'. The Council would not make the Beach Store available to the Festival, in spite of Bill's protests, and instead the Drill Hall was used. The number of song guests was extended to include the folk scene's two great harmony groups – The Young Tradition (Peter Bellamy, Heather Wood and Royston Wood) and The Watersons, plus Frankie Armstrong and Bob Roberts. Not all the guests were there all week: The Young Tradition came from Saturday to Monday but after a booking elsewhere they returned to the Festival without

further payment. In fact they offered to help in any way so that they could be part of the event, and The Yetties were impressed that Heather Wood helped to clean the toilets. The Watersons were booked for the Wednesday and Thursday only, but after performing at Beaulieu Festival on Friday afternoon, they returned to Sidmouth for the last-night party. Norma Waterson, Heather Wood and Rod Stradling wrote topical parodies of the epic poem 'Hiawatha' and the song 'The Holmfirth Anthem' which were performed at the party.

The Sunday concert featured The Young Tradition, The Wayfarers, The Yetties and Music of the Countryside, whilst a second concert with The Watersons, The Yetties, Bob Roberts and music from The Ranchers was held in the Methodist Church Hall on Wednesday. The Music of the Countryside was a concert performance led by Nan Fleming-Williams, one of the senior EFDSS musicians who spear-headed the music for square dancing from the 1940s and played regularly on BBC broadcasts. The other members

were Pat Shaw and Denis Smith. Nan wrote to Bill that they had 'some rattling good tunes guaranteed to reduce folk clubs to a state of rapturous hysteria without fail'.

In the decade leading up to the fiftieth Festival, the number of young singers and musicians involved in folk music, song and dance has rightly been applauded. It is easy to forget that in the mid-sixties there were just as many young singers and musicians – indeed there was a much greater proportion of young people back then. In 1966, all the members of The Watersons, The Young Tradition, The Yetties, as well as Frankie Armstrong were under the age of 31. The Yetties' folk club in Yeovil attracted a number of people who attended the Festival, including two young enthusiasts, Philip George and David Thomas – the latter better known as Taffy Thomas who was sixteen and had just completed his GCE O-levels. Philip and Taffy offered to help with sales, but Bill felt they should buy their tickets and asked Bob Common of the Yetties for a recommendation. Bill was re-assured and gave them free tickets after Bob said that he had had a 'fatherly talk' with them – Bob was then aged 25!

Taffy is one of the many people who recall an outstanding event on the Saturday that the Festival

Song Spot in the Drill Hall

Tony Capstick and Malcolm Fox from Sheffield at the camp-site bonfire

Royston Wood and Lal Waterson at the camp fire

started. This was the Football World Cup Final at Wembley when England beat Germany. Taffy watched the winning goal at home, just before Pete Shutler picked him up in his car to take him to Sidmouth. The Festival dancers attended a Council reception in the late afternoon, but one of the dancers had a transistor radio and relayed the score around the marquee as the game went into extra time. Ron Smedley remembers that the Chairman of the Council was still making his speech when the memorable words, 'They think it's all over – it is now!' were uttered.

Brothers Paul and Gerry Bates from Sheffield were on holiday in Teignmouth with their parents in 1964 when they made several evening visits to the Festival. They were already involved in the Sheffield folk club scene, and returned to the Festival in 1965 with their friends Malcolm Fox and John Civico. By 1966 there were a dozen people from Sheffield, mainly from the Barley Mow Folk Club: this was quite apart from the Cutlers. Gerry's photographs show Lal Waterson, Tony Capstick and Royston Wood standing round the bonfire on the camp-site on Edwin Hill's field at Bulverton Well. This may have been the year that Bill

Rutter was summoned to the campsite in his dressing-gown after complaints that the singing was keeping people awake.

The 1960s were, of course, a period of rapid social change, especially affecting young people. Fashion, hair length, musical styles, methods of political protest, campaigns for racial equality, anti-apartheid protests, the anti-Vietnam War campaign, relations between the sexes, alcohol and drugs were all challenging the established order. The folk scene was not unaffected by such change, and there was inevitable tension with a slightly (but only slightly) older generation of social dancers, not to mention the resident population of Sidmouth. Rod Stradling remembers the differences between the singers and dancers at this stage: 'we were hip, they were square'. The tensions were most clearly seen at the Festival in the general appearance of the singers, in the selection of songs for both private, but more importantly public consumption, and in the amount of alcohol being drunk.

After the 1965 Festival, Fred Austin from Newton Abbot had already commented to Bill that the singers should be reminded that they were the public face of the song revival and that they should not 'shock newcomers with songs that should be kept for the rugby club.'

By this he meant songs which had a sexual story line. Another festival-goer wrote that the first night audience at the Drill Hall in 1966 was presented with 'a monotonous succession of badly sung "public house" songs – many in poor taste, from a table loaded with bottles of beer and sung by apparently inebriated singers.' These accusations were denied by the participants. There was even a suggestion that the singers should submit the songs in advance to the compere, so as to keep tight control on the songs presented to a mixed holiday audience.

It is possible to see in these comments the changing nature of the Festival. The Festival's foundation was based on the premise that the performances were for the general public, to encourage them to take part and perhaps continue their new interest after the Festival, but at least to spread a little

> This may have been the year that Bill Rutter was summoned to the campsite in his dressing-gown after complaints that the singing was keeping people awake

knowledge and understanding about England's folk traditions. This was certainly the case with the dancing, but it also extended to song. But increasingly the singers, and indeed the dancers, wanted the opportunity to sing for each other and dance together. Fellow enthusiasts would understand the nuances of traditional style, the traditional basis for unaccompanied singing and the sometimes risqué repertoire within the tradition. The experienced dancers wanted to dance something a little more challenging than 'Cumberland Square Eight' and 'Circassian Circle'. In addition, it had always been assumed that all the festival-goers would contribute as volunteers to help with collections, make coffee, staff the sales table and information centre, as well as provide the dance displays. Some people, however, simply wanted to enjoy the music and dancing and just have a holiday. Nevertheless, that sense of belonging, of helping and of volunteering can still be seen throughout the Festival.

Bill Rutter, as ever, tried to follow a middle line: he was certainly keen to give great encouragement to younger performers, and was prepared to accept youthful exuberance. On the other hand, he was aware of the involvement and support of the general public, particularly the local residents. He felt that tradition should be receptive to new ideas, and that the 'traditionalists' were in danger of being exclusive, not entertaining and thereby 'no better than the Playfordites'. He was a traditionalist, but not a purist.

A comment from a folk dancer appreciated that the Song Spot generation were very similar to her own generation a few years earlier. 'We loved the Song Spot. How funny it was to see all of us in another generation. Nice things, teenagers.'

The Drill Hall may have lacked the intimate atmosphere of the Beach Store, but it did provide a better setting for the Night Club, which maintained the 'ceilidh' atmosphere with a mixture of social

English dancers at Port Royal

folk dancing, singing, displays by the Morris teams and overseas dancers. Nan Fleming-Williams described it as 'the spot of the week,' and felt that if festival-goers did not attend at least once, they were 'very definitely the losers'.

The downside of the slogan, 'the simpler the better' and the identical displays by both Trefusis and Storrow (they appeared at different shows) was that the public and the folk dancers in the audience commented that they had seen it all before. To vary the dances and make the displays a little less similar the quality of the dancers had to be further improved. The publicity leaflet for 1966 stated, 'If you wish to be considered for Display Dancing, please indicate on Booking Form, and make sure you are

present for the audition in the Rehearsal marquee on Saturday night, 30th July, when seventy-two couples will be chosen.' The leaflet went on to say that if you are not chosen, do not worry because there is much more to do than dancing in the displays. But for one person who wrote to Bill, being in the displays and official busking parties was the 'chief thrill and enjoyment of the Festival'. But Bill also had to consider the audiences, and increasingly the overseas dance groups were better rehearsed than the English displays.

The village square dances were repeated, with Colyford and Sidbury replacing Newton Poppleford and Otterton, and the overseas dance groups and Morris Men performed there during the evening. There was a desire by the English dancers to learn the dances of the overseas groups, and to teach them English dances. The previous year this had happened informally, after the Swedes were most anxious to swap their dances: Jenifer Barlow described the event as 'really marvellous' in a letter to Bill. The dances were formalised in 1966 and called the Swappers' Club, held from 9.30 to 10.30pm in the marquee, after the public displays. Each evening featured a different overseas dance group, plus a group of English musicians, and the whole event was compered by the person who suggested the event in the first place,

Westminster Morris Men

Chingford Boys' Morris

Griff Jones from Lutterworth. This was the start of the events later known as 'Meet the Team' and now as 'A Chance to Meet' and 'Dance Roots'.

Green Man's Morris were back at the Festival in 1966 – Bill often encouraged bands and Morris teams to come two years on the run – alongside Beaux of London City, Westminster and, for the third year, Headington Quarry Morris Men, plus the Sheffield Cutlers. There was a great deal of overlap between the Beaux and other people involved in the Festival that year – Ron Smedley and his assistant Bob Parker, as well as members of The Ranchers were all members of the side. John Tether as the team's hobby horse was a great asset to the Festival as a collector, and he subsequently became an effective MC at the Festival. There was, however, a general feeling of a London bias.

Bill was very keen to encourage youth dance teams, such as the pupils from Honiton School and the Lutterworth boys. 1966 saw the first

- First credit card
- Prices and incomes freeze
- Severn Road Bridge opens
- Aberfan Disaster
- World Cup: England 4, Germany 2
- Carnaby Street
- Chinese cultural revolution
- No 1 hits for The Troggs, Small faces, Beach Boys and … The Beatles.

1966

visit of a London team of schoolboys, Chingford Morris, who were inspired by Peter Boyce, a teacher at Chingford County High School, where he repeated the successes he had achieved at Weston-super-Mare Grammar School – encouraging an interest in folk music and dance amongst the boys. In some cases, Peter was responsible for starting a life-long passion for folk music and dance. His successor as folk enthusiast-in-residence at Weston was John Brock, one of his former pupils who returned to the school as a music teacher, and who still leads the Weston Country Dance Band.

The Chingford boys were away from home for almost three weeks – apart from Sidmouth they also went to one of Bill's Folk Camps. They were mainly sixth-formers and some of them, including Geoff Hughes, had actually started Morris dancing at primary school. In due course, Geoff became a clog-dancer, ran workshops at Sidmouth, met his future wife at the Festival and as a result moved to Lancashire where he founded the Rumworth and Abram Morris sides.

As well as the morning rehearsals for the country dancers, there was a Morris rehearsal. Bill's intention here was for the Morris men to rehearse their entrances and exits, plus any possible massed Morris displays. The reality was slightly

different, and Peter Boyce's comments are indicative of the changing nature of Morris. Peter took his boys out of the 'practice' because, 'We were being taught a particular style for the massed Morris. This was having an horrific effect on my boys, (a) they were confused, (b) they concluded that "sir" had taught them wrongly.' Peter believed that in the massed Morris displays, teams should be allowed to do their own style. 'Morris practice should not be used to standardise style.' Nevertheless, he felt that, 'the festival has had a tremendous effect on the juniors'. Peter's comments had an impact on the programme the following year.

The opening of the Festival on the Friday evening was billed as 'Young England' and featured the Chingford Boys and, once again, country dances from Honiton Secondary Modern School pupils.

> **The trunks with all the costumes were lost on the rail journey, but fortunately each dancer had a costume in their hand luggage**

The dances performed by the teenagers included 'Morpeth Rant', 'Jubilee Roundabout', 'The Rifleman', 'Devon Bonny Breast Knot' and the 'Circle Waltz'. Additional displays came from the Welsh group Parti Prifysgol, making a return visit, and international dance groups.

There were further advances with the overseas dance groups, and for the first time, an émigré group in England was invited to the Festival: the Latvian dance group Sakta who came from Bradford, and who were recommended by a Latvian resident of Sidmouth. The Boerke Naas Volkskunstgroep from St Niklaas in Belgium came for a long weekend and performed flag-waving and sword dances.

But the biggest impact in 1966

Torchlight Procession in Church Street

Skalitshan Ensemble, Czechoslovakia

came from the first Eastern European visitors: the Skalitshan Ensemble from Skalica, West Slovakia – then part of Czechoslovakia. The group had a memorable impact. Nineteen-year-old Bob West worked alongside Ted Poole who persuaded him to come to the Festival. Bob remembers teaching the Slovak dancers how to play darts in the Swan Inn, and that they sang everywhere they went. The trunks with all the costumes were lost on the rail journey, but fortunately each dancer had one costume in their hand luggage. During the Festival, Eva Kolesarova, a dancer who spoke excellent English, fell in love with a BBC film editor and member of the folk club in Plymouth, David Sharp. After a courtship which survived the Russian invasion of Czechoslovakia in 1968, they were married in 1969, and still live in Plymouth. Visits to Western Europe from Communist-bloc countries were rare and the group had no money. The Town-Festival Liaison Committee carried out some fund-raising and raised £30 which was given to the group as pocket money.

And once again, there were the Rory O'Connor Irish Dancers.

After the success of the Hobby Horse Club, Bill looked around to find someone to run the morning sessions. Stephanie Barlow was a local teenager who had helped with

the Festival whilst still at school. By 1966 she was at teacher training college, and agreed to run the Hobby Horse Club alongside Evelyn Summers from London who taught singing games and nursery rhymes to the youngest children. John and Mary Brock played for them, and there were visits from the Chingford Boys. The whole event really took off and the *Sidmouth Herald* carried letters of thanks from local parents.

Bill continued to struggle with accommodation. A new hostel was located in Cuddy's Nest, which was a youth club in the Globe Stables on East Street, another property that has since been demolished and replaced by the Ham Car Park. Cuddy's Nest was a nickname for The Globe, a pre-war pub. But with 200 people to accommodate in hostels – a figure which had doubled in two years – somewhere new had to be found to feed them. Bill obtained permission to use St Nicholas School for a hostel and as a canteen, but just before the Festival started, the number of rooms available was reduced and the school withdrew permission to use the kitchens. So the cooking continued at Halse's Yard, and a trolley ferried it across to a second, smaller marquee on the Ham Car Park.

Seemingly for the first time, a 'working programme' was produced alongside the souvenir programme. The former document included all the events, including those (such as the Night Club) reserved exclusively for the ticket holders and, as it was produced closer to the Festival, it was also more accurate. This practice continued until the souvenir programme was discontinued after the 1999 Festival, but it is the reason why the phrase 'working' programme is still used.

The Torchlight Procession was again the climax of the Festival. The procession came from the Blackmore Gardens, down High Street, Fore Street, then turned right up New Street, through the Market Square, up Church Street to the Triangle, and

then onto and along the Esplanade to Port Royal. The description of what happened next is almost exactly the same as today. When the dancers arrived on the Esplanade and the procession stopped, the dancers gave their torches to the by-standers whilst they danced. A rocket was then the signal for the dancers to retrieve their torches and continue to the water's edge. The difference in 1966 was that it was possible to jump, or even step, off the Esplanade onto the beach! When the second rocket went off, 'torches will be simultaneously doused in the sea'. In 1966, however, there were no fireworks.

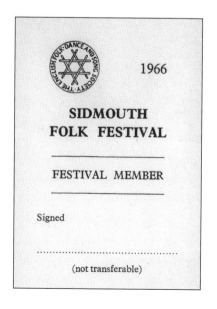

1966

SIDMOUTH FOLK FESTIVAL

FESTIVAL MEMBER

Signed

....

(not transferable)

Morris Dancing for Folk Singers

1967

The 1967 Festival saw some significant changes as far as Morris dancing was concerned, and these changes heralded an important re-focussing of the Festival in other areas of dance.

In the early years of the Festival, many male members of the company of dancers were also Morris men (this was before women started to Morris dance). There was a single 'correct' way of dancing each dance based on the volumes of Cecil Sharp's *The Morris Book*, and therefore a group of six men from different teams could perform the same dance in the same way. As the Festival became established, specific teams were invited, generally those with a high standard of dance who were attracted to the idea of a folk festival. The Morris men were no longer expected to dance in the country dance displays, although some of them chose to do so. The same situation applied to sword dance teams, although there were fewer teams that specialised in sword dancing. Morris dancing was still exclusively Cotswold or South Midlands Morris. There were very few North-West Morris teams, no Border or Molly teams, and no 'invented' traditions.

Increasingly, younger men were becoming interested in Morris dancing, some of them from the song clubs, and they wanted to re-interpret the dances, rather than follow the established 'Book' way of performing them. Roy Dommett played a vital role in encouraging dancers to think about how and what they danced. The need for a different approach to Morris dancing at the Festival could be seen in Peter Boyce's comments after the 1966 Festival. The Chingford team were back again in 1967 – by this time the membership extended beyond the sixth formers to include folk enthusiasts from the area, and the team was dancing Morris, rapper, longsword, clog, and the sailor's hornpipe clog, and they also had a mummers' play.

Chingford were joined by the other young 'stars' of the London Morris scene – Hammersmith Morris Men. Their squire was nineteen-year-old John Kirkpatrick, who had already been Morris dancing for seven years. The team had been founded and initially taught by Hugh Rippon, and included Tony Poile (ex-Sheffield Cutlers). Like Chingford, they offered a full repertoire, including a mummers' play ('owes more to Charlie Chaplin and the Goon Show than Cecil Sharp House – it includes a five-man dragon', wrote John Kirkpatrick) and the Abbots Bromley Horn Dance (they learned this especially for Sidmouth and borrowed the set of horns owned by the EFDSS).

A year or two earlier, the Sheffield Cutlers had danced non-stop rapper along the Esplanade for forty-five minutes and in 1967 both Chingford and Hammersmith set out to break the record. Chingford were first, dancing for sixty-two minutes, but this record was broken by Hammersmith who lasted for ninety minutes. Chingford had their revenge in 1970 when they danced two lengths of the Esplanade: two hours in total, with Geoff Hughes wearing out a pair of shoes. That record still stands.

Chingford and Hammersmith brought youthful exuberance to the Morris, and paved the way for the excitement of the seventies. But the significant change in the Festival's approach to Morris was that, instead of simply providing 'rehearsals' for established dancers, it started teaching people how to do the dances. We take this for granted now, but it was a novelty at the time, and indicated that the Festival was attracting a new type of folk enthusiast.

Hugh Rippon was asked to run two separate events – Beginners' Morris Practice (9.30am) and Morris Teams' Practice (10.00am), which laid emphasis on the entrances and exits for the displays. Hugh was the Public Relations Officer for the EFDSS, although this was his first visit to Sidmouth. In addition, Peter Boyce ran a 'Clog and Rapper for Beginners' session at 11.30am each day. Both events were a great success and captured the ever-increasing song enthusiasts. Indeed Bill wrote afterwards, 'We now hold Morris and rapper clubs for the folk singers'. These events were not yet called 'workshops'.

Hammersmith Morris Men with John Kirkpatrick second from right

Hugh was invited back in 1968, with the Morris Rehearsal at 11.15am and Beginners' Morris at 11.45am in the marquee, whilst Paddy O'Neill taught sword dancing. In the programme, Bill gave the Beginners' Morris events a variety of descriptions, starting with 'Morris for anyone including folk club types' on Monday, 'Morris for Inexperienced' on Tuesday, and 'Morris for anyone' on Friday. Hugh Rippon remembers that the numbers of people turning up were so large that they had to move out of the marquee and onto the grass on the Ham: Hugh taught from the tailgate of his Land Rover. A few years later, Hugh remarked to Bill that he kept 'bumping into the results' of these Morris sessions all over the country.

The impact of Morris dancing on the town is illustrated by a display at the final-night party, which was

Nautical Night in Blackmore Gardens

> ## With true civic dignity, they pranced about wearing flowers in their hats and bells on their rolled-up trousers

always the occasion for frivolity. The *Sidmouth Herald* reported that four Sidmouth councillors performed a Morris dance, 'With true civic dignity, they pranced about wearing flowers in their hats and bells on their rolled-up trousers. Instead of carrying sticks or swords for the carefully rehearsed Morris dance, they brandished buckets and spades.' The four councillors concerned were C.E.Fryer, Peter Ikin, Frank Lock and Alan Gibberd.

Both Ron Smedley and Tony Foxworthy had directed at the Festival for two years, and new people were now appointed. Peter Dashwood became Director of Dance and, as he was a member of the EFDSS staff – he was the Southern Area Organiser based in Bournemouth – Bill increasingly relied on him in the preparation of the Festival. Bill's EFDSS region had expanded and he was involved in Folk Camps and the purchase of

Halsway Manor in Somerset as a residential folk centre. In 1967 he also co-ordinated National Folk Week, a nationwide event in May, so he was grateful for Peter's help. First in the south, and later as EFDSS Eastern Area Organiser, Peter shared Bill's infectious enthusiasm and instigated a whole series of events, festivals and clubs – song, dance, Morris. He was also responsible for attracting many new people from the southern area to Sidmouth.

Like Ron Smedley, Peter was keen to improve the standard of dancing amongst the English company of dancers, and he was particularly concerned to have a fast-moving show with, for example, short bursts of Morris dancing in the displays, and a slick presentation. Peter Dashwood was also keen to vary the content of the displays in order to avoid the criticism that the shows were becoming too similar. On Tuesday evening, the whole show in

the Blackmore Gardens had a nautical theme, with singers performing songs such as 'The Leaving of Liverpool' and shanties whilst 'hoisting the mainsail' (actually, nets tied to ropes looped over a tree trunk), and the Chingford dancers performing the 'Sailor's Hornpipe'. The dances performed in the daily displays included more traditional dances from the *Community Dance Manuals* – 'Goathland Square', 'Speed the Plough', 'Ninepins', 'Dorset Four-Hand Reel' and 'The Wiltshire Tempest'.

Apart from the overseas dancers, the Morris teams and the dancers who rehearsed the social folk dance items, a different dance dimension was provided by the Reading University Playford Dance Display Team. Bill had seen them at the Inter-Varsity Folk Dance Festival, and amongst the dancers were Brian

Hammersmith Morris perform the Abbots Bromley Horn Dance

Bill Rutter as Beau Nash

Jones (the son of Cyril and Iris Jones), Stuart Ball, later the Festival's treasurer, and Ian Graham: both Brian and Ian were later Chairmen of the EFDSS National Executive. The group was introduced by Bill Rutter, dressed as Beau Nash the eighteenth-century Bath Assembly Rooms master of ceremonies. After one performance, the dancers, still in costume, went for a cream tea in a neighbouring village where Mary Gosling (now Meeks) remembers an American tourist being dumbfounded by her 'olde English' dress. The first Scottish dance group appeared at the Festival, the Westbury Scottish Dancers from Bristol, some of whose members continue to perform as Corryvrechan.

As for the dances in the villages and the Thursday night dance in the marquee, these were billed as 'ceilidhs'. Bill had written, 'We are trying to turn some of the square dances (a bit out of date) into ceilidhs'. Thursday was the 'Grand Festival Ceilidh' with The Yetties, Hugh Rippon, the dancers from the Canary Islands, Dave and Toni Arthur and Hammersmith Morris Men. The daily Swappers' Club continued, and on Saturday night, the marquee was the venue for a 'Public Folk Dance'. Increasingly, therefore, the marquee was being used for evening events, with the risk that the displays would have to be cancelled if it rained. Bill took out pluvius insurance which cost £77 for the week, based on expected collections of £40 a performance: one show was spoilt by rain.

Denis Manners was in charge of song events in 1967 and 1968. Well known as the founder of Towersey Village Festival in Oxfordshire, Denis was then a singer, song club organiser and Morris dancer, and also a member of the EFDSS National Executive, Chairman of the British Federation of Folk Song Clubs and involved with Folk Camps. He had first visited the Festival in the fifties. To assist him in 1967 was Festival regular Ted Poole from Swindon Folk Club. Ted was heavily involved with the Western Federation and was also one of the committee members organising the Keele Festival. Ted and his wife Ivy continue to run their folk club – the longest established folk club organisers in the country.

The song guests included The Trunkles, Irish singer Tim Lyons, Dave and Toni Arthur and The Yetties. Cyril Phillips from Sussex brought the traditional anglo-concertina player Scan Tester to the Festival for a couple of days. The Trunkles included Festival regular Brian Hayden, and it was during the Festival that Brian figured out how to improve his duet concertina which then led to the manufacture of concertinas with the Hayden Duet keyboard system. The Yetties had suggested The High Level Ranters from Tyneside as guests and although the whole group could not come, Johnny Handle and Colin Ross performed at the Festival, and Tom Gilfellon visited for part of the

> *Bill was canny enough to realise that some singers would welcome the opportunity of a holiday by the seaside, with free tickets, in exchange for inclusion in the programme*

week. Scottish singer Ray Fisher, who is married to Colin, also sang. Griff Jones managed the song events with Taffy Thomas as his assistant.

Not all of the song 'guests' were paid a fee. Bill was canny enough to realise that some singers would welcome the opportunity of a holiday by the seaside, with perhaps some contribution towards their travel or accommodation plus free tickets, all in exchange for inclusion in the programme. This continued to be a feature of the booking policy for several years.

For The Yetties, the summer of 1967 was a landmark, because in September they turned professional. Bill believed that he had taken them

Dave & Toni Arthur in the Beach Store

Stefan Grossman plays guitar watched by Denis Manners with Scan Tester (left), Ray Fisher (glasses) and Rod Stradling (standing).

for granted in the past, so offered them 'star billing', a fee and hotel accommodation. The group was very important to Bill – they were a bridge between the song and dance worlds, equally respected by both, and necessary for Bill to help improve the public and private image of the folk song events. They were also the Festival's unofficial ambassadors around the country. 'See you at Sidmouth' they would say up and down the country, and they did.

Tony Foxworthy had wanted to move the song events into the pubs, but Bill knew that they were not yet ready to welcome festival-goers to sing and play in their bars. Indeed, at the 1967 Festival there were several confrontations between some of the pubs and a few festival-goers, 'especially if they happen to be fashionably attired with a beard', wrote Bill. There were so many complaints that he wrote to the brewery about the treatment of festival-goers in The Black Horse and The Dove, in particular. The brewery responded with regret, stating that the tenants only refused to serve 'unwashed beatnicks of dishevelled appearance, with bedrolls slung over their shoulders who invariably ask for rough cider'. Bill, of course, distanced himself from the 'beatnicks' and tried unsuccessfully to meet with the local Licensed Victuallers' Association in the winter months. This was probably the year that Eddie Upton was refused service in The Black Horse for wearing jeans, and Peter Dashwood in The Dove because he had a beard.

Pete Coe made his first visit to the Festival in 1967. Born in Cheshire, Pete was at teacher training college in Cheltenham, and went to the

Roque Nublo from the Canary Islands

Festival with local folk club members, including the resident group The Songwainers whose members then included Dave Stephenson and Sue Burgess. Dave Hunt was another first timer that year, as was Eddie Upton who sang at the Festival with Derek Lockwood and Paul Holden in a group called The Juggs. Heather Wood took a few days off from her Young Tradition commitments to introduce American blues guitarist Stefan Grossman, in his first year in England, to the Festival. A photograph of Stefan was used on a subsequent Festival postcard.

The previous year, Rod Stradling had met Danny Greene, and they were married on 5 August 1967: their Festival visit was also their honeymoon. They were just one of many couples who have spent their honeymoon at the Festival over the years. Not many of them, however, had Taffy Thomas tagging along to a romantic meal during the week!

The Night Club venue was again the Drill Hall, and each evening there was a different band or couple of musicians to play for the dancing and some singers. Several of the nights were themed. Tuesday was Sheffield Night, which was led by Paul and Gerry Bates, who brought thirty-five other members and friends of the Barley Mow Folk Club to the Festival. Although Gerry is

now a member of Grenoside Sword Dancers, he then had no experience of folk dance and they asked Bill Rutter to call the dances, whilst they concentrated on the singing. They also performed a topical mummers' play with characters that included 'Old Father McCall' (a thinly-disguised Ewan MacColl, played by Gerry), 'Sir Bold Foxworthy', 'Good King Harold' (Harold Wilson, the Prime Minister) and the Conservative leader 'Edward of the Heath'. Wednesday was North Country Night, led by Johnny Handle, Thursday was Spanish Night with the Canary Islands dancers, and Friday was the traditional last night party – Peter Dashwood had unsuccessfully suggested a 'binge and barbeque on the beach'.

Away from Sidmouth, other international festivals had become established outside the EFDSS: The Folkestone International Folklore Festival and, in the north, the Billingham International Folklore Festival which was established by the local council under the direction of Philip Conroy. Links were established between Sidmouth and Billingham – links which continue today – because Billingham was just after Sidmouth, and groups could be shared. In 1967 one of the truly memorable groups appeared at both festivals – Agrupacion Folklorica Roque Nublo from the Canary Islands.

Package holidays were still in their infancy and the Canary Islands were

1967

- Breathalyser
- Abortion legalised
- Pound devalued
- Liverpool's RC Cathedral consecrated
- Sergeant Pepper's Lonely Hearts' Club Band LP
- First colour TV
- Arab-Israeli Six Day War
- Procol Harum's 'Whiter Shade of Pale', Bee Gees and The Monkees at No 1 … and The Beatles.

Roque Nublo musicians

not a holiday destination. Bill reckoned that they would have the same sort of impact as the Israelis – and he was right. The Roque Nublo dancers brought their own LP record, and quickly sold out. They gave out lapel badges in the form of little bunches of bananas, and these were much sought after. As Bill wrote afterwards, 'Everyone, as you must know, loved the warmth and excitement you brought with you'. A Sidmouth resident wrote to the *Sidmouth Herald*, 'Hail to our visitors and hosts! What an atmosphere of sunny carefree happiness created by the irresistible rhythm of the music and song of our friends from the Canary Islands.' They offered to perform at the local hospital, where by chance, the Chairman of Sidmouth Urban District Council, Ted Pinney, was recovering from an operation. The resulting photograph graced the front page of the *Sidmouth Herald*, and during the week, all the other groups made similar visits.

Alongside Roque Nublo were groups from Belgium – Reuzegom, performing Flemish dances and flag waving – and Germany. Die Trabanten Göttinger Tanz und Spielkreis was from a youth organisation in Göttingen. Bill booked them without knowing very much about them and then discovered that they intended to dance to gramophone records. Fortunately, Bill found the correct music in the EFDSS's Library and Kathy Upton was volunteered as a musician. It was clear that Bill had to be a little more selective in his choice of groups.

Accommodation proved to be a headache again, in spite of the addition of the Old Fire Station, close to the Radway Cinema, and Cherry Hayes, a large building on the site of the public library, which housed the Canary Islanders and the Belgians. Ten members of the German group stayed in the home of Alan Gibberd in Bowd, whilst the

Drill Hall was used as the canteen for all the hostellers. The camp-site location had to be moved at the last minute to a field beyond Greenway Lane at Bowd: this was further out of town than the usual site. The facilities were, however, a little better, thanks to the Council, and the working programme promised 'reasonable toilets'.

In a letter to the *Sidmouth Herald*, local resident Hazel Clapp wrote that the Festival was the only time the town really came to life, and was enjoyed by young and old alike, 'Long may we have the festival in Sidmouth'. The local residents, especially the younger ones, were also becoming involved in helping the Festival. Bill wrote that some of them were getting up at six in the morning and working through until one o'clock the following morning. Sandra Lang and Sandra Large were singled out for praise: they were both members of the town folk club, and worked hard washing up, helping with the meals for the overseas visitors, and making the coffee for the Song

> ### ... the working programme promised 'reasonable toilets'

Spot. Sandra Lang continues to support the Festival, alongside her sister Mandy.

The usual enthusiastic letters, often with constructive criticism, were received during and after the Festival. One comment was received by the Belgian group, and Bill quoted it over and over again in correspondence. 'The Belgians said to me, "We have been going to festivals for 22 years but this is the first real folk festival". They meant, of course, we do not merely show-off, but involve the people. We succeeded in doing this, this year. Originally a little festival for Society members, it became over the years Sidmouth's Festival. This year it became Devon's Festival. It will not be long before it becomes nationally known.'

Reuzegom from Belgium

English Teams within an International Festival

1968

'The Sidmouth Festival is unique and in accordance with its greater importance, next year will be known as the "Sidmouth International Folk Festival", Bill Rutter wrote in his report to Sidmouth Urban District Council in Autumn 1967. The change in name may have been due to the increasing importance of the international nature of the Festival, but 1968 also marked a real change in the style of English dance at the Festival.

In spite of the desire to improve the standards of the English dance displays in 1965 and 1966 under Ron Smedley, and then in 1967 under Peter Dashwood, there were still problems. Bill had urged his two directors to concentrate on the simple dances, but this led to some frustration amongst the performers and the more discerning audience members. There was still the fundamental problem of turning a group of enthusiasts from all over the country into a slick team of dancers whose displays would compare favourably with the overseas groups. Both the Morris teams and the overseas dance groups were based on all-the-year-round practising with the object of performing in front of audiences. The English country dancers could not compete.

Bill had already explored the possibility of inviting rehearsed groups of dancers. The Mercians came from the Derby area in 1965, and there were the Reading University Playford Dancers and Redbridge Folk Dancers in 1967. Compared with their European counterparts, English folk dance clubs were more interested in social dancing than in presenting displays, and generally they lacked the skills of choreography, or saw no reason why they should acquire them.

> There was still the fundamental problem of turning a group of enthusiasts from all over the country into a slick team of dancers

Bill Bush had identified the issues as early as 1965. He was a great Festival supporter and later the main organiser of the festival at Chippenham (then also held in Lacock). He wrote to Bill Rutter, 'I am well aware of the difficulty you are up against when inviting all and sundry to come along, charge them to join in, and in consequence unable to select your company. It now seems to me that Sidmouth is not just

another Society Festival and a kind of free-for-all, but it is something which is likely to have very wide appeal within the next few years. Foreign teams may be drawn to the festival in the same way as they are to Llangollen, if so we simply cannot afford to trail along behind. In other words the standard of *our* dancing has to reach a pretty high one. I am not convinced that you can do this by inviting anyone to come along providing they can dance. ... It is impossible to rehearse a hundred or so dancers in the short time there is for rehearsal and expect them to put on a first class show in front of the public. ... It would be a better idea to invite districts or even clubs to send along groups of dancers.' Bill agreed with these comments, but added, 'Let's face it – the English social dancing is a back-cloth to the special, such as Morris and invited teams'. And that is how Bill treated the situation until 1968 when the emphasis clearly switched to groups of display dancers being invited to the Festival. There was still a Festival company of dancers, but the emphasis was on the invited groups.

Brian Jones had just completed his finals at Reading University when he came again with the Playford display dancers, whilst his parents, Cyril and Iris Jones led the Tottenham Folk Dance Club's

Folk Dance Display

Tottenham Folk Dance Club at Port Royal

display dancers, described by Bill as 'good young dancers'. Also from London came the Phoenix Club dancers, led by Colin and Margery (Skip) Ellacott, the grandparents of Alison Ellacott who now plays in the folk dance band Alterations. The Berkshire and Oxfordshire Dancers were put together by Paddy O'Neill, and the members included Ian Graham and Jennie Manners, daughter of Denis and Sheila Manners. The Sedgemoor Dancers from Weston-super-Mare also danced at the weekend.

Bill put together the East Devon Dancers himself. Made up of members of the Willand Club and former pupils of Honiton Secondary School, part of their display was a Harvest Home set in the nineteenth century, with dancers representing the farmer, his wife, the squire, parson, Gypsies, poacher and farm workers. The women dragged the men up to dance, and then there was a blackout, and they were replaced in the same dances by young long-haired youths, and girls in the 'miniest of mini-skirts' who had been sitting on the front row. The blackout meant that the display had to take place in the evening.

These groups of social dancers performed their own rehearsed sets in the displays, and also came together to rehearse and perform 'massed' display dances. Bill promised them, 'a festival, a feast and an occasion for celebration and fun together; besides a show to the public. If the definition at the end of the week between performers and public becomes blurred then we have succeeded.'

For the first time, the word 'workshop' was used in the programme, and the wording made it clear the level of these events:

'Morris, clog, music and rapper workshops for the inexperienced'. The workshop for musicians had started in 1966 with the title The Players' Club in the Old Forge, led by John and Mary Brock. In 1967, it was renamed the Musicians' Club, with Barbara Wood of the Bristol Country Dance Band, who returned to lead the workshop in 1968 alongside a different band or musician each day. One of the event's purposes was to provide a group of musicians that would play for the village barn dances. The morning Song Spot every day was also described as a 'workshop'.

The Morris sides included Coventry Morris Men, whilst traditional longsword team, Loftus Sword Dancers, winners of the folk dance competition at the Llangollen International Eisteddfod, also appeared. Both Hammersmith and Chingford were again at the Festival. In addition to the full range of dance repertoire, the Chingford team also included three singers, Mike Clifton, Ray Worman and John Fordham, collectively known as Home Brew, a harmony trio, who later accompanied Shirley Collins on her seminal album *Anthems in Eden*. The impact of the newer breed of Morris team can be seen in a letter from Bill to Peter Boyce, 'It seems there are only two Morris sides in London these days ... Hammersmith and Chingford. At least with the necessary extrovertism for displays where ritual is at a discount.' On the last night, Chingford and Hammersmith danced rapper together, joining forces for a four man somersault and a combined lock.

But the real importance of the 1968 Festival for the Chingford team was that one of their dancers, Tony Roberts, was married to local woman Pauline French on the final day of the Festival. They had met at a previous Festival when Pauline had been a waitress at the hotel where Tony was staying. The afternoon Festival procession went via the Parish Church, where Chingford Morris provided a guard of honour,

and Home Brew sang 'Lord of the Dance' in the service. Meanwhile, at the Connaught Gardens, the display included dances and tunes on the theme of weddings, including 'Haste to the Wedding'. After a number of years in London, the couple now live in Sidmouth.

During the week, the audiences grew substantially, and mid-week Bill decided to run two parallel shows on the final evening in both the Blackmore and Connaught Gardens. To allow each group to perform in both venues, the programme was complex, and the *Festival News* – the first year there had been a daily newsletter – was invaluable for keeping everybody informed.

Bill had been impressed with Johnny Handle – 'Johnny's ideas fit in very well with the way we would like to see Sidmouth develop' – and The High Level Ranters were invited for the 1968 Festival. At the time, the Ranters comprised Johnny Handle and Colin Ross, as well as Foster Charlton and Tom Gilfellon, plus a new member, twenty-year-old Alistair Anderson. Here was another group that bridged the song and dance worlds and, like The Yetties, Bill used them across the Festival. Other singers in 1968 included Packie Byrne, Ray Fisher, Dave and Toni Arthur, The Broadside (formerly The Meggies) and Home Brew.

Bill Rutter's emphasis was on the Festival itself and on the club singers

Bill Rutter collecting from the audience

Floor singers in the Beach Store (Packie Byrne stood at back)

rather than on the guests. Each year, the initial publicity leaflet was issued in time for the EFDSS AGM and National Gathering in early November, but it deliberately carried no details of guests. An enquirer asked for details of the artists and was told, 'We have never sought to do this at Sidmouth, contenting ourselves with one or two names and making the Festival available to the rank and file singers of the country. This seems to have paid off as they are pouring in this year.'

The song events followed the familiar pattern – the Beach Store three times a day, the Sunday concert at the Manor Pavilion (which included the Sidmouth Accordion Orchestra whose conductor was local councillor and Festival supporter Arthur White), and a Drill Hall concert on Wednesday evening – the Beach Store at the same time had a 'Song Spot Ceilidh' with 'some of the best items from the festival members'. The *Festival News* announced that on Friday, the 11.00am Song Spot would be a competition for the Sidmouth Storyteller of 1968. 'Packie Byrne will be Story Leader and Adjudicator. Will anyone who can tell stories please come to this session. Warning. Only clean stories will be accepted.' The competition continued for many years and was the first story-telling event ever held at an English folk festival.

One folk group that sang at the Festival was the harmony group The Valley Folk, from the Bury Folk

Club in Lancashire, whose LP *All Bells in Paradise* was released by Topic Records in 1968. The four members were sisters Jean and Elaine Carruthers (plus former member, another sister Sheila), John Dickinson and seventeen-year-old Steve Heap. Steve had played the drum in a scout band and the cornet in the school brass band, but the idea of just standing up and singing really excited him. His first visit to the Festival had been in 1965, which he remembers as

> ## the idea of just standing up and singing really excited him

'unbelievable, magical, fascinating, and it was where I wanted to be.' Indeed, Steve has continued to be in Sidmouth during the first week in August ever since.

The Valley Folk came to the Festival, even though they were not booked, because they noted Bill Rutter's message that folk club organisers from all over the country attended the Festival, but in any case, they enjoyed the atmosphere. This may have been the year that a TV advert had the jingle, 'We're all a lot better for butter', and Steve remembers The Songwainers organising all the harmony singers in a special arrangement of the jingle, with the word 'butter' changed to 'Rutter'. Roger Watson, on his first visit and performing

floor spots with Colin Cater, also remembers a similar harmony rendition of 'My Old Man's a Dustman' to the tune of 'The White Cockade', possibly in 1968.

The Drill Hall had hosted the Night Club in 1966 and 1967, but in 1968, the number of season tickets sold by mid-July was 850 (plus at least another 200 performers), and Bill decided that no more would be sold. How would even half of these people fit in to the Drill Hall? The answer was to run two late night events. The Night Club was in the Drill Hall – a ceilidh with a display by one of the overseas teams. The second event – called the 'Late Night Extra' was in the Beach Store. In 1969 the Night Club was in the Beach Store and the Late Night Extra was in the Drill Hall. When the late night event moved out of town in 1971, it was called the 'Late Night Extra', and this title has endured through the decades and been adopted by other festivals. It is therefore strange to think that the name came about because it was an *extra* late night event, rather than because it was 'extra' to the day-time events, which is what is commonly assumed today.

To gain admission to the Drill Hall Night Club, season ticket holders had to have a green ticket. Pink ticket holders could only go to the Late Night Extra in the Beach Store. Bill considered that the compere of the Night Club was crucial: the programme of song, dance, Morris, rapper, music and visiting teams was put together on a day-to-day basis by the compere, and Bill asked Johnny Handle to take on this role. A variety of people compered the singing and music in the Late Night Extra. 'The public dancing at the Night Club is slanted towards the singers and is of the utmost simplicity,' wrote Bill. The last night parties were held in the marquee and the Drill Hall.

The change in the title of the Festival led Bill to write to Johnny Handle, 'As I strive for equality of song with dance, have you any suggestions for "internationality" on

Loftus Sword Dancers

the song side, apart from claiming that Northumberland is not England?'

Bill was very keen to have a group from West Germany that could dance the schuhplatter, and in 1968 Trachten Verein Ubersee-Feldwies came from Bavaria. They were recommended by Ruth Noyes, the Librarian at the EFDSS who, with her husband and daughter, helped as guides and interpreters to several groups in the late 1960s. The group was accompanied by the town's Burgermeister, whose daughter was a member of the group. Burgermeister Geschwender and his wife were guests of Sidmouth Urban District Council, and he was invited to open the Festival. An English group of

dancers returned to Germany later in August accompanied by Chairman of the Council, Ted Pinney. After the Festival, one of the German musicians wrote, 'Before coming to England I had a prejudice against her population. But already, after one day, I had to discard my prejudice. I have never met such friendly, nice people ... I am sure I will often remember the blue sea, the red cliffs, the green meadows and the lovely houses.' Bill himself wrote, 'One of the aims of the festival is to spread an understanding amongst the various peoples of the world, and we feel we were particularly fortunate to have this group. Their gaiety and fun

made them many friends and strong links have been forged.'

Four Dutch dancers had visited the Festival in 1967 and now they brought a dance group, Wageningse Dansgroep Wieledansers, of twenty-one people – as well as a 'fan club' of a further twenty-eight people. The following year two members of the Dutch group returned to the Festival to help with the Song Spot. After the failure to attract a group from Poland, Bill invited a group of Polish émigrés from Southampton, assisted by extra dancers from the Polish community in Trowbridge, called Karpaty. Peter Dashwood found them a musician, George Skipper, who was more used to playing for English dances. Two other groups at the Festival were Lo Solelh d'Or Groupe Folklorique from France and Porin Teinitanhuajat from Finland. And, of course, the Rory O'Connor Dancers.

> **'One of the aims of the festival is to spread an understanding amongst the various peoples of the world ...'**

The Festival has always had a confused approach to the start of the week. The official opening used to be on Monday, when the displays started, but this was pulled back to Friday. A display was not necessarily the best place to have an official opening with speeches from the councillors, and in 1968 the Festival inaugurated the Raising of National Flags outside the Ham Marquee, an event which continues in a similar way today. The preceding reception for the dancers was already established, and the flag-raising was added to make it a public event. As today, each overseas dance group danced briefly.

By 1968, neither Stephanie Barlow nor Evelyn Summers were available to run the Hobby Horse Club, so Bill asked the Tottenham Folk Dance Club and their leaders Cyril and Iris Jones and the overseas dance groups made daily visits.

Bavarian Schuhplatter

The Fourteenth Festival – Friday 2nd - Friday 9th August 1968

Peter Dashwood with two admiring French dancers opposite the Drill Hall

There was an ever-increasing demand for camping and fortunately, the Festival was able to return to its previous sites. The noisy site was opposite the former railway station, whilst the quiet site was on the field behind the present entrance to the site. There was fear that the noisy site would be too full, and Paul Bates from Sheffield was asked to be the unofficial warden for the site to prevent anyone who had not paid, from camping there. Edwin Hill kindly provided wood for the bonfire. A list of campers survives and includes Dave Hunt, Tony Engle (later of Oak, Webb's Wonders and now Managing Director of Topic Records), John Howson (who now hosts the Festival's In the Tradition events), The Valley Folk, Jim Boyes (later a founder member of Swan Arcade and now with Coope, Boyes and Simpson), Pete Coe, Christine Richards (later Chris Coe), Bill Rutter's son Julian, Dave Longly (who now manages the Rocking Chair CD sales at the Festival), Ken Langsbury and Dave Stephenson of

The Songwainers, Vic Gammon, Chris Bartram and June Tabor. This may have been the year when June Tabor sang 'Dido, Bendigo' round the late-night camp-fire.

After much lobbying, including letters to Devon's Director of Education and threats of Parliamentary questions, Bill finally gained access to the new secondary school at Primley for the overseas dancers. There was still a shortfall of accommodation, and in June Bill threatened to withdraw invitations to dance groups unless the matter could be resolved. He ended up using the former railway station buildings, as well as Woolcombe Hall, the Guide and Scout Huts, St Francis Hall, the Catholic school and the convent. In order to accommodate the increasing number of overseas dancers, Bill had to reduce hostel space for paying festival-goers and, later, for the English dancers. Thank goodness for the camp-sites.

The difficulties over the school were at county level, and contrasted with the close relations between the Festival and the Sidmouth Urban District Council. Those relations became even closer following the flooding of the town in mid-July. Although the town was quickly back to normal, the EFDSS, festival-goers and the Dutch team contributed to the town's Flood Relief Fund.

The Festival benefited considerably from the support of both councillors and council employees. In his report after the Festival, Bill wrote, 'The biggest single factor contributing to

the success of this year's Festival was the enthusiasm of Mr Pinney, supported by Mrs Pinney, who, during the Festival, inspired us all with all his extra, imaginative ideas.' Ted Pinney was then Chairman of the Council, and he continued to support the Festival through his distinguished political career on the District, County and Town Councils for the next thirty years.

Ted Pinney was not the only councillor to give his support. Alan Gibberd and his wife Vera worked hard in the town on the Festival's behalf – in 1968 they were thanked

> ### *... the Rory O'Connor Irish Dancers were awarded the Freedom of the Festival*

for helping with the washing up! Frank Lock was another enthusiast, and in 1968 he married Monica, whom he had met at the Festival. Peter Ikin and John Govier were other supporters at this time. The Town Clerk, Eric Howarth, the Publicity Officer, Eileen Allen, and the surveyor, Tom Chambers all helped the Festival over and above the requirements of their offices. Tom Chambers and his wife always helped to decorate the Beach Store.

The Festival made a special award in 1968. After appearing at the Festival in four out of the previous six years, the Rory O'Connor Irish Dancers were awarded the Freedom of the Festival.

Folk dancers from France

The Rory O'Connor Irish Dancers

A Company of Fools

The Company of Fools

1969 The fool was an integral part of many Morris teams, and an important aspect of the dance displays at Sidmouth. Douglas Kennedy had been intrigued by the role of the fool in folklore and folk dance, and at the first post-war Stratford-upon-Avon Festival had told the dancers to forget themselves, lose their inhibitions and become fools! Bill Astley attended those early Stratford Festivals and was a regular festival-goer at Sidmouth: he was the Betty for the rapper-dance performances by Jockey Morris and at Sidmouth, and he was one of the people who inspired Taffy Thomas, originally the fool for his school Morris team.

During the changeovers between items at the displays at the Connaught and Blackmore Gardens, the MC would introduce the next performers, but there was often a need for something more to fill the gap, and a need for someone to aid communication with the audience. This was an opportunity for the fools to entertain the crowds, and Geoff Hughes remembers the Chingford Morris doing 'little skits' between the items: spoof ballet dancing, leapfrogs and other improvised tomfoolery. There was also the opportunity for similar fooling in the processions. Taffy joined in all these antics, but the whole idea of performing in this way to entertain an audience intrigued him.

In 1969, Bill Rutter asked Taffy to put together a group of people to link the dance items with fooling, and the Company of Fools was created. Although the phrase had previously been used for a similar purpose at the EFDSS's Royal Albert Hall Festival, Taffy was responsible for taking the idea, adapting and extending it far beyond a collection of Morris fools. Taffy was assisted by Dave Greenwood from Yeovil who did a contortion and tumbling routine. He dressed up as a rag doll and was placed in a box which was carried in – the sides collapsed and Dave did his routine. Taffy now observes, 'That year was the start of traditional street theatre. There is a straight line from that to Magic Lantern to Salamis to Chipolatas.' It is difficult to believe it now, but street theatre was virtually non-existent in England prior to the 1970s, but Taffy was to seek his inspiration from French street theatre, as well as from people with circus and fairground skills. By this time, Taffy was at teacher training college in Dudley in the West Midlands where he met his first wife, Sheila Metson.

Dave Wood, then employed by the EFDSS in the North-East office in Darlington, was in charge of song,

> *... spoof ballet dancing, leapfrogs and other improvised tomfoolery*

with Tony Rose as his assistant, and the principal song guests were Martin Carthy and Dave Swarbrick. The partnership of Martin and Dave had excited the folk scene since 1965 when Dave left The Ian Campbell Folk Group and joined Martin. But early in 1969, just as Fairport Convention were in the process of changing musical direction, Dave was invited to play on their *Unhalfbricking* album, which was released just before the Festival started. This led to an invitation to join Fairport permanently, and the week at Sidmouth saw the final Carthy-Swarbrick appearances. In his review of the Festival in *English Dance and Song* magazine, Tony Rose wrote of Martin and Dave, 'Perhaps what audiences enjoyed most was the fact that through the week they were able to sample the whole repertoire of these talented musicians'. Performers certainly needed a large repertoire if

Taffy Thomas

The Songwainers

they were to sing for the whole week. Another memorable duo performed at the Festival for free tickets and no fee – Tim Hart and Maddy Prior. For the second year, the Yeovil Folk Song Club (home of The Yetties) organised a 'Pre-Sidmouth Ceilidh' in Yeovil on the Friday night that the Festival started. The intention was that people would stop off on their way to Sidmouth and the previous year there had been 350 people in the audience. In 1969, Tim and Maddy and Packie Byrne were the guests.

The members of The Songwainers were now Dave Stephenson, Ken Langsbury and Ron Taylor, and they established their reputation during the week: 'Their esoteric material, improbable harmonies and rural wit brought the house down every time,' wrote Tony Rose. John Kirkpatrick sang as well as Morris danced and his recently self-composed song 'Dust to Dust' was the song of the Festival: he wrote out the words for Martin Carthy, June Tabor and many more.

The song events themselves were now diversifying. No longer was there simply a single event at any one time, with a similar format. Fred Austin from Newton Abbott was asked to run a Ballad Singing event at the Festival in 1969, and the venue was the Old Forge. The event was intended to appeal to the Festival song enthusiast rather than to the general public, and to encourage new singers. Fred kept a detailed report of the event, which indicates that attendances varied between fifteen and 100, with an average of about fifty. 'The best

singers were the young ones, 16 to 20, and they also gave the better material.' Repertoire was not limited to the classic ballads, but included industrial songs, Scots songs, music hall and parody. 'Many of the young ones had obviously come hoping to sing something good and were desperately nervous to do so. Great credit to the good manners of the body of experienced singers. ... An important piece of missionary work which should bear fruit.' The singers included June Tabor and Manchester's Marie Little, as well as Martin Carthy.

The youthfulness of the festival-goers seems to have been a feature that had run right through the sixties. The archives for 1969 include a large number of the initial enquiry letters from people who bought tickets, and over and over again, the address is given as a

hall of residence or a teacher training college. Although there are a large number of enquiries from the South-East, there are significant numbers from Lancashire, Yorkshire (especially Sheffield), Northamptonshire and Scotland. Car ownership was increasing, even if the motorway system had not yet caught up, and this led to even greater attendance: the railway station had closed in 1967.

Karpaty returned to the Festival in 1969, one of six international dance groups. Another émigré group, the renowned Orlyk Ukrainian Folk Dance Ensemble from Manchester, was also invited, as were still more Belgians – this time, Gilde Sint Sebastiaan Keerbergen whom Bill had seen at the Leuven Festival. He wrote to them, 'It will be a tiring festival for you, not because we work you hard, but because there is so much on, people will not go to bed!' The musicians must have created quite a stir, because after the Festival Bill wrote to them, 'Our public houses will never be the same again. They are all wanting bands to play in their bars next year.' Presumably, they did not wear jeans or sport beards! The Skansen group from Sweden was recommended by the Phoenix Folk Dance Club from London who had earlier visited the group in their own country.

The return of the Israeli dancers from Haifa caused considerable excitement. The usual arrangement at this time was to pay for meals and

Orlyk Ukrainian Dancers

Israeli folk dancers

After the two shows on the final night in 1968, Bill programmed the same pattern on Saturday, Tuesday and Friday, and Festival staff used their cars to ferry the performers between the two sites. Some of the evening shows were billed as, for example, 'Israel Night' or 'Sweden Night', although other dance groups were also featured. The accommodation of the overseas dance groups had been eased in 1968 by the use of the secondary school at Primley, although the Festival also used Woolbrook School and other smaller halls, as well as some private homes. In 1969, however, the Festival was able to concentrate the catering at Primley, which was a significant step forward.

As for the English dancers, 1969 was the final year in which the 'company of dancers' rehearsed and then danced in the displays. The two groups were called The Willows and The Oaks. The company had been a feature since the very first Festival, and one of the continuing difficulties remained until the end – how to pair up the 'unattached' dancers. One of the women dancers wrote to Bill before the 1969 Festival to suggest that the 'pairing up be done more quietly than at the initial get together which tends to be a case of the few males looking over a herd of cows – that is exaggerated.' Bill replied mischievously that the pairing could be done by 'blind mating in the office, lists on a pole in the marquee, free for all or public auction'.

The social dance displays were, in any case, becoming a less significant aspect of the shows. The Kentish Travellers led by David Jex, The Exe Valley Dancers and the Benfieldside Folk Dance Club led by Malcolm Doughty all performed English social dances, although the latter also performed longsword and rapper alongside their North Country folk dances. Orange and Blue Band from Bedford played throughout the week and band members Roger and Daphne Nicholls remember that half-way through the general dancing on the last night, it poured with rain and the torchlight procession was a wash-out, with many dancers refusing to take part. Frances Carder later recalled that on the Esplanade only one torch remained lit, held by a man in swimming trunks. The Festival ended just as it had begun: the speeches had just finished on the opening night when it poured with rain and the audience and performers ran from the Connaught Gardens to the Ham Marquee and the Drill Hall where the shows took place.

Roger Nicholls was a French teacher and had encouraged one of his pupils, Richard Brecknock, to play the fiddle. But when he was fifteen,

accommodation of the overseas dancers, plus travel from the point of entry in England. It was not usual to pay any sort of fee, but the high cost of air travel from Israel led Bill to offer them extra money, and then he set about raising it from synagogues in London and local community groups. After the group had performed for the Night Club in the Drill Hall, as usual bare-footed, Lyn Squance remembers the dancers pulling the splinters out of their feet. As with the previous Israeli visit, the dances were more choreographed than with other groups. The comment in the *Sidmouth Herald* by a local resident that 'they were not traditional' was evidence to Bill of the increasing knowledge of the local audience, but Tony Rose wrote of their 'grace and elegance' and 'tremendous vitality and freedom of movement'.

Finally, in 1969, there were the Irish. Not the Rory O'Connor Dancers this time, but St Enda's School of Irish Dancing in Bristol. They camped but had their meals provided, and afterwards the leader, Pam Leahy, wrote, 'I have been to many *feisanna* both in Ireland and England, but there has never been a week like your Sidmouth Festival.' Over thirty years later, Pam, now married to Bob Common, still agrees with that statement.

English dancers

The Fifteenth Festival – Friday 1st - Friday 8th August 1969

Richard's family moved to Bournemouth, and he was soon playing his fiddle for local folk dances. Peter Dashwood and Dave Williams invited him to Sidmouth – 'What's Sidmouth?' asked Richard. He was asked to report to the Drill Hall at 9.00am on Friday and his father dropped him off just outside the town at about 2.30am. He found the Drill Hall but then slept in the shelter at Port Royal. As dawn broke, he realised there was someone else in the shelter – a young man with a banjo – and they swapped tunes until the police moved them on. A butcher offered them a free breakfast if they cleaned his shop. Richard spent all day Friday putting up beds in the hostels and signs around the town, and the rest of the week playing his fiddle whenever he could, including a solo spot at the Night Club. The Festival had quite an impact on Richard's development as a musician.

'All the kids in the town cannot stop talking about it'

The Morris and sword teams included the Jockey and Exeter Morris teams who had appeared before, plus newcomers Manchester Morris Men, performing North-West and Cotswold Morris and, from the North-East, Monkseaton, under the leadership of Alan Brown, performing their rapper-sword dance as well as Morris, longsword, Manx and country dances. Bill also invited another school Morris team – this time, from Burford Grammar School. The Minehead Hobby Horse also visited the Festival, whilst Graham and Mary Cole gave clog dance displays and ran a workshop.

More and more festival-goers were arriving early and there was so much excitement in the town by Thursday that an impromptu performance, featuring the Swedes and a Morris team, was laid on in the Market Square in the evening. This early welcoming event is a feature which continues to the present day.

The Hobby Horse Club in Connaught Gardens

The children's events became more popular in 1969. In addition to the Connaught Gardens' Hobby Horse Club, Bill bowed to the pressure from local parents who wanted a more central location, and a parallel Black Horse Club in the Blackmore Gardens was arranged. As in 1968, the Tottenham Club led by Cyril and Iris Jones was involved in the Connaught Gardens, whilst Bob and Rose-Marie Bowker organised the Black Horse Club. Bill leafleted all the schools within a ten-mile radius, and both events were a great success. Afterwards Bill wrote to Cyril Jones, 'Your contribution was a wow! All the kids in the town cannot stop talking about it.'

Bill's report to the local council contained some examples of the informal, fringe events which helped generate the festive atmosphere in the town and which also helped the Festival's image. Fred Tedbury was a local enthusiast for the Festival and each evening he cleared a space in

his cafe, the Winter Gardens (now Carinas), for a session of song and dance and allowed the Festival to take a collection from his customers. Busking displays were held each evening in the Market Square and outside the Marine, whilst The Orange and Blue Band played from the balcony of the Wyndham Hotel, to the delight of the passers-by. By now, some of the pubs had relented, and they welcomed singers and musicians for informal sessions. The overseas dance groups were given coach tours and were also entertained by various organisations in the town – the Town Band hosted an evening with the Belgians, the Swedish dancers met up with the Methodist Church goers and the Young Conservatives had the Israelis.

Bill was able to report to the Council that all the hotels and guest houses were full, and that the town's businesses were benefiting financially from 1400 festival-goers

Orange and Blue Band

Graham and Mary Cole

(1000 of them on the camp-sites), plus a large number of day visitors. The *Sidmouth Herald* pointed out that if each camper spent £10 during the week, the Sidmouth economy would have benefited by £10,000 – a huge sum. Bill also felt however that the Council was not exploiting the impact of the Festival, and suggested that by providing a car-park in a field on the edge of town, the Council could recoup some of the money it was investing in the Festival, and increase the number of day visitors.

By 1969, the Festival was regularly being featured in the media, with coverage on the regional programmes of both BBC and ITV – the latter lasting almost ten minutes. All the regional and local newspapers reported on the Festival, with daily news items in the *Express and Echo*.

In spite of the growth of the folk revival, dance and song, the EFDSS was failing to expand its membership at the same rate.

- *Riots in Belfast and Derry*
- *Investiture of the Prince of Wales*
- *Isle of Wight pop festival*
- *Concorde maiden flight*
- *Man walks on the moon*
- *No 1 hits for Fleetwood Mac ('Albatross') and Rolf Harris ('Two Little Boys') ...and finally for The Beatles 'Ballad of John and Yoko'*

1969

Increasingly the dance and song worlds were growing apart, and the interest in folk dance from the song enthusiasts was not always to the established dancers' liking. The dancers who came to Sidmouth seemed to be younger and a little more outgoing and eclectic than the EFDSS membership as a whole, especially at a local level. EFDSS staff, particularly Bill Rutter and Peter Dashwood, could see the need to be outward-looking and welcoming, but there were now fewer staff to encourage this. The Sidmouth Festival was certainly growing faster than the EFDSS as a whole, and the Executive was becoming concerned at the size and budget of the Festival, especially as income was still dependent on voluntary donations at outdoor displays which were therefore dependent upon the weather. By the time staff costs were taken into account, the Festival was hardly covering its costs. The national economy was becoming less stable, with expanding inflation, which placed considerable strain on organisations such as the EFDSS.

Through 1969, there were rumours that Bill was about to leave the staff of the EFDSS, and some people thought that he might run Halsway Manor, Folk Camps and Sidmouth outside the EFDSS, and perhaps even set up a Western Folk Society. In the event, Bill and Sidmouth stayed within the EFDSS. Nevertheless, his work commitments had grown, and local resident Antony Brunt acted as Bill's personal assistant at the Festival: Antony was able to use his local contacts to involve many more townspeople. Margaret Grant had returned to England after a couple of years in Ireland and had spent a few years on the EFDSS's National Executive. She also came to the Festival and helped Bill with the organisation. She thought the whole event was 'grand' and thoroughly enjoyed herself. Bill responded that he now wanted 'to encourage the rank and file dancers to come to Sidmouth as the singers do'.

Then as now, Sidmouth was clearly the market leader amongst the ever-increasing number of folk festivals. Broadstairs Folk Show had been established in 1966 by Jack Hamilton in a seaside town that was similar to Sidmouth. The emphasis was on English dance displays, rather than on overseas groups or dance and song events for participation. In North Yorkshire, Whitby Festival had started in 1966 and was mainly a song event for northern folk enthusiasts. Both festivals were week-long events in August. Weekend festivals were becoming more popular – Keele, Cambridge and Towersey have already been mentioned, but by 1969, there was also Bromyard, Falmouth, East Coker and Cleethorpes. All these festivals started at a base level of what Sidmouth had already achieved, and all of them benefited from Sidmouth's experience. Jack Hamilton at Broadstairs, Tony Foxworthy at Whitby, Bill Meek and John Conolly at Cleethorpes, Denis Manners at Towersey: all these people had been to Sidmouth, which provided a role model for how to run a festival. Increasingly, of course, all these festivals provided competition, but Sidmouth was still the market leader.

Manchester Morris Men

The Knowle Arena

Setting up the Knowle Arena, 1970

1970 Once Bill Rutter had secured the use of Sidmouth Secondary School for the overseas dance groups, and once he had reduced the provision of hostel accommodation for English festival-goers, he could invite more overseas dancers. The two evening shows, using both the Blackmore Gardens and the Connaught Gardens, helped to cope with the larger audiences, but the space in the Gardens was limited and many people could not see the dancing properly, even when tiered

> **Alongside the Knowle was a thirteen-acre site which, in the 1830s, had been used as a zoo, with kangaroos, camels and pelicans**

seating was provided. Moreover, the crowds were spoiling the flower beds and the dependence on voluntary contributions meant unpredictable levels of income. In 1970, however, one of the most significant changes to affect the Festival was accomplished.

The Knowle was once a private residence, but for a number of years it had been a hotel. It had been rumoured for some time that the owners wanted to sell the property and Sidmouth Urban District Council was interested in buying it for council offices. Alongside the Knowle was a thirteen-acre site which, in the 1830s, had been used as a zoo, with kangaroos, camels and pelicans. When the council discussed the purchase in 1967, Ted Pinney had said that the site would make a marvellous centre for the folk dancers, although it is possible that Bill Rutter had already placed

the thought in Ted's head. The purchase went ahead and in Autumn 1968, the council acquired the property.

Bill started to lobby the Council during the 1968 Festival. In the *Sidmouth Herald* report of the Festival, under the heading 'Next, A Festival Arena?', Bill was reported as saying, 'On the land fronting Station Road you already have half a natural amphitheatre where the grassy bank rises to the hotel buildings. An Arena in that position would relieve pressure on other parts of town'. This was referred to as the 'lower site' as opposed to the 'upper site' which is where the two council car parks are now located. Bill envisaged the development in three stages covering as many years. In stage one, an area 'about the size of the Connaught Gardens' would be levelled, 'using surplus soil for a platform along the railings for a

bandstand'. Stage lighting would be needed. In stage two, the bank would be terraced, with seating being provided on the terraces in stage three. Bill hoped that the upper site could be used for changing tents. The wheels of local government turned slowly, and Bill was still trying to persuade the council to let the Festival use the site a year later. A stumbling block was whether or not the council would allow cars to be parked on the site.

The Knowle was not the grassed parkland that it is today, but rather an area of scrubland: a 'nursery for weeds', Bill called it. During his 1969 summer vacation from teacher training college in Dudley, Taffy Thomas worked for Bill in the Festival office. On one occasion Bill took Taffy to a council meeting and on the way back, they stopped to look at the site. Taffy remembers, 'We walked down the hill to this

The Knowle Arena in 1970

Esbart Dansaire de Rubi from Spain

scrubby piece of ground and he said. "The displays are getting too big now so we're going to have an Arena here, there's going to be a stage there" – pointing to a patch of ground with animal droppings – "and there's going to be 20,000 people sitting on the bank over there." I couldn't see it, but he had the vision.'

In the months following the 1969 Festival, the Council finally gave permission for the use of the Knowle as an Arena, although the Blackmore and Connaught Gardens continued to be used for the children's events in the mornings. The provision of adequate car parking proved ellusive and visitors had to use existing facilities in the town or park in side roads.

A wooden dancing platform was laid close to the existing site of the stage, council staff having first levelled the ground with soil. There was a small stage for the musicians and two canvas marquees were erected behind the stage as changing tents. There was no backdrop to the dance platform, and the audience was therefore distracted by the movement of dancers waiting to perform. The *Festival News* had to ask dancers not to walk around behind the dance platform: 'This year, we are trying to be a little more professional in our presentation.' There were two side stands either side of the dance platform, and deckchairs, which were brought up from the Esplanade and people queued up to collect them from the

open lorry. There was no designated area for the deckchairs and people arranged them

> *... deckchairs were brought up from the Esplanade and people queued up to collect them from the lorry*

haphazardly up the side of the bank. The public was charged an entrance fee at the gates and could then roam

the site at will. The thick foliage at the top of the bank did not exist so that the buildings could be seen clearly. It was perfectly possible to avoid payment and watch the dancing from the pavement or walk up the road to the council offices and watch from the top, and many people did just that.

The previous year David Mills, who had just finished his teacher training course at St Luke's College in Exeter, volunteered to help at the Festival and found himself moving chairs, looking after one of the hostels, team-guiding the Israelis and stewarding in the Gardens. At the end of the Festival, Bill asked him to organise a team of stewards for the new Arena and these included Michael Barraclough, now a well-known dance caller, and Mark Ferris. Mark, or 'Gaffer' as he is usually known, has become a distinctive figure at the Festival. Dressed in a clown's costume and with a wild, rather unkempt beard, few would guess that during the rest of the year he is a medical doctor in North Wales. Gaffer was also described in the programme as the 'Noisy Camp Warden', a description which had two interpretations. David Mills went on to organise

Raising of National Flags

London Festival Dancers

EFDSS events, including the Hobby Horse Club (the name was eventually used for the children's section of the EFDSS) and as he now says, 'Bill Rutter and Sidmouth sure changed my life!'

Barbara Graham, a teacher in Reading, was asked by Bill Rutter to provide a team of programme sellers for the Arena: 'a squad of 12 mini-skirted girls from a Reading school' was the *Sidmouth Herald's* description of this team. One of the sixth-form girls was Pat Emerson, and the sight of Pat (in her mini-skirt) climbing over the fence at the Arena was too much for Richard Brecknock, who chased after her to ask her to the dance at Newton Poppleford. Instead of playing fiddle in the band, Richard danced with Pat all night, and now, over thirty years later, and happily married, they are both involved in the organisation of the Festival. But this was not Pat's first visit to the Festival. Her grandfather, Frank 'Pop' Ingerson had been to the first Festival in 1955, playing melodeon, and Pat visited the Festival with her mother Joyce.

- *18-year-olds given the vote*
- *Equal Pay Act*
- *Edward Heath becomes Prime Minister*
- *Jesus Christ Superstar premiere*
- *The Beatles disband*
- *'Bridge over Troubled Water' (Simon and Garfunkel) and 'In the Summertime' (Mungo Jerry) at No 1*

1970

Richard and Pat's daughter Robyn is therefore the fourth generation of the family to visit the Festival. Richard was also responsible for persuading musician Ted Hutchinson from Bournemouth to become Hostel Manager, and Ted was succeeded by Pat's sister Sue and her husband Terry Reeves. Ted's son, Paul Hutchinson, has been attending the Festival off-and-on for thirty years as a band musician.

Having secured this new venue for the displays, Bill had to find dance groups to fill it. With the English displays, he was finally able to invite the London Festival Dancers, directed by Ron Smedley. Ron's commitment to high standards of display dancing was

Tropical Harmony

well known and the group was the basis for the displays at the Royal Albert Hall Festivals each year. The London dancers were supported by groups from the South-East, arranged by Brian Heaton, who was the Director of Dance, and from Tottenham Folk Dance Club, Nottingham University Dancers and The Mercians. As in previous years, Bill talent-spotted dance groups at the Inter-Varsity Folk Dance Festival, and he particularly wanted the Nottingham dancers because of the sense of fun they projected.

There were two groups of Scottish dancers, two of Irish dancers, and West Indian and Punjabi groups from England, as well as groups from six other countries. Festival supporter Bill Poll lived in the Midlands, and Bill Rutter enlisted him to find a steel band and Tropical Harmony was the result, although a lorry had to transport the musicians and their pans in the processions. A newspaper headline was 'Steel Band Steal the Show'. The Punjab Bhangra Dancers from Wolverhampton had already performed at an EFDSS festival in Birmingham. At Sidmouth, Bill Rutter was particularly impressed with the way in which the group spent the mornings teaching the dances to the Sidmouth youngsters in the Primley area: 'that is what the festival is all about'.

The London Festival Dancers represented England at international

Punjab Bhangra Dancers

festivals in other countries, and in Romania in 1969 they spotted the Joza Vlahovic group from Zagreb in Yugoslavia, who were invited to Sidmouth and who created a great deal of excitement in the town. Other dance groups came from Denmark, the Netherlands (thanks to a Dutch resident in Sidmouth), Switzerland and Spain. There was clear disappointment that the Spanish group, Esbart Dansaire de Rubi from Barcelona, had to rely on recorded music because of the prohibitive cost of bringing professional musicians. The Swiss group, Mon Pays de Fribourg, was a choir.

Newcomers to the Festival were the Faithful City Morris Men from Worcester, who had their origins in a ceilidh club that was inspired by Sidmouth, West Somerset Morris, as well as the traditional side from Chipping Campden and another boys' team: Heston Boys' Morris. Chingford Morris returned after a year's absence. The daily processions from Port Royal now had a little

Tony Rose, Dave Williams and Roger Watson in the Beach Store

further to go, and it was at about this time that the banner was introduced to lead the processions which paraded in front of the dance platform when they arrived at Knowle.

Hugh Rippon suggested that the demand for learning Morris dancing was large enough to justify two sessions – 'just starting' and 'more experienced' – requiring a second teacher: 'Needs to be someone from a lively team, much in touch with folk song clubs, who can teach well, but isn't too poncey about it'. Roy Dommett was enlisted, but unfortunately, he was ill just prior to the Festival and was replaced by Geoff Hughes, still a teenager. Hugh's view was that 'Morris should have something of the "elemental" or "earthy" about it. This should contrast well with Ron Smedley's not-so-elemental London group!'

In 1970, Bill recognised the increasing demand for musicians' workshops, and put on three sessions a day. He looked to two young exciting players to join the established team: David Kettlewell, who was the Director of Music, and John Kirkpatrick, who joined the experienced musician Barbara Wood. Each of the three sessions had a different emphasis – John Kirkpatrick looked after experienced players and developed their ability to play for dancing, Barbara looked after the new musicians, whilst David's workshop gave musicians the opportunity to listen to, and play, different styles of music, including jazz, classical and non-English music. All three leaders had

to provide bands of musicians for various performances around the Festival: the barn dances in the villages, at the head of processions, the Arena overtures and at the Late Night Extra in the Drill Hall.

In addition to the Morris dance and music events, there were also clog dance workshops (beginners and advanced, again with Graham and Mary Cole), rapper sword with Paddy O'Neill, a talk on folk customs from Tony Foxworthy and, for the social dancers, a Display Workshop, led by Brian Heaton. Once the Festival was underway, additional workshops were arranged and listed in the *Festival News* – mummers on Wednesday, guitar on Friday with Bob Axford and concertina with Louis Killen. Attempts to run a daily square dance workshop were only thwarted by the lack of a venue. There was a desperate desire to learn.

For the dance enthusiasts, Bill adopted Peter Dashwood's suggestion of a daily Tea Dance in the marquee, even if it did mean that Peter's wife Janet was in charge of making the teas just after their honeymoon! The admission was 5/- (25p) with tea, and although season-ticket holders were admitted free, they were surcharged 2/6 (12.5p) for tea. With Peter as MC, the music was once again the responsibility of the music workshop. On Monday evening, the dancers could choose between the Barn Dance at Sidford, the Swappers' Club in the Drill Hall and the Playford Ball in the marquee. At last, Bill felt that he could offer a good programme to the dancers.

The song events diversified further in 1970 with the introduction of a nightly Music Hall. Tony Foxworthy, who by now had left the employment of the EFDSS, organised a collection of singers – himself, Bob Davenport, John Foreman and Martin Winsor – although the venue, a small marquee on the Ham, was not ideal. Music hall evenings became popular at festivals in the 1970s but Sidmouth was again the first. The Song Director was Tony Rose, with Roger Watson as his assistant. Tony was a local lad from Exeter, who then lived in London and had recently become a professional singer. Such was the reputation of Sidmouth, that many folk club singers, residents, semi-professionals and even a few professionals, were prepared to come to the Festival for complimentary tickets and free camping. The Tuesday evening concert of 'distinguished visiting singers by invitation of Tony Rose', as the programme put it, included the local harmony trio Staverton Bridge, Rosemary Hardman and Bob Axford, John and Sue Holman and The Songwainers. But apart from the music hall singers, only one guest singer was booked and paid a fee – Louis Killen.

There was quite a collection of singers from the Derbyshire area at the Festival, especially from the Druids Folk Club in Derby. A photograph taken in a highly-decorated Beach Store shows John Gibson (Gibbo) in shorts with Gordon Atkinson on his right, and then Keith Kendrick, Tony Lloyd, Tom Addison, Tufty Swift, John Tams, Andy Swift and Roger Watson, all but Tom being from the Derbyshire area.

The management agency for The Spinners tried to get the group a booking on their way down to a concert in Plymouth, but they were out of Bill's price league. Rather cheekily, Bill suggested that they could pop in and have a look at the Festival – and they did, appearing briefly at the Beach Store.

The Arena solved one of the

The Derbyshire folk scene support John Gibson in the Beach Store

Festival's problems, but another one remained. It was becoming impossible to accommodate even a fraction of the festival-goers in the late night events in the Drill Hall and the Beach Store, and Bill enquired with the owners of the Radway Cinema about using it as a venue for

> ## 'I have never packed so much fun and excitement into one week before'

late night concerts. 'Quite impossible,' said the owners. There were now well over 1,000 festival-goers and Griff Jones expressed the view that Bill was allowing the Festival to become too big. 'Tell me how to make it smaller without stopping it', Bill replied. The late-night festival-goers spilled out into

the town and there were complaints about the noise. Solving this problem became Bill's priority for 1971.

But experienced festival-goers thought that it was the greatest and most successful Festival ever, and one of the Nottingham University dancers summed up her feelings: 'I have never packed so much fun and excitement into one week before.' Geoffrey Cohen reviewed the Festival in *English Dance and Song* magazine and although the music sessions that he described are now familiar, his reference to them suggests that they were a novelty at the time. 'Wherever you went you found small groups getting involved. One musician would start playing and before long there was an impromptu band – and possibly next time you passed a group would be dancing, singing – or just discussing and exchanging tunes … caught up in the spirit of the thing – the spirit of Sidmouth!'

Yugoslavian Dancers

Late Night Extra

1971 In Bill Rutter's report to the Sidmouth Urban District Council after the 1970 Festival, he acknowledged the disruption of holding the late-night events in the town – by now, the venues included not only the Drill Hall and the Beach Store, but also the Old Forge. In addition to the noise, these Festival events were attracting hangers-on, hoping to gate-crash the events. These included local youths and Bill expressed his regret that the Festival had so far been unable to provide for them.

Bill had always been aware of the need to keep the festival-goers quiet late at night. He negotiated with the Council for the use of halls and permission to erect marquees, and he knew that the goodwill of the townspeople was vital. He also appreciated the youthful exuberance of the newer festival-goers, particularly amongst the song enthusiasts. He had rigidly enforced the curfew on the late-night events, even to the extent of stopping Tony Rose in mid-song on one occasion.

The late-night noise came to a head in 1970, partly because the opening of the Knowle Arena had increased the profile of the Festival, and therefore the number of visitors to the town. After the pubs shut, the late-night events close to the Esplanade were bound to attract attention. The residents near the Ham started a petition to ban the Festival, although they stated, 'we are not being critical of the Folk Festival performers, but we deplore the behaviour of the riff-raff who are attracted by the event'.

For a couple of weeks, the *Sidmouth Herald* carried correspondence from critics of the Festival, critics of the hangers-on and supporters of the Festival. There was no doubt that a number of the residents (often people who came to Sidmouth to retire) clung to standards of behaviour in society that had been overtaken by more modern ways. Not surprisingly, they were shocked when they came face-to-face with those modern ways. Some people assumed that anyone

> **'One wonders why no immediate action was taken to stop alleged public copulation'**

with long hair was lazy, unemployed and needed a good bath! One of the strong Festival critics blamed the Festival for a 'complete decline in morals', even though youths who later appeared in court for vandalism were locals. One of the complaints was against the Ham Hop, a pop music concert in the Ham Marquee on the Saturday after the Festival finished (the precursor of Caribbean Night at the Knowle), but this was clearly nothing to do with the Festival. The minister at the Methodist Church, which had hosted the Festival service, wondered if it was a good thing that Sidmouth was so insulated from the outside world. The vicar of Salcombe Regis felt that it was impossible to keep the modern world at bay, and that the answer lay in improving the Festival facilities. Both men supported the Festival.

Behind this controversy lay a recurring theme which could be seen in the pages of the *Sidmouth Herald* and elsewhere right through the sixties and beyond: how best to promote Sidmouth as a holiday resort and what sort of entertainment is appropriate for the town in order to retain its charm and character? Nobody wanted fun fairs and amusement arcades, but some people appeared not to want any attractions for the holiday-makers.

A public meeting was held in the town, at which Festival supporters challenged some of the wilder assertions of the critics. Bill himself wrote, 'one wonders why no immediate action was taken to stop alleged public copulation'. The meeting led to more local people offering their services as volunteers at the Festival. Pelham and Lyn Squance and Sheila Guest, for example, had supported the Festival for several years, but now offered to help with the setting up and management of the Knowle Arena. Lyn and Sheila continue today as volunteer stewards, helping with the Arena seating, alongside Maurice Dunsford and Mandy Lang. Other local supporters included Alistair Hay, who arranged the lights at the Arena, and from further afield there was John Faiers who managed the Beach Store.

Arena audience

Antony Brunt was a local resident and folk dancer who became an enthusiastic Festival supporter. Increasingly, he helped on the administrative side of the Festival, and was about to become Bill's permanent assistant a year later, until work commitments took him away from the town. Amongst the people he brought in were local bank employees: each bank took responsibility to steward one of the village barn dances. His parents were also great Festival supporters and frequently entertained overseas groups at their home on Salcombe Hill. Other parents were brought into the Festival by their children, most notably at about this time, Tom McCulloch, father of Mac from The Yetties who helped with the torches and the Late Night Extra, and John Kirkpatrick senior, and his wife Beryl.

But Bill realised that he had to take action against the late-night noise, and decided to oppose all extensions to licensing hours in the pubs, to end all events in the town at 10.30pm apart from on the last night, and to provide alternative late-night events that would not disturb anyone. Bill foresaw immense problems with this last promise, but he kept his word.

A late-night event that would not disturb the residents meant an out-of-town venue, which meant a marquee in a field. Antony Brunt and his friends used bells and whistles to determine the best location for the marquee: if the sound could not be heard in the town, then they had the right place. The field at the top of Greenway Lane off Bulverton Road in an area called Bowd seemed perfect, especially as it met the other criteria – space for cars and a separate entrance and exit. Antony used his contacts and persuaded the land-owner to let the Festival use the field. He also persuaded Devon County Council employees to dump fifty lorry loads of

Massed Morris at the Arena

soil to fill a dip at the top of the field.

The same field was used for the late-night event for thirty years, using exactly the same one-way traffic system – the entrance up Greenway Lane, and the exit down the lane through the orchard at the bottom of the field. In those early years, the exit was just a dirt track,

> **The canvas sides of the marquee were pulled down, and cars were lined up to shine their headlamps into the marquee until power was restored**

and when it rained the journey became quite hazardous, several cars ending up in the ditch. Power for the marquee came from a very noisy generator, which malfunctioned on a couple of occasions, plunging the marquee into darkness. The canvas sides of the marquee were pulled down, and cars were lined up to shine their headlamps into the marquee until power was restored.

The first late night event was on Saturday and was described in the programme as follows: 'Late Night Extra. Compere: Jim Brannigan. A Ceilidh. Compere takes initiative for good programme. The Yetties will play. Anjana display. Martyn Wyndham-Read will sing. Known

MCs can be asked to take dancing. Performances should end at 1.00am but this is only an approximate time. No need to vacate field. There will be wood provided for bonfire singing and Tony Vokes's Hot Dog Stall will be in attendance. Toilet facilities officially described as "primitive". There was no bar, and the marquee was not used for any other event during the day, so it was an expensive solution to the problem - but it worked. With the Festival removed from the town centre after 10.30pm, and a bus to transport the festival-goers up to the Bowd Marquee, the town was considerably quieter.

In 1970, the Festival made a small profit, but after an allowance was made for EFDSS staff costs, the balance sheet showed a loss of £500. Attendance at the Festival by both season-ticket holders and day visitors may have been growing year by year, but this required more events, and therefore more guests, accommodation and venues. Income and costs were chasing each other ever upwards and Bill was under pressure to make the Festival financially secure.

The first year that I attended the Festival was 1971. I was just twenty years of age, and an undergraduate at Manchester University where I developed my interest in folk music which had started back home in Liverpool, inspired by The Spinners. I was a frequent visitor to folk clubs in

Music session in the Horse and Groom

Rosie Hardman and future husband Rob Ixer

Manchester, especially Harry Boardman's club, and I ran the university Folk Song Society. I joined the EFDSS and in the summer of 1970 I listened to BBC Radio's *Folk on Friday* feature on Sidmouth and resolved to visit in 1971. Fellow student Ian 'Boot' Ankers came from Crewe where there was a lively folk club. He had come across the Festival in 1968 whilst on holiday with his parents, and persuaded them to let him stay whilst they continued their holiday.

There he met up with Colin Harris from Honiton and the following year about half-a-dozen people from Crewe came to Sidmouth, one of whom later became Colin's wife. The numbers grew in 1970, and by the time I tagged on to the group in 1971, there were over twenty of us from, or associated in some way with, the Sing Out Folk Club in Crewe. This experience was not unusual: many people accidentally 'discovered' the Festival, and one person's enthusiasm has often led to more and more of their friends coming to the Festival. All of us in the Crewe crowd were in our early twenties, and for most of us Sidmouth was our main holiday. It was one aspect of our collective social life and by coincidence, the first job I was offered as a newly-qualified teacher was in Crewe.

Sidmouth was almost 250 miles from Manchester and the M5 motorway then only went as far

south as Bristol. On Friday evening we all crowded into the small public bar of The Black Horse for what I recorded in my diary as, 'a tremendous singing session'. Indeed, The Black Horse continued as a base throughout the week, and I sang at several of the lunch-time and evening informal singing sessions there, as did Kitty Green (now Vernon) and John Forrest (a noted Morris historian now living in the States). The repertoire relied on the chorus songs popularised by The Watersons and Young Tradition and sea shanties. Clearly, the pubs now welcomed informal music and song, although the lounge of The Black Horse, with its 'smart dress only' sign on the door, was kept for the regulars. At the back of the pub was a yard which was a gathering place for the folk enthusiasts to chat. The Horse and Groom was another pub which welcomed the Festival: it had a small bar, but a large skittle alley and a garden where musicians gathered to play. None of the

> ... the lounge of The Black Horse, with its 'smart dress only' sign on the door, was kept for the regulars

Festival venues had bars, so the pubs were well patronised. Afternoon closing time was 2.30pm, but this meant that the afternoon Festival events were well supported.

My diary also reveals the official song events that I attended. The Music Hall was repeated, this time in the Guide Hut, with Tony Foxworthy, Redd Sullivan and John Foreman, plus the Lancashire singer Harry Boardman who often joined us for the singing in The Black Horse. The Music Hall was undoubtedly popular because, on the night I tried to get in, it was full. The Ballad Sing moved to one of two vacant shops on the site of what is now the NatWest Bank on High Street: the Folk Shop (selling books, records and other items from the EFDSS's main shop in Cecil

The Druids in the Drill Hall – Dave, John, Mick, Keith and Judi

Sharp House) was next door. The focus for the song events was the 4.00pm Song Spot at the Drill Hall: there were a limited number of seats and most of the audience sat on the floor. The main guests for the week were Dave and Toni Arthur and Martyn Wyndham-Read, and they were supported by such performers as Chris Richards and Pete Coe, Colin Cater, Rosemary Hardman (another Manchester singer), Muckram Wakes (Roger Watson, Helen Wainwright and John Tams did a single Drill Hall appearance), The Songwainers, Tony Rose, Staverton Bridge and Oak – all of whom performed without fee. The Derbyshire contingent grew, and The Druids came to sing and play during the week: the members were John Adams, Keith Kendrick, Mick Hennessy (later of Roaring Jelly), Judi Longden and Dave Broughton (a former member of the Sheffield Cutlers). Roger Watson, then living in Derbyshire, was the Producer of Song with Mike Price from Gloucester as his deputy.

The afternoon Song Spot was run like a folk club, but one with some excellent floor singers supporting the main guests. The format for the Beach Store at the same time was a 'Come All Ye'. This meant that anybody could turn up, put their name on the list, and then be called up from the audience to sing. The Come All Ye format alternated at the evening Beach Store session with a more formal event with a guest. The difference depended on whether

The Yetties with Oscar Burridge on fiddle

there was a separate concert – The Manor Pavilion concert on Sunday evening continued, and there were further concerts in the Ham Marquee on Tuesday evening and the

> ## *... adults were catered for in the evenings, especially Tuesday which was X-rated*

Methodist Church Hall on Thursday. The 11.00am session in the Beach Store had a workshop format, concentrating on instrumental accompaniment of songs, although on Wednesday Dave and Toni Arthur gave a lecture on witchcraft.

I was completely unaware of a fringe festival that took place in Sidmouth in the few days before the Festival started and on the Saturday after it finished. This was the Sidmouth Festival of Music, held in

the Secondary School and organised by four local men, Jon and Tim Shardlow, Bob Perry and Greg Charlton. The guests included Michael Chapman, Jo-Ann Kelly, Spirogyra, The Scaffold, Roy Harper, Gawain (with Paul Downes and Steve Knightley) and Steeleye Span (Maddy Prior, Tim Hart, Martin Carthy, Ashley Hutchings and Peter Knight). Quite a line-up!

Taffy Thomas was now married to Sheila and together they had formed Magic Lantern with Pete Collard and Diane Bevan. Magic Lantern was a shadow puppet show: members of the group sang songs which were illustrated by the shadow puppets. They also performed linked programmes on a theme, such as 'The Fair', involving songs, dialect poems, sketches and music. The show was not very portable, and needed black-out, so they were based all week in the Woolcombe Hall next to the Guide Hut: Taffy's friend Dave Greenwood also helped with the shows. An extra matinee show was added because they were so popular with the children, whilst the adults were catered for in the evenings, especially Tuesday which was X-rated. Magic Lantern continued performing at festivals and folk clubs for several years and, alongside the indoor show, Taffy soon introduced the whole concept of street theatre to the folk revival.

By 1971 ceilidhs were seen as different events from the other dances. The working programme has the following event on Saturday evening: 'The Ham Marquee. Festival Barn Dance. This is NOT a Ceilidh although Twisted Yarn will

Festival Singers

sing at about 9.45pm. MC Dick Witt with the Rangers Band.' So, a ceilidh was not always a dance with song or display interludes – it was a description of a type of dance.

Other evenings in the Ham Marquee featured a Ceilidh with The Yetties and Martyn Wyndham-Read on Sunday, an Anglo-Scottish Ball on Monday, the concert on Tuesday, a Playford Ball on Wednesday with Jan Willcocks and the Blake Band, and a Grand Festival Barn Dance with Hugh Rippon and the Weston Country Dance Band on Thursday. The Swappers' Club continued each evening in the Drill Hall under Griff Jones, so that there were now plenty of events for the dancers. Yet, my diary reveals that the Yetties Ceilidh was 'packed out' and the 'full up' signs were displayed at the Newton Poppleford village barn dance on Tuesday before we could get in. My interest was at the ceilidh end of the dance scene but there was a good deal of overlap between the barn dances and the ceilidhs.

John Kirkpatrick led the experienced musicians, and Peter Fox from Manchester offered to run the beginners. John encouraged Bill to use the booked bands, rather than the workshop musicians, for the Arena overtures.

The Arena displays were affected by some bad weather. There was now no alternative indoor venue so that if the weather was really bad (as on Sunday afternoon) the show had to be cancelled and refunds made to the day visitors. Peter Dashwood, who had returned as Producer of Dance, earned himself a reputation by stating that, when he had danced a solo Morris jig at a previous Festival, it had caused a thunderstorm. Alas, he repeated the trick on Friday evening and the show was rained off just after the Chairman of the English Tourist Board had officially opened the Festival.

The Festival suffered a blow in June with the cancellation of the group from Hungary. Luggudegillet from Sweden made a second visit, as did the Orlyk Folk Dance Ensemble from Manchester, whilst the group from Germany, Sudmahische Sing und Spielscher, were South

Magic Lantern

Moravians who had been expelled from Czechoslovakia after the war. The Derry Ceilidhe Band came from a Nazareth House orphanage in Northern Ireland, and had already appeared on Hughie Green's television talent show *Opportunity Knocks*. Anjana performed bhangra dances and were led by a former member of 1970 guests, Punjab Bhangra. The Pestalozzi Children's Village Trust was based in Sussex and visited the Festival whilst camping at Upottery to perform dances from Jordan and Thailand. The ground on which the dancing platform was laid had been flattened and a canvas backdrop was erected. I remember watching a couple of the afternoon shows, which still ended with the audience being invited up for a final dance or two. The music came from bands appearing at the Festival, and they also played the overture. For several years the Friday evening overture was provided by the singers, who later also sang in the Torchlight Procession.

Bill Rutter continued with his policy of inviting different areas of the EFDSS to provide displays of social dancing. The North-West Dancers were drawn from Merseyside, Manchester and Lancashire and were directed by Ethyl Anderson, shortly before her retirement as the EFDSS's regional organiser. Her comment that some of the best dancers had left the area to

go to university was indicative of the age range of some of the dancers. Geoff Hughes, the Chingford Morris dancer who was running the rapper and clog workshop, was in the same hotel as the North-West Dancers, and at dinner on the first evening shared a table with Ethyl Anderson. Cecilia Bailey from the North-West Dancers was late down and filled the only empty seat at the same table. Two years later, Geoff and Cecilia were married and Geoff moved to Lancashire where he eventually formed the Rumworth and Abram Morris teams. The other display group came from East Anglia, where Peter Dashwood was then based. Hammersmith was the only official Morris team, although Giffard, Herga (both based on folk clubs, the former team included Dave Hunt) and East Suffolk Morris Men also performed throughout the week.

The Experienced Morris workshop was led by Roy Dommett who also took several social dance workshops. Every morning my friend Ian Ankers and I attended the Beginners' Morris workshop, probably the same year that Keith Chandler, who was also a newcomer to both the Festival and Morris dancing, attended: Keith is now the recognised authority on the social history of Morris dancing. Under Griff Jones's skilful leadership, we learned a selection of Adderbury dances, but at the time we were unaware of the controversy surrounding the event.

Morris Dancing for Women

1972 When Griff Jones was asked to lead the Beginners' Morris workshop in 1971, he was at first a little reluctant. He was interested if it was a serious attempt to teach Morris to beginners, but he was not very thrilled with the thought of a 'free for all for every Tom, Dick and "Harriet".' Bill assured him that the first session would be crowded but that the numbers would ease when it was realised that hard work was required. Bill had missed Griff's point: 'I do not think that women ought to be allowed to participate in this. I am not really happy about their being present even.' Bill agreed to barring women, but jokily warned, 'Lord have mercy on you, you misogynist'.

Monday's *Festival News* carried a letter of complaint from Kit Fray, Jane Miles, Marion Steward and Marion Hancox who, as teachers, wanted to watch the workshop. 'Bring back Hugh Rippon!' was their cry. Roy Dommett was happy for the women to watch his Experienced Morris workshop instead, and Hammersmith came to the women's defence. After the Festival, Roy Dommett wrote to Bill suggesting a 'Ladies Ritual Dance Workshop', at which dances from the Cheshire Plain could be taught, leading to an Arena performance at the end of the week. Bill agreed, and Roy was asked to lead the workshop at the 1972 Festival. There were, however, only two such events, and the

- *Pocket Calculators introduced: £70 each*
- *'Bloody Sunday' in Derry*
- *Miners' strike and power cuts*
- *Watership Down published*
- *Munich Olympics*
- *'Amazing Grace', 'I'd Like to Teach the World to Sing' (New Seekers) and Alice Cooper's 'School's Out' at No 1*

Beginners' Morris workshop was now labelled 'men only'.

In the twelve months between the 1971 and 1972 Festivals, the first women's Morris team had started to practise. This was the Bath City Morris which started in October 1971. A men's side, taught by Tubby Reynolds and attached to the university, was already in existence, and the Morris practice was followed by social dancing. The women were not very happy to sit

'Bring back Hugh Rippon!' was their cry

around waiting for the men, and Betty Reynolds started teaching them some dances. Both Tubby and Betty played a vital role in the development of the women's Morris movement. At first, there was a desire to teach dances which had originally been danced by women, for example from North-West England, or from Ilmington.

The second women's side, England's Glory Ladies' Morris, started after a conversation involving Marianne Glover, Dickie Major and others in the Marine Bars at the 1972 Festival. Some of the dancers

were drawn from the Cheltenham Folk Club, many members of which came to the Festival, and Bernie Cherry taught the first dances. Ruth Fraser and her daughters Fi and Jo were also involved.

This was the start of a period of intense controversy amongst Morris dancers. Some of the men's teams argued that traditionally, the Morris was danced by men and not by women, and that this should continue. The women countered that social circumstances would have prevented women from Morris dancing prior to the twentieth century, but that society had changed and now there was equality of the sexes. Some of the men felt that it was hard enough persuading the general public and the media that this was a 'manly' pursuit: they felt that Morris dancing would be attacked as 'effeminate' if the women danced. The women said that some of the dances were traditionally danced by women, especially in the North-West of England. The Morris Ring, as an organisation made up of men's clubs, objected to women being taught to dance the Morris, and put pressure on the EFDSS to keep women out of Morris workshops at festivals.

Garstang Morris in 1975

Sidmouth was caught in the middle of the row, but was an event which attracted many of the chief protagonists on both sides. Whatever Bill Rutter did would be wrong in someone's eyes. As there were, as yet, no women's Morris teams that had sufficient experience to be invited as guests, Bill could avoid that issue for a few more years. He eventually took the view that the workshops should be for everyone, and that even if he wanted to stop women dancing Morris, which he didn't, there was nothing he could do. Better to use the very best workshop leaders to make sure that, if they were going to dance, they did it properly. All of this was in the future – for 1972, the women had to be content with the two workshops.

As in 1971, Roy Dommett also led the Experienced Morris workshop,

and in both years he also did some social dance workshops. Each of his Morris sessions was devoted to a different Cotswold tradition, but on Thursday he taught Border Morris dances from Worcestershire and Herefordshire. At the time, there were no Morris teams specialising in these dances and the first ever Border workshop, taught by Roy, had only taken place a few months earlier – as ever, Roy was pushing at boundaries. The invited Morris sides were Exeter Morris, Martlet Sword and Morris Men from Sussex and the Garstang team.

Bill heard about the Garstang Morris Men from Lancashire in a letter from a Festival enquirer – her husband danced with the team. Garstang Morris were then quite new, and still developing their repertoire of North-West Morris

dances from the Preston area. Bill was a little hesitant about booking them, but Tony Foxworthy saw them dance in Preston and reported back enthusiastically to Bill who wrote, 'all my hesitations are a thing of the past'. With a band of musicians, and the precision of the Lancashire Plain style of dancing, Garstang created a tremendous impression wherever they danced, especially in the processions and on the Arena stage at Sidmouth. Roy Dommett remembers that they were 'incredible in their impact'.

The Garstang dancers shared accommodation with the first Basque group to visit the Festival – Argia Euskal Dantzari Taldea. Roger Edwards, the leader of Garstang, regarded his team as young, defiant and energetic, but he was knocked out by the Basques: 'They possessed

The capacity audiences in the small venue made the atmosphere hot and sweaty, but nevertheless deeply desirable

all the ingredients that I wanted for Garstang – visual and audible excitement, love of what they stood for, identity, self respect, integrity and the highest standards.' Roger still remembers their joint end-of-the-week party. As Garstang dancers individually arrived back to get changed, they entered a silent and darkened building. But as soon as they opened the door, there was a 'sudden riot of noise and light' with members of both teams cheering and waving. The Basque flag (then banned in Franco's Spain) and the Union Jack hung in the hall, and there was a barrel of beer. Then the house went quiet again as they waited for the next unsuspecting arrival.

The Late Night Extra gave the opportunity to see one of the overseas dance groups each evening: they generally appeared out of costume and at least one dance was for everyone to join in.

Tubby Reynolds

Roy Dommett

The Swappers' Club was dropped and each evening in the Drill Hall, Tubby Reynolds ran a ceilidh, called Albert All At Sea.

For a couple of years Tubby and Betty Reynolds had been running a ceilidh in Bath the same weekend as the Royal Albert Hall Festival in February, called 'Albert Out of Town'. For Sidmouth week, Albert moved to the seaside. The music was provided by the experienced music workshop and Tubby was encouraged to feature anything from the Festival that took his fancy. One evening the dance music was provided by a group of singers performing 'mouth music'. Bill Rutter saw the event as a 'sort of Festival Club'. This was the start of a whole succession of ceilidh events held over the years in the Drill Hall until it ceased to be used as a venue in the 1990s. The capacity audiences in the small venue made the atmosphere hot and sweaty, but nevertheless deeply desirable.

Bob and Rose-Marie Bowker had led the Hobby Horse Club in 1971, but Cyril and Iris Jones were back running the event in 1972, again assisted by several families from the Tottenham Folk Dance Club, including Harry and Sadie Stone and their son Brian who later played in Hoedown, Junction 24 and Fiddlin' Around, Mick and Nita Mulford (whose sons set up the Oakapple Band) and Helen Stefani, later Helen Holt, who formed The Reelists.

The Songwainers

Three generations of the Mulford family still come to the Festival. On Wednesday evening, there was a Mardi Gras in the Market Square for the children. The Bowkers still had a role to play at the Festival. They organised dance tours for the 'unattached dancers' – those social dancers who wanted to rehearse some dances and perform them along the Esplanade and in neighbouring towns and villages. They had done this more informally the previous year, and felt that it was a definite social success.

Vin Garbutt established his reputation during the week ... and folk club organisers up and down the country filled his diary for months ahead

Jan Willcocks was the Arena Producer – the first time this title was used and she had a methodical approach to devising a balanced programme to keep the audience's interest. The last night, featuring all the dance groups, always attracted a large audience, and Jan capitalised on this by having a similar show on Thursday as well. Jan organised a group of rehearsed social dancers from the South-West, whilst Ellis and Christine Rogers brought the dance group Folkweave which rehearsed in Hammersmith in London and featured dancers from London and the Home Counties. Geoff Hughes and Brian Jones did a clog dance in a pantomime cow outfit as part of Folkweave's performance. Brian Willcocks, husband to Jan and a member of The Ranchers, played for both groups. Beryl Marriott returned to the Festival and led the experienced musicians, whilst Ian Graham looked after the beginners.

The Spanish dance group Esbart Dansaire de Rubi from Barcelona made a return visit, encouraged by

Fred Jordan (Mike Price behind)

Mark 'Gaffer' Ferris. Since their previous appearance in 1970, Gaffer had been over to Spain to visit them, and had developed a keen interest in the dance and music of Catalonia. Ever since this time, Gaffer has helped the Festival with the overseas groups. Other dance groups came from the island of Madeira, Switzerland, Sweden, Italy and the Netherlands, as well as the Basques. The Rory O'Connor Dancers returned, and a group of Polish dancers from France also appeared. Each group was offered hospitality by a different voluntary organisation in Sidmouth.

Dave and Toni Arthur were again the main song guests in 1972 – 'a great hit with campers and holiday-makers alike,' the new Song Producer, Mike Price wrote. By this time, Dave and Toni had been joined by John Harrison, one of the original members of The Watersons. Fred Jordan, the traditional singer from Shropshire, made the first of several visits to the Festival, continuing a line of traditional singers and musicians that had started with Bob Roberts and Scan Tester, and which continues today under the banner 'In the Tradition'. The nightly music hall of the two previous years was replaced by a Friday morning 'Miscellany of Music Hall' featuring many of the Festival song guests, including Geoff and Pennie Harris, the three

'The sun will rise
this morning at
6.30am. Antony
Brunt to arrange'

members of Muckram Wakes (Roger and Helen Watson and John Tams), and Rod and Danny Stradling.

The Stradlings were now part of the seminal English music and song group Oak, together with Tony Engle and Peta Webb, and they came straight to Sidmouth from an appearance at Cambridge Festival. On Thursday evening in the Beach Store, the singers not only included The Yetties but also Pete Shutler and his wife Marion, who was an excellent singer and also managed The Folk Shop during the Festival. Magic Lantern returned, just at the point when they were turning professional. Pete and Chris Coe replaced Pete Collard and Di Bevan in the line-up, and Magic Lantern were joined by a Punch and Judy show from Derbyshire, featuring Derek Pearce, later a member of Umps and Dumps and Roaring Jelly. The Druids also returned to sing at the Festival and also to play for Ceilidhs and a Tea Dance.

Vin Garbutt established his reputation during the week with his song 'The Valley of Tees' and 'The William Tell Overture' played on the whistle, and folk club organisers up and down the country filled his diary for months ahead.

With more and more events taking place, the working programme was becoming thicker and thicker: it was produced on an ink duplicator and laboriously collated and stapled by hand. Produced after the souvenir programme, the working programme was more accurate and included more events, especially those intended only for season ticket holders. Of course there were no mobile phones in the early seventies, and even photocopying was not generally available. Bill used the working programme as a sort of Festival instruction manual, and it bore the unmistakable imprint of Bill Rutter – written exactly as if he had spoken it. In the listing for the Sunday night Manor Pavilion concert, he wrote, 'Will all singers please note this is in the main an unconverted audience. Please entertain and not be erudite or esoteric!' The programme also listed who was to do the collection at a Market Square display, who was to collect the banners for the procession, where to collect the key for the hall, and where to drop it off afterwards. The style was lampooned in the daily *Festival News*: for example, after several days of bad weather, the message appeared, 'The sun will rise this morning at 6.30am. Antony Brunt to arrange.'

There was recognition of support for the Festival in the town when Alan and Vera Gibberd were awarded the Freedom of the Festival. After the Festival, Fred Austin praised Bill Rutter, 'Your great flair for showmanship makes this a real festival and great entertainment'.

The Execution of William Rutter

FOUL DEEDS AT SIDMOUTH

EXECUTION
of
WILLIAM RUTTER

1973 One event which is recalled over and over again by festival-goers from the early seventies, was the mock hanging of Bill Rutter. Pete Coe was largely behind this idea to stage a coup against the Director, and he enlisted the designer John Crane to produce a broadside which listed Bill's alleged 'crimes'. Headed 'Foul Deeds at Sidmouth', amongst the 'diabolical crimes' were abducting the matron of the Sidmouth Hospital and demanding a ransom, breaking and entering the Bowd Inn and stealing casks of 'spirituous liquors', robbing the Lord

Bill is led away to be tried

Mayor of Sidmouth of his chain of office and the showing of 'Art Films for Connoisseurs' in the Guide Hut.

Pete circulated hundreds of copies of the broadside and on the appointed day, Bill burst into the Beach Store, pursued by Morris men carrying an enormous noose. Bill, also in Morris kit, was led away to meet his fate – in the Ham Marquee. Pete was amazed to see that the whole event had taken on a life of its own, with a marquee full of people, prosecution lawyers and witnesses all carefully briefed. During the trial, Bill's wife Terry called out, 'Who's going to weed my garden?' The judge responded, 'Over-ruled', to which someone shouted, 'Over-grown!' During the trial, which was at lunchtime, Bill stood nonchalantly eating a bag of chips. Amongst the people involved were Derek Elliott, Keith Chandler, Fi Fraser, Chris Coe (who played the Matron) and Chris Turner.

The event indicated the affection with which Bill was held amongst all the festival-goers. He could be cantankerous, he rubbed people up the wrong way at times, but there is no doubt that he had a heart of gold

The Director enjoys a last meal – with Derek Elliott, Brian Jones, Keith Chandler and Chris Turner

and dedicated his life to the cause of folk music and dance. He and his wife Terry turned their own cottage over to the early guest and Sidmouth staff arrivals, and usually let someone from the Festival live in the cottage while they were staying in Sidmouth. Terry herself worked tirelessly during Festival week.

Bill's letters were so open and there are frequent indications of his philosophy. In 1973, for example, he wrote, 'My whole life has been dedicated to beginners. I don't care about the people who know how to do things. I'm only interested in those who don't'.

The hanging was an example of why a week-long festival was different to a weekend event. John Tams reviewed the Festival in *Melody Maker* and wrote, 'It has time to get going, the momentum building up day by day, as Devonshire cream teas give way to song spots, workshops, concerts and dances.' He also pointed to the opportunity for singers to join forces, and for a Festival fringe to develop.

Jan Willcocks was again Arena Producer, with Colin Cater in charge of song events. Colin had previously performed in a duo with Roger Watson and by this time he was living in Chelmsford in Essex, where he continued to perform mainly English songs and tunes, with melodeon accompaniment. This was obviously a very strong team, and Colin's letters to Bill were gushing with ideas.

After the 1972 Festival, a correspondent to *English Dance and Song* complained about the lack of variety in the song guests. Bill responded privately saying that many of the song performers were

Hobby Horse Club at the Arena

not booked, but they just enjoyed coming, and he could not stop them. Nevertheless, Bill looked to Colin Cater to introduce some new faces. Bill wrote to Colin that Sidmouth had 'built up its reputation on the song side by the fact that it gave ample opportunity for floor singing' and wanted to see at least one session a day that was a Come All Ye. Colin agreed, but felt that no advantage was gained by having 'a lot of dead sessions'. Something more than a succession

> **'My whole life has been dedicated to beginners. I don't care about the people who know how to do things. I'm only interested in those who don't'**

of Come all Ye events was needed, and even the Ballad Shop had featured singers. The guest list was still expanded using the complimentary ticket offer, but many singers – particularly those who were semi-professional, or even professional – were happy, honoured even, to accept the offer. So alongside the main song guests The High Level Ranters, Tony Rose and Derek and Dorothy Elliott, there was strong support from June Tabor, Chanticleer, Bob Stewart, Mike and Jacquey Gabriel, Pete and Chris Coe, Keith Kendrick and many others.

Colin was keen to develop beginners' instrumental workshops and even ceilidh band workshops – the fact that these were being suggested in the song part of the Festival was indicative of where the enthusiasm for ceilidhs lay.

One instrument that was gaining in popularity was the concertina. Neil Wayne was a concertina fanatic who helped develop the instrument's popularity in the folk scene under the banner 'Concertina Consciousness'. There was a newsletter, conventions, bags and t-shirts. Eventually Neil set up his own record label, Free Reed and the first dedicated mail order service for folk music records. He offered to run daily concertina workshops, assisted by Alistair Anderson who was at the Festival as part of The High Level Ranters. Neil's enthusiasm was beginning to run away with him, with suggestions at every turn, and at one stage Bill wrote, 'I wish I had never got involved with concertinas'.

In 1973 Fred Austin decided to bow out of the Ballad Sessions, and he was replaced by Dave Jones, assisted by Tom Addison (who was just about to join The Songwainers) and Keith Chandler. This event might only have drawn small audiences, but Keith wrote, 'For me, as for Fred, the Ballad Shop is the high spot of Sidmouth.'

1973 was the first year when the correspondence, the programme and the newsletter, all give the impression that a 'guest list' of singers was being used to promote

the Festival. As such, it was trying to attract people for the guests just as much as for the experience, the event, the atmosphere, the opportunity to find out more about your particular interest.

The Fettlers came from Teesside, and one of their members was Vin Garbutt. Jan Willcocks had seen them at the Billingham International Folklore Festival where they appeared on the main stage in amongst the dance groups, drawing a great response from the audience, so they were booked at Sidmouth to appear on the Arena. Bill was seeking to replicate The Yetties: he liked this sort of group – instrumental music for listening to, good singalong songs, a sense of humour, and the ability to play for ceilidhs: a group that had the ability to hold a large, general public audience, as well as have the integrity which would impress the folk enthusiasts. The High Level Ranters had all these features, and he seized on The Fettlers as another group in the same mould.

The High Level Ranters wanted to do more than just play for dances, or appear in brief song spots, and as a result they were programmed for a solo concert in the Methodist Hall on Monday, plus a Northumbrian Ceilidh, with the group themselves providing the dance music (mainly for North-Eastern dances), songs, stories and instrumental solos.

Although Bill was anxious to avoid the criticism of repeating guests, he could not conceive of a Festival that did not include The Yetties, and he settled on a single concert performance.

After the success of the women's ritual dancing workshops in 1972, one might have expected a re-run in 1973, but nothing was scheduled.

- *Britain joins EEC*
- *VAT introduced*
- *Vietnam ceasefire*
- *Pablo Picasso dies*
- *Donny Osmond, David Cassidy and Slade's 'Merry Xmas Everybody' at No 1*

1973

Some of the American dancers

John Kirkpatrick and his then wife Sue Harris organised some unofficial women's Morris workshops which culminated in an outdoor performance on Friday – the processional dance they performed ended up in the garden of the Horse and Groom, and when the wooden gates were shut behind them, the male dancers who objected to women dancing hammered on the gates.

The first few days of the Festival were marred by torrential rain – it started late on Saturday morning and continued virtually non-stop until Monday lunchtime, by which time many campers had been washed out. Dozens of local residents came to their rescue and put them up in their own homes. One casualty was Fi Fraser who came to the Festival with friends from Cheltenham and a chocolate cake from her fourteenth birthday. Her tent blew down and, along with another girl, she was rescued whilst walking into town at 5.00am by a local butcher – perhaps the same one that looked after Richard Brecknock in 1968. There were just two of us in the Crewe contingent – myself and Chris 'Jake' Jaycott – but fortunately our tents survived the downpour, although Chris remembers that the entrance to the camp-site was thick with mud. The exit road to the Late Night Extra site was closed, and the one-way entrance was reversed at midnight. After Monday, the sun came out.

In 1973, the Grenoside Sword Dancers visited the Festival. Inspired by seeing the Cutlers at Sidmouth, Gerry Bates, Pete Civico, Dave Brookes and others had formed the Sheffield Apprentices, a city-based rapper team, which later merged with the Cutlers. By this time, John Parsons had settled in Sheffield and married Pam, his girlfriend from Grenoside, and he was the first

> ...the male dancers who objected to women dancing hammered on the gates

outsider to be invited to join the Grenoside dancers. He was followed by other dancers including Gerry, Pete and Dave. Another traditional dance side, Bampton Morris, visited the Festival for the weekend. Led by Arnold Woodley, the team was largely comprised of teenage boys.

Now that the Arena had become established, Bill invited back some of the overseas groups that had visited in the past. All such invitations emphasised the changes and the new Arena. The flag wavers and sword dancers of Boerke Naas in Belgium returned for the full week, whilst a group from Feldwies in Germany's Bavaria repeated the 1968 visit from the town. Kujawy Polish dancers from Trowbridge visited the Festival – some of the dancers had come with the Karpaty dancers in the sixties.

Two of the groups had been at the Royal Albert Hall Festival in the sixties – Orce Nikolov from Skopje in Yugoslavia (Bill unsuccessfully tried to get them on BBC's *Blue Peter* to help pay their expenses) and Les Tambourinaires de Brignoles from Provence in France, featuring dancing hobby horses accompanied by giant pipes and tabors. A second group from France, Lou Cieri from Orange, made the first of several trips to Sidmouth.

In Greece the right-wing military dictatorship, the 'colonels' junta', was coming to an end. The regime did not enjoy a good press in this country, so the visit of Kerkiraikon Chorodrama from Corfu was anxiously awaited. After the Festival, they wrote, 'None of us felt like leaving, we felt the warmth of the people, we very much appreciated everybody's kindness, but most of all we liked your sense of humour'.

Les Tambourinaires de Brignoles

The Nineteenth Festival – Friday 3rd - Friday 10th August 1973

The Fettlers, with Vin Garbutt second from left

But the biggest impact came from the Hubert Hayes Mountain Youth Jamboree from Asheville, North Carolina in the USA. Most groups sent under thirty dancers – any more and Bill tried to persuade them to limit their numbers. This American group sent ninety people! Fortunately, they paid for their own accommodation – some in the hostel and the rest in the Fortfield Hotel. The Jamboree was actually a folk dance event in North Carolina, and several groups made up the team that visited the Festival. As the President of the EFDSS was then Princess Margaret, the group expected to meet her – either in Sidmouth or afterwards in London – if not her, then the Queen! Bill had to dissuade them from playing the American national anthem at each performance, complete with a young girl dressed to represent the

Statue of Liberty. This was the first time that the so-called 'Appalachian dancing' style had been seen at the Festival, or probably anywhere in this country – they performed clog squares, smooth squares and buck dancing – and they also sang. On Wednesday, they hosted an American Night in the Ham Marquee. Bill summed up their visit: 'We were overwhelmed by the tremendous delegation, the like of which had not been seen before at this great Festival'. By this time, each overseas dance group was allocated a team guide, and Griff Jones's two daughters, Sian and Eluned, were allocated to the Americans. The experience led directly to Elenud going to study in the States, where she still lives.

In anticipation of local government re-organisation, each evening Arena show was named

after one of the towns that were going to form the new East Devon District Council. The English displays were led by the Sedgemoor Dancers from Weston-super-Mare, who included John and Jacquie Clegg, Rowland and Susan Cook with John and Mary Brock providing the music. Sam Sherry made his first visit to a folk festival, and danced at the Friday morning Music Hall and elsewhere. After two years of presenting Magic Lantern at the Festival, Taffy Thomas concentrated on activities at the Arena, and the title 'Company of Fools' was resurrected.

1969 had been the last year that the camp-site opposite the old railway station had been used. The present-day site at Bulverton became the main, or noisy, site, and the quiet site was located at Fortescue, just over a mile out of town. By 1973, this was called the Family Site and Dick and Janet Stanger had become the wardens. The site had a very steep slope, which made it difficult to pitch the tents and during the night many campers slid to one end of their tents. Some of the local residents were nervous about the camp-site, but Dick and Janet invited them to a tea-time ceilidh on the site, and the ice was broken. The ceilidhs continued each year, and many of the children were able to show what they had learnt in the workshops. Other performers over the years included Erik Illot, Woodfidley and Vin Garbutt. One character on this site was Peter Irving, known as Peter

Peter the Red in 1976

Family camp-site ceilidh

the Red. Dressed all in red, with a white beard, he drove around the Festival on a very small moped, which he called his 'monkey bike'. He had been making cine films of the Festival since the sixties, and

> *'None of us felt like leaving. We felt the warmth of the people. We very much appreciated everybody's kindness, but most of all we liked your sense of humour'*

gave film shows, first in the Drill Hall then the Balfour, as well as on the camp-site after it went dark. Outside his tent, he had plastic inflatable chairs, and generations of children sat there listening to his stories. Peter was a regular feature of the story-telling competition, as was Dennis Byers, who amused generations of children with his origami skills. Within a couple of years there was a third Festival camp-site, at Salcombe Regis over two miles from Sidmouth.

Craft workshops were also introduced in 1973 – the first time such an event had been held at an English festival. Chris Coe ran two events, for copper enamelling and jewellery making and soon afterwards, Chris and Megan Rose formed the Craft Guild to promote craft-making on the folk scene. The Day Centre for senior citizens at Twyford House on Coburg Road welcomed musicians each morning, and this became a daily programmed event which continued until 1995: Alan Gibberd was behind this initiative.

Alison Potts had lived in Cornwall and visited the Festival in the late sixties. She then moved to York and offered to come and teach songs and singing games to the four to eight-year-olds, and this was the start of several years' involvement for Alison – now better known as Alison

The first craft workshop – Chris Coe (left) teaches enamelling to Margery Thomas

McMorland, a well-respected Scottish singer. Amongst the songs that Alison taught were 'Father William', 'We're Going on a Bear Hunt', and 'I Have a Bonnet Trimmed with Blue' and she used finger puppets and cut-out images to illustrate the songs. Later Alison produced books, an LP and a film of children's songs and rhymes and she was featured heavily on BBC's *Listen with Mother*.

With so many changes affecting the folk movement, Bill proposed a

Folk Parliament each morning in the skittle alley of the Horse and Groom. Topics for debate included 'What makes a good club?', 'Who cares about tradition?', 'Electric Folk', and 'Sidmouth – where do we go from here?' led by Bill himself. It may have been at this latter event, or at a similar session a few years later, that Rod Stradling asked if song and music groups from other countries could be booked in order to make other areas of the Festival 'international'.

Alison Potts

International Song

1974 'We still hanker for some real internationalism on the song side,' Bill Rutter wrote in the run-up to the 20th Festival in 1974, and this internationalism came from a distant shore – Australia. The Bushwackers and Bullockies Bush Band were spending the summer in England, and caused a minor sensation on their visit to Sidmouth. They wrote to Bill Rutter on the recommendation of Nigel Bonallack who had helped at Sidmouth and was then living in Australia. They were already well known back home, with several records to their credit, and even before they arrived in June, Bill was receiving letters from club and festival organisers wishing to contact them. Their repertoire was described as 'traditional, Australian and Irish songs and tunes' and their instruments included accordion, melodeon, concertina, fiddle, banjo, bones, whistle and lagerphone – a long pole covered in bottle tops which was struck with a stick. The five-piece band played all over the Festival, represented Australia at the Raising of National Flags, and teamed up with song guest Martyn Wyndham-Read, an Englishman who had lived in Australia and who specialised in Australian songs, in the Market Square on Monday evening.

After the Festival, the Bushwackers described their visit as 'a most amazing experience and one we shall never forget.' In response, Bill wrote, 'if you got something out of the festival, you certainly gave a tremendous amount'.

Australia was not the only Commonwealth country to be represented: from Canada came the top-rated dance group Les Sortileges. Ron Smedley and London Folk had seen the group at a festival in Israel and recommended them to Sidmouth. They performed a repertoire of French-Canadian dances and music many years before the English folk scene fell in love with the music of Quebec, and the group summed up their visit, 'the festival was fantastic and the people marvellous'.

In keeping with similar international festivals in other countries, the Festival was re-titled the 'Sidmouth International Folklore Festival'. For the first time, a dance group from Asia visited the Festival, in the form of the National

In mid-July, three dance groups all cancelled their appearances in the same week

Folk Dance Federation of Japan, whose music included the samisen, a three-stringed banjo-style instrument.

Elsewhere, however, there were international dance group headaches for Bill. In mid-July, three dance groups all cancelled their appearances in the same week. There was a political crisis in Turkey, a revolution in Portugal and, yet again, a dance group from Poland cancelled without reason. Fortunately, there were dance or music groups from another five countries: in addition to Australia, Canada and Japan, there were groups from Hungary and another Basque group, and Bill managed to persuade a group from Belgium to come at very short notice to fill the gaps. There was also a Ukrainian group from Manchester: Sokil

Bushwackers and Bullockies Bush Band on the Ham

Basque dancers

Ukrainian Folk Dancing group which was an offshoot from Orlyk.

Ever since Bill Rutter had visited Hungary in 1966, he had wanted to welcome a group from that country, and finally he achieved this wish in 1974. The Vadrozsak Dance Ensemble created a tremendous impression and on Wednesday tea-time there was a special performance in the Ham Marquee.

There was really no event at which the international dance groups could give an extended performance. The former Swappers' Club had been an opportunity for the English dancers and the overseas groups to exchange each other's dances, and the Arena at the Knowle gave the opportunity to really see the dance groups, but there were few opportunities to see extended performances. In 1972, the Basque group and the Irish had given longer performances in the road at Port Royal, but the setting was not ideal. As with many of the Eastern European dance groups, Vadrozsak had an extensive repertoire and they wanted to show it. So, in 1974, the Wednesday Tea Dance was brought forward, and Brian Jones and a team of helpers had just thirty minutes to take down the canvas walls of the marquee, and arrange 200 seats around the edge of the dance floor. The audience was charged 20p a seat

and there was a collection from the people who stood outside the marquee itself. The Hungarian dancers gave a magnificent two-hour performance, and then the helpers had thirty minutes to set up the marquee for the evening ceilidh from The Fettlers.

All of these arrangements were made during the Festival and announced in the *Festival News*. In 1976, the event was extended to every day and to all the dance groups, with the title 'Meet the Team'.

John Brock from Weston-super-Mare and leader of the Weston Country Dance Band became Arena Producer, whilst his predecessor, Jan Willcocks, put together the Western Dance Team to perform social dances in the displays.

The Starters' and Advanced Morris workshops were led by Jack Brown and Johnny Burke, who were both from Stafford Morris. Although Jack and Johnny were ready to welcome women to their workshops, Bill decided to run a separate women's Morris workshop and John Kirkpatrick and Sue Harris were invited to formalise the events that they had led in 1973. They were assisted by Marianne Glover and Richard Major from the new women's team, England's Glory from Cheltenham. John Kirkpatrick wrote to suggest that the women could perform at the Friday Arena show if the standard was good enough, but Bill replied tongue-in-cheek, 'I think you want me drummed out of office with my pants off'. After the Festival, Bill wrote to tell Keith Glover that a woman had danced in the advanced Morris workshops and had even danced in the massed Morris on the Arena. Not everyone had realised that she was a woman, and Bill wrote, 'Jack Brown was not sure and didn't like to ask. I wasn't going to tell him what to look for! It proves, however, that a woman can dance sufficiently like a man to prove a nonsense of the official attitude. I do not hold the view that she has to, but here she did.'

The town was full of Morris dancers in 1974. The official guests were the Albion Morris and the Sheffield University team, whilst Benfieldside Folk Dance Group also performed rapper-sword and Morris

Japanese musicians

Sokil Ukrainian Dancers

dances. Albion Morris was an off-shoot of Chingford Morris, formed when Ashley Hutchings invited dancers to perform on the 1972 seminal album *Morris On,* and subsequently with the Albion Country Band. Their musicians at Sidmouth included Ashley Hutchings. Then, in addition, the Stafford, Broadwood and Chelmsford Morris teams came and busked around the town. But perhaps the greatest impact came from two fairly new Morris teams who did not even feature in the working programme – Gloucestershire Old Spot Morris and Great Western, who both made their Sidmouth debuts.

Exeter-based Great Western Morris made an impression on the Festival in two ways. Firstly, they

danced at the first event in the Market Square on Thursday evening, which was described in the working programme as, 'Bill Rutter will meet any teams in the Market Place to loosen up for an informal display'. They have danced at this event every year since. Secondly, they created something of a stir at the Folk Dance Competition.

There were three separate competitions at the 1974 Festival – for an original song, tune and dance. The panel of judges, which included Roger Watson, Dave Williams and Eric Winter, chose Peter Prytherch's song 'I am a Bold Sailor', a dance by Ron Beeson, and Colin Cater's tune 'General Amin's Retreat' as the winners. One of the youngest competitors was fifteen-year-old Alison Ellacott (now leader

of Alterations country dance band) who wrote three tunes including 'The Wombles' Morris Dance'. But the entry which won the greatest applause for its humour was Great Western Morris's send up of 'Bean Setting' called 'Brain Setting', performed with rolled-up newspapers in the style of the 'My Brain Hurts' sketch from BBC TV's *Monty Python's Flying Circus.* They were suitably rewarded with a prize – an empty baked-bean tin, decorated with ribbons, and the dance was repeated in the fun and games of the final night Late Night Extra – by this stage frequently referred to simply by its abbreviation, LNE. It was the start of a whole series of humorous antics by Great Western Morris at the Festival.

The Gloucestershire Old Spot Morris Dancers busked around the town, and appeared at Monday

> *It was the start of a whole series of humorous antics by Great Western Morris at the Festival*

evening's LNE. The members included Ken Langsbury, Keith Glover, Paul Burgess, Rod Stradling, Martin Brinsford and Bernie Cherry. They were the first revival Cotswold team to concentrate on a single tradition, and their dancing of the Longborough village tradition was energetic, enthusiastic and breathtaking. Alongside teams such as Garstang, they displayed the deep commitment that was often characteristic of the 1970s Morris revival. 1974 was probably the year I remember Old Spot dancing, in kit, on the camp-site on Saturday morning as everyone packed up their tents: a symbolic ending to a fantastic week.

England's Glory also made their Sidmouth debut – an improvised appearance in the Beach Store as none of them had their kit with them in Sidmouth.

Vadrozsak Dancers from Hungary

Bill wanted to get into the routine of Song Producers spending one year as producer-designate, followed by two years doing the job. So Colin Cater returned for a second year with Keith Glover from Cheltenham as his deputy, learning what to do and planning the following year. Keith was a song club organiser, a Morris dancer with Gloucestershire Old Spot, his then wife Marianne was a dancer with the new women's Morris team England's Glory, whilst their children also became involved as dancers and performers, most notably Tristan who is a member of The Chippolatas.

Having left the Teesside Fettlers in the previous twelve months, Vin Garbutt was a guest as a solo singer in his own right. He was joined by Martyn Wyndham-Read and Harry Boardman, plus the singers who were offered complimentary tickets and who were listed separately in the working programme – 'we anticipate the following will also be at the Festival'. They included the Scottish singer then living in Sussex, Isobel Sutherland, The Songwainers (by now Festival regulars), June Tabor, Muckram Wakes (whose members were now Roger and Helen Watson and John and Susie Adams), Heritage from Dingle's Folk Club in London, Pete and Chris Coe and Martin Graebe (then best-known as a song-writer). The BBC Radio 2 *Folkweave* programme recorded at the Festival during the week, mainly from the Beach Store, which was the setting for a live broadcast on Thursday. The line-up for that evening included some of the above singers, plus Graham and Eileen Pratt and Johnny Coppin.

The Festival hosted the first

1974
- *Miners' strike and three-day working week*
- *Harold Wilson returns as Prime Minister*
- *Watergate scandal – Nixon resigns as US President*
- *David Essex, Mud and Abba's 'Waterloo' at No 1.*

themed song event in 1974 – a performance of the 'Maypoles to Mistletoe' show with Martyn Wyndham-Read, Geoff and Pennie Harris, Arkey's Toast and the Broadwood Morris Men. Darlington Mummers performed several different styles of mummers' plays and, as with Coventry Mummers who appeared in the sixties, the Darlington group performed at song spots, ceilidhs, in the streets and they also ran a workshop. Increasingly, the folk scene was becoming aware again of regional identity, and several of the song guests gave talks or workshops on this theme: Harry Boardman on Lancashire songs and folklore, and Pete and Chris Coe and Muckram Wakes on songs from the Midland counties. This awareness paved the way for the Morris revivals in the North-West and the increased interest in customs through the seventies.

Two members of Albion Morris were John Watcham and Mike Clifton, formerly members of Chingford Morris and the song group Home Brew. The two men had now formed Mr Gladstone's Bag. Dressed as Victorian gentlemen, they performed a full song set in character – Victorian parlour ballads and a great many double-entendres – and were the precursors of performers such as The Kipper Family. They wrote, in character, to Bill Rutter asking to be featured at a song event, and Bill –

Ken Langsbury of Old Spot in 1975

always one for joining in the joke – replied even more formally and hilariously. They performed at the Sunday evening Manor Pavilion Concert, which was now billed as 'Director's Choice', and compered by Bill himself. The high demand for song events was illustrated by the Performers' Concert in the Ham Marquee at the same time. John Kirkpatrick and Sue Harris performed at both concerts.

A new song venue was brought into use – the Council Chamber at

Old Spot Morris in 1975

the Knowle above the Arena. This was known as the Assembly Rooms at the Festival, and it hosted a concert on Thursday evening.

The Drill Hall in the evenings had become established as a ceilidh venue and Dave Williams was put in charge of the week's events, called All Together Now. The usual line-up was a band, a couple of singers, a Morris team and one of the overseas dance groups, and the event was now licensed. Thursday evening was a Hampshire Special, with the band Lumps of Plum Pudding, and performances by Woodfidley, Tim Radford (later a well-known Morris dancer with Adderbury Morris), and Ian Ferguson who sang at informal events and played his bagpipes in Festival processions for many years.

There were very few bands that concentrated on ceilidhs, but in 1973 the Garden Gnome Ceilidh Band played at the Festival. The band grew out of The Druids and included John Adams. They returned in 1974, and on Wednesday

> *At one stage during the ceilidh, different dances were done at each end of the hall, and when a whistle blew the sets changed dances*

afternoon turned the normal song spot into a ceilidh with a Garden Party theme: A Fete Worse than Death. The event was opened by Lady Vinegar-Butty (Vin Garbutt in a frock!) who was presented with a bouquet of weeds by June Tabor, dressed as a schoolgirl. The afternoon included a beauty contest for men dressed as women, won by Ken Langsbury. At one stage during the ceilidh, different dances were done at each end of the hall, and when a whistle blew the sets changed dances. The band was supplemented by Pete and Chris Coe, and Roger Watson was the caller: the seeds of the future New Victory Band were sown that afternoon, as were the

Hobby Horse Club in the Blackmore Gardens

themed and fancy dress ceilidhs in subsequent years.

Other dance bands at the Festival included Country Custom from the Midlands, Woodley Yeomen from Reading and Itchen Scratch Band from Southampton. Itchen Scratch was a family band, with Paddy and Joan Searle and their children Mary-Jo, John, Peter and Lizzie. Several years previously the whole family had been stewards and programme sellers, and at the Hobby Horse Club, the children asked if they could play alongside the band. The band played for several years in the Market Square on Thursday evening, as well as at other events, including the Drill Hall and Late Night Extra. By 1974, when they played for the Hobby Horse Club again, the band included some non-family members and Mary-Jo was at university in Swansea. Mary-Jo has continued to be involved at the Festival as a

Morris dancer, workshop leader and musician with The Committee Band.

Eileen Phelan had moved away from Sidmouth several years before, but returned to the Festival to lead the Starters' Social Dance workshop, aimed at the singers. At a Folk Forum discussion on 'Where does the revival go from here?' the comment was made that there was a need for a dance revival akin to what had happened to song over the previous ten years, to make the dancers more critically aware of what they were doing. Eileen Phelan wrote in the *Festival News* that there was a need for callers to 'indicate a step other than the hell-for-leather-knees-up: after all, the least important factor in an English folk dance is the pattern'. These comments all anticipated the changes in English dance that were about to take place, and it all started with the musicians.

Great Western Morris

English Country Music and an Assistant

Dave Hunt

1975

John Kirkpatrick's new band Umps and Dumps had played for Thursday's Grand Festival Dance in the Ham Marquee in 1974, and when Bill Rutter invited the band back in 1975, John was very precisely describing them as a traditional English band. 'We play in a style (we hope) based very strongly on the traditional musicians of Southern England, as you can hear on *Boscastle Breakdown* and *English Country Music from East Anglia* [two memorable albums released by Topic in the two previous years]. This is as opposed to the revival mish-mash of styles which is neither English nor American nor historical but something weaker and less marked than any of them,' John wrote in a letter to Bill.

The members of Umps and Dumps were John Tams, Tufty Swift, Derek Pearce, as well as John Kirkpatrick and Sue Harris, whose son Jobie was born a few months before the Festival. They played at two dances in the Ham Marquee, with callers Nibs Matthews and Hugh Rippon, a Drill Hall Ceilidh and an LNE, as well as in the processions.

This interest in the style and repertoire of English traditional musicians was not isolated. Oak had played at Sidmouth in 1971 and 1972, mainly as a concert band, although they also played for dancing. The members were Tony Engle, Peta Webb, Rod and Danny Stradling. Their inspiration was the songs, tunes and style of playing and singing that they found amongst English musicians such as Scan Tester, the Sussex anglo-concertina player, Oscar Woods from Suffolk and Dartmoor's Bob Cann. By early 1974, Oak had

> '**It does seem extraordinary, now, that we were able to play together for some six days on the trot**'

split up, with Tony and Peta forming Webb's Wonders in London. Rod and Danny Stradling moved to Wiltshire, where they both became involved in playing and singing in the Cheltenham area. Rod played for Old Spot Morris, and they came into contact with a number of similarly-minded musicians. By 1975 some of

these musicians had become The Old Swan Band: Rod and Danny Stradling, Martin Brinsford, sisters Jo and Fi Fraser and Ron Field.

Meanwhile, in London, a group of young men, some of them students at City University, played and danced with Angel Morris. One of these musicians, Dan Quinn, had seen Oak, and then in 1974 he 'fell hopelessly in love' with the music played by some of the musicians who became The Old Swan Band when they played in London. Dan's fellow musicians were Roger Digby, Mike Bettison, Bob King, Alex West, Ted Stevens and Australian Graeme Smith, who was the inspiration for many of their tunes and songs.

These London musicians arrived at the Festival on the Friday and started playing tunes in The Old Ship, a pub that had not hitherto been a venue for informal music at the Festival. Rod Stradling now recalls that while he was putting up his tent on the Saturday morning, someone told him that there was another group of musicians playing 'your sort of music' in The Old Ship. Rod and the rest of Old Swan Band went straight to the pub, and were immediately welcomed and the playing began. Dan Quinn remembers a more reserved start to the proceedings – each group of musicians playing tunes to each other from different ends of the pub – before they came together as one. Rod recalls, 'It does seem extraordinary, now, that we were able to play together for some six

Umps and Dumps

Bob Davenport in the Horse and Groom garden

days on the trot, given that our repertoires were somewhat more limited back then. Probably the most memorable thing was how enthusiastic we all were. And certainly, we all knew their tunes and they knew all ours, by the end of the week. Beyond that, it's all a bit of a glorious blur!'

The week has passed into the history of both bands – the London musicians were then unnamed, but became Flowers and Frolics within a few months. But it was a highly significant event for the Festival and for the development of English Country Music nationally. The emphasis on English tunes and style of playing, and the complementary impact on dance repertoire and

style, did have the profound effect on English folk dancing that had been called for the previous year. And the Sidmouth Festival was an important venue for showcasing the bands and bringing these changes to a national audience.

The Festival programmes and the *Festival News* give no indication of these sessions in The Old Ship, and the only mention of either band is a brief thank you in the *Festival News* to The Old Swan Band for playing in the music hall. Four of the London musicians did a spot in the Beach Store.

Other musicians played in the sessions in The Old Ship (both in the bar and the back garden) including all the members of Umps and Dumps, and John Tams's playing of the euphonium encouraged Alex West to take up the tuba which then became part of the Flowers and Frolics sound. Dave Hunt, Hugh Rippon, Roger Edwards of Garstang Morris (booked again in 1975) and singers such as Ken Langsbury, Alison Potts and Taffy Thomas also called in. Martin Ellison of Garstang was only seventeen years old and had just bought his first melodeon when he played at those sessions. Even though he only knew a few tunes, Martin still remembers the thrill of playing in the same session as John Kirkpatrick and the sessions had a profound effect on his development as a musician. Over the next couple of years, the number of musicians

playing in a similar style increased, encouraged by the Cricklade English Music Weekends organised by the Stradlings. One of the musicians from Los Jairas from Bolivia also played in The Old Ship in 1976 and joined Flowers and Frolics on stage. There was disappointment that his favourite tune, 'Woodland Revels' was not added to Los Jairas's repertoire.

Sidmouth had been promoting music hall songs several years before the folk revival as a whole had recognised their place in the broad spectrum of 'traditional' music. The interest in surviving village musicians also highlighted the fact that music hall songs were part of the repertoire of country singers. After a few years of being programmed in the mornings, the music hall moved to the Drill Hall in the evening. Umps and Dumps played, Magic Lantern entertained and Sam Sherry performed the clog dances that he and his brothers had made famous on the variety stage. Dave Hunt was an occasional member of Magic Lantern and the photograph of him dressed in clown's outfit and carrying a bass drum featured on the front page of the *Sidmouth Herald's* first Festival Souvenir, and later in Festival publicity.

In the *Festival News* in 1974, the position of Assistant Director had been advertised. The intention was that the person appointed would succeed Bill some time in the following few years – Bill was now over sixty years old. John Dowell was appointed in the Autumn, and moved up from Bournemouth, where he had been working as a surveyor for the local authority. 'Having two left feet, unable to play an instrument and often asked not to join in choruses, I inevitably ended up running a folk club, I got involved in Christchurch Festival, first doing

The London musicians in the Beach Store

- First radio broadcasts of Parliament
- Snow on 1 June, 90 degree heatwave in August
- North Sea oil flows to UK
- Bay City Rollers, Billy Connolly and Queen's 'Bohemian Rhapsody' at No 1.

1975

Fi Fraser and Martin Brinsford in the Old Ship

the publicity and then as song director,' John recalls. He was not, however, a Sidmouth regular. In 1973, he was due to go to Cambridge Festival, but his car broke down and he went to Sidmouth for a weekend instead. In 1974, he called in on his way back from a holiday in Cornwall, and saw the advert. It seemed to be the perfect opportunity to turn one of his hobbies into a job, although it meant a cut in salary. Unknown to John, Bill was in trouble with the EFDSS because they had not agreed to the appointment. Bill's defence was that the salary was included in his budget which they had approved.

In the event, John's appointment in November 1974 was not a moment too soon. In early 1975, Bill became ill with arthritis and heart problems, and he was away from the office for several months. Away from the office, but that did not mean he was not working. Correspondence was taken to him at his cottage in Clyst Hydon and later the replies (written

in Bill's unmistakeable green ink) were collected for typing up in the Exeter office. But it did mean that John was given a great deal of responsibility at a very early date.

During the Festival week, the organisers of eight folk festivals met briefly to discuss common issues. This meeting led to an annual conference, organised by John Dowell and Tom Brown, which later became the Association of Festival Organisers (AFO). The initiative for this development came from Sidmouth.

Unlike today, the song events were not structured in advance with a running order and time allocation for each performer. The style was far more casual, and the size of venue meant that most of the time, a sound system was not needed. Bill had always recognised the importance of using the right MCs and comperes for all the Festival events – the right person in the right event to create the atmosphere

required. With more song events taking place, there was an increasing awareness of finding the right MC, whether it was the Ballad Shop or a concert or a Come all Ye, and the new Song Producer, Keith Glover from Cheltenham, was careful in his selection of comperes. Keith also acknowledged the ever-increasing number of folk club singers and aspiring guest performers who wanted an opportunity to sing.

As for guests, Keith Glover was keen to bring in some Irish performers. At the time, Irish music conjured up images of the Clancy Brothers and the Dubliners, although The Chieftains had paved the way for bands such as Planxty,

> *'Having two left feet, unable to play an instrument and often asked not to join in choruses, I inevitably ended up running a folk club ...'*

which combined Irish traditional songs with ensemble arrangements of tunes. The novelty of something which we now take for granted can be seen in a comment in the folk press, 'a welcome development in [Irish] folk music in recent years is the small close-knit group relying on traditional instruments'. One such group was Na Fili from Cork, a

Na Fili in the procession

Roaring Jelly in the Drill Hall

Strawhead on the Esplanade

trio of musicians playing fiddle, whistle, accordion and uillean pipes, whom Keith invited.

Trotto was a band comprising David Kettlewell, Richard Brecknock and David Lochner who were coming to the end of a period as musicians-in-residence at the Arts Centre at Loughborough University: Richard was only just as old as the undergraduates. They were keen to play and sing at the Festival and they led a series of workshops, The Five Ages of Music. As they were professional performers, David Kettlewell felt that they had to ask for a fee, 'but Richard and I particularly feel we've had a lot of benefit from Sidmouth and all it means, and the goodwill is more important than the money'. Bill replied that it was 'these sort of sentiments which make me fearful of taking advantage'.

Other guests included Bob Davenport, Magic Lantern and Freda Palmer, a traditional singer from Witney in Oxfordshire. The Festival still relied on the singers and groups who came for complimentary tickets: the Song Producer usually drew up a list of names in the Autumn but more were added during the year. The surviving correspondence reveals just how grateful, honoured even, many of the singers were to be offered the tickets. The people who accepted tickets in 1975 included Strawhead (who lost their voices singing along the Esplanade), Alex Atterson, Bill Caddick, Sean Cannon, Crowdy

Crawn (with Brenda Wootton), Erik Ilott (The Bristol Shantyman), Alison Potts, The Songwainers, Rod and Danny Stradling, June Tabor, Kevin Mitchell (an Irish singer living in Glasgow), Mervyn Vincent from near Padstow, English Tapestry and the hilarious Roaring Jelly. The complimentary ticket performers alone would have made a decent festival line-up in the mid-seventies.

At the time Roaring Jelly were largely unknown outside their home area of Derbyshire, but as Derek Pearce was already coming to the Festival with Umps and Dumps, Keith Glover was keen to have the whole group, so Mick Hennessy and Clive Harvey also came. Clive was the main songwriter and was responsible for many of Jelly's funny songs: 'Family Christmas', 'Valerie Wilkins', 'Christmas in Australia' and 'Cajun Gumbo', the latter hinting at Clive's later membership of England's first Cajun music band, R. Cajun. Derek had earlier visited the Festival with a Punch and Judy show.

Hugh Rippon and Nibs Matthews led the starters' and advanced Morris workshops respectively, whilst Sue Harris and Marianne Glover ran the Women's Ritual workshop. The number of women's sides up and down the country was now increasing, and the Sidmouth workshops gave a great boost. Festival newcomer Jenny Howard wanted to ensure that all the Morris workshops would be open to men and women. She is now happy to reveal that she was the person who contacted the Equal Opportunities Commission, which wrote to the EFDSS and the letter was referred to at the first workshop. The women's workshop was held in the Arena Marquee and Kate Rose remembers male dancers lining the railings to sneer and shout abuse. The Squire of the Morris Ring, Morris Sunderland, addressed the women, telling them that they were 'spoiling it for the men'. This of course stiffened their resolve to continue,

Hobby Horses in the Hobby Horse Club

and several more teams were formed as a result of those workshops, including Kate's first side, Flowers of May, Holdens Goldens in the Midlands and Poynton Jemmers in Cheshire. Alan Whear and Jenny Joyce went back to their already-established Windsor Morris 'filled with enthusiasm'. Derby Crown had already been established using the notes made at the workshops in 1974.

A social dance display group, Woodfidley from Hampshire led by David Slater, had visited the Festival informally in 1974 after David (then the Religious Education Adviser for Hampshire Education Authority) had heard about what he now calls 'a good gig' in Devon. They returned as guests in 1975 and on one occasion there was a downpour of rain just before they were due to perform at the Arena. Musician Richard Carver appeared on stage dressed only in swimming trunks, flippers, snorkel and goggles – plus his accordion – but the rain stopped for the duration of their dance. Not to be outdone, The Fettlers followed Woodfidley on

Woodfidley

Musician Richard Carver appeared on stage dressed only in swimming trunks, flippers, snorkel and goggles – plus his accordion

stage pushing a small wheelbarrow carrying a large Fettler dressed in a sou'wester and gumboots.

Some of the dancers from North Carolina who had been at the Festival in 1973 returned as the Carolina Cloggers and Carolina Country Boys. The Rory O'Connor Dancers returned and Denmark, Switzerland and the Netherlands were all represented. But the Festival was unlucky with the groups from

John Brock tries dancing on stilts, 1979

Czechoslovakia (their government decided that they were not good enough) and from Nepal, who were refused permission to travel.

But the most spectacular dance group came from France – Lous las Aygues from Les Landes, although simply called 'the stilt dancers' by those who saw them. The group had been spotted by John and Mary Brock whilst holidaying in France in 1974. On their return, they described the group to Bill as 'quite spectacular when twenty-eight of them danced on stilts, with a further twelve girls dancing between the stilts.' With fifty-two people, thirty pairs of stilts, thirty long poles and the men's distinctive but bulky sheep-skin waistcoats, the group needed a great deal of transporting around the Festival. They had a memorable impact on the audiences and, of course, some of the festival-goers wanted to 'have a go' on the stilts. Even the prospect of a few broken limbs did not dissuade them. One of the French dancers came off the Arena stage in tears after an overwhelming response from the enormous crowd. The audience at the Torchlight Procession were amazed to see the dancers walking across the pebbles, still on their stilts. On a later visit, the dancers insisted on performing in the rain on the slippy stage, and several of them fell off the stilts: Peter Boyce remembers audience members shouting at them to stop. Bill

Lous las Aygues

Rory O'Connor Dancers on the Ham

Helping Sid Reach the Sea

wrote to the group after the Festival that they had 'a special place of honour in our festivities' and the following year, he arranged a trip of English dancers to France to meet up with the group.

A silly event was held during the week. Perturbed that the River Sid disappeared into the pebbles as it approached the sea, a group of festival-goers held a 'Help Sid Reach the Sea' workshop, but after an hour or so trying to dig out the pebbles and find the river, they gave up. 'Whose crazy idea was this anyhow?' one of them asked.

FIRE! Beacons, Barrels and Bangs

1976

In 1975, Bill Rutter casually asked Taffy Thomas if he had any ideas for developing the Arena. Bob Common overheard the conversation. 'Have you thought of a fire festival?' Taffy suggested, plucking a wild idea out of the air. 'Fine', said Bill, 'how much would it cost?' Taffy responded, 'Oh, about £100.' 'Great,' said Bill. Bob quizzed Taffy, 'What do you have in mind?' 'No idea,' said Taffy, 'but I've got £100 to do it with'.

The result was one of those events that is vividly remembered by everyone who saw it.

Beacons, Barrels and Bangs was billed as 'a celebration of fire' on the special poster-cum-programme. Taffy wanted to do something better than the mediocre fire shows performed by community arts groups that he had seen and he based the show on customs that use fire, bonfires, fireworks and the burning of effigies. Magic Lantern's amazing forty-five minute performance came at the end of the Monday evening Arena show. The event was split into five parts,

starting with fire for light and warmth, with torches, lanterns and a beacon in the middle of the audience, accompanied by Dan Claiden from Dartmoor on primitive percussion and a song by Leon Rosselson sung by Tim Laycock. The second part was fire as ritual: Flowers and Frolics played 'The Bonfire Tune' from the Surrey one-man band Albert Farmer and Dave Hunt and Taffy swung fire chains, which are part of the New Year festivities in Stonehaven in Scotland, around their heads. Suddenly, there was a gasp from the audience as what looked like two big bonfires at the top of the Arena bank burst into flames. The bonfires were, in fact, the tar barrels.

'he's mad' was all he could say

This was the most memorable section: the November the Fifth Tar Barrel 'Rollers' from neighbouring Ottery St Mary. The wooden barrels are soaked in tar, filled with straw and set on fire. The barrels are then

carried on the shoulders of the men (and women and boys) through the streets of Ottery until they collapse round their heads. For their Sidmouth appearance, the Ottery men simply picked up the barrels and ran down the hill, in front of the stage and back up the opposite side. As Taffy now remembers, 'Nobody in the audience could believe how anybody could run with a bonfire on their shoulders that big'. Roped-off avenues kept the audience away from the tar barrel rollers, but it was frightening and spectacular. The fourth part used fire as celebration and entertainment and included The Great Rolando as a circus ring-master with Lester Simpson leaping through burning hoops. Finally, there were the fireworks on and around the Arena stage, captured on a photograph with Flowers and Frolics cowering on the bandstand. The whole show was dramatic and amazing, but everyone remembers the tar barrels.

The Yetties were performing elsewhere on the night, but watched the audience walking back to town. Bob Common remembers that they were white-faced – he asked a friend how it had gone. The friend shook his head: 'he's mad' was all he could say.

The fireworks only just made it to Sidmouth. Taffy had a chest full of them in his van and, driving towards Sidmouth, a trailer full of

Fire Chains

Tar Barrel

Burning Hoop

hay caught fire ahead of him. The policeman apologised for the delay, explaining casually that they were just going to let the trailer run back into the ditch. The plans were hastily changed when Taffy told him what was in his van.

By this time the members of Magic Lantern were Taffy, Sheila Metson, Jeannie Harris, Dave Greenwood and Tim Laycock. Bill Caddick had been a member of the group and they still collaborated on some projects. For this performance they were joined by Dave Hunt, Philip Jay, Major Mustard (Mike Frost) and The Great Rolando – Billy Beresford, a former circus and music hall entertainer, who taught many of his skills to Magic Lantern. The 1976 Festival came just as Magic Lantern were relocating from the Midlands to a new base in Suffolk. By this time, the company was not only doing the Magic Lantern shows, but had also

developed the street theatre performances to include fire-eating, tumbling, stilt walking, escapology, magic and illusion. Dave Greenwood was the stilt walker, wearing a top hat from which smoke often billowed. The whole

> ## 'we're enjoying the music, you leave him alone,' she cried

company assembled for a photograph, but who could have guessed the identity of the person in the bear suit. Another photograph reveals the truth – June Tabor. On one occasion the bear sat on the bonnet of a van as it went up towards LNE. The police stopped the van: 'I'm the mascot,' the bear declared. 'And I'm the spare tyre,' said Dave Hunt sitting in the boot holding the bass drum. On another

occasion Taffy was dressed as Boris the Bear and ran up to the policeman on duty in the procession. 'Grrrrrrrr,' said Boris. 'Piss off Taffy!' said the policeman.

By 1975 and 1976, the members of Magic Lantern were so busy at the Festival with so much equipment, that Taffy managed to persuade Bill to let them live on the Arena site in caravans. Dave Hunt also came from the Midlands, and was brought along to help with the catering, but he also performed with the group: known as Ramo Sami, he excelled at fire-eating routines. In 1976, Dave was just in the process of starting his own street theatre and children's show with Vic Baker – Dr Sunshine's Pavement Show.

Another Magic Lantern initiative in 1976 was their Border Morris performance. In spite of Roy Dommett's 1972 workshop, there was only one revival Morris side specialising exclusively in Border

The Magic Lantern Company

The bear is revealed – June Tabor

Morris: they were to make their Sidmouth debut in 1977. Taffy had a copy of the 1909 photograph of the Brimfield Morris, and decided to perform the dance in costumes similar to those in the photograph. Magic Lantern toured the dance round all the venues at the Festival and the pubs in a single evening: it was a one-off show, but it had a lingering impact.

The previous year Magic Lantern was part of the Sunday evening show in the Manor Pavilion. As the audience assembled outside, Major Mustard busked the queue. The Theatre Manager appeared and told him to stop, at which point a policeman arrived on the scene and a row developed. By this time, an old lady in the queue had joined in – 'we're enjoying the music, you leave him alone,' she cried. The people in the queue only found out that they had been set up and that the whole incident was a Magic Lantern sketch when the individuals got up on stage later in the evening. Fortunately, the *Sidmouth Herald* was there to capture the event, including the old lady.

1976 enjoyed one of the hottest and driest summers for many years. There was a drought in many parts of the country, with restricted water supplies. During the Festival, the sun shone all day long, the temperatures were into the eighties and there was not a hint of rain. Ticket sales reached a new all-time record. By early April, 1,200 season

- *Jim Callaghan succeeds Wilson as Prime Minister*
- *Emergency Drought Act limits water usage in scorching summer*
- *Ulster Peace Movement*
- *National Theatre opened*
- *Mao Zedong dies*
- *Three number 1s for Abba, and The Worzels' 'Combine Harvester'.*

1976

tickets had been sold and two of the three camp-sites were full. It was decided to put on extra events and sell another 200 tickets. The Festival was sold out by May and hundreds were turned away. There were also about 1,200 performers, stewards and volunteer helpers.

After the success of Na Fili in 1975 Keith Glover recommended The Bothy Band. Now regarded as one of the all-time great Irish bands, The Bothy Band had only been in existence for a year, and the members – Donal Lunny, Matt Molloy, Tommy Peoples, Paddy Keenan, Michael and Triona Ni Dhomnaill – became giants of the Irish music scene. The Festival paid its highest ever fee to the band, who visited from Monday to Friday. As if that wasn't enough, the Festival also booked the duo Jackie Daly (all Ireland button accordion champion) and Seamus Creagh (fiddle). An Irish Concert in the Assembly Rooms (Council Chamber) also featured Packie Byrne who was

joined by Bonnie Shaljean on harp. There were seats for 200 people, but 300 were squeezed in or watched through the open windows, and dozens of people were turned away. The Bothy Band's next two appearances were the Drill Hall and the Beach Store, and it was evident that the venues were not big enough to handle such popular guests. They did, however, do a twelve-minute spot on an afternoon Arena show. In addition to these performances and an Irish music workshop, they also played in sessions in the bar of The Balfour Arms.

Roaring Jelly went from strength to strength and Swan Arcade – Dave and Heather Brady and Jim Boyes – were also a great success. The complimentary guest list included Lancashire's Tom Tiddler's Ground (which included Chris Parkinson), Flowers and Frolics, Old Swan Band, Graham and Eileen Pratt, John Bull Outfit (including Roger Edwards and Derek Atkinson from Garstang Morris), Martin Graebe, Steve Ashley, The Songwainers ('we are pleased to come and help out again'), June Tabor and the Celebrated Ratcliffe Stout Band. And the Bushwackers made an eagerly-awaited return.

After moving venue each year – the Boat House, the Arts Centre (used for the first time as a Festival venue in 1974), Brunt's Wine Shop on Fore Street – the ballad event became the 'Song Swop' and was held in the Lower Methodist Hall.

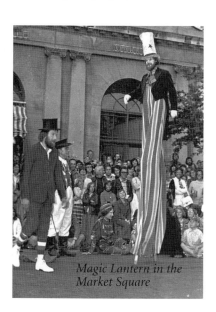

Magic Lantern in the Market Square

Outside the Manor Pavilion, 1975

England's Glory at the Arena

It was led by people such as Jacquey Gabriel and Keith Chandler, whilst in the Horse and Groom, there was a daily session of shanty singing led by Jim Mageean. With the addition of the Drill Hall and Beach Store events, the song enthusiasts had plenty of choice. Two music halls were held in the Drill Hall during the week – on Monday and Thursday, both presided over by Dave Stephenson.

Flowers and Frolics and The Old Swan Band both played in the Music Hall, and returned to The Old Ship to repeat their English music sessions. They were joined by an ever-increasing number of like-minded musicians, including booked band Webb's Wonders (Peta Webb, Tony Engle, Ken Lees and Alan Ward). Both Old Swan and Flowers and Frolics played for Tuesday's Licensed Ceilidh in the Drill Hall, and on Wednesday evening at a Concert of English Country Music at the Assembly Rooms, which also included English fiddler Chris Bartram and the Bampton Morris Dancers.

The traditional Bampton dancers were led by Francis Shergold with both Reg Hall and Rod Stradling as musicians. The side complained in the *Festival News* about other teams dancing Bampton dances, leading to further comment, including the observation that one of the Bampton men was wearing brown, rather than black, shoes. The incident is now part of Bampton's own oral history! Other guest teams

included the village revival team in Adderbury, three locals (Taunton Deane, Exeter and Great Western), as well as Leeds University. The scale of Morris at the Festival can be gauged by a quote in the *Festival News* from a policeman on the Esplanade, 'I'm even dreaming Morris men now!'

John Kirkpatrick and Sue Harris were not available to take the women's Morris workshops because they were expecting their second child, Benji, in August. Marianne Glover of England's Glory led the workshop with assistance from Sheila 'Shoz' Spencer and their daily sessions included Wheatley and North-West dances. On Saturday, England's Glory became

> ### *The incident is now part of Bampton's own oral history!*

the first women's Morris team to perform on the Arena, with a dance from Ilmington and the Abram Circle Dance from Lancashire. Dance Producer John Brock, a Morris dancer himself, was surprised at the level of opposition. One Morris man wanted his money back. 'Like sex, women's Morris is a fact of life,' wrote Bill. Meanwhile, Windsor Ladies' Morris appeared at Thursday's Late Night Extra. There were enough women's teams, or individual dancers, to permit a women's

massed Morris session at noon on Thursday on the Esplanade.

In spite of the Women's Ritual Dance workshop, some women wanted to learn the Cotswold dances with the men, and Tubby Reynolds and Roy Dommett, who ran both the starters' and experienced workshops, welcomed both sexes. There were now separate starters' and experienced rapper workshops.

There had already been a divergence in the folk dance scene between the ceilidh dancers and the experienced country dancers. By and large, the ceilidhs generally appealed to the younger dancers, the folk song enthusiasts, the dances were the simpler traditional dances and the emphasis was on having fun. The events also had song spots or Morris displays. The country dances were no less fun for the participants, but generally there was more emphasis on correct execution of the dance figures, the dances appealed to a wider age range, and the repertoire included dances from the Playford collections, plus recently made-up dances with more complex patterns.

As far as Sidmouth was concerned, the same bands often played for both events. Country dance bands The Squarecrows played for the Playford Ball and Silver and Gold did a Tea Dance, but the former also did a Drill Hall Ceilidh and the latter played at LNE. On the ceilidh side, Webb's Wonders played at LNE and in the Drill Hall, but also did the Friday Tea Dance. Rhona Hitchcock of Silver and Gold found the prospect of playing at LNE in 1975 'a little daunting' but she had been impressed by the improving standard of the dancers.

The English bands such as Old Swan Band, Flowers and Frolics, Umps and Dumps, Webb's Wonders and, later, New Victory Band changed the musical style of ceilidhs, and made them distinctively different to the established folk dance scene. The tunes were from traditional English musicians and there was a determination to play them in a style derived from those same musicians. The instruments used, such as the melodeon, fiddle and anglo-concertina, were more suited to the strongly-rhythmical style of music, in contrast to the smoother, chromatic piano-accordion favoured by the established bands. The new bands played more slowly, and there were more polkas and hornpipes and fewer reels. The dancers responded by putting more stepping into the dances and they rejected the walking step favoured by the country dancers. The callers attracted to the English bands included Tubby Reynolds, Roy Dommett, Dave Williams, Hugh Rippon and Dave Hunt and they concentrated on the traditional English dances in the EFDSS's *Community Dance Manuals.*

One of the great strengths of Sidmouth was that it catered for both the major folk dance styles, and all the grey areas in between. For the country dancers, the morning and afternoon workshops at this time included square dancing, Playford, American running set and Scottish dance, and later in the day there were the afternoon tea dances and evening dances in the Ham Marquee (including the Playford Ball and an Anglo-Scots Dance). For the ceilidh dancers, there was the ceilidh in the Drill Hall and the Late Night Extra. In 1975, Keith Glover as Song Producer also chose the ceilidh bands, but in 1976 John Brock, having done his two years as Arena Producer, became Dance Producer (a new post) and Brian Jones took over at the Arena. John may have been an accordion player from the Weston Country Dance Band, but he found the music of the new-wave English bands 'exciting with the style giving great lift to the dance.' He remembers that it was the dancers that made the distinction between the two styles, but that musicians like himself were enthusiastic for the 'new' music.

Sidmouth was not, of course, the only event or opportunity to experience the English bands and

Los Jairas

ceilidhs, and the informal music and song sessions, but the Festival did have the greatest concentration of 'new wave' enthusiasts. But if your dance and musical tastes lay in the established folk dance scene, then you could ignore the new styles and carry on with your own feast of music and dance.

The favourite ceilidh band at Sidmouth, and indeed at many

> *One of the great strengths of Sidmouth was that it catered for both the major folk dance styles, and all the grey areas in between*

festivals, was The Yetties, although they successfully appealed to the country dancers as well. At the time that the new English bands were emerging, The Yetties were moving out of the folk clubs and into the concert halls, and they were playing for fewer ceilidhs and country dances. Bill Rutter could not imagine a Sidmouth Festival without them so the Festival promoted concerts in neighbouring Exmouth, Seaton, Exeter and Axminster on different evenings, plus a Wednesday ceilidh and Friday

Late Night Extra in Sidmouth itself. This was partly a response to local government reorganisation which had meant the disappearance of the old Urban District Council, and the creation of a Town Council and East Devon District Council. The appeal to the rest of the District was also helped by the village barn dances, and appearances by the overseas teams at places such as Exmouth sea-front and Branscombe.

The Festival has always relied upon volunteer help, and some contributions have been considerable. Clive and Hazel Morgan and their two young daughters first came to Sidmouth for a family holiday in about 1970, and for the first week it was quiet and peaceful. When Clive saw the folk enthusiasts arrive with their beards and hats, he was not impressed, but his eldest daughter was thrilled by the music and joined in the dancing. Later in the week the children's event was short of the back legs for a dragon and Clive found that his daughter had volunteered him. They were hooked. Hazel sadly died several years ago, but more than thirty years after the first visit, Clive and his daughters are still coming to the Festival. Clive says, 'It's important to me and the family – it's a meeting point. I don't dance or sing, but I love the atmosphere, meeting friends and being able to contribute'. That contribution benefited several areas of the Festival over the years, initially at the Arena.

Prior to 1976 Antony Brunt, Pete Smith, the team guides and a group of local residents helped set up the hostels and prepare the venues, but the amount of work was increasing, and it was clear that a specialist team of people was needed. Ted Hutchinson suggested that a Task Force be set up for the week before the Festival, and in return the volunteers would receive free Festival tickets. John and Jane Hill were both in Task Force that year and, alongside Roger Saunders, they are still helping almost thirty years later. George Stuart was brought in

> *the children's event was short of the back legs for a dragon and Clive found that his daughter had volunteered him*

by John Dowell as a steward, but soon he became the Festival's maintenance engineer and part of Task Force.

Over the years, Task Force have set up the hostels and the various venues, whilst at the Arena, they erected the lighting towers, side stands and fences.

In the mid-seventies, the Festival purchased the Arena side stand seating but had nowhere to store it. Clive Morgan was then a Senior Probation Officer in Newport and offered storage. In the spring, Clive's community service offenders sanded and painted the seating, and some of them came to Sidmouth to erect it. They also helped with the Arena fencing, but were not very fast. Task Force sent a couple of women to show them how to knock in fence posts. The men rose to the challenge and the fence was erected in record time. Clive remembers that the young offenders had great job satisfaction and, not surprisingly, the re-offending rate

Les Madras

was very low. Clive later made further contributions at the Arena, as the 1980s will reveal.

Close contact with the Czechoslovakian government and with the British-Czechoslovakian Friendship League guaranteed that the invited group, Zavadka, was allowed to travel to the Festival. The Festival was not so lucky with the group from Nepal. Sidmouth resident and Festival volunteer Sandra Lang was working for Voluntary Service Overseas (VSO) in Kathmandu and she tried hard in both 1975 and 1976 to get the Bhairab Dance Ensemble to Sidmouth. Problems with work permits caused last-minute cancellations each year. The *Festival*

News included humorous items about 'Sherpa Dowell' going in search of the Nepalese dancers on the mythical fifth camp-site and finding only the Tibetan recluse Rut-Er. Of course, the Yetties were blamed! The jokes lasted for several years.

Other overseas dance groups were from Austria, France (two groups, Bretons and Catalans) and Finland, whilst Les Madras was a group made up of Caribbean Islanders based in Paris. Always on the look-out for international singers, the Festival invited Los Jairas from Bolivia – the first of many visits by the group. We may now take pan-pipes for granted, but then their music was described as 'little-known' in their publicity.

Windsor Ladies' Morris

Pogo and Protest

23rd INTERNATIONAL FOLKLORE FESTIVAL SIDMOUTH

29 JULY ~ 5 AUGUST

1977 By the time of the 23rd Festival in 1977, Bill Rutter was looking towards retirement, confident that John Dowell was well able to succeed him as Festival Director. It is therefore an opportune moment to reflect here on what the Festival had to offer to the various enthusiasts.

Publicity for the Festival was sent out in January each year. The leaflet was accompanied by a typed news-sheet with a list of guests and a request for stewards who were offered free tickets in exchange for four to six hours of stewarding each day. The 1977 mail-shot also contained details of the first Reunion Ceilidh, which was held at Cecil Sharp House on 29 January with the Bushwackers Band and Taffy Thomas. A second news-sheet was issued later in January and separate leaflets were aimed at the Arena audience. Residents of Sidmouth and surrounding villages were offered cheaper season tickets: £4.50 instead of £12.00. EFDSS members also received a discount: they paid only £9.00. Camping was £5.00 for the week. Season tickets for children were £2.00 with an extra pound for camping. These were all pre-April prices, but as the Festival

was selling out each year, most people took advantage of the cheaper prices to guarantee getting a ticket.

The working programme was still produced on an ink duplicator: foolscap-size sheets of paper stapled together. The arrival of the programme in early July was – and is – always an exciting experience.

In 1977, as now, there were three official starts to the Festival. On Thursday evening in the Market Square there was an informal display featuring one or more of the overseas dance groups which, in 1977, was Jan

> *A professional sound system was used, although by today's standards it was quite primitive*

Pirrewit, a children's dance group from Belgium. Great Western Morris were the residents, and Itchen Scratch Band played. The second start was the Arena Show on Friday evening, featuring all the overseas dance groups, and attended by the Chairman of East Devon District Council and other councillors. And

then on Saturday, there was the Breaking of National Flags on the Ham, with one-minute displays from each of the dance groups. These were all very public occasions and elsewhere at the Festival, groups of enthusiasts would return to their favourite venues to meet with friends and welcome newcomers.

The camp-sites were open from Wednesday, allowing campers to arrive as and when work commitments allowed. Friday evening saw a Come All Ye in the Beach Store for the song enthusiasts, a Late Night Special in the Market Square for the children and a Morris display outside the Marine Bars by Great Western Morris. Many people, including the guests who were in hotel or other accommodation, could not arrive until Saturday.

The Arena shows continued twice a day, at 3.00pm and 8.00pm, throughout the week with the same mix of overseas and British dance groups. The format included an overture from one of the English bands, who also played during the ten-minute interval and again at the end of the show as the audience was leaving. General dancing by the public had disappeared by 1977. The only variation was that on Monday evening, The Yetties hosted a Song Show, featuring singers from the overseas groups. The staging of the Arena shows had improved year by year, with the dancing platform laid flat on a concrete base. There was

Turkish dancers

now a separate covered bandstand and the canvas backdrop was laid out to give clear entrances and exits at each side. A professional sound system was used, although by today's standards it was quite primitive, and the sound was mixed in a caravan slightly behind the bandstand. There were two lighting towers and the deckchairs were now permanently laid out in rows. Car parking at the Arena was still a problem and although the Council had created a car park for its employees in 1975, this was only available to the Festival in the evenings.

The Meet the Team events took place at 6.00pm each day in the Ham Marquee as a one-hour opportunity to get a bit closer to the dancers. The overseas dance groups also performed at the Late Night Extra, not necessarily in costume, and they were expected to include a dance which could be taught to the audience. The groups were no longer included in the village barn dances but they were not yet being

programmed for the Market Square in the evening. From 1975 onwards, a special show of overseas dancers took place on Sunday afternoon at Exeter Cross (on the recreation ground where the main road towards Sidford divides into Arcot Road and Sidford Road) 'for the benefit of residents in the area'.

In addition to Jan Perrewit, the dance groups included Lou Cieri from France, two groups from Italy, a marching band from Bavaria, a group of Ukrainians from Canada and the first ever group from Norway. The Festival anticipated problems with the groups from Greece (Lykion Hellinidon Kavalas from Eastern Macedonia) and Turkey (Turizm Ve Folklor Egitim Merkezi – abbreviated to TUFEM) because relations between the two countries had worsened in the mid-seventies over Cyprus. Apart from the first and last two nights, the two groups were on different Arena shows, and the Festival always

transported them in different buses. But in one of those heart-warming illustrations that music and dance can transcend international crises, the members of the two groups crowded into each others buses and socialised, played and danced together throughout the week.

The dancers were catered for with a variety of different events. For the country dancers, there were the Tea Dances in the Ham Marquee from 3.00 to 5.30pm each day with bands such as Hoedown, Silver and Gold and the Weston Country Dance Band and callers including John Chapman, Cyril Jones and Gay Gaylor. In the evenings, the same venue hosted a general dance on Saturday, the Playford Ball on Monday with the Weston Country Dance Band and Kate Coombes, a Square Dance on Tuesday with Culver Griffin from the USA, whilst the Grand Festival Dance maintained its position on Thursday.

Further afield, the village Barn Dances continued in Sidford each evening Monday to Thursday, plus Colyford on Monday, Newton Poppleford on Tuesday, Sidbury on Wednesday and Tipton St John on Thursday. The bands for these events included The Reelists, The Squarecrows, Redbridge Band and the musicians from Woodfidley, whilst other callers included Walt Tingle and David Slater.

The dance workshops were most likely to appeal to the country dancers. There were experienced and starters' social dance workshops, with different bands and callers each day, as well as Running Set and American Square (with Culver Griffin). The social dance workshops varied each year depending on which bands and callers were booked.

There were no ceilidhs during the day, so that the ceilidh dancers could

Greek dancers

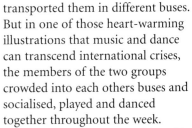

- Queen's Silver Jubilee
- Punk rock
- Red Rum wins Grand National for third time
- Elvis Presley, Bing Crosby and Charlie Chaplin die
- Wings 'Mull of Kintyre' No 1.

The Punk Ceilidh

Len Evis behind the bar

indulge their other interests. On Wednesday evening, the Ham Marquee dance was a Ceilidh with The Yetties and John Chapman. Each evening in the Drill Hall, Taffy Thomas presided over 'Taffy's End of the Pier Show' with Flowers and Frolics, Travel by Steam (a band linked to Great Western Morris) and Hoedown taking two evenings apiece.

Taffy was also responsible for another of those events which is remembered by everyone who was there. Acknowledging one of the recent fashions in popular music, Wednesday was Punk Ceilidh Night. Flowers and Frolics were recreated as a band called Mentally Negligible and the whole audience came dressed in black bin liners, ripped t-shirts and safety pins. Even the landlord of the Balfour Arms, Len Evis, who provided the bar in the Drill Hall, dressed up, and Sheila Finn and Alan Weird (Whear) won the worst-dressed Mr and Mrs Punk competition, although in Sheila's case, there was not a lot of costume: just a couple of large, and strategically placed, cardboard razor blades. The favourite punk dance was the pogo, which simply involved leaping up and down in time to the music, so the folk dances were done in the pogo style, although I remember that this was rather exhausting after the first dance or two. The joke continued at the Late Night Extra, but whatever did the German marching band think when they were followed up and down the marquee by a crowd of crazy

English people pogoing in time to their music!

The Late Night Extra featured bands from both the ceilidh and country dance sides of the Festival: Flowers and Frolics one night, the Weston Country Dance Band the next, reflecting the mixture of audience from right across the Festival spectrum, but all the dances were relatively easy and accessible.

> ... one of those heart-warming illustrations that music and dance can transcend international crises ...

Clog dancers, including Joss Mellor, Geoff Hughes, and Graham and Mary Cole, had been performing at the Festival since the sixties, but now groups of clog dancers were emerging. Reading Cloggies carefully researched clog and step dances, and they performed at the Arena in 1977. The booked Morris teams included Manchester Morris, Bourne River, Great Western and Newcastle Kingsmen. Steve Mitchell from Manchester Morris led the North-West Morris workshops. Roy Dommett and Tubby Reynolds took the Experienced Morris workshops, with Richard and John Brock taking the starters. Dave 'Buttercup' Robinson took the Women's Ritual Morris workshop and although

there was no rapper workshop programmed, an impromptu event was organised at the Balfour Arms.

But the greatest interest arose from a couple of relatively new Morris dance teams from Shropshire. John Kirkpatrick and Sue Harris had moved to the county in 1973, and started looking for local songs, tunes and dances. John had become disillusioned with the Cotswold Morris scene, feeling that it lacked energy and passion. A group of local sixth formers, with no preconceptions of Morris dancing, wanted to start a team, and John seized the opportunity to use the available information on Border Morris as the basis for a fresh approach to Morris dancing in the revival. He took elements from the available notations, invented the step, adapted the costume descriptions and introduced a generous helping of spectacle to create The Shropshire Bedlams. The companion women's team, Martha Rhoden's Tuppenny Dish, adapted dances from the area and further afield to 'suit their femininity'. Apart from some appearances locally, and one Festival visit, the two groups were almost completely unknown, but John and Sue's high reputation resulted in an invitation to Sidmouth, and even a couple of spots on the Arena.

They were a sensation at Sidmouth – the appearance, the energy, the flamboyance of the men, and the fresh approach of the women. At the time, it was very unusual to have joint teams, men and women, performing

Shropshire Bedlams

alongside each other. John had just joined Steeleye Span and the band had to turn down a tour of Australia because John would not back out of the Sidmouth visit. Over the following few years, the Bedlams inspired new and existing teams to turn to the Border Morris and interpret the dances differently, other teams copied the Bedlams' style rather too slavishly, whilst some teams realised the possibilities of adaptation and creation in other styles.

Official venues for watching the Morris teams apart from the Arena, were the Market Square at 8.30pm (although most of these displays were moved into New Street because of the new traffic system) and opposite the Marine Bars at 10.00pm. All the dance teams were encouraged to dance along the Esplanade on Sunday at noon, a feature which still remains.

'Unattached' Morris dancers used to congregate and dance in the road outside The Swan, but with more cars and the new traffic system, the Morris dancers had to move. For several years, these unattached dancers had formed into sides and busked in Sidmouth and elsewhere – they became known as the Odds and Sods (or Sids) Morris, and one year The Dommetteers. The *Festival News* also reveals the large number of full Morris teams that danced during

the week, including Windsor Ladies, Derby Crown women, Derby Morris Men, Pilgrim, King John, Red Rose,

> **Steeleye Span had to turn down a tour of Australia because John Kirkpatrick would not back out of the Sidmouth visit**

Bristol, Hartley, Cardiff, Cardiff Ladies, Taunton Deane, Bathampton, Headcorn and Chelmsford.

To help the non-booked dancers, the Festival identified busking sites,

with teams booking these in advance and advertising them in the *Festival News*. Venues included Port Royal, the Esplanade opposite the Tourist Information Centre (then located west of the Bedford Lawn car-park) and the Marlborough Hotel forecourt after 7.00pm. There was also an attempt via the *Festival News* to improve the appearance of the dancers: 'scruffy costume lets down the Festival, and the dance, more than a poor standard of dancing as far as the public is concerned. Aspiring Morris Men please note.' Presumably the women were never scruffy!

So as far as the dancers were concerned, whether the interest was in watching the Arena displays and the dancers on the Esplanade, or in taking part in workshops, tea dances and barn dances, or in dancing at the ceilidhs and Late Night Extra, or in learning Morris and rapper dances or taking part with the rest of your team or busking with fellow dancers, there was more than enough to keep them occupied.

The new Song Producer was Barry Lister, who lived in Sidmouth. Bill Rutter wrote, 'It gives me a great deal of satisfaction to find a local lad in charge of this part of the festival'. Barry was a member of Isca Fayre, a song group resident at The Jolly Porter Folk Club in Exeter, and he also carried the hobby horse for Great Western Morris. As a resident, Barry obviously knew a great many people in the town and had personal contacts with, for

A dance in the marquee

John Foreman

Battlefield Band in the marquee

example, the pub landlords. The Anchor was a pub which had always been rather hostile to the Festival, but in 1976 Festival regular Fred Rooke persuaded the new landlord to let him and Derek Reid use the upstairs room for some impromptu song workshops. The pub found that the festival-goers were quite well-behaved, and Barry negotiated the use of the room for three sessions a day – workshops in the morning and the Ballad Spot in the afternoons and evenings, led by Jacquey Gabriel and Keith Chandler.

The Beach Store was a central venue for song sessions. There was the Come All Ye each morning from 10.30 to 12.30, which provided an opportunity for anyone to put their names on the list and sing a couple of songs. The 3.00pm session was also billed as a Come All Ye, but there were generally three guests alongside a more limited number of

singers from the floor. The evening 8.00 to 10.30pm session featured three guests. The venue was rough and ready and small, allowing fewer than a hundred audience members. There was no bar, but coffee was available.

The Drill Hall was used for two song events a day with the lunchtime one-hour At Home events featuring just a single performer. During the week, the guests were Battlefield Band, Swan Arcade (just prior to splitting up for the first time), Fred Jordan, Brenda Wootton, John Foreman and Peter Bellamy. Brenda Wootton, however, turned her session into a pasty-making workshop: coming from Cornwall, she was not impressed with Devon's attempts to make her native dish. And Peter Bellamy held a Folk Quiz, an event which has had many manifestations over the years.

Later in the afternoon, the Drill Hall was used for a song event from 4.00 to 6.00pm, featuring three guests a day.

In the evenings, concerts were held in the Assembly Rooms at Knowle with generally six guests squeezed into two-and-a-half-hours. Monday was an English concert with Fred Jordan, The Songwainers, Ken Langsbury, Chris Bartram, Bob Cann and the MC Tony Rose, and Tuesday was a Celtic concert with Brenda Wootton, Ar Log from Wales, Bob Stewart, Battlefield Band and Kevin Mitchell. There were no themes on Saturday (with Swan Arcade, Peter Bellamy, Strawhead, Tony Rose, John Foreman and Frankie Armstrong) and Wednesday (some of the guests already mentioned plus Mick Ryan and Jon Burge and Mick and Sarah Graves). Other performers included Spredthick, Tickler's Jam, Tom

Swan Arcade in the Beach Store

Peter Bellamy

The Twenty-third Festival – Friday 29th July - Friday 5th August 1977

*Hobby Horse Club
on the Ham*

McConville and The John Bull Outfit. In addition, there were Sunday evening concerts in the Ham Marquee and the Manor Pavilion for the event now called Director's Choice: for the rest of the week it was used for live theatre. The Arts Centre was used for the Folk Shop, rather than for events.

For the children, the Festival was on the verge of offering a great deal more choice. The folk enthusiasts were bringing their children to the Festival in greater numbers, and the events continued to attract the local children. More was needed than the playgroup for three to seven year olds, and the Hobby Horse Club for children over seven. Bill Rutter continued his policy of decentralising responsibility, and appointed a Children's Producer, Paul Weir, another of the Festival supporters from Cheltenham. Paul had been involved with Folk Camps, another of Bill's initiatives which had many links with Sidmouth. Paul wanted to provide the children with their own events, rather than simply providing a creche whilst their parents enjoyed the Festival. He introduced the title 'Sid Kids' to give the events a separate identity.

It was Paul who suggested the Morris Minors event to cater for the demand for Morris dancing for children. Dick Rendell, from Manchester Morris Men was in charge and he had run similar events at Folk Camps. Morris Minors was

so popular that it became a regular feature for many years.

Children could choose the playgroup (with different guests each day), the music workshop led by Brian Stone from Hoedown, a children's singalong with Alison Bloomer and Alison McMorland (formerly Potts), children's crafts with John and Nancy Lomax and

> **'For six days, there is a friendly international atmosphere in what must be the perfect setting'**

children's games, plus the Hobby Horse Club. Since 1975 the Friday afternoon Arena Show had been a 'Children's Special' but there was increasingly the opportunity of including more items featuring the children. A marquee on the Ham was used for children's events, plus the Arena Marquee, the Chapel Street Hall and the Lower Methodist Hall. Bill was immensely pleased with the range of activity and wrote to Paul 'to congratulate you on the first really organised Children's Sidmouth'.

It was at about this time that Tristan Glover (son of Keith and Marianne and now a member of Chipolatas) took part in the children's events alongside Barnaby Stradling (son of Rod and Danny)

and Ken Langsbury's children. He remembers singing the Songwainers' 'Whose Pigs are These?', 'The Bumble Bee' and 'The Bear Hunt', and that the adults teaching the songs included Dave Hunt and Taffy Thomas.

In the weeks prior to the Festival, there were calls for East Devon District Council and Sidmouth Town Council to cut their financial support for the Festival. Then, as now, some people only looked at the balance sheet when the Festival was doing well and making a small surplus, which was certainly the case in the two or three years prior to 1977, thanks to the weather. The Festival received support from local councillors, including John Govier, Ted Pinney and Frank Lock, but Robin Pocock remained firmly against the Festival. Indeed, Mr Pocock took a week's holiday so that he could 'investigate the ins and outs of the Festival', and John Dowell sent him a free season ticket. He believed that seventy per cent of his electorate did not want the Festival, although he admitted that, at a Town Forum, he had been out-voted ninety to one.

Mr Pocock asked for a referendum, and Colin Healey, owner of the Prospect Newsagency obliged by organising a petition. The result was over 6,000 in favour of the Festival, and just twelve against. Omitting the festival-goers from out of town, about one third of the votes came from local residents. Colin Healey said at the time, 'Apart from the boost to business, the town comes alive with colour and music. For six days, there is a friendly international atmosphere in what must be the perfect setting. Dancers and singers are gentle, good-humoured and happy people.' Ted Pinney, as Chairman of East Devon District Council, thanked the residents for being such 'gracious hosts' and for leaving the visitors from other parts of the world 'with a lasting impression of Sidmouth's unfailing courtesy and hospitality'.

Midnight Jig

1978 All the overseas dancers were now being accommodated and fed at Sidmouth Secondary School at Primley. Some English dancers and volunteer staff also stayed in hostels in the Woolbrook area and in some cases had their meals at Primley as well. Some hotels were moving away from full board and instead provided evening meal, bed and breakfast, or simply bed and breakfast. Not all of the hotels had yet embraced the Festival, and dance performers who booked into the Byes Links Hotel were told by the manager that it 'would not go down well' if they went in and out of the hotel in costume. Increasingly, there was a demand for self-catering accommodation, although this was difficult to find. So the accommodation selected by most festival-goers, whether from preference or necessity, was the camp-site.

The Festival was on a high locally. The resounding vote in favour of the Festival in Colin Healey's petition and Robin Pocock's own experience of the event in 1977 curbed the criticism. But it was suspected that anti-festival residents were behind the sudden interest in the camp-site by the local fire officer.

Beneath the page one headline 'Midnight Jig', the *Sidmouth Herald* reported, 'Festival campers were angered this week when they were ordered at midnight to shuffle 150 tents around on the main festival camp site.' Bill Rutter and John Dowell had been tipped off that the fire officer would be checking the camp-site on Tuesday morning, so Bill made his unpopular announcement at the Late Night Extra on Monday. The requirement was that tents had to be at least fifteen feet apart, and that outside each tent there had to be a bucket containing not less than two gallons

> *... it was suspected that anti-festival residents were behind the sudden interest in the camp-site by the local fire officer*

of water. The arrangements were supervised by the long-standing camp-site warden Alan White. The public health inspector had already visited the site, and was perfectly satisfied with the arrangements. It was gratifying to note that the local authorities were so concerned for

the campers' well-being! The incident led to a tightening up of the camp-site lay-out with the more clearly defined, and named, lanes between the groups of tents.

Not surprisingly, the festival-goers were not too pleased with the disruption, but they quickly saw the funny side and Wednesday's *Festival News* carried a parody of a well-known folk song, re-titled 'The Wild Camper', with the chorus:

So it's no way, never,
No way, never no more.
Will I move my tent over,
No, never, no more.

And the wags who contributed to the *Festival News* also suggested new rules for melodeon players: twenty feet apart, with a bucket of beer in front of each player!

Looking through the correspondence, the programme and the copies of the daily *Festival News*, there are many seemingly small incidents and events which led to significant developments at the Festival and in the wider folk scene in the following years.

There is a large interest today in West Gallery music and singing: the arrangements of church music for instruments and voices which were led from the West Galleries of churches, rather than from the later organs and formal choirs. Linked to this is the music of the village bands, including the marching bands from the Whitsun Club Walks. Rollo Woods from Winchester was a pioneer of this music, long before

Bill Rutter asks the LNE audience to move their tents

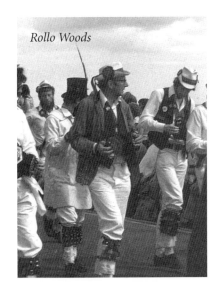
Rollo Woods

Apple Chill Cloggers

the West Gallery Music movement started. In 1978, he brought the Victorian Village Band and Choir, which was renamed The Madding Crowd, to Sidmouth to lead the hymn singing in the Blackmore Gardens on Sunday evening, and he gave a talk on the subject on Tuesday morning. From tiny acorns ...

As already noted, there were no ceilidhs during the day. But in Tuesday's *Festival News* an impromptu event was announced: a ceilidh to be held in the Anchor Garden at noon, 'weather permitting', with Old Pull and Push, one of whose members was Paul, son of Ted Hutchinson. The experiment was successful and ceilidhs were also held on Thursday and Friday. From 1979, the Anchor Garden at lunch-time became a regular ceilidh venue. From tiny acorns ...

The Festival had already welcomed a couple of clogging dance groups from the USA, and in 1978 it was the turn of Apple Chill Cloggers (a spoonerism for their home town, Chapel Hill). The group offered to send a video-tape: the first time this had happened. They had been inspired by the Green Grass Cloggers who had taken a radical approach to clogging by combining the clog stepping with square formations rather the conventional big circle sets. It was a style that appealed to the younger dancers in the States, and the Apple Chill Cloggers were keen to teach the style to new dancers. For the first time, an overseas dance group led a week-long series of workshops, every morning in the Drill Hall, and the friends they made later corresponded with group members across the Atlantic. The

leader, Susan Gramling, wrote to Bill, 'It seems that some of them are continuing to practice what they had learned and even passing clogging on to others. Isn't that marvellous? I guess it's that kind of sharing that your festival is all about.' At the time, there were no Appalachian clogging groups in England. This single series of workshops did not, however, lead to the immediate establishment of such dance groups – that came later in the 1980s. But from tiny acorns ...

Taffy hosted his End of the Pier Show again in the Drill Hall each evening. Wednesday was Music Hall night and, as with the previous year, there were two Music Halls – one in the Assembly Rooms and the other in the Drill Hall. The former was respectable and had no bar, whereas the latter was much more fun. Flowers and Frolics were the pit orchestra in the Drill Hall, but made a much greater contribution. The climax of the evening was a performance of Shakespeare's *Macbeth*, which had been abridged – actually to eight minutes – by Flowers and Frolics. Roger Digby played the title role, with Ted Stevens as all three witches, Bob King as Burnham Wood and Vin Garbutt as Malcolm. Paul Weir and I reviewed the Festival for the principal national folk magazine at the time, *Folk News*, and wrote, 'This had the audience rolling about in hysterics. The time and effort spent

Paul Weir at the first Anchor Garden Ceilidh

Vin Garbutt as Malcolm in the Scottish Play

Ken Langsbury and the Camel

on the music hall attests to the energy and commitment that this festival induces.' Other items in the Music Hall included The Ancient Egyptian Team – an enlarged Dr Sunshine's Pavement Show which included Dave Hunt's two daughters. They performed the

> *... a performance of Shakespeare's Macbeth, abridged – to eight minutes – by Flowers and Frolics*

sand dance (with John 'Tool' McIntosh, Phil Ashworth and Vic Baker as Wilson, Keppel and Betty respectively) and the camel dance: the camel was in the style of a pantomime horse, and its appearance had been well trailed in the *Festival News*. Flowers and Frolics frequently appeared with Bob Davenport, but as he was not appearing at the Festival, there was a ventriloquist's dummy to represent him. Operated by Lester Simpson (then a member of Gingers Street Theatre and now part of Coope, Boyes and Simpson) the dummy, complete with Bob's characteristic shock of wild sandy hair, sang one of his signature songs 'Moving Day'.

The Music Hall in the Assembly Rooms had a variety of guests including Tim Laycock, Ken Langsbury and the Oyster Ceilidh Band.

In 1978 the Oyster Ceilidh Band comprised John Jones, Alan Prosser, Ian Telfer, Will Ward, Chris Taylor, Ian Kearey and caller Cathy Lesurf. Although John Jones had been to the Festival before (he danced with an embryonic Great Western Morris) this was the first visit for the rest of the Kent-based band. Ian Telfer now remembers, 'We had a truly wonderful time. There was a sense of discovering a wider social scene that was also heavily into English music, and we made lots of friendships and connections that persisted.' The membership of the band overlapped with Fiddler's Dram, who were also at the Festival, and whose song 'Day Trip to Bangor' became a Top Three Chart hit the following year. The ceilidh band played at various venues: a ceilidh in the Drill Hall, an Arena overture,

Late Night Extra, a barn dance in Sidford and a Tea Dance.

Tuesday's End of the Pier Show was Lancashire Night with Garstang Morris and The John Bull Band, and there was even Lancashire hot-pot for everyone. Friday's theme was Sixties' Hippy Night. Two Scottish bands appeared at the Festival: Bully Wee and Ossian, with the latter having a great impact. Magic Lantern had split up as a touring company in 1977, and Tim Laycock came as a solo singer. Dr Sunshine's Pavement Show's street theatre helped fill the gap left by Magic Lantern, and they also ran some of the children's events. The *Folk News* review noted that Dr Sunshine's 'worked like Trojans all week'. *Folkweave*, BBC Radio 2's folk music programme produced by Peter Pilbeam, recorded at the Festival throughout the week.

Old Pull and Push in the Anchor Garden

Poynton Jemmers

The festival scene nationally was expanding with more and more festivals being started up and down the country. Yet the focus for professional and semi-professional singers was still the folk club. Nevertheless, singers had to be adaptable. Festivals had a greater variety of events, and many performers realised that they had to offer more than the thirty to forty-minute sets that were standard in folk clubs. Many of the invited singers, whether they were paid a fee or receiving complimentary tickets, were also offering workshops or talks. Tim Laycock presented 'Dorset Dialect Verse and Village Entertainments', John Wright and Catherine Perrier: 'French Traditional Folk Styles', Dave Surman talked on 'Folk Songs of the Upper Thames', Tundra (Doug and Sue Hudson): 'Broadsides and Street Literature' and Jon Raven talked on English Canals. The guests were offering more talks than the Festival could accommodate, and impromptu talks (and other events) were held in the Winter Gardens (Carinas) and announced in the *Festival News*. The Anchor and the Horse and Groom were scheduled for morning talks or singarounds, but shortly before the Festival started, the Horse and Groom suddenly closed temporarily and all

the events were moved to The Black Horse. This pub had been used for informal gatherings of singers over the years but there was the opportunity of using it for official events once the skittle alley had been built in the backyard. Later, the pub was completely altered and the skittle alley was incorporated into the main pub.

Women's Morris became a controversial issue again in 1978. After the 1977 Festival, the Moulton Morris Men from Northamptonshire complained about the appearance of a women's Cotswold Morris side, and the matter of whether or not the EFDSS should promote women's Morris in this way at festivals and events was referred to the Society's governing body, the National Executive Committee (NEC). Bill was clear that on the basis of both equality and the development of a living tradition, women's Morris should be included. He was, however, not sure what conclusion the NEC would come to. In May, he wrote to the new Arena Producer, Les Willcox from Bristol, 'It would be wise for us at Sidmouth this year to see that Cotswold is not danced on the Arena by women. ... Practically this would mean, say, Poynton rather than Windsor and a firm understanding as to the repertoire to be danced. ... Sidmouth led the field in the development of women's Morris. It will not hurt for once that we drop back in the crowd.'

Poynton Jemmers came from Cheshire. Ann Mettam had attended

the women's Morris workshops at Sidmouth in 1975 and discovered that England's Glory did a dance called Knutsford, close to where she lived. A few weeks later, Poynton Jemmers were founded and after a visit to the EFDSS's Vaughan Williams Memorial Library and a search of the notations of the newly-established Women's Morris Federation, some of the Jemmers started to research the dances of their own area. In 1976 they performed at the EFDSS National Gathering in London and, as a result, Bill invited them to dance at the 1978 Sidmouth Festival. By this time, their repertoire included dances from several Cheshire towns and villages such as Goostrey, Mobberley, Holmes Chapel and Runcorn. They created quite a sensation, and the *Festival News* was filled with jokes about 'Grab a Jemmer'. Ann wrote of a 'particular thrill' at being invited because the Sidmouth workshops had been responsible for her starting the team, and her favourite moment of the whole week was when Bill Rutter walked onto the stage after their last-night Arena performance and declared, 'They're British – aren't you proud of them?'

Morris-wise, there was a definite northern emphasis. Garstang Morris returned for their third visit, whilst other newcomers were Poynton's nearest neighbours in Cheshire, Adlington Morris Men who danced Cotswold dances, and from Staffordshire, Keele Rapper, based at the university. The latter included a young Chris Pitt, now a dance caller and a recent Arena MC.

Meanwhile, the EFDSS Executive did make a statement about women's Morris. Whilst recognising the EFDSS's 'conservation of tradition' role, the Executive also believed that the Society had to 'watch for, and nurture, the traditions as they develop. By forbidding Women's Morris we might be applying a false influence to the natural development of a living tradition.' The EFDSS policy, therefore, did not forbid the public performance of the Morris by women. Of course, this statement did not please some men's sides who were members of The Morris Ring.

Dr Sunshine's Pavement Show always looked for the humour in any situation and their spoof of women's Morris, performed around the Festival, was well-received by people on both sides of the argument.

The two processions a day were cut back to just two for the whole week because of traffic problems, although on Wednesday there was an attempt to set a world record for the most Morris dancers performing at the same time, with the 'Winster Processional'.

In addition to dance groups from the Netherlands, France, Switzerland (duelling alpenhorns played from the Arena stage and the top of the bank) and the Basque Country, there was the first visit from a Tibetan group – The Bod-rigs Dos-ghar Tsog-pa dance group which was based in Switzerland. The performances included a yak (like Dr Sunshine's camel, it appeared to owe something in style to the pantomime horse), and Bill wrote after the Festival, 'The children were excited with your Yak dance, and it was not only the children'. The Irish dancers were fairly local, the Yetminster group taught by Pam Common.

But the Sicilians created the most impact. Gruppo Folk Canterini della Riviera Jonica came to the Festival courtesy of a friend of a work colleague of a Festival regular. A distinctive feature of the group was the man who alternated between blowing into and throwing in the air a large decorated jug. Blowing into the jug added a percussive element to the music, whilst throwing it in the air added to the spectacle. The jug thrower had only broken five jugs in ten years, but this became five and a half when he broke a handle at the Arena.

After Great Western Morris's Festival debut in 1974, they continued to perform at the Festival informally until being booked as guests in 1977. The side took their dancing very seriously, displaying enthusiasm and energy and being

> ### The jug thrower had only broken five jugs in ten years ...

very concerned that the audience was suitably entertained. After the Brain Setting dance of 1974, they devised a funny dance each year for the final LNE. In 1975 there was Flashers' Morris in dirty raincoats and strategically placed bell-pads, the following year they dressed as ballet dancers and in 1977 there was the One-Legged Morris. In 1978 they discovered that they were programmed for Thursday's LNE where they were sharing the bill with Sicily. The Mafia Morris was the result, with the dance floor littered with dead bodies by the end of the dance. Great Western were not the only people to do something special at LNE. After the local councillors had performed their impromptu Morris dance in the sixties, it was the turn of the local policemen. For several years in the seventies, they did the Police Morris, using truncheons as sticks. The Festival enjoyed great co-operation from the police at this time, especially from Sergeants Bob Seldon and Doug Holsgrove, and in spite of the number of visitors, the police made fewer arrests in Festival week than at any other time.

The LNE layout did not change very much over the seventies. The stage was sited on the side, with the top end popularly known as the 'bog end'. As there was no bar, many people brought their own beer, including the Cheshire and Manchester contingent who 'imported' their own supplies of Boddington's beer, in the distinctive four-pint Bodcans. One year they ran out and had to send someone back to Manchester for fresh supplies. Dave 'Crocket' Houghton mimicked the Sicilians with his own 'Bodcan throwing'. Fortunately, the generator was now less noisy and slightly more reliable, but the only catering was still Tony Vokes's hot dogs.

For those festival-goers who were still bursting with energy after LNE there were always the late-night private parties at The Balfour Arms. Landlord Len Evis and his wife Margaret put members of Garstang in charge of the invitations and as the pub was fairly close to the hostel, many overseas dancers joined in. The music sessions in the skittle-alley frequently lasted until dawn, when breakfast was served. We all thought we could dispense with sleep for the week.

Sicilians

The Sicilian jug thrower and Ted Pinney

Silver Jubilation

1979

'We are celebrating with a mixture of nostalgia and the current scene', Bill wrote in the first newsletter to publicise the Festival in January 1979. By the end of February, the Festival was sold out. Preparations for the Silver Jubilee had started a couple of years earlier, with letters to some of the overseas groups that had made the greatest impression. It was always going to be a memorable occasion for Bill Rutter who retired as Regional Development Officer for the EFDSS and as Festival Director on 1 September 1979.

The overseas dance groups were a selection of the best and most popular guests from the previous dozen years, so that the Festival was guaranteed to have a whole series of show-stoppers.

As in 1975, the contact for the French stilt dancers, Lous las Aygues, was John Brock who visited the group in 1978 to discuss their return visit. They were enthusiastic, even though their own festival (which was itself inspired by their first visit to Sidmouth) started as Sidmouth finished. The group made new costumes and stilts especially for their visit and after their first day, the new team members were telling Bill Rutter that, 'The festival is fantastic! We have never experienced anything like it!'

Also from France came Lou Cieri from Orange in Provence. When they were last at the Festival, in 1977, they met up with the Bavarian marching band featuring brass instruments and drums, Ebersberger Spielmannszug, and the friendships forged that year led to exchanges between the two groups. They met up again in 1979 when both groups were invited back to Sidmouth. Also from the 1977 Festival came TUFEM: Turizm Ve Folklor Egitim Merkezi, from Turkey. Once again they had a five-day coach trip to get

Zavadka

here, which they felt was well worth it, and they found the Festival to be more enjoyable than ever.

Zavadka from Czechoslovakia repeated their success of 1976 and were the only Eastern European

> ## By the end of February, the Festival was sold out

country to be represented. Afterwards Bill wrote to the group, 'The Festival is about friendship between everyone whatever nationality and the attendance of your group at our 25th birthday helped to re-affirm our motivation'. Les Sortileges from Montreal in Canada were last in Sidmouth in 1974, and their leader wondered if the return visit would be as good,

and their reception as enthusiastic. 'After 24 hours back in Sidmouth, we found that the festival is something particular that we do not find anywhere else. There is a spirit, a feeling and a flavour particular to this festival.' In addition to the French-Canadian step dancing, they performed a Moose Hunt Dance that enthralled the Hobby Horse Club.

Esbart Dansaire de Rubi from Spain had already proven themselves to be firm favourites on their two previous visits, and they prepared a special performance. On Sunday evening they performed Mooshiganga, a dance-drama which depicted the last days in the life of Christ. The dancers entered the darkened Arena bearing torches, whilst the character depicting Christ was illuminated by a single spotlight.

Prelaz, the Dutch musicians

The performance held the audience completely spellbound, and at the end the group's leader was brought onto the stage to receive an ovation from the audience. 'One of the most impressive sights of the Festival for many years', declared the *Festival News*. The demand from the Sidmouth audiences was such that the performance was repeated on Tuesday night, although John Brock recalls that the group was surprised by the audience's response.

Hupsakee from Amsterdam had been to the Festival (with different names) in 1972, 1975 and 1978, but they were so determined to come again that they offered to camp when they found out the hostel accommodation was full. Two of the dancers even came to London in February for the Festival Reunion. A surprise item was the 'long-umbrella' dance in the style of the long-sword dance, which they composed after some of their dancers attended the sword dance workshop in 1978: bowler hats and waistcoats completed the costume. Their musicians, Prelaz, were even more popular, and who could forget the double bass on wheels in the processions. The Czechoslovakians had a double bass on legs and 'Gaffer' Ferris asked in the *Festival News* if the French had a bass on stilts.

The Sicilians – Canterini della Riviera Jonica – had made such an impression in 1978 that they were brought back in 1979, with, of course, the jug thrower. The song and pan-pipes group, Los Jairas from Bolivia, was another group that just had to be invited back for the celebrations. Ten groups from overseas – the highest number either before or since. No, eleven ... there could not be a Silver Jubilee without the Rory O'Connor Dancers from Ireland.

Great Western Morris on stilts

From the United Kingdom came the Westbury Scottish Dancers, who provided photographic evidence to answer the often-asked question

> **Councillor Ted Pinney, Chairman of East Devon District Council, was to be seen up a ladder erecting flags and bunting**

about what a Scotsman wears under his kilt! English social dance displays were provided by London Folk (now directed by Mike Wilson-Jones) and Woodfidley, directed by Sonia Carver and led by David Slater. Coincidentally, both Sonia and Mike had been to the same school, Weston-super-Mare Grammar School where Peter Boyce had been a teacher. Other ex-pupils of the school included Sonia's husband and Woodfidley musician, Richard Carver and Ian Anderson, then a member of Hot Vultures and now editor of *fRoots*, one of the Festival's sponsors. Hot Vultures came to the Festival in 1979 and Ian remembers that although their repertoire of American blues was unusual for the Festival at that time, they were 'welcomed with open arms'. Ian recalls, 'It was such a great experience'.

The Morris teams included both the local teams – Exeter Morris Men and Great Western Morris – as well as Beaux of London City, rapper dancers Hoddesdon Crownsmen and Handsworth Traditional Sword Dancers from Sheffield. Women's dance was represented by Yorkshire Chandelier who determinedly did not want to be described as Morris dancers, preferring the term 'display dancers'. Great Western's contribution to the last night LNE was a Morris dance on stilts.

The town was in celebratory mood even before the Festival started. John Govier, Chairman of the Amenities Committee and his wife (both strong Festival supporters), Mr and Mrs Peter Hook of the Royal York and Faulkner Hotel and Councillor Ted

Westbury Scottish Dancers

The 1955 Dancers

Cyril Jones with the Hobby Horse Club

Pinney, Chairman of East Devon District Council, were all to be seen up ladders erecting flags and bunting in Fore Street and Old Fore Street. The Thursday informal display in the Market Square attracted its largest audience. 'Long before it was due to start, the two Devils [dancers] from the Rubi, Spain, team were dancing to the Dutch, who were playing a Yugoslav tune, backed by Itchen Scratch from Southampton. Bolivia, Turkey and the Band, Ebersberger, showed a bit of the Festival to the joy of the crowd and with all the children doing Bonny Green Garters with Great Western Morris, the Festival was on,' reported the *Festival News*.

Bill Rutter offered some advice to both new and regular festival-goers, 'Expect nothing. Create everything anew.'

Monday was designated the Festival's birthday to celebrate the first public displays at the first Festival in 1955. The day was a series of marathons, with the Arena show started at 3.00pm and continued until 10.30pm, with two

main shows and a two and a half hour Yetties' Concert in the middle.

Special stages were erected either end of the Knowle site and dance groups from all over the Western Region of the EFDSS were invited to perform. Dozens of them responded – folk dance clubs, Morris teams (men and women), clog dancers, international dancers, school groups, mummers and Irish dancers. The groups came from the extremes of the Western Region, including the Shrewsbury Lasses who came on a coach for the day and whose members included a very pregnant Bev Langton, now Producer, with her husband Ray, of the Children's Festival. From outside the region came the Seven Champions Molly Dancers (their first performance at the Festival), Windsor Ladies' Morris and Derby Crown women's team. At least one of the men's Morris teams who were against dancing on the same occasions as women, put aside their objections for the day. These displays started at 2.00pm and continued right through until 8.30pm. In addition to the usual tea

tent and ice cream van there were was a ram roast, although the request in the Monday *Festival News* for 'advice from anyone who has experience with Ram Roasts' was a little disconcerting.

The whole Arena experience was preceded by a procession from Port Royal – the longest procession ever in the history of the Festival – which was led by the 'Founding Members'. Bill had tracked down as many as possible of the original dancers from 1955 to invite them back to the celebrations. Colin and Mary Mayfield now recall that they were treated as 'Festival veterans' in the procession, even though most of them had been in their early twenties in 1955 and therefore scarcely fifty years of age in 1979! There was a commemorative performance on Monday afternoon in the Connaught Gardens, compered by Nibs Matthews, with performances from the 1955 dancers (who busily rehearsed in the morning), London Folk, Morris teams and songs from Cyril Tawney.

Guest of honour was the EFDSS's Vice President, Douglas Kennedy, whose vision for popularising folk

Los Jairas

Umps & Dumps in the Anchor Garden

dance after the Second World War had made the Sidmouth Festival possible. He had been taught to dance by Cecil Sharp himself. Afterwards, Douglas wrote to Bill, 'It really was borne in on me ... how the seeds that Cecil Sharp sowed and were cultivated by me and you and many others, have blossomed and fruited over the years. A final word of congratulations on a masterpiece and the wide recognition it deserves.'

The sizes of the audiences were, alas, somewhat affected by the damp and chilly day, but the spirit and enthusiasm of the performers were not affected.

Elsewhere, the marathons continued. The Ham Marquee hosted a Silver Jubilee Concert, starting at 3.00pm and ending at 10.30pm. At the same time, there was a Come All Ye in the Beach Store, a Ballad Session in the Anchor and a Drill Hall ceilidh featuring three different bands.

At 9.00pm the Esplanade was closed to traffic and all the overseas and British dance groups performed. At 11.00pm the evening reached a climax with a magnificent offshore firework display. One of the town's strongest Festival supporters, Colin Healey of the Prospect Newsagency, wrote, 'Thank you for a truly memorable night on the seafront. The atmosphere was not electric, it was atomic. It reminds me of a saying by Sydney Smith, "Mankind are always happier for having been happy; so that if you make them happy now, you make them happy twenty years hence, by the memory of it." What a festival this is.'

When it came to the song guests, some of the significant singers from the past were invited – Cyril Tawney and Louis Killen, Tony Rose and Martin Carthy, Na Fili from Ireland and Ar Log from Wales and Roaring Jelly. John Foreman and Roy Harris had both been to the Festival several times, and The Songwainers – Dave Stephenson, Ken Langsbury and Ron Taylor – re-formed especially for the Festival. Shirley Collins had not previously appeared at the Festival, but was one of the revival's foremost singers: she performed for the week with her sister Dolly. Louis Killen dueted with Cyril, with Martin and with Shirley at different times during the week. And finally The Yetties of course: the celebrations would have been incomplete without them.

Other song guests included Strawhead, Tickler's Jam, The

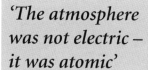

> ## 'The atmosphere was not electric – it was atomic'

Celebrated Ratcliffe Stout Band, Curates Egg, Lancashire female singer Pat Ryan, Crows (two duos: Ralph Jordan and James Patterson – known as Silas – and Mick Ryan and Jon Burge), Jim Mageean, Derek Schofield, Hot Vultures, Kevin Mitchell and Sam Stephens and Anne Lennox-Martin. Derbyshire trio Six Hands in Tempo made their Sidmouth debut with their

Martin Carthy in the Beach Store

repertoire of songs from the thirties and forties, and established a national profile. Rod Ferguson was the new Song Producer, with John Heydon as his assistant.

After Magic Lantern had disbanded as a touring company, Taffy Thomas continued to live in Suffolk, whilst the name Magic Lantern continued with Sheila Metson, Jeannie Harris and Chris Foster running it as a community-based programme. They all came to Sidmouth for the Silver Jubilee and there was a revival of the shadow puppet shows on Sunday, street theatre performances around the Arena on Monday, and films about traditional singers, musicians and step dancers on Tuesday. 'Time and Tide' on Friday was a show about the Suffolk coast.

The bands at the evening Drill Hall ceilidhs included regular favourites Flowers and Frolics (with their Big Band, a one-off

Louis Killen and Cyril Tawney in the Horse & Groom

Roy Harris at LNE

The Twenty-fifth Festival – Friday 3rd- Friday 10th August 1979

John Dowell, Terry & Bill Rutter, John & Jacqueline Clegg and Tom Brown

performance for Sidmouth which included all past members) and Umps and Dumps, plus Tickler's Folk Circus, The Wayfarers (later known as The Ripley Wayfarers) and Peeping Tom. Other folk dance bands included Orange and Blue (who also played for London Folk) and Four Leaf Clover (John Patrick and Chris Dewhurst from the Midlands).

The Arena was the setting, for the first time, for the Sunday Morning Christian Service, arranged with the Sidmouth churches and the Sicilians, Bavarians and Woodfidley all contributed to the service.

Jim Reynolds, son of Tubby and Betty, had taken over from Paul Weir as the Children's Producer. The Hobby Horse Club was split with Cyril Jones continuing to lead the club for the older children and Kate Powell running a junior Hobby Horse Club for seven to nine year olds. There was also a playgroup; a music workshop led by Barbara Wood, who based her sessions on her book *Join the Band*; a singalong with Alison Bloomer; Morris Minors; drama; crafts; games and the children's very own Late Night Extra – in the Market Square at 8.30pm on Thursday.

Cyril Jones had realised that teenagers were not really being catered for at the Festival – too old for the children's events, but needing something separate from the adults. On Wednesday evening, he organised a teenage folk dance in the Methodist Hall aimed mainly at former Hobby Horse Club members. 'Teenagers only please' read the notice in the *Festival News*, and fifty of them turned up to dance.

Bill Rutter described himself as 'the chap who was directed by the Sidmouth Festival'

The first twenty-five years of the Festival were commemorated in a booklet, a history of the Festival. At the 1978 Festival, Bill Rutter asked festival-goers for memories of the Festival. Sounds familiar!

By this time, Bill was suffering badly with arthritis and walked with the aid of a stick, but Taffy Thomas wanted to mark his retirement with something spectacular. On the final night at the Arena, Taffy prepared a vanishing trick. Bill was helped up a set of steps and stood on a pedestal in the middle of the Arena stage. He was surrounded by paper screens and Dave Hunt and Taffy did a fire-blowing act which culminated in setting fire to the screens. When the paper burnt away, all that was left on the pedestal was Bill's walking stick. Taffy announced, 'We appear to have vanished Bill Rutter,' at which point Bill's booming voice called out from the top of the bank, 'You don't get rid of me that easily'.

Then John Dowell appeared and awarded Bill and Terry the Freedom of the Festival.

So many people have described the important impact that Bill Rutter had on their lives: 'a formative adult', 'a father figure', 'the first person to discuss new ideas with'. Taffy says now, 'He had an open, warm, liberal attitude, he was very open to debate and discussion. He never thought that anyone in the room was more important than anyone else. I had huge respect for him.'

At both the last night Arena show, and the final Late Night Extra, there were emotional farewells to Bill Rutter, who described himself as 'the chap who was directed by the Sidmouth Festival'. He had earlier been given a special Silver Jubilee Award, the citation for which simply read, 'To Bill Rutter, For Sidmouth', and he was later awarded the EFDSS's Gold Badge for his outstanding contribution to folk music. Bill described the Festival as 'the most consistently happy and inspiring folk event in the country', and his greatest wish was that 'you will carry the inspiration home and pass it on'.

He ended his introduction to the Silver Jubilee booklet with the words, 'Wherever people sing, dance or play Sidmouth is remembered with affection. It is written on my heart.'

Sidmouth Olympiad

1980 I reviewed the 1979 Festival for *Acoustic Music* magazine and ended with the words, 'Here's to the next 25 years of the Sidmouth Festival'. But with its Silver Jubilee celebrations and the emotional retirement of Bill Rutter, the 1979 Festival was going to be a hard act to follow, as the newly-appointed Festival Director, John Dowell, quickly realised. Although only thirty-two years old, John had been groomed as Bill Rutter's successor but, unlike Bill, John was the full-time Festival Director and he did not have substantial EFDSS responsibilities.

Bill was replaced in his EFDSS roles by Tom Brown, who was based in Exeter, so that John and Tom were able to bounce ideas off each other. Tom also became the Festival's Dance Producer for 1980 and 1981 and, as his interest was mainly at the ceilidh end of the dance scene, he was able to look at that aspect of the Festival from a different point of view. Bill Rutter himself was elected to the EFDSS's governing body, the National Executive Committee.

It was not in John's nature to make radical changes and, in any case, the town and the festival-goers would not have approved. Nevertheless, there was a fundamental examination of the Festival and its future development, and changes were introduced over the following few years. The archives contain a sheaf of papers with John's ideas for the future. One of the critical aspects was finance. The 1979 Festival had lost over £5,000 and although this had been anticipated, the reserves were now at a low level. Tight financial control was needed although there was little obvious impact on the ordinary festival-goer. The country was in the grips of inflation, and was about to plunge into recession.

> ### ... dance movements quite unlike anything the Festival had previously seen

Bill had relied upon a large number of hard-working volunteers, but inevitably new and younger blood had to be brought in to maintain the Festival. John was able to draw upon his contacts in the area and beyond, particularly in the song, Morris and ceilidh worlds, but he also had to maintain the support of the EFDSS and the experienced folk dancers. David Slater, with his background in social dance display, was therefore an excellent choice as the new Arena Producer.

The 1979 line-up of overseas dance groups had been so sensational, that John and David decided to look further afield for some of the groups in 1980. This was helped by the Festival's admission to membership of CIOFF – Conseil International des Organisations de Festivals de Folklore. The Billingham International Folklore Festival was already a member and indeed, Billingham's Director, Philip Conroy, was Secretary-General of CIOFF world-wide. Through CIOFF, the Festival was able to invite a Mexican group on an extended tour of Europe – Grupo Folklorico de la Universidad de Guadalajara. But with fifty members, 300 costumes and one and a half tons of equipment, plus substantial transport costs in England and onwards to their next festival in Switzerland, there were at first some doubts that Sidmouth could afford the group. But they came, and were, 'The hit of this year's festival', declared a review in *The Guardian*, a rare acknowledgement of the Festival's existence by the national press.

From Sri Lanka came Pulasthi Art Circle, whose dance movements were quite unlike anything the Festival had previously seen. Even on the Arena, their intricate hand and body movements were most impressive and John Dowell, quoted in the *Sidmouth Herald*, described their fire-eating dance as 'fantastic'. David Slater and John were keen to have an authentic group from Hungary, rather than a heavily-choreographed Eastern European group, and the Bokreta Ensemble from Szany was just right: a genuine village group. One evening, when rain caused the Arena show to move inside the marquee, the Bokreta

Mexico at the Flag Raising

- Moscow Olympics
- Greenham Common protests against Cruise missiles
- Iraq-Iran War
- John Lennon shot dead
- Police and Blondie at No 1

1980

Meet the Team – Sri Lanka

group were the sensation of the evening, the climax being when the dancers spontaneously involved the audience.

The Festival had already welcomed flag-throwers from Belgium, but in 1980, a group which displayed the more flamboyant Italian style was invited. Sbandieratori dei Borghi e Sestieri Fiorentini were from Florence, and Taffy Thomas earned an ovation from the audience the first time he announced them, faultlessly and without notes, from the Arena stage. But the group members were overcome with grief when a bomb explosion in Bologna led to deaths and injuries: there was a minute's silence at the Arena on Sunday afternoon.

An Israeli group from Upper Galilee – the Safad Dancers – also came to the Festival. Then, as now, Israel was at the centre of world tension and conflict. The Israeli Embassy was in close contact with the Festival and the local police regarding security, and David Slater remembers one particular Arena

show when a solo Israeli female dancer stood alone on the stage, illuminated by a single spotlight. David sensed the Israeli security man at his side nervously reach for his gun, just in case.

Le Berry, a group from north of the Massif Central in France, had been seen by John at a festival in

> ## David sensed the Israeli security man at his side nervously reach for his gun

Norway. With hurdy-gurdies and bagpipes, they performed bourrées at a time when the English folk dance movement was just becoming interested in these dances. The basic description of the different forms of the bourrée published in the *Festival News* was an indication of this emerging interest.

Busking had always been an important feature of the Festival – informal dance and music displays

helped to create a festive atmosphere in the town and the collections boosted Festival income. The Bill Rutter Award was inaugurated in 1980 as an annual presentation to the group or individual who collected the most money from busking. The award was won in 1980 by the Danish dance group, Danica Truppen.

The British dance groups included the Boyle-O'Dowda Irish Dancers from Hampshire, Headington Quarry Morris, Old Spot Morris, Preston Royal Morris, and Derby Crown women, who performed garland dances. In the rough plans for the dance guests in the archives there are the words 'No female Cotswold Morris'.

Taffy's fellow Arena compere was Dave Williams, who had been coming to the Festival since the sixties. His talents were many and varied and, like Bill Rutter, he enthused and encouraged others. He had already been a singer, musician and caller at the Festival, and had spent several years as an Arena compere. Taffy remembers that he had the knack of 'talking to audiences of thousands of people as if he was speaking to a couple of friends from the armchair of his living room'. He appreciated the tradition at a domestic level, but understood the professional presentational requirements of the Arena. 'He was always professional, but never slick,' Taffy remembers.

John Dowell decided to repeat one of the successes of the Silver Jubilee year, and on Monday evening the Esplanade was again closed to traffic so that all the dance teams could perform. The climax to the evening was again a firework display, this time partly sponsored by the South West Trustee Savings Bank. Alas, the weather, which was described in the *Festival News* as 'foul', had an adverse effect on the dancers, crowds and collections. Earlier on Monday evening, the Arena Show had included song items from the overseas dance groups, compered by The Fettlers, who had been re-formed with just two of the original members.

An earlier idea had been to feature Fiddler's Dram at the Arena on Monday evening – by this time, the

Hungarian dancers in Blackmore Gardens

Italian Flag-throwers

group had enjoyed chart success with 'Day Trip to Bangor', but had also ceased to function as a touring band. The Oyster Ceilidh Band played at the Festival all week, including Monday evening's Kent Ceilidh at the Drill Hall with song spots from band members as well as from the duo Tundra. The band even brought some of the local beer, Shepherd Neame, for the bar to sell.

Two new bands catering for the different dance audiences appeared at the Festival – Hemlock Cock and Bull Band were booked through Steve Heap's agency, Mrs Casey Music, whilst The Falconers catered for the experienced dancers. Hemlock Cock and Bull were about to record their first album, on Topic, with dance descriptions by their favourite caller, Eddie Upton, who remembers the enthusiasm and knowledge of the dancers at their Drill Hall ceilidh – he had previously called mainly with novice and sometimes reluctant dancers, but at Sidmouth, the floor was full as soon as he announced the dance. The members of the band then were Jean-Pierre Rasle, Paul Martin, John Maxwell and Dave Whetstone, and they were just starting to play some French tunes, although the French dances came later. Roger Wilkins, leader of The Falconers, afterwards expressed his surprise at the number of people attending the Playford workshop – there were too many people to fit in the Drill Hall. On Friday the band played for a dance on

the lawn of Hunter's Moon Hotel, an un-programmed event which continued until 2001.

The demand for song events of all types was increasing and there was a greater move to the concert-style event. Lunchtime 'At Home' events in the Drill Hall continued with performers such as Packie Byrne and Bonnie Shaljean, Sean Cannon and Nic Jones, and later in the afternoon there were the 4.00pm to 6.00pm song events featuring several song guests. Also in the afternoon, the Assembly Rooms was the venue for a series of song and music events: Hungarian and Mexican music and Ar Log from Wales, whilst on Wednesday Flowers and Frolics introduced two films on traditional music and dance made by the Arts Council – *The Bolden Lad* and *Sam Sherry: Stepdancer*. Sunday lunchtime at the Drill Hall saw a performance of London Pride, a show featuring songs, music and recitations about London,

presented by Flowers and Frolics and Andrew Frank.

1980 was Nic Jones's first appearance at the Festival, although there had been several earlier attempts to book him. His album *Penguin Eggs* was released that year, but in 1982 he was severely injured in a horrific car accident and has never performed in public since. His Friday lunchtime 'At Home' featured a series of other singers and musicians, including Silas, Nigel Chippendale and Gerry Hallom, and there was a rare opportunity to hear Nic's fiddle playing.

Dave Goulder was another singer making his debut at the Festival. Best known for songs such as 'The January Man', Dave was then living in Sutherland in Northern Scotland – 800 miles from Sidmouth. He was also known for his railway songs, some of which he sang at the Tuesday evening Railway Ceilidh in the Drill Hall with the local Exeter band Travel by Steam and songs and monologues from Eddie Upton and Roger Brazier.

There was no Music Hall in 1980, but Friday night at the Drill Hall was Fifties Night with the Oyster Ceilidh Band, Sean Cannon, Nic Jones, Martin Bloomer and others. Performers and audience dressed in bootlace ties, drainpipe trousers, drape jackets, circular skirts and petticoats, with bouffants, pony tails and a large amount of Brylcreem. Highlight of the evening was the dramatic entry of Taffy Thomas on a motorbike, which he rode straight into the Drill Hall, and his subsequent rendition of 'Hound Dog'. His motorbike was partly for effect

Headington Quarry in the Market Square

Nic Jones and Sean Cannon relive their youth

and partly by necessity – he was compering the Arena Show and had to perform between introductions.

The Winter Gardens had become Carinas Disco in the previous twelve months and was used for various informal and unprogrammed events. There were some ceilidhs at lunchtime, a couple of afternoons of jazz with musicians who included Alex Atterson, and three afternoon Macedonian dance workshops led by Blowzabella. The workshops were publicised only by word of mouth and there is no mention of them (or the band) in the programme or the *Festival News*. But they were mentioned in *Acoustic Music* magazine, where the Festival was reviewed by staff reporter Pippa Todd.

The events for children – it was not yet called the Children's Festival – featured a puppet show 'Happily Ever After' which took part in several of the events during the week as well as hosting a children's party. Cyril Jones bowed out as host of the Hobby Horse Club, which was run by John Middleton with

different bands each day, including the Oyster Ceilidh Band and Flowers and Frolics. Cyril did, however, informally organise again two Teenage Barn Dances in St Francis Church Hall. The Children's Late Night Extra in the Market Place on Thursday evening featured the Sid Kids' Kaylie Konsort, made up of thirty young musicians from the children's music workshop which had been led by Nigel Chippendale. One of the tunes was Nigel's own composition, 'The Sid Kids' Polka'.

1980 was the year of the Olympic Games in Moscow, and the Festival staged its rival event – 'Sidmouth

> *Highlight of the evening was the dramatic entry of Taffy Thomas on a motorbike ...*

Olympiad 1980'. Needless to say, this was not totally serious! Several of the events were centred on the ford – there was the tug of war (won by the Men of Kent) and the back stroke (running backwards through the ford, with some competitors using skateboards and spacehoppers). Elsewhere there was the decathlon (a pub crawl of ten pubs for teams of six people), bum volley ball (won by the Israelis), equestrian events for hobby horses, egg throwing (shot put), throwing the dustbin lid (discus) and the marathon from the camp-site to Port Royal. The

winners received medals, and some people still have them. The ford became the venue for another wacky event the following year.

The Festival continued to attract an ever-increasing number of Morris dancers, both full sides and individual dancers. Outside the Mason's Arms, Morris dancers would gather to practise the dances taught in the Advanced Morris workshop, or to start a tour of the Esplanade or simply to dance together for their own amusement. The pub was situated in Chapel Street, just behind the Hotel Riviera, and the road was virtually traffic free. Stroud Morris and Seven Champions both danced there on their tours of the town. Morris dancers from New Zealand also used Sidmouth as a place to meet up and dance whilst over in England. This started a trend and from the early 1980s to the present day past and present members of Hong Kong Morris meet up at the Festival every year.

The Mason's Arms had also become the venue for the English music sessions. After three years in the Old Ship, the Old Swan Band and Flowers and Frolics and their friends moved to the Mason's Arms in 1978, although like the Old Ship, it only had a small bar and back garden. With restricted pub opening hours, the sessions were more concentrated than they are today. Baz Parkes remembers that the Mason's attracted musicians who became the second wave of English bands, and he particularly remembers John Gasson, Paul Hirst

Taffy Thomas and his motor-bike

Dr Sunshine's Pavement Show

and other Seven Champions musicians who became the band Melons for Ecstasy, as well as members of the local band Travel by Steam – Bob and Kate Powell and Barry Lister. The Mason's experience had a 'seminal influence' on Baz's own playing. Other musicians continued to play English music in The Old Ship, and in 1980 the *Festival News* carried this anonymous jibe at the quality of the musicians: 'Ship Inn Top Ten: 1 Curly Headed Ploughboy (badly), 2 Oyster Girl (very badly) …', ending with instructions to the musicians to 'collect their L-plates from the Angel, Islington', the area in London where Flowers and Frolics played.

The pub sessions were an essential part of the Festival atmosphere. Song sessions had taken place through the seventies in The Black Horse and the Horse and Groom, and by 1978 Alan White and Chris Haytor were singing in The Black Horse, whilst Dave Bryant was hosting a lunchtime session in the Anchor. Those Anchor sessions were repeated in 1979, with a plea in the *Festival News* for the melodeon players to stay away – it was a strictly unaccompanied song session. At the end of the week, thanks were given in the *Festival News* to 'all the harmony singers who filled the middle bar with beautiful sounds'. By 1980, Alvin and Jackie Barrett and Alvin's brother John had moved from the Mason's Arms to be landlords of the Anchor. Alvin was keen on folk music and had been a regular at The Jolly Porter Folk Club in Exeter. In 1980, the singers sang in the middle bar all week, and have returned each year since. Known as the Middle Bar Singers, they have evolved some elaborate rules, a list of fines and a system for ensuring that everyone gets a chance to sing. A twig is passed from singer to singer – whoever has the twig, it is their turn next. The twig rules! Sometimes there were joke twigs such as the peacock feather in the photograph.

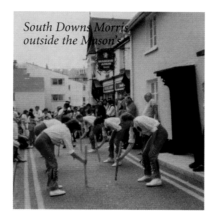

South Downs Morris outside the Mason's

Musicians in the Mason's

Over the years the Middle Bar Singers have contributed substantially to the Festival atmosphere. One of their strong supporters has been Colin Healey from the Prospect Newsagency. Colin told me a story about one of his customers, an old lady who just wanted to pay her paper bill and stay at home until the Festival was all over. It was mid-day so Colin invited her across the road to the Anchor. 'She clung to my arm

'The Middle Bar made one dear old lady very happy'

and I found her a stool in the corner. She was apprehensive but asked for a Dubonnet and ice. After ten or fifteen minutes I looked at her and noticed she was crying, visibly and strongly. She said, "It's this song, my brother used to sing it, he was the coxswain of the Whitby Lifeboat". The song was "Three Score and Ten" about a mighty storm when seventy

were drowned on the East Coast. She hadn't heard it for thirty-five years until that day in the Anchor. We left shortly afterwards, but every day for the rest of the Festival she came into my shop, "Can we go over the road again?" We did and on the last day she sat near the front and they sang her song. She cried every time. The Middle Bar made one dear old lady very happy.'

The folk enthusiasts may have donned their rock 'n' roll gear on Friday evening, but the rest of the week, they wore a different 'uniform'. In fact there was a 'Spot the Folkie' competition in the *Festival News*: I wonder how many of the following are still features of festival-goers? Waistcoat with badges, tankard with clip, pouch on belt, faded tatty jeans, beer gut, clogs, printed t-shirt, unkempt beard, red spotted handkerchief and silly hat! It was a recurring theme: Ted Stevens's alternative newsletter, *Sidmouth Harold*, in 1978 had a fashion page which highlighted many of the same features.

Anchor Middle Bar Singers – led by Lynne Tann

The Sidmouth Invasion

1981

During the 1981 Festival, BBC Television filmed all week for an hour-long documentary broadcast on BBC2 in October. Entitled *The Sidmouth Invasion*, the programme was seen by an estimated two to three million people. The excellent response to the programme led to a further series of excerpts from the Festival, broadcast in the Spring of 1982. It was the sort of national media coverage that the Festival deserved. BBC Radio 2 was also at the Festival all week – the producer of the folk programme Peter Pilbeam was even used as a song compere.

The Arena site at the Knowle is rather different today than it was in the seventies and eighties. Catering facilities on the site were limited – there was a tea tent staffed by members of Exmouth Folk Dance Club and friends, and you could buy an ice cream, but there was not the range of catering available today, and there was no bar. There was no real attempt to encourage people to go to the Arena site unless there was a performance. The all-day displays of Silver Jubilee year had indicated the possibilities, but it was several years before those possibilities were turned into reality. There was not the high level of security that is necessary today. A simple wooden fence about four feet high was placed at either side of the Arena bank, although extra stewards were always requested for the last night to patrol this perimeter fence.

The Arena dancing platform was still the flat boards laid on top of the concrete base which had been laid specially for the Festival, although the slight slope, to drain rain water off the concrete, has been the cause of some surprise to dance groups over the years as they gradually gravitated to the south of the stage. The bandstand was a raised area at the back of the stage. The sound system was provided by a Devon company, D.C. Conybeare, whose sound desk was located in a caravan which was slightly behind the north end of the stage. There were two lighting towers, and local resident Alistair Hay was still using his amateur dramatics' experience to provide the lighting for the evening shows. The lights were hired from Stage Electrics, the same company that provides the Festival's sound and stage equipment today.

There was grandstand seating either side of the stage, with deck chairs in front of the stage. Pel Squance was now Arena Manager, whilst the gates and tickets were under the control of John Clegg and Rowland Cook, two prominent folk dancers from the Weston-super-Mare area: John's wife Jacqueline Clegg managed the Folk Shop at the Festival for many years.

For several years there had been a Craft Marquee on the Arena site. The emphasis had been to encourage people to make crafts, with demonstrations and opportunities to have a go. The craft demonstrations included basketry, raku pottery, leatherwork, clog making and screen printing, but as these activities were only publicised in the *Festival News*, it was obvious that they were aimed at the festival-goers and not the general public. The sale of crafts was concentrated on just two days – Monday and Friday.

The hot, dry weather of the mid-seventies was a thing of the past. Certainly, there were years of sunshine, but the unpredictable English weather could always result in rain which meant that the Arena shows were affected. For several years, there was a complex wet weather procedure: if it was likely to rain, then the Arena show would be moved to the Ham Marquee, and the event in the Ham Marquee was moved to the Late Night Extra Marquee at the Bowd. The Bowd Marquee could be used in the mornings, typically for dance workshops, but it had to be kept clear in the afternoons and evenings in case it rained. In the days before mobile phones, one can only imagine how the decision to move the

The Arena site in 1979

The Rainbow Dancers

Dance workshop in the Ham

performance was communicated around the Festival. Tony Wiggins, now the Deputy Arena Manager, was a steward at the top Arena gate when a long queue formed for the evening show. He remembers that they grew restless as the sky became overcast, although one the steward's attempts to lighten the atmosphere through community singing seemed to be working. Then the message arrived – the show was being transferred to the Ham Marquee. Tony organised the queue into a 'crocodile' and marched everyone down Station Road and along the Esplanade to the Ham, picking up the queues from the middle and bottom gates en route. Then the audience had to be squeezed into the marquee, sensitively recognising the existence of three separate queues and the priority of season-ticket holders. By the time the show started, everyone was soaked to the skin!

But in 1981, a marquee was provided on the Arena site. This was to be the new wet weather marquee, but of course this meant that it could not be used for any other events in the afternoons or evenings. Unlike at the Ham, the marquee was eventually set up in concert format with seats and a large stage for the dance displays. The Ham Marquee events would now be undisturbed, and the Bowd Marquee could be used more extensively: the Morris workshops in the morning, clog dance workshops in the afternoon and dances in the evening. All the dance marquees had inconveniently-placed poles in the middle of the dance floor.

The freeing up of the Bowd Marquee allowed the venue to be used for a new

style of dance event. 'Experienced Dancers Only' was the label that was attached to the evening dances, which allowed the experienced dancers to develop their interests separately from the ceilidh dancers and the new dancers. It also gave the experienced dancers the reputation of exclusivity. The Ham Marquee was used for several different events: concerts, ceilidhs and

> ## Tony organised the queue into a 'crocodile' and marched everyone down Station Road

barn dances which were all aimed at the general festival-goer and the casual visitor. Surprisingly, the Playford Ball, which one might have expected to have been held at the Bowd Marquee, was also held on the Ham.

Four of the overseas dance groups in 1981 were from countries that had often been represented at the Festival: France, Czechoslovakia, the Netherlands and Sweden. The groups from both Sweden and France had been seen by David Slater at the Brunssum Festival in the Netherlands. The Czech group, Kasava, had been recommended by John Braithwaite, who was a folk enthusiast, Morris dancer and member of the British-Czechoslovak Friendship League dance group, and he had seen the group in Czechoslovakia. John's interest in international folk dance later led to him becoming an Arena compere and recently the announcer at the Dance Roots events. Kasava was

extensively featured in *The Sidmouth Invasion* programme.

For the first time, a group from Africa came to the Festival. Louga Folk Ensemble from Senegal were making an extended visit to Europe under the auspices of CIOFF. The suggestion by one of the local newspapers that the women might dance bare-chested proved to be unfounded. After Sidmouth, John Dowell took the group to Bob Cann's Dartmoor Folk Festival, where the village fete atmosphere contrasted with the large-scale Sidmouth Arena shows. After a gap of several years, the Festival once again invited émigré groups within England to perform at the Festival. Ekome was a dance company from the St Paul's area of Bristol which specialised in Afro-Caribbean dance, whilst Czuplak was a Ukrainian dance company from Nottingham, led by Stepan Czuplak, a former member of Orlyk Ukrainian Dancers.

1981 was the International Year of Disabled People, and David Slater was keen to invite a group of wheelchair dancers. He had seen The Rainbow Dancers on BBC TV's *Jim'll Fix It*, and wrote to Jimmy Saville for contact details for the children's group, which came from Princes Risborough in Buckinghamshire. The group was delighted to accept the invitation, and they made a great impression on the Sidmouth Arena audiences.

Clive and Hazel Morgan, who helped with a club for disabled people in Ebbw Vale, had brought a group of club members to the Festival for a holiday in 1980. Realising that there were no facilities for the disabled at the Arena, Clive and Hazel brought a converted double-decker bus to Sidmouth in 1981 for use as a temporary toilet and rest room for disabled people. Soon, this was also used as a parent and baby facility, and the bus was a familiar sight at the Arena for many years. Clive subsequently set up his own business, European Heritage Tours, and has given great assistance to the Festival with transporting dance and music groups to Sidmouth from ferry terminals and airports. He has also represented the Festival at the Sidmouth Chamber of Commerce.

Carlisle Morris Men made their first of many visits to the Festival, concentrating mainly on rapper and longsword dances, and Downes Morris from Croydon and Great Western Morris also appeared. Berkshire provided both Kennet Morris Men and the Reading Traditional and Step Dance Group, the full title of the Reading Cloggies, who gave displays of clog dances and step and country dances from Scotland, the Lake District and Southern England.

O ne of the Reading Cloggies was Julie Williams, who had first visited the Festival as a teenager in the early seventies. Accompanied by her parents, Ron and Frankie Rudd and sister Claire, the family knew little about folk music and dance apart from a folk dance club in Bridgwater that Julie and Claire went to as a spin-off from their Girl Guides' folk dancing badge. Julie now recalls, 'Little did we know it, but our lives were about to be changed irrevocably by our introduction to the Festival. There are now four generations of the Rudd family who are so addicted to

Louga Ensemble from Senegal

the Festival that we can't imagine life without it.' Julie went from one dance workshop to another all day, and recalls the 'sense of achievement at the end of the week having mastered a new set of steps'. Before

> ## The suggestion that the women might dance bare-chested proved to be unfounded

long, Ron and Frankie were on the stage of the Arena with the South West Area Dancers and later the Isca Dancers. Julie and Claire were both keen on clog dancing, and this developed into an interest in other forms of percussive dance, and the whole family took part in the Apple Chill Cloggers' workshops in 1978. The Rudd family made further contributions to the Festival as will soon be apparent.

The Shropshire Bedlams and Martha Rhoden's Tuppenny Dish made a return visit to the Festival. Without being consulted, the Bedlams were programmed for one

of the Advanced Morris workshops. They declined, arguing that they did an original interpretation of Border Morris dances, not a faithful reconstruction, and that they saw no reason to let others in on their secret. Imitation may be a form of flattery, but they were irritated with by-standers who scribbled in note-books during their performances. At their LNE display, the Bedlams ended the dance by 'mooning' at the audience – an incident captured on film by the BBC.

Bedlams and Martha Rhoden's were not the only dancers from Shropshire, which was extremely well represented at the Festival. Indeed, the county has had a huge presence at the Festival ever since. The Ironmen and Severn Gilders danced informally around the town, whilst The Shrewsbury Lasses led the women's ritual dance workshops. They devised a dance especially for the workshop called 'The Shrewsbury Flourish', and in the years since, Lasses' member Bev Langton has been pleased to see that the dance has entered the repertoire of several dance teams.

The pages of the *Festival News* are an indicator of the number of Morris and other display groups that could field a side sometime during the

Kasava being filmed

- 'Gang of Four' sets up Social Democratic Party
- Toxteth riots
- Pound coins replace pound notes
- Charles marries Diana
- First London Marathon
- John Lennon's Imagine at No 1

1981

Building the whale

Launching the whale

week: Seven Champions, Stroud Morris Men, Windsor Morris, Fidler's Fancy from Cheshire, Herga, Shrewsbury Bull and Pump, Flowers of May, Barnstaple Morris, Whitethorn, Ilfracombe Cloggies, Frome Valley, Magog Ladies, East Saxon Sword and Bantam Cocks. Even though there were so many dance groups, the audiences crowded round to see them dance on the Esplanade. The usual dance venue outside the Marine Bars had to be moved across onto the Esplanade pavement in the aftermath of Councillor Robin Pocock's attempt to drive his car through the middle of Great Western Morris's dance set.

The demise of Magic Lantern led to an increased role for Dr Sunshine's Pavement Show, and also for a new street theatre group, Gingers Street Theatre, who had first performed at Sidmouth in 1979. The basis of Gingers was Val Carman and Lester Simpson, who often brought in extra people such as John 'Gibbo' Gibson,

and their performances included processions, music, stunts, fire shows and mime. One of their items was the spoof overseas dance group from Morocco. They arrived suddenly at the Hostel and changed into their long black costumes and yashmaks. Hostel Manager Dick Stanger was

Fortunately, the yashmaks hid their laughter

very angry that he knew nothing of this newly-arrived dance group, especially as they could not speak English. They were transported to Port Royal for the afternoon procession, and the Arena audience truly believed that they were genuine. Their performance was a marriage ritual which involved releasing a dove (actually a homing pigeon) from the middle of the stage. Fortunately, the yashmaks hid their laughter, and the

display looked terribly serious. The cover was almost blown when they could not speak French to the dancers from Senegal. After it was over, Val and Lester had to explain the joke to the Senegal dancers, and to Dick Stanger!

Like Gingers, Scaramouche was a street theatre group from Derbyshire and they featured Chris and Rose Timms, Derek Pearce and Kate McCrae. The two groups worked closely together during the week, and their projects included the whale-building workshop. Taffy Thomas was also involved when his Arena compering duties allowed. The whale was built on the Arena site as a project involving adults and children to celebrate the wedding of the Prince and Princess of Wales. The whale was welded from steel tubes, floats of expanded polystyrene and polydrums and was covered in thick black polythene sheets. It was given large white teeth. Then the whale had to be transported from the

Gingers' Fire Show in the Market Square

Morocco?

Arena to the beach. John Dowell's wife Mandy telephoned the police and asked politely for permission to close the road. 'What's it for?' asked the police officer. 'To launch a whale,' replied Mandy. 'That's fine, what time would you like to do this?' asked the policeman in a voice which suggested it was an everyday occurrence. *The Sidmouth Invasion* captured the procession to the beach with costumed musicians and whale-carriers. Dick Stanger recalls that it was launched 'with full dignity, to the strains of "We'll (Whale) Meet Again" and a rowing boat towed it out to sea'. What the TV failed to capture was the mysterious appearance of a model whale on the beach at Prestatyn in North Wales ten weeks later. It could only have been the Sidmouth whale!

John Heydon brought his experience of running Herga Folk Club in Harrow and the Haddenham Ceilidhs to the role of Song Producer. The Herga was one of the country's top folk clubs and at one stage in the seventies, John Heydon was ordering a hundred tickets for club members. Ruth Fraser's birthday fell during the Festival and through the seventies and into the eighties, Herga club members held a Cream Tea Workshop Birthday Party with everyone dressed in Alice in Wonderland costumes. The Mocha and The Marlborough were two of the venues, but there was always a parade on the Esplanade, and as the processions were for 'costumed performers only', they joined in.

There was a distinctive slant towards traditional singers amongst the guests, with the Stewarts of Blairgowrie – Belle Stewart and her daughter Sheila – retired Brighton fisherman Johnny Doughty, a return visit from Bob Roberts, Jeff Wesley and Ulster singer Len Graham, as well as clog dancer Sam Sherry.

Scottish singers Cilla Fisher and Artie Trezise performed in concerts and Drill Hall song spots and also arranged the singers for the Country and Western night in the Drill Hall on Tuesday. Other singers included Vin Garbutt, always a Festival favourite. Eddie Upton remembers compering the LNE when Vin was a guest. 'How long do you want?' asked Vin. 'Oh, about three songs,' said Eddie, forgetting the length of Vin's introductions. Forty-five minutes later, Vin was still there, but the audience loved him. Sam Stephens and Anne Lennox-Martin (who performed at the revived Music Hall), Tim Laycock, Geoff and Joy Lakeman (then residents at Herga Folk Club – their three sons became members of Equation and are now performing with Kathryn Roberts and Cara Dillon), the Dead Sea Surfers and Derek Brimstone performed. The song MCs included Steve Heap.

Monday evening at the Arena saw the first in the series of shows that did not involve the overseas dance teams. Ashley Hutchings, who had been a member of Fairport Convention, Steeleye Span, and Etchingham Steam Band had established The Albion Band and worked extensively at the National Theatre in such productions as *Lark Rise*. 'The Albion River Hymn' depicted the life and times of the River Thames, as seen through the eyes of its admirers, workforce and London residents, and included readings from Jerome K. Jerome, Lewis Carroll and traditional and contemporary songs. Amongst the performers were Ashley himself and June Tabor, plus the distinguished actor Howard Goorney. The evening was a successful innovation for the Festival, although it stretched the technical resources at the Arena to their limits.

As for dance bands Hemlock Cock and Bull Band returned to play for ceilidhs (just prior to the dropping of 'Hemlock' in the title). Oxfordshire-based ceilidh band The Woodpeckers made their Festival debut – although as they shared a name with a local country dance band, there was some confusion for some of the dancers.

A small group of sixth formers from Moulton Comprehensive School in Northamptonshire chose the Sidmouth Festival for their summer holiday. It took thirteen of them over ten hours to travel by service bus. With one adult and twelve children's tickets, they camped on the third site, and successfully managed to get into LNE, which then was only for adult season-ticket holders. Disappointed that they could not get into the Drill Hall Ceilidhs, they organised their own event and the ford seemed a good location. The sixth formers included the band Aunt Thelma's Candlelight Orchestra, headed by melodeon player Simon Care, and they played for the ceilidh in the ford. The Festival disassociated itself from the event, and in spite of continuing to do so, the ceilidh in the ford has taken place every year since. Simon Care is absolutely amazed that it is still going.

By Monday, the *Express and Echo* was announcing 'Sidmouth Gripped by Festival Fever', whilst the *Sidmouth Herald* summed up the week in its page one headline, 'It Was Magic'.

Dancing Feet and Happy Voices

1982 The Sidmouth Invasion on the television, and the subsequent series of six programmes in March and April 1982 led to more requests about the Festival than ever before. Similarly, East Devon District Council received many more enquiries about the town as a holiday destination, and not just during Festival week. The council's Amenities Committee decided to spend more money on publicising the Festival – surprisingly perhaps, the council actually made a profit from the Festival.

John Dowell had already turned his attention to Festival marketing, and for 1982, he used the slogan 'Dancing Feet and Happy Voices' as well as commissioning the design of the 'Sidmouth Fiddler' which has remained a Festival logo, in various guises, ever since.

It was not just the publicity from the television programmes which prompted John to sharpen up the marketing. The folk music scene was going through a period of change. There was concern that the folk clubs were staid and past their peak, the leading folk agency run by Jean Davenport had folded, there was a recession, and there was perceived to be an ageing audience with very few younger people coming into the scene. The two national folk music magazines, *Folk Review* edited by Fred Woods, and *Acoustic Music* (formerly *Folk News*) edited by Karl Dallas had both stopped publication, whilst *The Southern Rag* was still operating as a quarterly magazine for the south of England prior to its transformation into the monthly *Folk Roots* (now

fRoots). However, informal sessions were becoming popular, and more and more people were joining and starting Morris teams.

A round-table discussion on the folk scene published in *The Southern Rag* in 1980 had centred on folk clubs, but editor Ian Anderson noted that there were far more festivals than in the early seventies and he wondered if people now preferred to go to a couple of festivals a year rather than a weekly folk club. His co-editor, Lawrence Heath, himself a Sidmouth regular, observed that the folk enthusiasts were not always able to get to a weekly folk club because of family responsibilities, but that they could take the children to a folk festival. 'Festivals are a growth

'Festivals are a growth industry'

industry', he felt. Indeed, the English Folk Dance and Song Society's 1982 *Folk Directory* carried a list of sixty festivals, but there were undoubtedly many more. Increasingly, however, they were operating outside the auspices of the EFDSS. Sidmouth was still the leader, but it was no longer the only player in the field. John Dowell understood that there was no room for complacency and

that to stay ahead, Sidmouth had to be the best. He understood the importance of marketing and presentation, and alongside marketing to the folk enthusiast, John had to consider the Festival's wider audience amongst the general public in East Devon – residents and holiday-makers.

John Howson had first visited the Festival in the late sixties when he was still a teenager in Liverpool, but was now living with his wife Katie Howson in Suffolk. He arranged for traditional melodeon players, Oscar Woods and Font Watling, dulcimer players Reg Reeder and Billy Bennington and singer Ted Chaplin to come to Sidmouth. Other traditional performers included Fred Jordan from Shropshire, making his third visit, and veteran shanty-singer Stan Hugill who made his Festival debut to join Jim Mageean and Johnny Collins in the Festival's regular shanty sessions.

Travel by Steam in the Market Square with Roger Watson on tuba

- *Falklands War*
- *Prince William born*
- *Pope visits Britain*
- *Home computers and video recorders dominate Christmas sales*
- *Musical Youth's Pass the Dutchie at No 1*

Kate Powell

The Bampton Morris Dancers appeared at the Arena and elsewhere and a meeting in the Marine Bars with the Suffolk singers and musicians led to reciprocal visits between Oxfordshire and Suffolk which have continued ever since. The Suffolk musicians and singers were central to an East Anglian evening in Sidford Village Hall on Monday, which also featured Taffy Thomas, who had lived in Suffolk but was now in the Lake District, and Peter Bellamy. This was before the 'In the Tradition' sessions and the various traditional singers and musicians were featured in the normal programming of song and music events.

Peter Bellamy presented a song and slide performance, 'We have fed our sea for a thousand years' in the Drill Hall, one of several themed shows in the 4.00pm slot in the venue during the week. Strawhead was a Lancashire trio that had a strong following in Sidmouth, and in 1982 they also brought the Northern Brass Consort to accompany them. Dick Gaughan was a first-timer to Sidmouth – the previous year he had been instrumental in establishing Perform, a new organisation which attempted to unite the British folk movement. Cajun music hardly featured in the British folk revival before the 1980s, and the pioneers in introducing the style were guests in 1982: R. Cajun. This was still music to listen to, although there was a growing interest in Cajun dancing as well.

Rod Stradling had a busy year: he was one of Bampton Morris's musicians, and also played in the new English Country Blues Band with Chris Coe and Ian Anderson and Maggie Holland. He and his wife Danny were also playing their final gigs before leaving The Old Swan Band.

The afternoon Assembly Rooms concerts were extended, the evening concerts continued, the Beach Store had song events three times a day, singarounds led by Ian Woods and Charley Yarwood were held twice a day in the Horse and Groom, and there were song events in the Black Horse and Ballad Swaps in Trumps (a shop opposite the Anchor). But the largest venue was still only capable of holding a couple of hundred people.

> ... *dressed in a hyper-intelligent shade of the colour blue ...*

Continuing the themed ceilidhs, the Drill Hall Ceilidh on Tuesday evening was billed as 'Drilliways: The Infinite Improbability Ceilidh Band. If you've done six impossible things this morning why not round it off with a dance at the "Ceilidh at the End of the Universe"'. This was a tribute to Douglas Adams's *The Hitch Hiker's Guide to the Galaxy* which had started as a radio series in 1978 before being published and then televised. The band was actually Travel by Steam, and amongst the people behind the evening were some of the 'usual suspects': Taffy Thomas, Gingers Street Theatre, Martin Bloomer, Ian Carter and Mike Bettison. Drilliways was, of course, Milliways – The Restaurant at the End of the Universe, and one of the characters in the book, Hotblack Desiato, was named after a London firm of Estate Agents. Trevor Bennett drove all the way back to London to collect a Hotblack Desiato sign which was hung outside the 'Drilliways'. Sid Long remembers that several people – himself included – were dressed in a hyper-intelligent shade of the colour blue, and Steve Mansfield recalls that several people dressed as either Zaphod Beeblebrox III, with the extra head, or Trillian with a silver foil dress, wig and silver make-up. Several people had babel fish coming out of their ears. The bar served pan galactic gargle blasters, which was rough scrumpy and crème de menthe: 'People tried one, but never two,' Sid remembers. Caller Kate Powell sat on a silver crescent moon which was suspended from the ceiling, and the whole of Drilliways was decorated with silver and white streamers.

Other bands at the Festival included Pyewackett, Jumpleads (described as a 'Rogue Folk' band by *The Southern Rag*) and Ram's Bottom from Derbyshire, as well as Silver and Gold, The Falconers and Four Leaf Clover. Pyewackett's first album had just been released: the members included Rosie Cross, Bill Martin, Mark Emerson and Ian Blake, and the instruments included woodwind and brass. An increasing number of bands were using brass in their line-ups (following the lead of John Tams and Flowers and Frolics), and John Adams, Nick Barber and Barry Lister led a workshop for brass instruments. The following day, John presented

Basques

Turkish dancers at LNE

an experimental music workshop, exploring the use of reggae and soul for country dance.

Cathy Lesurf, who had been a member of Fiddler's Dram, the Oyster Ceilidh Band and the Albion Band, became the Arena Producer. Sidmouth favourites Canterini della Riviera Jonica from Sicily returned with their jug thrower, whilst other countries whose dancing was popular at Sidmouth, Turkey (BITI Academisi Folklore Group), Ireland and Denmark, provided groups. Goizaldi was the latest dance group to come from the Basque Country, and in his role as Arena compere, Taffy Thomas was able to announce, at the end of one of their performances, the magnificent spoonerism, 'Ladies and gentlemen, there you have all the Basques in one exit'. From Eastern Europe came another popular Hungarian dance group – Delep Napsugar Tancegyuttes – but the Bulgarian group had last-minute problems with their visas and failed to appear. As replacement, John Dowell invited a group of English dancers who performed Yugoslavian dances, as well as a group of Vietnamese refugees.

The Vietnamese 'boat-people' were frequently in the news: they were refugees who settled in a variety of countries. The Sopley Reception Centre in Hampshire had welcomed almost 3,000 Vietnamese refugees since 1979, and a group of eleven to sixteen-year-old girls performed the bamboo dance at the Festival, with accompaniment from some English musicians on flute and guitar. The

> ## 'Ladies and gentlemen, there you have all the Basques in one exit'

experience had a remarkable impact on the confidence of the young girls. Within weeks of the Festival, they had dispersed to various parts of the country, but as the *Sopley Newsletter* recorded, 'Over the past few months they have shown to tens of thousands that the Vietnamese have a contribution to make to the enrichment of our lives'.

The precedence of 'something different' at the Arena on Monday evening had been set the previous

year, and in 1982 there was a performance of 'The Everlasting Circle'. This was a touring show of English dance, song and music devised by EFDSS employee Tom Brown to celebrate the Golden Jubilee of the merger of the dance and song societies to form the EFDSS. Sponsored by the bus company National Express, the show had toured theatres earlier in the year, and amongst the performers were Cathy Lesurf, Roger Watson, Barry Coope, Jo Fraser, Fi Fraser, Kerry Fletcher, Keith Kendrick, Barry Lister and Nigel Chippendale.

Having busked around the Festival the previous year, The Ironmen and Severn Gilders brought their interpretation of Border and Cheshire Morris dances to the Arena stage from their home of Shropshire, whilst Chanctonbury Ring returned after many years to perform North-West Morris.

Bantam Cocks was a young Morris side from a school in London, and their repertoire of Morris, rapper, longsword and clog dances came from their teacher, Pete Saunders, who danced with Chingford Morris.

Vietnamese dancers at the Arena

Clog dance from Bantam Cocks

The Bantam Cocks had danced informally at Sidmouth in 1976 when team member Gary O'Mahoney was just twelve-years-old. In 1978, Gary and two other Bantams had danced a clog routine at the Sidford barn dance, not knowing that his future wife, Carolyn, was in the audience, aged twelve. She noticed him though, and pointed him out to her mother. Three years later they met at Cecil Sharp House and Carolyn became one of the Bantam's musicians. Gary now dances with Hammersmith Morris whilst Carolyn dances with Broken Ankles and Stepback.

The new Dance Producer was Eddie Upton who had been a member of the Etchingham Steam Band and was then better known as a dance caller than a singer. In addition to arranging the workshops and dance programme, Eddie also led the jogging 'workshop' each morning at 7.15am starting outside the Drill Hall. There is even film of a very slim Eddie Upton in running shorts doing his exercises before leading the joggers along the Esplanade. Chris Rose recalls that members of Seven Champions Molly Dancers took it in turns to jog each morning so that they could persuade Eddie to invite the group in 1983. In fact, their early mornings were wasted because Eddie was not responsible for inviting the dance groups. Someone must have appreciated their endeavours, however, because they were invited. Although he was the Dance Producer, Eddie also had responsibility for song and music workshops, and he arranged a Harmony Singing workshop led by himself and Vic Gammon. Vic also led the Band Musicianship workshop which used *The Sussex Tune Book*, published by the EFDSS, which he had edited with Anne Loughran.

The interest in dance was diversifying. The various Morris and other display dance workshops (clog, rapper and longsword) continued, although there was some frustration that Beginners and Advanced meant Cotswold, whilst Women's Ritual meant North-West, and there were calls for the North-West workshop, and indeed the other workshops, to be more obviously for both men and

> *Eddie also led the jogging 'workshop' each morning at 7.15am*

women. Nibs Matthews returned as the leader of the Dance Technique workshop, and he also hosted the Dance Study workshops which had a different theme each day – Irish, display, creating new dances and Pat Shaw dances for example. Hugh Rippon led a workshop for callers with a different band each day. There were separate American and Playford dance workshops, but also Renaissance and International Dance, and Macedonian Dance and Music workshops. The latter were presented by Chris Gunstone who brought Dave Roberts, a fellow member of Blowzabella, to help. The workshops were an indication of the upsurge of interest in the dances of other countries amongst the younger folk enthusiasts.

At this time, workshops were always presented in a series – each day from Sunday through until Friday. The impact of workshops as the impetus for starting new interests, developing existing interests, setting people on the road to becoming singers, dancers, musicians, and for starting new Morris teams, new bands and new dance clubs cannot be underestimated. Sidmouth was certainly the first Festival to set up these workshops, and the pattern has been copied over and over again, but it is only at a week-long Festival such as Sidmouth that themes can be developed and real progress made. Dancers such as Lynne Render, a Festival regular for thirty years, would run between the Drill Hall and the Ham Marquee for the various dance workshops, and she feels that her changing interests over the years have been well catered for by the variety of Sidmouth's workshops. Pat Hoban from Birmingham recalls that she would always take new dances back to her club from the workshops, which she describes as 'a training ground' for bands and callers.

The Festival ended on a cautious note. The EFDSS was clearly in financial difficulties and, although the details had not emerged at the time of the Festival, there were fears for the Festival's future. The *Festival News* article by the EFDSS Chairman below the headline, 'EFDSS Goes Bust!' was designed to shock rather than describe the truth, but the *Sidmouth Herald* picked up the story in its Festival round-up. Under a front-page headline of 'Festival Needs a Lifeline', John Dowell was quoted as saying that local businesses that benefited from the Festival should be prepared to offer support. It became a familiar theme.

Gingers Street Theatre returned and in one of the Festival processions, they and Taffy Thomas paraded a huge model of Neptune. This provided an idea for a future Drill Hall Ceilidh.

Suffolk musicians: from left: Adrian Turner, Billy Bennington, Katie Millard, Oscar Woods, Font Watling, Reg Reeder, Jeannie Harris, John Howson, Ted Chaplin, Katie Howson

Songs for Europe

1983 The increased media exposure, especially through the BBC, led to Sidmouth being selected to host the European Broadcasting Union's Fourth Folk Music Festival. Seven countries, including Britain, sent guests who were featured not only in the special EBU radio concerts, but also in other Festival events. Most of the performers had never been heard before in England and Rosie Cross of Pyewackett remembers that the Festival was 'a tremendously successful cultural exchange of music', which had long been a Festival aim. Even though some of the European bands had been put together specifically for the recordings, they produced music of the highest calibre. Ale Möller from Sweden was one of the musicians, and shortly afterwards the band Filarfolket was formed, with Ale as a member. The British performers were The Boys of the Lough, Pyewackett, guitarist John James and Dave Cousins and Brian Willoughby. Dave was a member of The Strawbs and Station Controller of the local commercial radio station, Devon Air, which set up a mobile broadcasting unit on the Bedford Lawn car park and broadcast live throughout Devon.

The EBU concerts had the effect of persuading East Devon District Council to allow the Festival to use the Manor Pavilion all week, instead of just the Sunday evening. The EBU held three evening concerts in the Manor Pavilion, and it was the venue for a BBC Radio recording of The Boys of the Lough on Monday, part of which was broadcast in the regular *Folk on Two* programme later in the week, presented by Jim Lloyd. The Festival also featured elsewhere on

> **'... a tremendously successful cultural exchange of music'**

Radio Two, including the John Dunn programme, and John Dowell and Alan Titchmarsh did a live commentary of the Torchlight Procession on Alan's late-night radio programme. BBC Radio Devon broadcast twice a day from the Festival, including the Sunday morning Interdenominational Service at the Arena. The BBC's *Holiday Programme* was filming in Sidmouth during the Festival, which was included in the subsequent broadcast.

As if the EBU recordings, BBC Radio Two, BBC Television, Radio Devon and Devon Air were not enough, the commercial television station, TSW (Television South West) filmed throughout the Festival and later in the year broadcast three half-hour programmes. Most of the filming was of performers singing and playing to small gatherings of people away from the Festival venues – Andrew Cronshaw and Ric Sanders playing on the jetty opposite the Drill Hall, Roaring Jelly singing 'Christmas in Australia' in the Connaught Gardens, Huw and Tony Williams performing on the Alma Bridge – all giving the impression that the whole Festival was similarly low-key and small-scale. The third programme in the series was at the other extreme, and showed the overseas dance groups at the Arena.

On several occasions, the Festival audiences had enjoyed Ukrainian dance groups from various parts of England. For the first time, the Festival was able to invite a group of Ukrainian dancers from the USSR. Vesna was the first of many groups from the former USSR and, more recently, from Russia and the new independent countries. With their colourful costumes and their energetic dances, especially the hopak, the group was an instant success. On the Friday evening

Banevolks from the USA

Vesna Ukrainian Dancers from the USSR

The Fabulous Salami Brothers

claim that they could pull that back on the return leg was, alas, mere wishful thinking. Keith remembers, 'It was great fun, with both sides entering into the spirit of the game and the Festival. Although we would never meet each other again, for that first week in August we were great chums, and will always remain so, even if it is only a memory. But there again, that's Sidmouth!'

Keith Rusby was also known as Mussalami. After Magic Lantern had folded as a touring company, Taffy Thomas developed his street theatre interests through The Fabulous Salami Brothers – apart from Keith Rusby, the other members were Mike

opening Arena performance, they ended the show, and were called back for an encore. They then launched into the song 'My Bonny Lies over the Ocean' in English, and the audience's applause could be heard on the Ham.

> ## *... we were great chums, and will always remain so, even if it is only a memory*

There was also an American dance group at the Festival, Banevolks from Indiana performing American clogging and flat footing as well as the more modern Charleston and jitterbug. Although the Soviet group was heavily protected with 'minders' the dancers and musicians mixed freely with the other groups, and during the week a Ukrainian dancer performed with the Americans, and an American performed with the Ukrainians.

A football match was arranged between the Ukrainians and some of the English festival-goers, and Keith Rusby filed a match report twenty years later. 'Picture the scene: 10.30am, a team of bedraggled and hung over "artists" took on the super fit dance team from the Soviet Union, with Taffy Thomas refereeing – the only referee to give an LBW decision on a football pitch. We made two elementary mistakes – discussing tactics at 4am in the Balfour and turning up.' Keith's fellow players included Roy Harris, Gaffer Ferris and Pete Coe, and the result was a 2:0 win for the visitors. The English

Isla St Clair

Bettison, of Flowers and Frolics, Jim Woodland and Richie 'Three Balls' Taylor. They continued to collect circus skills from former performers, and their routines included illusion, fire-eating, juggling, dancing over broken glass, smashing a paving stone over someone's groin – 'feats of strength, skill and stupidity' – whilst Jim provided songs of social comment. They appeared at the 1983 Festival and their performances included a lunchtime show in the Drill Hall. One of their routines was the Foreign Legion sketch. Massive Foreign Legion hats hid their heads and shoulders, they were bare-chested with eyes drawn on their

Manley Morris at LNE

• *Seat belts compulsory*
• *Breakfast TV starts*
• *Compact Discs*
• *Flying Pickets, Culture Club and Billy Joel's Uptown Girl at No 1*

1983

nipples, with huge papier mache noses and a mouth drawn around each of their belly buttons. Their shorts had little arms either side, and after marching around to the music, they stood in line and rippled their stomachs, thus appearing to whistle the tune 'Colonel Bogey' through their belly buttons. Keith recalls that, although Jim was the only one to make this look realistic, the audience went wild.

Pulasthi Arts Circle from Sri Lanka returned, and there were also groups from Portugal, Brittany, Belgium, Finland and the Kalarrytes group from Greece.

The English dancers included two long-established Morris teams – the Manley Morris Dancers from Cheshire with their distinctive North-West dance, and the rapper dancing of the Monkseaton team. The Monkseaton men brought with them a largely unknown, sixteen-year-old Northumbrian piper as part of their Arena performances. This was Kathryn Tickell's debut at the Festival.

1983 saw a number of changes to the Festival, not the least of which was in the catering. The Ham Marquee already had a snack-bar which, for some strange reason, had only been available to season-ticket holders in 1982. The only refreshments at the Arena were in the tea tent, but for the first time permission was granted for a licensed bar. The Bowd Marquee was now being used for workshops for most of the day, as well as a dance in the evening and the Late Night Extra, and something more than hot-dogs was needed. 'Food for Folk' provided the catering up at the Bowd, with a barbeque, curries and soups. A full-scale Craft Fair with over thirty stands operated throughout the week – but only just before and during the Arena shows. The concept of the all-day showground was still several years in the future.

Car parking was – and of course still is – a problem in Sidmouth at the best of times. There had been frequent calls for extensive car-parking facilities on the edge of the town, and finally, in 1983, a field beyond the Arena, now occupied by houses, was used.

The *Festival News* had previously been produced on an ink-duplicator, with a team of helpers running off the copies and stapling the sheets together late into the night. In 1983, the *Festival News* was properly printed, which allowed the more extensive use of illustrations, as well as making it easier to read. Lawrence Heath had been contributing a cartoon strip to *The Southern Rag* called Borfolk and for several years in the eighties, there was an occasional Borfolk strip in the *Festival News*. The hero of the strip, Frank Ingnobody, was shown in various events at the supposedly fictitious Midsouth Folk Festival.

Nationally, there was concern about the quality and presentation of Morris dancing. John Dowell had helped to adjudicate at a Morris dance competition in Bath and decided to introduce a Ritual Dance Competition at Sidmouth. The Morris Ring was still not too pleased

> ### The Monkseaton men brought with them a largely unknown, sixteen-year-old Northumbrian piper

about women dancing the Morris, so that when Nibs Matthews (as a former Squire of the Morris Ring, but also Director of the EFDSS) attended a meeting of the Ring Advisory Council, the EFDSS came in for some harsh criticism for promoting the competition. No doubt there was a fear that a women's team might actually win! 'Who would judge the competition?' was the cry from the Ring officers, to which Nibs replied, 'Well, any of you could be the judges'. In the event, Nibs himself, plus David Slater, David Anderton (who led the advanced Morris workshops) and Rod Stradling, Bampton's musician, were the judges. Thankfully for the Morris Ring, the winners were Monkseaton. The competition is also remembered for the torrential

Sri Lankan dancer

downpour in the middle of the event, leading to the Arena Marquee coming under several inches of water.

The Ritual Dance competition continued for several years, and the seriousness with which the performers and audience viewed it could be seen by the vehemence of the complaints over the adjudication. The judges were sometimes booed by the audience, and harangued afterwards by the dancers and their supporters. Fortunately, the seriousness was tempered by some very funny entries – often from the Boughton Monchelsea dancers and later the Fabulous Fezheads.

It was decided to book a singer who would attract a general audience for Monday evening's Arena show. Isla St Clair had been a performer at folk clubs since she was a young teenager, but in more recent years she had been the hostess on BBC television's *The*

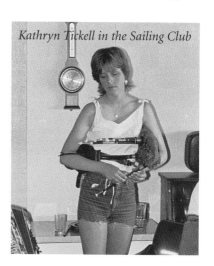
Kathryn Tickell in the Sailing Club

Seven Champions in the procession

Generation Game, presented by Larry Grayson. This had led to a series of TV programmes, *The Song and The Story*, which dramatised traditional songs which were sung by Isla. She was accompanied for her performance at Sidmouth by musicians who had performed with Cliff Richard and Paul McCartney. Support performers were the Scottish singer exiled to Norwich, Alex Atterson, and Kent duo Tundra.

The Old Ship Inn had been closed during the 1982 Festival, and the musicians who had gathered there found a new home in the York Tap. It re-opened in 1983, but The Mason's Arms had closed the previous November, much to the distress of Seven Champions who arranged a requiem preceded by a wreath-making workshop. An alternative English session had been held in The Radway Inn in 1981, judging by this *Festival News* item: 'No Reels in the Radway Wednesday night'. *No Reels* was the name of the Old Swan Band's first album, so it was a coded message for English musicians. Although the Radway did not want any music in 1982, the pub became the main venue for English music in 1983 after the Mason's closed. Early musicians included Mick Brooks, Martin Nail, members of Seven Champions Molly Dancers and Taz Tarry. Taz was making his first visit to Sidmouth and, as he had been playing the fiddle for a year or so, he went to a fiddle workshop led by Paul Burgess, Fi Fraser and Flos Headford (all members of the Old Swan Band). Afterwards they all went across the road to the Radway Inn and, as Taz (now a member of the band Grand Union) recalls, 'I've never looked back and the Radway became a second home during Festival Week – I can definitely say that Sidmouth changed my life'. The pub has continued to host the English music sessions ever since.

> **'I can definitely say that Sidmouth changed my life'**

The news that the Horse and Groom was also threatened with closure led to a petition to the brewery from the folk enthusiasts. Elsewhere, the pubs were booming. The Anchor's landlord, Alvin Barrett, was quoted as saying that a fifth of his annual turnover came from the ten days around the Festival. The Marine Bars did four times as much business as normal, and the grocery store, Trumps, described trade as 'fantastic'. One of the publicans suggested that 'Every shop and pub in the town relies very heavily on the Festival'. Such comments may have been self-evident, but they had not been stated so emphatically in the *Sidmouth Herald* before.

There was the 'traditional' letter of complaint about the Festival to the local newspaper, and although the financial benefits of the Festival were put forward in subsequent correspondence, the letters page also extolled the benefits of the Festival as a joyous occasion, spreading international understanding, and enriching the lives of the local population. 'All joined together in the common aim for peace', as one correspondent wrote. 'A week when the town comes alive', wrote another.

Ian Carter from Derby was the new Children's Producer, and he had to contend with not having the Methodist Halls as a venue. Alvin Barrett made the upstairs room at The Anchor available to the children for Kaleidoscope, an event which was open from 10.00am until 10.00pm and aimed mainly at the older children in their teens. This was an age group that Cyril Jones had tried to cater for with his teenage dances, although they had to wait until the 1990s to have control over their own events. A kaleidoscope keeps changing its pattern and that was the intention of the event – a constantly changing array of activities was planned.

One of the big successes at the children's events was the clown Albert the Idiot and his amazing car, Henrietta. The children crowded round him and the car, which was remote-controlled, every time they appeared and they were very popular at the Children's Special at the Arena on Friday afternoon. This event had been running for several years and was a combination of overseas and British dance groups, children's entertainers and performances by the children of what they had learned at the workshops. Dozens of children from the music workshop stood by the side of the stage and played for

Tundra in the marquee

Andrew Cronshaw and Ric Sanders with members of Pyewackett in the Drill Hall

the dancing of the Hobby Horse Club. Jeff Dando (ex-Bath City Morris and now a member of Bampton Morris and The Woodpeckers band) was well-established as the leader of the Morris Minors, who performed in the Arena show, and this was probably the year that a very young Saul Rose (later a member of Waterson:Carthy and Seven Champions) danced a jig on the Arena stage. Saul was also making his stage debut as a musician that year with his parents' team Whitethorn Morris, one of the invited groups. He played a bass drum (on a stand) but it was too big for him to carry in the processions.

The storytelling competition continued and in 1983 a new competitor arrived from the States. 'I would like to enter the story-telling competition: Pat Ryan (I'm from the Chicago Story-tellers Guild)' ran the *Festival News* item. Pat eventually made his home in England and became a crucial figure in the storytelling movement, although he did not win the competition in 1983.

Just before the start of the 1983 Festival, John Dowell received a letter for the *Festival News*. He did not understand what it was about and, in spite of its mis-spellings and bad grammar, it was published. The letter read, 'Dear Mr Doorbell, My Uncel Henry and his boy Sid will be a coming down to your Festival at Sidmouth. They now lot's of old

song's and wandered if they could sing some. Mr David Bellamy have seen them in Norwich and he thinks there very good, also Mr Jim Souza, Mr Taffy Thompson and Mr Alex Atkinson, the flying Scotsman. … There song's go back a long way to time immoral and Im sure youll agree they ougt to be preserved. … They call thereselves the Kipper Family, from somewhere near Trunch in Norfolk.' At this stage, the Kipper Family had only

> *Dear Mr Doorbell, My Uncel Henry and his boy Sid will be a coming down to your Festival at Sidmouth ...*

performed a few times in Norwich and had not done a proper folk club booking. Henry and his son Sid arrived, and did floor spots in the Beach Store and the Horse and Groom, with songs such as 'The Male Female Highwayman', 'Dido, Fido' and 'Joan Sugarbeet', and by the end of the week they were the sensation of the last night LNE. Of course George Kipper maintains that he had been invited to perform at the Festival, but that he was unavoidably detained at Her Majesty's Pleasure, and the other two family members stole all the glory. With George still being

unavailable, Henry and Sid were the ones invited back the following year.

Pyewackett played modern arrangements of tunes published in the Playford collections, whilst Mike Barraclough was interested in introducing the accompanying dances to the younger ceilidh goers. Together, they presented a 'Playford Balls-up' in the Drill Hall, which contrasted nicely with the more sedate Playford Ball with the Sussex Bonny Men and caller Dick Reed in the Ham Marquee the previous evening. Mike wanted to place the seventeenth century dances in a modern context, which – with youthful boisterous energy – was closer to the original context than the current folk dance club Playford scene. Rosie Cross recalls that during the 'Pyewackett Gallop', the dancers refused to stop when the musicians tried to end the dance. After playing the tune in waltz time to put the dancers off, the musicians eventually left the stage – and still they danced, singing the tune themselves. Finally, the musicians struck up again and by mutual consent the dance came to an end – after more than twenty minutes. The Drill Hall was packed and the atmosphere was hot and sweaty, but that evening is still recalled by dancers as a pivotal moment.

There was a constant desire to introduce new workshops to reflect changing tastes, but with limited resources this inevitably meant that some workshops would be dropped, but of course this disappointed some people. Cathy Lesurf and the Oyster Ceilidh Band had led three workshops on mediaeval dance in 1980, and then a series of Renaissance dance workshops in 1981 whilst Will Ward ran the Early Music workshops. When these workshops were dropped in 1983, there were messages in the *Festival News* asking for them to be reinstated. At the end of the week, John Dowell, writing in the *Festival News*, acknowledged the difficulty of achieving 'the right compromise between changing with the times and providing better facilities and a wider range of performances, whilst maintaining the relaxed, friendly, traditional "Sidmouth" atmosphere that we all know and love'.

The Streets of Sidmouth

1984 Well, not quite! It was the London streets that singer Ralph McTell made famous in a song that he had first recorded back in 1969. Later issued as a single, it reached number two in the British charts (when they were still called the Hit Parade) and it made Ralph a household name. In addition to his concert appearances, he was performing on children's television in a programme called *Alphabet Zoo:* he wrote the songs about the animals.

When he was running a folk club, it had been one of John Dowell's ambitions to book Ralph McTell, but as he was such a 'big name' John never thought it would happen. He was therefore overjoyed to be offered the chance of presenting Ralph McTell in the Monday evening Arena show. In spite of a weekend affected by rain, in an otherwise glorious, sunny summer, Monday evening stayed warm and dry and a very large audience packed the Arena to hear Ralph sing a range of his best-loved songs, including, of course, 'The Streets of London'.

The singer-songwriter was not a new concept to the Sidmouth Festival. But the presence of Ralph

Packie Byrne

McTell on the line-up of what many people saw as a firmly 'traditional' folk festival highlighted the growing breadth of the music to be heard at Sidmouth, and it was an indication of the greater variety to come.

The venues for song and music were generally small-scale, and this was a limiting factor in the booking of big name guests, especially as the Festival still preferred guests to come all week. This preference was, however, changing because of the cost and the need to provide variety. With the decline of folk clubs, the festivals were becoming the main source of bookings, and income, for professional and semi-professional performers. The days of enticing

> ... *the growing breadth of music to be heard at the Festival* ...

professional performers to Sidmouth on the basis of free tickets and seaside holiday accommodation were long gone.

Over the years, there had been some opportunities for the English folk enthusiasts to learn dances from the overseas groups, for example, in the popular Meet the Team events, but there was a demand for much more. In 1982, there had been the Macedonian dance workshops, led by musicians from Blowzabella, and the Society for International Folk Dancing (SIFD) had been involved in the workshop programme in both 1982 and 1983, but they were not always able to provide live music. The 1983 *Festival News* carried adverts from SIFD clubs up and down the country, which indicated the increasing interest, and a band called Rosbif played for a workshop of French dances in the Dance Study series of events.

There were no SIFD workshops at the 1984 Festival, but the guests did include Blowzabella and Rosbif, and French dances were included in Dave Williams's Meet the Caller workshop, with music from Rosbif. The band also played at the Saturday lunchtime Anchor Ceilidh and their French dances drew enthusiastic comments in the *Festival News* from SIFD members and others. Blowzabella's repertoire was drawn from several different European countries, with the drone instruments of the hurdy-gurdy and the bagpipes very much to the fore. At this stage the band consisted of founder members David Armitage and Jon Swayne, plus Cliff Stapleton, Paul James, Dave Roberts and Dave Shepherd. There was also considerable interest in the music. A series of workshops on Pipes and Whistles included Paul James and Jon Swayne of Blowzabella on bagpipes and Jean-Pierre Rasle of Cock and Bull on pipes, whilst the instrument workshop included a session on the hurdy-gurdy from Cliff Stapleton.

It was not just European dances that were becoming more popular. There were still no groups in England performing Appalachian clogging, although the appearance of the Banevolks group in 1983 had led to requests in the *Festival News* for a workshop. In 1984, two members of the Limberjacks Appalachian Cloggies from New York visited the Festival, performing informally on the Esplanade and they organised three impromptu workshops in the Arena Marquee.

English dance was not, of course, forgotten. The 'Experienced Dancers Only' events continued at the Bowd Marquee, there was a dance most evenings in the Ham Marquee, a barn dance and a ceilidh in the village halls each evening, as well as the Drill Hall Ceilidhs and the LNE ceilidh. Not to mention the Anchor

Taffy Thomas as Neptune

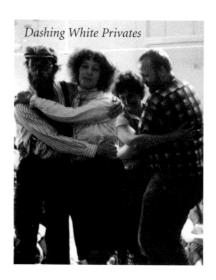

Dashing White Privates

Garden lunchtime ceilidhs and the Tea Dances. There may have been a choice, but most of the venues were quite small. The Oyster Band returned, and although the word 'ceilidh' had been dropped from the title, they still played for dances. Other bands included Ram's Bottom and The Ripley Wayfarers.

The latest in the long line of fancy-dress ceilidhs was the Underwater Ceilidh on Tuesday evening in the Drill Hall, with The Oyster Band and Taffy Thomas. A face and body painter was 'in residence' outside the Drill Hall for the dancers to complete their appearance. In the *Festival News* there was an apology that the Drill Hall could not, as planned, be flooded because of the water shortage (another drought), although sea weed was hung from the ceiling. During the evening, Anne Lennox-Martin, Kerry Fletcher and Chrissie Thomas gave a synchronised 'swimming' display in bathing costumes, in spite of the fact that Chrissie was over seven months pregnant. The announcement for the ceilidh was full of dreadful puns – the Drill Hall is the *plaice* to be, the Oyster Band will play *sole* music, Taffy Thomas, the caller who was dressed as Neptune, is a *dab* hand and a *whale* of a time was promised. At the end of the ceilidh, 'Neptune' led all the dancers out of the Drill Hall … and into the sea.

Actually getting from the Esplanade onto the beach was fraught with

difficulty. During the previous year, the height of the beach had fallen dramatically, so that instead of the former two-foot jump onto the beach, the distance was now more like ten feet, although there were no railings. The Torchlight Procession arrangements had to be changed, and for the first time the groups processed along the Esplanade and down the ramp at the Sailing Club, instead of simply jumping off the Esplanade. But with thirty-one groups, the middle section of the procession had to get onto the beach at the York Steps, whilst the back used the Bedford Steps. This was before the groyne of rocks opposite the Royal York had been built, so the dancers could spread out right along the beach from Port Royal to the Bedford Hotel.

The singers had an opportunity to dress up as well, with a South Sea Islands Fancy Dress Party on Sunday evening in Carinas featuring Six Hands in Tempo, Eric and the Dead

> *there was an apology that the Drill Hall could not, as planned, be flooded, because of the water shortage*

Sea Surfers. Judging by their description in the souvenir programme – 'They claim that their biggest contribution to the folk scene has been to popularise the wearing of gaudily coloured Hawaiian shirts!!' – the Dead Sea Surfers would not have spent much time on selecting a fancy dress costume.

The increasing variety of the guests, and the mixed programming of venues, led to varied line-ups for the song events. In a single event, the audience might have heard Sussex traditional singer Johnny Doughty singing unaccompanied songs about the sea, Six Hands in Tempo, the Oyster Band and The Kipper Family.

After the previous year's stunning debut, The Kipper Family were officially booked and one of their

performances was a Friday lunchtime Drill Hall special – 'Trunch Traditions: the songs, dances, folklore, rituals, customs and excise of Trunch'. This was probably the occasion when the 'Dashing White Privates' was danced for the first time.

The other song guests included Pete Bond, Cosmotheka, Packie Byrne, English Tapestry, Andrew Frank, Jo Fraser, Rory McLeod, Watson, Draper and Locke, Jim Woodland, and Chris Pitt and Gavin Atkin. Chris and Gavin had performed informally the previous year and realised that if they went to The Dove at about 6.00pm each evening, the Song Producer would be meeting up with the comperes. Gavin and Chris hung around and offered to fill any gaps in the programme. Their repertoire was funny music hall songs sung by Chris with Gavin playing concertina. This was some years before Gavin was a member of the folk dance band Florida. The term 'singaround' was well established in the wider folk scene, but the Festival now programmed a series of 'tunearounds' led by Dan Quinn in the Balfour Arms each evening. Len and

---

- *Miners' strike*
- *Cable TV*
- *Brighton bombing during Conservative Party conference*
- *Band Aid's Do they know it's Christmas?*
- *Torvill and Dean*
- *Frankie Goes to Hollywood (Relax), Wham and Stevie Wonder at No 1*

1984

Andy Turner receives his prize from Shirley Collins

Glyncoed Welsh Dancers

Margaret Evis had retired from the pub the previous year – there was an emotional *This is Your Life* event chaired by Keith Rusby – but the late evening private parties continued: a further opportunity for the overseas dancers and musicians to relax and meet the English musicians.

Alongside the Ritual Dance competition, a Sidmouth Singer competition was introduced. With heats every afternoon in the Beach Store, and Shirley Collins as the judge, the eventual winner was Andy Turner, who had been visiting the Festival with his parents Bob and Jean from the age of seventeen, and who continues to come every year with his own children. Andy plays in the dance band Geckoes and is also a singer with the band Magpie Lane.

The Horse and Groom pub had shut for good earlier in the year, and informal song sessions became concentrated on the Anchor Middle Bar. Although it was a free session, the Middle Bar had nevertheless always had a collecting tin for donations which was then handed to the Festival. After a few years, the singers realised that they could put their names on the collecting tin and receive an honourable mention in the *Festival News*, which listed all the collections as part of the Bill Rutter Award. For several years, the Award had been won by 'Captain Morgan's Pirates' which was another of Clive Morgan's contributions to the Festival. His daughter, Deborah, danced with the Glyncoed Welsh Dancers who came to the Festival and performed around the town, and Clive supervised their collecting tins. Once, when Clive realised that a dance team was late arriving at the Festival, he arranged for the Glyncoed group to dance outside the Drill Hall so that John Dowell in

> ### an attempt to see who could dance as far south as possible ...

the first floor office would hear them. The trick worked and they appeared on the Arena the same day.

In 1984, the Middle Bar Singers initiated a list of fines and charges for misdemeanours such as forgetting the words or singing 'The Wild Rover' and at the end of the week, they were surprised to learn that they had beaten Captain Morgan and so received the prize – a specially inscribed walking stick – at the Friday night LNE. Rivalry with 'Captain Morgan' continued for several years, and in 1985, when they won again, the Middle Bar Singers had collected almost £1,000 for Festival funds, and in all, they were awarded six walking sticks.

For several years, Seven Champions had been behind the 'Marine Morris' displays. This was an attempt to see who could dance as far south as possible, which of course meant dancing in the sea. 1984 was the year of the Los Angeles Olympics, and Seven Champions organised the 'Marine Ritual Dance Competition Sidmouth Olympics Watersports' which seemed to be an excuse for everyone to get very wet.

Barry Lister became the new Arena Producer – a former Song Producer, he also had experience of

Marine Morris

Miorits Ensemble

High Spen Blue Diamonds

dance (as a member of Great Western Morris) and the theatre, through the local amateur dramatic society in Sidmouth. After the previous year's success with a group from the USSR, the formula was repeated in 1984 – this time with the Miorits Ensemble from the state of Moldavia, whom John Dowell had seen at the Billingham Festival. The group Lany from Poland brought so many costumes, that they would not all fit on the bus sent to Heathrow to collect them.

French stilt dancers returned – a different group called Lous de Bazats. Unfortunately, they left their long poles at home, but the ever-resourceful George Stuart made them a set. A group from Spain withdrew in June, but Hora Galim from Israel was able to fill the gap. Los Jairas from Bolivia returned, whilst other groups came from Norway and Reunion Island: Les Etincelles de la Jeunesse Panonaise.

Jing Ying was a group from Hong Kong that lived up to its name, which translates as 'the best'. Their Lion Dance featured a fluorescent orange lion that winked at the audience, and the performance of their musicians at the Tuesday evening Assembly Rooms concert moved Song Producer Barry Coope to tears.

The English groups included Garstang (their final appearance at the Festival) and Poynton Jemmers, Gloucestershire Old Spot Morris (who won the Ritual Dance competition), High Spen Blue Diamond Rapper Dancers (their first of many appearances) and Woodfidley. High Spen became the latest team to teach rapper sword at the annual workshop, which was invariably held at the Balfour Arms. It became the practice for the rapper workshop to perform on the Esplanade at the end of the week, and on High Spen's most recent

visit to Sidmouth in 2000, the group's leader, Ricky Forster, is proud to remember that no-one dropped out during the week, and nine sets of dancers performed on the Friday.

'Nations of the World Unite' and 'Town Opens Doors to Peoples of the World' were just two of the newspaper headlines. The *Sidmouth Herald's* comment, 'In a world where there is often conflict and unrest, how refreshing it is to see people from the different nations and cultures joined by the friendship of song and dance', suggested that one of the messages of the Festival was finally getting through. In the Autumn, the Festival won the 'Carnegie Interpret Britain Award' presented by the Society for the Interpretation of Britain's Heritage, which sat alongside East Devon District Council's 'Flag of Honour' awarded by the Council of Europe in 1979.

Reunion Island

Jing Ying

Folk Aid

1985 In June, the folk scene was shocked to hear that Festival stalwart Taffy Thomas had suffered a stroke. From the Company of Fools, through Magic Lantern, the Arena Fire Show, and The Fabulous Salami Brothers, to the Drill Hall Ceilidhs and the Arena, Taffy Thomas had played a crucial role in many aspects of the Festival. This was the era of the massive fund-raising of Band Aid and Live Aid, and the folk scene joined in with 'Taff Aid' aiming to raise money to help Taffy's family – he faced the prospect of a year without income.

In Sidmouth, a variety of fund-raising activities took place – raffles and a Salami Brothers' cassette for example – although the most novel initiative was 'Buy a Pebble for Taffy' which involved John Maxwell selling pebbles from the beach, on the dubious basis that Taffy had once sat on them! In The Dove, when buying a round of drinks, some people added 'one for Taffy' and the money went into a glass behind the bar. The regular Marine Morris remembered Taffy's role as Neptune at the Underwater Ceilidh, and announced their own 'Dive Aid', which included the usual dancing in the sea, plus male wet t-shirt and 'ritual song' competitions, the latter involving the Middle Bar Singers.

But most of the fund-raising energy went into organising a benefit concert which was scheduled for Thursday at 6.00pm. One concert quickly became two – in different venues at the same time. The performers included many of the Festival guests, plus a few extras, and the audiences contributed large sums of money.

> **Taffy could not be prevented from offering suggestions by telephone from his sick-bed**

One of the concerts was held in the SWEB Building, a new venue in 1985. This was owned by the South West Electricity Board and was located just beyond the Beach Store on Ham Lane – the site is now part of the Ham car park. Apart from the Taff Aid concert, the SWEB building was used for some of the children's events as well as lunchtime and evening singarounds with Charley Yarwood and Ian Woods.

During these singarounds, the second fund-raising event of the Festival took place. Band Aid and Live Aid were, of course, the rock and pop music's response to the famine in Africa. Ray and Wendy Lee at London's Capital Folk Club mobilised the folk scene under the banner of 'Folk Against Famine' and their main initiative was to knit or crochet blankets for Help the Aged, and at the same time obtain sponsorship for the campaign. Many people have recalled sitting in the SWEB building, enjoying the music and knitting furiously.

Another event at the SWEB Building was the series of workshops for the Percy Topliss Show. This event had been planned by Mike Bettison and Taffy Thomas as a 'street musical' based on the book *The Monocled Mutineer*, the true story of Percy Topliss, the leader of a First World War mutiny before the Battle of Mons. The story was later turned into a major television drama. Taffy had written the story as a mummers play, aimed at the youth season ticket holders, and it included a dragon because the MI5 Christmas card at the time showed the 'dragon of subversion' – the enemy within. Mike ran the workshops himself, and Ian Blake helped with the music, but Taffy could not be prevented from offering suggestions by telephone from his sick-bed.

There were improvements to the Arena, with a new raised stage, instead of the boards laid flat on the ground. This improved the visibility for everyone, but especially for those on the deckchairs at the front who, ironically considering that they paid more for their seats, previously had had the worst view. The bandstand, sound and lighting systems were also upgraded, but the improvements

The Percy Topliss Play

- *Live Aid concert*
- *Bradford City stadium fire kills 55 people*
- *Microsoft launch Windows version 1.0*
- *Jennifer Rush's The Power of Love at No 1*

1985

Ponte Caffaro from Italy

were largely wasted in the first year because the bad weather led to many of the shows moving to the marquee. One outdoor show that was saved was the Monday evening concert, with The Dubliners, whose former chart success with 'Five Nights Drunk' guaranteed a large audience of season ticket holders, residents and holiday makers.

The most spectacular overseas dance group was from Italy – the Ponte Caffaro Carnival Dancers. This was their first ever visit outside their local community in Northern Italy to perform their carnival dances. The costumes, especially the hats and masks; the hypnotic music, played mainly on fiddles; and the distinctive dances, with stepping, pointing fingers and nodding heads, created a sensation amongst the folk enthusiasts. Many friendships were made that week, and since then a number of dedicated people have travelled to Italy at Shrovetide to experience the dances in their village setting.

1985 was also the first time that a group from Egypt, Sharkiah, had visited the Festival. Links were made with Sidmouth's twin town in Switzerland, Le Locle, when a group from the town, Les Francs Habergeants, visited the Festival. From Yugoslavia, the Shota group danced at the Arena and there were also groups from Sweden and Spain.

Several of the British dance groups had visited the Festival before – The Shropshire Bedlams and Martha Rhoden's Tuppenny

Dish, Grenoside Sword Dancers, and Ekome – whilst Irish dance was represented by the stunning Clann na Gael from Newcastle-upon-Tyne, the first of many visits by the group. South Downs Morris from Sussex was a young team, mainly drawn from a sixth form college, featuring Roger Watson as musician. Their studied style, slow and athletic, contributed to them winning the Ritual Dance Competition.

Even before Taffy Thomas's illness, it had been decided to run a more conventional series of ceilidhs in the Drill Hall – no themed or fancy dress ceilidhs were planned. Nevertheless, the music was provided by some of the best bands on the ceilidh circuit at the time — Cock and Bull, Peeping Tom, Red Shift and the Oyster Band, and the latter band played at the final Drill Hall Ceilidh of the year on Friday evening. In the early days of the Anchor Garden Ceilidhs, the band

had played from in front of the wall on the left hand side when entering the Gardens. Alvin Barrett had transformed the area several years previously, which meant that the bands could then play from the raised grassy area at the far end, as the photograph of Cock and Bull Band in 1985 shows. There was no stage and the band had to set up on the edge of the children's play area. Two years earlier, Rosie Cross of Pyewackett was terrified throughout the ceilidh, fearful that the children were going to trip over the cables, injure themselves or damage the valuable musical instruments.

The Song Producer was Pat Ryan, a female singer from Lancashire, who had been visiting the Festival for many years – she was the first female Song Producer. Several of the song guests were from the North West, although performers such as Harry Boardman, Strawhead and Alan Bell had all visited Sidmouth before. Packie Byrne was now performing alongside Jo Fraser, and Alistair Anderson was another guest. Sadie Green Sales Ragtime Jug Band from the USA, was previously unknown in this country, but their appearance meant that band member Timothy Walker could meet up with his sister, Sally, who owned the Avalon Guest House in the town. A feature of the Festival in 1985 was 'Desert Island Discs', an event where Festival guests chose their favourite recordings, following the format of the long-running BBC Radio 4 programme.

Having previously been Arena Producer, David Slater now became

Clann na Gael

Jean-Pierre Rasle of Cock & Bull playing for an Anchor Ceilidh

the Producer of the Children's events – the term 'Children's Festival' had not yet been adopted, although there had been a separate programme for some time, proclaiming the events as 'Kids' Capers'. By now, Dr Sunshine's Pavement Show was involved in the children's events every year, and generations of children remember their hilarious sketches, their songs and the workshops. On Sunday afternoon they took part in a children's party in the Connaught Gardens. Dave Hunt and Vic Baker often added other people to the Dr Sunshine's line-up for the week.

The EFDSS was on the eve of a period of turmoil. It had always failed to attract the total support of the song enthusiasts, and a clear division now existed within the dancers – the country dancers and the ceilidh goers. The bulk of the support for the EFDSS came from the former through the folk dance clubs, but their members were getting older and few new people were coming forward to serve on the EFDSS District Committees, which were having even less impact on the folk scene at a local level. This picture was not universal: some Districts did combine the various interests, and the Devon District was certainly one of the more successful local organisations. The Sidmouth

Festival had always attracted a mixture of dancers, and the 'EFDSS dancers' who came were generally more out-going than in the clubs. The cause of the EFDSS's turmoil was financial. Income had failed to keep up with expenditure and new sources of income had not been tapped into. The headquarters building in London, Cecil Sharp House, required more spending on maintenance, but it was failing to maintain its position as a national folk centre.

Nibs Matthews was due to retire as Director of the EFDSS in November 1985, and his replacement, the BBC Radio Two folk programme presenter Jim Lloyd, spent several months as 'Director-Designate'. Jim visited Sidmouth and set up an EFDSS information caravan on the Ham: surprisingly, this was the first time that there had been a separate EFDSS promotion at the Festival for many years.

The Sidmouth Festival had continued to grow, with ever-increasing budgets. There was competition between festivals, and indeed, between the festivals organised by the EFDSS. Sidmouth was a potential source of income for the EFDSS, through the Festival itself, through the sale of membership (members received a discount on tickets) and through the Folk Shop. But it was also the potential source of financial ruin for the EFDSS, especially as income from the Arena was so dependent on the weather.

The weather in the summer of 1985 was the worst for many years and the Festival did not escape the rain. One of the press reports suggested that the Festival was planning to erect a mammoth marquee over the whole Knowle Arena, although the reporter may have just misunderstood the existence of the Arena Marquee. It rained on Friday and Saturday, then on Sunday it was worse – 'strong winds and driving rain' reported the *East Devon Extra* – and the Esplanade dancing, Arena shows and Anchor ceilidh were all washed out. As has often happened in these circumstances, local residents

offered accommodation to any campers who had been washed out of their tents. Monday was rain free, but the rest of the week was affected by the weather although it was dry for the final night Arena show and the Torchlight Procession.

John Dowell put on a brave face for the local press when he hoped that the Festival would break even. In fact, it made a net loss of £10,000 instead of a budgeted surplus. The financial position was instrumental in the commissioning of a report on the future of the Festival by the EFDSS's National Executive Committee, and this was considered at the June 1986 meeting. The report was written by John Dowell after consultation with a range of Festival supporters and EFDSS members.

John's report gave a clear overview of the Festival in the mid-eighties.

Purpose: The basic purpose of the Festival was to further the aims of the EFDSS and present folk music and dance to a wider audience. For the folk enthusiasts, it gave an opportunity to enjoy the music and dance they loved, and

> ... *generations of children remember their hilarious sketches*

also to meet like-minded people, but importantly, it provided an opportunity for experimentation and cross-fertilisation. For the local residents, it was felt that the event generated international friendship.

Audiences: It has always been very difficult to calculate the size of the total audience, which included people attending the Arena shows, watching the processions and Esplanade displays. An estimate was 30,000 to 50,000 people. About ten per cent were folk enthusiasts – including 1,500 season ticket holders and 1,000 performers and stewards. Day tickets were not sold because of limits on the size of venues, even though there was a demand. With over 300 events, spread over eight days, almost all folk music and dance interests were

Ian Kearey & John Jones of the Oyster Band in the Drill Hall

catered for, and there was always the potential to arrange extra events during the week and publicise them through the *Festival News*.

The ageing profile of the folk enthusiast audience was recognised, with fewer young people becoming interested. Only basic facilities on the camp-site meant that more people wanted indoor accommodation, which was expensive and limited. Some people could not afford tickets as well, so attended the informal and free sessions and paid on the door for occasional events. Audience expectations were increasing – better camp-site facilities, better staging, sound, lighting and seating – but audiences were not prepared to pay for them.

Artistic Policy: The Arena was seen as a 'shop window' for folk music and dance – the largest in the country. It was also seen as the 'entry level' and the rest of the Festival had to be equipped to cope with the interest generated by the Arena shows – accessible events for beginners, as well as the established events for the enthusiasts. The lack of a large song venue was seen as a strength because

Ian Telfer & Alan Prosser of the Oyster Band in the Drill Hall

the result was a proliferation of 'human-scale' events and venues.

In the past, the Festival had attracted artists on the basis that although the fee would be small or non-existent, the exposure would lead to folk club bookings throughout the year. The club scene was diminishing, and artists were increasingly asking for decent Festival fees as well as accommodation. It was becoming too costly to book artists to appear all week. Sidmouth was instrumental in promoting many of the new developments in the folk scene, for example women's Morris, English country music and street theatre. Increasingly, the new developments were now coming from outside the folk scene and the Festival was struggling to keep up with, for example, the new interest in roots music.

The Festival was a risk to the very existence of the EFDSS

The way forward, the report argued, was to book a smaller number of top artists for one or two performances each, with a larger number of up-and-coming artists who would use the Festival as a springboard. It was recognised that this required greater skills and imagination from the producers, at a time when it was becoming more difficult to find new producers and stick to the 'two-year rule'. The advantage of this rule was the variety and geographical spread that the turnover of staff could bring to the Festival. Workshops were seen as crucial, with a steady increase in demand for greater variety.

Ancillary Services: The financial contribution from the Craft Fair and from the concession on the refreshments was recognised, although the sales at the Folk Shop (over £14,500 in 1985) were not credited to the Festival.

Marketing: The report indicated the extent of the local marketing to a wide range of community organisations, and the use of the

local press, radio and regional television. There was the potential for more visitors from overseas (the 1985 Festival had been previewed in the *New York Times*) but there were problems providing them with accommodation.

Income: The report indicated the problems that had been encountered in trying to obtain both sponsorship and grants. The accounts revealed that neither Devon County Council, nor East Devon District Council nor Sidmouth Town Council gave any direct financial assistance to the Festival in 1985, in spite of the massive contribution the Festival made to the local tourist industry and to enriching the lives of the local residents. Help was given in kind.

The EFDSS: In 1975, at £17,500, the Festival turnover represented only 8.3 per cent of the EFDSS's turnover. By 1985, at £116,500, that proportion had increased to twenty-one per cent. The EFDSS was becoming more dependent on the Festival for income, whereas the Festival needed to build up its reserves after recent losses. The Festival was a risk to the very existence of the EFDSS, and similarly, the EFDSS was a risk to the continuation of the Festival. 'Either could very easily bankrupt the other', stated the report. A possible solution was to separate the Festival from the EFDSS, with the Festival covenanting a proportion of income or profits back to the EFDSS.

No sooner had the report been distributed to the EFDSS National Executive, than an offer was received to take over the running of the Festival. The offer was from Steve Heap and John Heydon, and was considered by the EFDSS National Executive immediately after discussion of John Dowell's report. The initial proposal was to set up a new company with the same aims and objects as the EFDSS to run the Festival, with John Dowell as Festival Director. The EFDSS Treasurer, Roger Barnes, recommended the offer, which was accepted by the National Executive. There were then several months of discussion to reach a final agreement, but in the meantime, there was the 1986 Festival to organise.

The End of an Era

Gaffer Ferris

1986 'Surely the weather can't be as bad as last year! Can it?' wrote John Dowell in his 'Welcome' message in the first *Festival News*. Alas, yes. It rained for much of the week, and the Arena shows were greatly affected, as were the informal dancing along the Esplanade and the collections. At the time, the only collections allowed in the streets were for the benefit of the Festival, and these were small, yet significant, items of Festival income. 'Probably a financial disaster', John wrote in the final *Festival News* on Friday.

By this time, the news about the probable change in 'ownership' of the Festival was out in the open and, although some EFDSS members especially in the South West, were saddened that the Festival was losing its links with the Society, there was also some relief that the Festival would hopefully be more secure under the new arrangements.

The changes were made more poignant by the death in June 1986 of Bill Rutter. Since his retirement in 1979, Bill had been far from inactive. He had been elected to the EFDSS's National Executive Committee, and had continued to encourage the volunteers in the Districts and Clubs. As far as Sidmouth was concerned, Bill clearly recognised that a new man was in charge and, although he visited the Festival, he let John run it his way. Since Silver Jubilee year, there had been a show of all the English dance groups on Monday afternoon in the Connaught Gardens, and during the 1986 performance, a commemorative seat was dedicated to Bill. It is still there, looking out over the area where the

> ## '... the Turkish group exhibited a feral power the others lacked'

dancing had taken place since the first Festival. The dedication was attended by Bill's widow, Terry, who is still a familiar figure each year at the Festival, and also by Bill's son Julian and family, and by Taffy Thomas and family. Taffy was recovering well, and was able to thank the festival-goers in person for their support the previous year.

In the summer of 1986 the Commonwealth Games were held in Edinburgh, and the accompanying arts festival attracted dance groups from many Commonwealth countries. A couple of these groups were invited to Sidmouth. But the Games and arts festival were hit by controversy and boycotted by several African countries, because of the British government's refusal to impose sanctions on apartheid-ridden South Africa. The groups from Guyana and Sierra Leone withdrew from the Sidmouth Festival, to be replaced by groups from Tanzania and Ghana, who then also withdrew. The Gambian National Troupe was already in England and, thanks to Lucy Duran and Ian Anderson, the Gambian government allowed them to perform at Sidmouth. They arrived in the

Taffy and Sam Thomas with Julian Rutter and family and Bill's wife Terry on 'Bill's seat'

Dembo Konte

town almost a week early, and Clive Morgan helped to arrange extra performances around the area to pay for the additional costs.

One of the musicians from The Gambia played the kora, a multi-stringed instrument, and his name was Dembo Konte. Within a year, Dembo and another musician Kausu Kuyateh from Senegal had released their own album, *Tanante*, in Britain and their tour of this country was sold out. They later recorded *Jali Roll* with 3 Mustaphas 3, John Kirkpatrick and Ian Anderson as backing musicians, and this album was World Music Album of the Year in *Q* magazine. For a while, the music of The Gambia, and the kora in particular, became one of the most popular and sought after examples of the newly-merging 'world music'. The *Festival News* carried a comment about the Gambian musicians from a group of young festival-goers, 'the best thing we have ever experienced at Sidmouth; the atmosphere when they play is the atmosphere we would love to see more of here'. *The Southern Rag* had become the monthly *Folk Roots* in mid-1985, and the magazine championed a greater awareness of world music. A correspondent to the magazine wrote of the 'wildness' of the Gambians' reception at their Late Night Extra spot, and editor Ian Anderson still recalls Dembo's panic-stricken face when he was whirled round the dance floor during the ceilidh.

...'a significant and most wonderful part of my life'

Lou Cieri from France and Hupsakee from the Netherlands both returned to the Festival, and other overseas groups came from Czechoslovakia and Canada whilst Ozel Cavusoglu Lisesi came from Turkey. Veselka was a group of Ukrainian dancers from near Manchester, and the other English dance groups included Handsworth Traditional Sword Dancers, Derby Crown, King John's Morris and Oyster Morris. According to Nick Beale, the *Folk Roots* reviewer of the Festival, the Turkish group was 'fast and furious in music and dance, exhibiting a feral power the others lacked'.

By now, all the overseas dance groups were being accommodated in Sidmouth College, the comprehensive school situated in the Primley area of the town. Known as Primley Hostel, the school also accommodated members of Task Force during build-up week. A team of local residents, for many years led by Alice Brooks, provided all the meals for the dancers. In addition to the Hostel Manager, the Festival volunteers included the hostel staff, who provided security and attended to the general welfare of the overseas dancers, and the team guides. The longest-established team guide was Viv Smith, who first came to the Festival in the early seventies to look after a group from Turkey. Indeed, as she had a particular interest in Turkish folk dancing, she was the team guide for every Turkish group the Festival has ever invited. In the late eighties and nineties, three sisters – Anna, Helena and Louisa Guest – were all team guides and Helena and her husband Jeremy Mitchinson were Hostel Managers for several years. Naomi Martin was another long-standing team guide whose fluency in Russian was a great asset.

For Viv the Festival has been 'a significant and most wonderful part of my life' and although the Hostel

Bob Copper and Eddie Upton in the Dove's silent singaround

Lou Cieri from France

The Thirty-second Festival – Friday 1st - Friday 8th August 1986

Gambian dancers in procession, 1986

disappeared several years ago, Viv and her daughter Hannah continue to come to the Festival every year. She feels that the friendly atmosphere in the Hostel was an important factor in bringing out the best in the groups in performance. She was always interested to observe how the groups got on with each other and she enjoyed facilitating the camaraderie. Viv remembers that one of the cooks in the hostel married an Italian flag-waver and, that as a result of the Silver Jubilee Festival, one of the Turkish dancers married one of the Canadians. In addition to the friendships forged between the groups, several of the team guides later visited the countries of their groups, most spectacularly Carolyn Booth who spent her honeymoon in Borneo. Gaffer Ferris is another

long-standing hostel volunteer, and was always one of the first people to meet each group as they arrived – his clown's outfit was guaranteed to make the dancers smile and put them at their ease.

The two-year rule meant that each of the four producers – Arena, Dance, Song and Children – served just two years, so that two of them changed every year. Eddie Upton, who had previously been a Dance Producer took over as Arena Producer. The 1986 *Festival News* carried a feature from each of the Producers about their approach to their role. For Eddie Upton, the Arena was the feature that made the Festival unique amongst British folk festivals. He regarded the public

face that the Arena presented as vital in preventing the folk movement from becoming introspective. 'It provides a rare opportunity for presenting folk as a spectacular entertainment.' With his recent experience of five months working with a theatre company, Eddie was concerned about presentation – a feature that he felt was sometimes lacking in folk music and dance performances – and he believed that the Arena could heighten awareness.

Gordon Potts was the new Dance Producer: he was a member of Hammersmith Morris and one of the organisers of the 'Knees Up Cecil Sharp' ceilidhs at Cecil Sharp House. Gordon may have been from a ceilidh background, but as a former manager of the Folk Shop at Cecil Sharp House, he knew about the EFDSS club dancers. His approach to each of the events he was responsible for was to put himself in the position of someone he knew – what would that person want in terms of callers, bands and workshops? One of his concerns was to encourage new bands and callers, and the final Drill Hall ceilidh featured musicians from the 'Playing for Absolute Beginners' workshop and callers from the 'Calling for Absolute Beginners' workshop. It was a theme that he has promoted at the Festival through to the present day. Two unscheduled workshops were advertised in the *Festival News*: a couple of Appalachian flat-foot style clogging workshops led by Ira Bernstein who just turned up at the Festival.

Edward II and the Red Hot Polkas made their Sidmouth debut in 1986, the members being Rod and Danny Stradling, their son Barnaby, John Gill, Tom Greenhalgh, Dave Haines and Jon Moore. The band combined mainly English traditional tunes with Caribbean rhythms. From Scotland

Ozel Cavusoglu Lisesi from Turkey

- *Chernobyl disaster in Ukraine*
- *3.25 million unemployed*
- *Privatisation of British Gas*
- *GCSEs replace O-levels and CSEs*
- *Perestroika in USSR*
- *Spitting Image's The Chicken Song and Living Doll from Cliff Richard and The Young Ones at No 1*

came The Wallochmor Ceilidh Band, who included accordion player Freeland Barbour, and who were challenging the established Royal Scottish Country Dance Society approach to Scottish dancing. Gordon Potts remembers their 'superb' LNE with Hugh Rippon calling. Country dance bands included Richard Smith's Blue Mountain Band, Wild Thyme and The Quarry Turners, whilst the Playford dancers again had a contrast of approaches, this time from Tom Cook and Mike Barraclough.

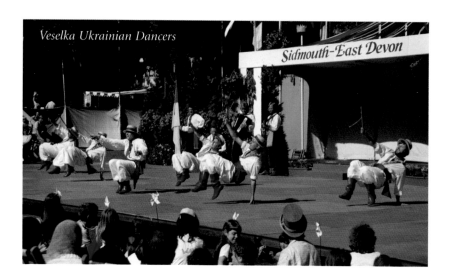

Veselka Ukrainian Dancers

Sidmouth-East Devon

The song side of the Festival lost one of its long-standing venues, when the Beach Store was demolished, along with the garage on the Esplanade, to make room for the new housing development on the corner of Ham Lane. In his report, John Dowell had described the Beach Store as a 'dirty old shed with a sandy floor and broken seats' whose 'demise is probably long overdue'. But it did have character and was once described as the 'spiritual home of the English folk revival'. It is remembered now with nostalgia, not only by the audiences, but also by the children who played in the sand and subconsciously absorbed the music – Jim Moray is just one example.

SWEB had already joined the list of venues in 1985, and now the Radway Cinema was used for the first time. This was more than a replacement for the Beach Store – it represented an improvement in comfort and capacity, and had the potential for better presentation and higher quality guests. But of course it was more costly to hire and equip than the Beach Store. It was also a concert venue rather than a 'club' venue, but the change seemed to be symbolic of the way the folk scene was shifting. Nevertheless, The Marlborough, SWEB, Carinas and the Sailing Club all had 'come all ye' events so that an intimate singing environment was available. The cinema had previously been a theatre so that there was already a good stage, and Song Producer Pat Ryan became the first performer to sing in the venue, which

was just used in the evenings.

Many people remember the comfort of the Radway Cinema. 'I missed half the concerts I went to because I fell asleep – it was so comfortable', remembers Marion Percy, who contrasted it with Carinas – 'dark, airless and uncomfortable but wonderfully atmospheric'. A few years later, Margaret and Peter Vipond were on holiday in Sidmouth during the Festival and, although they had no knowledge of folk

> ... 'dark, airless and uncomfortable but wonderfully atmospheric'

music, decided to join the queue outside the Radway Cinema. All the seats were taken, so they sat on the floor and watched 'an amazing performance' by Token Women. 'We were hooked and now come to Sidmouth every year – and it all began on the floor of the Radway!'

Carinas was now being used throughout the day, with a morning talk, 'Meet the Band' concert at lunchtime, afternoon Come all Ye with guests, a tea-time event such as 'Juke Box Jury' with Ian Anderson playing the part of David Jacobs, and panellists who included Jim Lloyd, Kathryn Tickell and Barnaby Stradling, and an evening concert. The Drill Hall still hosted the 'At Home' events at lunchtime and late afternoon mini-concerts. The

Assembly Rooms hosted concerts in the afternoon and dances in the evening, whilst the Sailing Club became the Song Swop and Ballad Session venue.

Whilst The Anchor was full of singers, musicians and dancers, The Dove remained a music-free zone. Although the pub welcomed festival-goers, the publican did not want any music or singing, and over time its central location meant that it became a meeting place for the producers, comperes and some artists. In the days before widespread ownership of mobile phones, it was the quickest and easiest way of contacting people or leaving messages. From the mid-eighties, the jokers in the pub started their own silent singaround, and the photograph shows Eddie Upton and Bob Copper silently 'performing' one of the Copper family's classics in 1985. Bob was the judge of the song competition that year, and in 1986 he and Ursula Vaughan Williams, widow of the composer and Vice-President of the EFDSS, were guests of honour at the premiere of the EFDSS's film of The Copper Family.

The song guests included Dave Burland, the Kipper Family, John Kirkpatrick and Sue Harris, traditional singers Charlie Hill from Dartmoor and Shropshire's Fred Jordan. Dave Swarbrick's band Whippersnapper, made their Festival debut, as did Sheffield duo John Leonard and John Squire, and Cockersdale. John Leonard is now director of the independent radio production company Smooth Operations that produces the Mike Harding folk music programme. Nineteen-year-old Kathryn Tickell made her second Festival visit – since 1983 her first album had been released, she had been appointed piper to the Lord Mayor of Newcastle-upon-Tyne and had become a professional musician.

The Monday evening Arena concert featured The Yetties, now minus Bob Common who had left the group in 1979. They were supported in the concert by Tony Rose, and by the re-formed Isca Fayre from Exeter whose members included Barry Lister and Martin Bloomer.

Bits of Kids were, according to the Souvenir Programme, a 'group of young musicians whose childhood was spent being taken to festivals and folk clubs – they are now old enough to fight back'. The members included Barnaby Stradling and Tristan Glover. There seemed some hope for the future.

There was some discussion in the Festival News about where the 'real' Sidmouth Festival was – was it the Late Night Extra, along the Esplanade or up at the Arena? David Slater, in his second year as producer of the children's events, dismissed such discussion as 'erudite' and a diversion. 'The fact is that the "real" Sidmouth of the year 2000 and onwards is very easily identified and its nurture and growth ought to be very important to all of us', David wrote. Indeed, his concern for the folk music and dance activities of the children has borne fruit in the Festival of the twenty-first century.

David laid out his 'objectives', which included providing fun, developing skills, identifying and encouraging real talent and helping the children to distinguish clearly between what he called 'come all ye' and 'advanced' and between 'folk' and 'display'. He also highlighted the fact that, for the children, there were fourteen separate workshops and nine other major events attracting, on the Monday, sixty children to the Morris Minors, 180 to the Hobby Horse Club, ninety to the singalong, eighty-five to the maypole dancing,

fifty-five to the clog workshop, sixty-five to street theatre, and almost 250 to the other workshops: of course some children attended more than one event. One of the events that started in David's time was the evening Family Ceilidh or Concert in St Francis Hall beyond the Balfour Arms. It was David who decided that 'Children's Festival' was an appropriate term for the collection of

> **Sid was surprised they had Rod Stradling in Sidmouth because he thought it was an old custom that was confined to Norfolk**

events he had been organising.

David was of course a Church of England minister, and during the week, when the rain was affecting yet another day's events, he was heard to mutter, 'Lord, if this is what you do to your friends, it's a miracle you've got any!' David Slater's clerical duties were in evidence on Tuesday when he conducted the marriage of Ken and Naomi Jones, who were at the Festival with the Preston Royal Morris Dancers. The desire to celebrate the occasion with a few of their fellow folk enthusiasts ended up with large crowds at the Parish Church and displays from four Morris sides.

The Festival News appeared to contain less trivia than in former years – some bemoaned this change, but it

was essential in order to present the Festival as open and welcoming, rather than the preserve of an 'in crowd' clique. Whether by design or accident, the Festival News also contained some longer features by festival-goers, including reviews or comments on aspects of the Festival. Gavin Atkin, now of the ceilidh band Florida, wrote a review of the informal sessions in the pubs, whilst anonymous critical comment on the wider folk scene and some aspects of the Festival was written by 'Mouth of Sid'. On several days, the Festival News managed to intercept postcards home from Henry and Sid Kipper and the contents were published. Sid was surprised that they had Rod Stradling in Sidmouth because he thought it was an old custom that was confined to Norfolk. But as Sid was the All-Trunch Champion Rod Stradler of 1978, he thought he might win. Some of Les Barker's poems were published in the Festival News as well, although he was not officially booked at the Festival.

The Festival was a financial disaster for the EFDSS, and this contributed to a financial crisis and some difficult decisions, most controversial of which was the proposal to sell the London headquarters building Cecil Sharp House. Opposed by some members, the protracted campaign to 'save the House' cost the EFDSS its credibility, many of its members and a great deal of money. In the end, the House was not sold, but the EFDSS as a national organisation has been slow to recover. But that is a different story: after thirty-two years, the Sidmouth Festival was 'under new management'.

The Gambians enjoy a cream tea in the Mocha

Under New Management

1987 Steve Heap and John Heydon recognised that changes to the Festival were necessary, but that the changes had to carry the existing audiences as well as develop new ones.

East Devon District Council supported the new arrangements, and after various assurances, was happy to switch its support to the new organisation. That support even extended to under-writing the Festival for up to £7,500 plus services and assistance to the value of £10,000. But with a budget that had now reached £130,000, there was still a huge financial risk which had to be borne by the new organisation. Change had to take place within the limits of a clear and tightly-controlled budget. To help boost ticket sales, day tickets were introduced for the first time. Local residents had long been able to buy discounted season tickets.

Steve Heap's involvement with the Festival went back as far as the sixties. Although he had sung at the Festival, and later compered song events, Steve's recent involvement had been in resource management. For several years he had been involved in setting up the Festival infrastructure with Task Force, and in dealing with venues and sound systems. The strengths he brought included a deep commitment to the Festival itself, a love of the music, a vision for the future and the ability to manage change.

Like Steve, John Heydon had a great passion for the music. He was a former Festival Song Producer,

- *Herald of Free Enterprise car ferry capsizes: 188 people die*
- *Hurricane hits southern England*
- *King's Cross tube fire: 31 people die*
- *Terry Waite taken hostage in Beirut*
- *Pet Shop Boys, T'Pau and Rick Astley at No 1*

organiser of the Herga Folk Club in Middlesex and the Haddenham Ceilidhs in Oxfordshire and director of Dragon Records. John also had his own accountancy firm in Aylesbury, so his financial skills were a great asset, although the day-to-day involvement with the Festival fell to Steve.

John Dowell continued as the Festival Director, but a new Song Producer was needed and John selected Alan Bearman. Organiser of London's Chestnuts Folk Club and Festival, Alan was unlike all his predecessors in that he was neither a singer nor a compere. He had the ability to select guests that would fill a

> ## ... there was a huge financial risk which had to be borne by the new organisation

venue, was an excellent and meticulous organiser, and a Sidmouth Festival goer for several years. At first, Alan was, like all the other Producers, a volunteer, doing the work in his spare time. Nigel Barrell from Hampshire became the new Children's Festival Producer after several years working in this part of the Festival.

Alan immediately set about tackling the three interconnecting issues of artists, venues and events. Two letters written by Alan in September 1986 and September 1987 set out many of the proposals for change which were put into effect over the following few years. Alan considered that festivals were different from folk clubs at both ends – there was the opportunity to invite traditional performers who could perform in a relaxed setting, but also to invite top-rated concert performers. Alan felt that themed events were something that festivals could do that clubs or one-off concerts could not, and they made

for more interesting programming than a succession of concerts. Other festivals booked too many middle of the range guests, Alan believed, but Sidmouth had the potential to do something different. More guests were booked for just part of the week, or increasingly, for just a couple of events. It was to become a feature of Alan's policy to book artists, or combinations of artists, who were not generally seen on the concert or festival scene – it has become a feature that has make Sidmouth unique. In arranging individual concerts, Alan was concerned to choose performers who would complement each other and share the same audiences. He also wanted to agree on the sort of shows that were wanted, and then book artists who would fit the bill. This was rather different to the established approach of booking a set of guests, and then programming them into a succession of concerts and club-style events.

There was a clear need to find a larger concert venue which would then make it feasible to book some bigger-named guests. But at the same time, there was a need to protect the small-scale events which contributed to Sidmouth's unique atmosphere, and which gave the

Michelle Shocked

Blowzabella in the Drill Hall

opportunity for audience members to sing and play. There was a need to attract larger audiences, but it was not simply a matter of finding new venues so that existing events could be duplicated – new venues would mean new styles of event, attracting new, but perhaps different, audiences. It was also important to make better use of existing venues.

The Arena Marquee was the wet-weather venue for Arena shows – thankfully, after two years of extensive usage, it was hardly needed in that capacity in 1987. It was available before the 3.00pm Arena shows and, with the Meet the Team events concentrated at the Ham Marquee, in the tea-time gap between the afternoon and evening shows.

On Tuesday and Wednesday, tea-time concerts in the Arena Marquee featured first Home Service and then Michelle Shocked. Home Service was made up of musicians who had worked at the National Theatre on such productions as *Lark Rise* and *The Mysteries*, so that concert gigs

outside London were rare. Band member John Tams was ill, and his replacement as singer, John B. Spencer, disappointed John Tams's many admirers. Michelle Shocked was a singer-songwriter from Texas whose first LP, recorded in a field on a Sony Walkman, had gone to the top of the independent charts in Britain. Problems with sound-checking, long queues and a single entrance meant that both concerts started late, and obviously something different was needed for the following year.

The Radway Cinema had a capacity of 400 people, and its use was now extended to the afternoons as well as the evenings. Carinas continued to be used throughout the day with themed events in the evening – one night was blues, jazz and skiffle, another was a concert of artists 'From the North'.

The Manor Pavilion had generally only been used for the Sunday evening concert, with the summer repertory company using the theatre during the week, whilst the Arts

Centre had been used for the Folk Shop. But now the closer links with East Devon District Council meant that the whole Manor Pavilion and Arts Centre complex was available to the Festival for the whole week. The Folk Shop moved to the Lower Methodist Hall, so that the Arts Centre could be used for events. The Manor Pavilion hosted talks and the occasional concert at lunchtime, and afternoon and evening concerts. The Arts Centre was mainly used for the less formal events – children's singalongs in the morning, family singarounds at lunchtime, song workshops in the afternoon, the Sidmouth Singer competition at tea-time, and a Folk Club in the evening. The approach was to use a venue as much as possible throughout the day and evening.

Singarounds were also held in the Marlborough Hotel in the morning, and in the New Tavern at lunchtime and in the evenings. The licensing laws still meant that the pubs closed at 2.30pm, which determined a finishing time for many events both in and out of the pubs. SWEB was now used for Festival Information, rather than for events.

For the uninitiated, the programme explained the subtleties of the event titles: the Come All Ye and Folk Club included floor singers – a couple of songs each – whilst a singaround was one song each round the room (including booked artists). Alan wanted to make it clear what customers could expect from an event.

Some of the previously-unbooked performers in 1987 were Roy Bailey,

Christine Collister and Clive Gregson in Carinas

Cosmotheka and Andrew Frank 'In the Box'

Siverko

Christine Collister and Clive Gregson, 3 Mustaphas 3, Roger Wilson, Jez Lowe and Sileas. Roaring Jelly came out of retirement for a Festival appearance, whilst Chris Wood and Andy Turner performed as a duo. Amongst the special or themed events were 'Christmas at Mellstock' with Dave Townsend and the Mellstock Band, Ashley Hutchings's 'An Evening with Cecil Sharp' show, a Dartmoor Concert with Bob Cann and friends, and two shows featuring Cosmotheka – 'The Black Sheep of the Family' and 'In the Box' with Andrew Frank.

There was a series of women's song sessions, featuring Peta Webb, Janet Russell and others, under the labels 'Finding a Voice' and 'Sisters in Song'.

The Parish Church also became a venue for the first time in 1987. The aim was to include performers who would appeal more to the casual visitor as well as to the local residents: it was an extension of the Festival into the community. A series of evening concerts, which attracted financial support from Devon County Council, included the television actor David Kossoff, who repeated his television and radio success with his Old Testament 'story-telling'; Dartington Gamelan Orchestra and The Yetties with their music, songs and readings based on Thomas Hardy.

For the dancers, there was a full range of workshops plus the lunchtime ceilidh in the Anchor Garden, a Typhoo Tea Dance (sponsored by the tea company) in

the Ham Marquee which overlapped with a Connoisseurs Dance in the Drill Hall in the late afternoon. In the evening, the 'Experienced Dancers Only' events continued in the Bowd Marquee, and there were

> **What was needed was a sensational dance group that would capture the attention of the general public**

dances in the Ham Marquee, where the callers and bands were given clear instructions that the events were aimed at the general public, and that dances should be chosen accordingly. The village hall dances continued and during the week there were three dances in Sidford, billed as ceilidhs or barn dances. There were Ceilidhs in the Drill Hall (although on Monday there was a Cajun Night with R. Cajun and the Zydeco Brothers) and, of course, at the Late Night Extra. For a few years alternative late night events were held in Carinas. Blowzabella had already added Nigel Eaton and Ian Luff to the line-up, but Jon Swayne had left, to be replaced by Jo Fraser and the Blowzabella sound became more saxophone-based.

Across the Festival, there appeared to be a more clearly structured series of events appealing to all interests and all levels of interest: something for the beginners and the

experienced, something informal and formal, something for those who wanted to participate and something for those who wanted to sit and listen.

More time, energy and money were spent in publicising the Festival. This was not just in the specialist magazines to reassure the folk enthusiasts that the new management was going to produce an even better Festival, but there was also more publicity in the tourist and arts publications. What was needed was a sensational dance group that would capture the attention of the general public – and the Festival found one: Siverko.

Siverko came from Arkhangelsk, inside the Arctic Circle in the Soviet Union. With their blonde hair, the women appeared to be identical, and the *Sidmouth Herald* described them as having 'porcelain-fair skin' which made them 'pretty as dolls'. The folk enthusiasts were a little sceptical of their highly choreographed style, especially with the pretend accordions and balalaikas, but the Arena audiences loved them. On Wednesday evening, they had the whole Arena Show (billed as 'Soviet Night') to themselves – the first time this had ever happened. Their two-hour concert ended with a standing ovation and three encores. Siverko's visit to this country was arranged by Irena Novikova, who went on to organise visits from several other groups from the Soviet Union, and later Russia.

Incantation

John Dowell being interviewed by Jenni Murray

There was a return visit from the Greek group Kalarrytes, plus dance groups from Poland, Sicily and Germany. The Malgache group from Madagascar only just managed to arrange their visas, thanks to the intervention of the local MP. Another Basque group, Itsasi, again had the English audiences wondering about the similarities with the English Morris and sword dances. The leader of the Patrick Farrington Irish Dancers, who also appeared, had first visited the Festival in the mid-sixties with the Rory O'Connor Dancers.

Festival guests Mr Jorrocks Morris were faced with the tragic death of their musician John Gasson in a car accident on his way to the Festival. John was also a member of the band Melons for Ecstasy and of the Seven Champions Molly Dancers, who went on to win the Ritual Dance Competition the day after John's death. The solo English jig competition at the Festival was started the following year and named in John's memory. Tracey Rose has organised the competition each year since. Tracey's husband Chris is a member of Seven Champions.

David Slater's dance group Woodfidley plus Wakefield Morris, Green Ginger Clog Dancers and Carlisle Sword and Morris Dancers all danced at the Arena. Stroud Morris became the first women's Cotswold Morris team to dance at the Arena since England's Glory in the seventies.

Monday evening at the Arena saw Incantation, a band that had enjoyed chart success with 'Cacharpaya'. Their music came from the Andes Mountains in South America and had been featured on the soundtrack of the film *The Mission*. The original line-up had been extended to include three Chilean musicians.

The Festival achieved some valuable publicity when it played host to a live broadcast, from the Arena stage, of BBC Radio 4's *Woman's Hour* programme on the Friday the Festival opened. The guests included television chef Keith Floyd.

A new organisation, The Friends of Sidmouth Festival, was established and the launch in April attracted over 200 people, with a number of local businesses becoming members of the Patrons' Scheme. Lord O'Hagan, the local Euro-MP, became the President. Members of the Friends were able to attend the late night Festival Club at the Assembly Rooms, featuring some of the Festival guests, but the lure of LNE was too strong to attract large numbers of people.

Perhaps more important than any of the changes to the Festival, was the fact that the sun shone, and there was no rain. The Festival almost broke even, and the loss of £334 could have been wiped out if just ten more season tickets had been sold. The Festival's future was more certain, and the new management could set about planning another year.

Musician from Kalarrytes, Greece

World Music

Hassan Erraji

1988 One of the key changes to the wider music scene in the 1980s was the recognition and appreciation that the classical, popular and folk musics of America and Western Europe were by no means the limit of world-wide musical expression. *Folk Roots* magazine, edited by Ian Anderson, increasingly featured world or roots music. WOMAD (World of Music and Dance) was a new organisation in the promotion of the music, and their festivals provided both competition and a different approach to the established folk festival scene.

Sidmouth was of course very experienced in dealing with performers from a wide variety of countries and the audiences expected a strong international dimension. The Welcome message in the first daily *Festival News* summed up the position: 'Sidmouth Festival has presented musicians from dozens of countries over the years, usually accompanying dance groups, so we are delighted at the interest being shown in world music at the moment.'

After the 1987 Festival, Alan Bearman had observed that relying on the musicians of overseas dance groups for concert spots was too problematic. 'We must feature more world music', he wrote.

So, in 1988, in addition to the eight dance groups from four continents, the Festival also booked bands or solo performers from six additional countries. These performers were Gwerz from Brittany; Hassan Erraji from Morocco; Gambian kora player, thirteen-year-old Pa Jobarteh (sponsored at the Festival by *Folk Roots*); The Barra MacNeils from Nova Scotia; Ritmia from Italy and Filarfolket from Sweden. This represented a large commitment to capture a new audience, as well as to develop the enthusiasm of existing audiences. Paul James of Blowzabella played a major part in bringing some of the European bands to the Festival.

> '... we are delighted at the interest being shown in world music'

Gwerz plus Bernard Lasbliez and Rosbif presented a Fest Noz – an evening of Breton dancing, following a workshop earlier in the day. Ritmia was one of Italy's top traditional music bands, featuring the excellent melodeon player Riccardo Tesi, and they appeared at 'Meet the Band', a Radway concert, a melodeon music concert, a workshop and a 'Latin Evening' in the Ham Marquee alongside the Sardinian dance group Salesiano – all in two days. Filarfolket also played for a Swedish dance workshop, as well as appearing in concert.

The overseas dance groups included The Wild Goose Chase Cloggers from the USA, whose dancing was derived from the Green Grass Cloggers which was also the style favoured by the emerging British Appalachian dance groups. The group led a series of morning workshops in the Council Chamber at the Assembly Rooms which further extended the growing interest in this dance form. From New Zealand came the first Maori group to visit the Festival: The Tumatauenga Maori Cultural Group, whose tongue-pulling war dance, the haka, was a big hit with the audience. For the first time, a group from Malaysia visited the Festival. English groups included Adderbury Morris Men and Seven Champions. My own visits to the Festival during the eighties had been occasional: after attending the Festival every year from 1971 to 1980, I returned with the Manley

The Wild Goose Chase Cloggers

The National Folk Dance Group of Grenada

Morris Dancers in 1983, and visited for a few days at a time in 1986 and 1987, but in 1988 I joined John Braithwaite as one of the two Arena comperes. This was the start of my involvement with the Arena and the dance groups which has continued in various guises to the present day.

Steve Heap did not regard the two-year rule as sacrosanct, and Eddie Upton became the first Producer to continue beyond the two years. In fact he stayed as Arena Producer from 1986 through until 1991, although during that time the role changed. After the 1987 Soviet Night, Eddie continued the themed evenings with a Caribbean Night on Thursday, featuring the group from Grenada and a steel band.

The policy of including dance and music groups from the non-indigenous communities in England continued, and London-based Taxi Pata Pata, led by Nsimba Foguis from Zaire visited the Festival. Some of the British folk bands were also opening up to multi-cultural influences – Roger Watson's band Chequered Roots, Tiger Moth (Ian Anderson, Maggie Holland, Rod Stradling, Chris Coe, John Maxwell

and Jon Moore), as well as The Oyster Band were all booked at the Festival. In the *Folk Roots* Readers' Poll in early 1988, The Oyster Band came first in the group, dance band and album categories.

This expansion of the Festival into world roots music did not mean

> ### *the loud event they were complaining about was ... the Spinners in the Arena*

that the traditional music of Britain and Ireland was neglected. Indeed, 'In the Tradition' had been used in 1987 for a couple of events featuring The Old Hat Concert Party (John and Katie Howson's band plus Suffolk traditional singers such as Ted Chaplin), and this was extended dramatically in 1988. The title was used for a daily lunchtime music and song session in The Volunteer Inn as well as for other events, mainly in the Manor Pavilion, and John Howson was the master of ceremonies.

'In the Tradition' guests in 1988 included Sussex singer Gordon Hall, Jeff Wesley, the three Northumbrian shepherds Joe Hutton, Willy Taylor and Will Atkinson plus Alistair Anderson, Dave and Betty Campbell, Bob Davenport and Jim and Lynnette Eldon.

The Spinners were the best known folk group in England, especially through their television appearances, but in 1988 they embarked on their farewell tour before retirement. They were therefore a natural choice for the Monday night Arena Concert, which was their last performance in Devon. Tiger Moth played for the Ham Ceilidh the same evening, and Ian Anderson remembers that on Tuesday morning the police received complaints about the volume of the music the previous evening: 'Just as I was puffing up with pride, it turned out that the loud event they were complaining about was ... the Spinners in the Arena!'

Other guests included return visits after several years' absence for June Tabor, accompanied by Huw Warren, and Frankie Armstrong. The Kipper Family had now fallen into the habit of being booked every two years (a situation which continues with Sid Kipper's solo bookings) and on each occasion they presented a new show. In 1988 it was The Crab Wars, their epic folk opera. Most afternoons in Carinas, there was a Showcase event for visiting singers and musicians, plus a guest. The evening Carinas concerts were for season ticket holders only, in order to increase the value of the season tickets, and these events were generally themed: 'Puffing and Blowing' (based on how people played their instruments), 'From the North of the A57' and a songwriters' concert. Elsewhere there were concerts for pipers and for box players as well as an Early Music concert.

The Arena Marquee was again used for a couple of concerts, at lunchtime, featuring The Oyster Band and Taxi Pata Pata. Alan Bearman and John Dowell were clearly testing out the best times to run such events.

'The Festival in the Church' continued with concerts by a silver band, The York Waits (commemorating the 400th anniversary of the Armada – they also played for The Dancing Master's Ball) and an evening of 'Tall Tales' from the radio and television personality Johnny Morris, well known for his *Animal Magic* programmes. The Vicar welcomed the Festival to his church, and David Slater helped with the arrangements.

Late Night Extra on Thursday saw a one-off appearance by the 'Dan Quinn All-Stars', which was a thinly disguised *first* reunion of the original members of Flowers and Frolics. Bob Mallindine became Dance Producer, and other bands included Ran Tan from Lancashire (with Martin Ellison), the all-female band from Sheffield Airs and Graces, as well as Hoedown from London, and Sidmouth favourites Orange and Blue and the Weston Country Dance Band. Callers included Charles Bolton, Bernard Chalk and Colin Hume, as well as Dave Hunt, Mary Panton and Hugh Rippon.

Steve Heap had a long-term vision for the Knowle Arena site, a vision which has come to fruition over a fifteen-year period. The Craft Marquee was becoming very popular and the Sidmouth Chamber of Commerce, observing the increasing number of visitors to the Arena site, was keen to have its own marquee so that local shops could have a presence. Over the following few years, first Trade Stalls and then a Music Fair joined the Craft Stalls on the Arena site.

For the first time, the Children's Festival had a theme – Down on the Farm – which involved workshops and a Fancy Dress Procession prior to the Showcase Ceilidh in the Blackmore Gardens on Thursday evening. The showcase had been incorporated into the Friday afternoon Arena Show which was aimed specifically at children, but the diversity and number of workshops now meant that a smaller-scale event was needed, hence the Thursday ceilidh. For the first time, Sidmouth Town Council gave a special grant towards the Children's Festival.

In about 1986, John Dowell and Tony Day of the Middle Bar Singers met by chance on a train to

Dave Burland, Jim Boyes, Dave Brady, Pete Morton and Ralph Jordan in Carinas

Birmingham, and John explained the financial problems besetting the Festival. This led to the Middle Bar Singers' Winter Reunion Weekend, which was first held in February 1987, and which took the form of a twenty-four hour sponsored singaround in The Anchor. In the first year, over £500 was raised for the Festival and 470 songs were sung, increasing to almost £700 and 513 songs in 1988. The Reunion Weekend continues to this day.

There were further events in the town during the winter months. The Friends of Sidmouth Festival organised a ceilidh in December 1987, in February Christine Collister and Clive Gregson performed at Carinas, and in March Sidmouth Accordion Orchestra, Pete Shutler from The Yetties, and the Devon Youth Jazz Orchestra featured in

two concerts in the Council Chamber. These events were intended to appeal to the local townspeople as well as attract festival-goers to enjoy a weekend break in Sidmouth. The Friends soon had 1,000 members.

The Folk Shop was relocated to the SWEB building: for a few years, the EFDSS still operated the shop in conjunction with Projection Records. Across the road on the Ham, Chez Nous took up residence as the caterer, whilst up at the Arena a local business, JKL Video, started to video the Arena shows.

And the 1988 Festival had another name change – 'Sidmouth International Festival of Folk Arts'. The sun shone again and the Festival's renewed success and higher profile were acknowledged in reviews in both *The Guardian* and *The Independent* newspapers.

A Wealth of Workshops

1989 The big-name concert artists and spectacular overseas dance groups may have caught the headlines year after year, but for many season ticket holders the workshops were a major attraction, providing the opportunity to pick up or develop skills and learn more about the folk music and dance of Britain and beyond.

The individual producers now had responsibility for programming workshops in their particular areas, and although the early years of the workshop programme had been predominantly instrumental music and English dance, the range of events had diversified over the years. In the Festival Newsletter sent out early in the year to potential ticket buyers, John Dowell suggested that the Festival had tended to take the workshops for granted and, although this was perhaps a little harsh, this area of the Festival was further developed in 1989, with the philosophy 'if there is a demand, we will put it on'.

At the 1988 Festival, Chris Wade from the Adastra agency and Beverley Folk Festival had had the job of overseeing the workshop programme. A survey and questionnaire revealed some startling facts: about 2,000 people each day took part in the workshops, with a staggering 11,500 attendances covering 165 individual workshops. Clearly the Festival was providing a major programme of

training and education, and over the years many people have derived inspiration from the workshops to start their own dance groups, play a musical instrument, or have discovered hidden talents that they never knew they had.

The workshops at the 1989 Festival give an idea of the range of interests covered. The social dancer could start at 9.30am with a choice of Beginners' Country Dance with Hugh Rippon, or American Dance with John Chapman, moving on at 11.15am to Dance Technique or Dances of the British Isles (two days each on Celtic, Welsh, Scottish and Irish). After a fifteen minute break,

> ### ... a staggering 11,500 attendances covering 165 workshops

the dancing continued at 1.00pm with Playford dances from John Lagden, followed by two separate workshop series covering a variety of dance styles (Wessex, Breton, Italian, Arab, Indian, one led by Blowzabella and four covering Cajun dance, the latest dance craze).

The display dancer had the choice of Morris dancing (advanced at 9.30am or beginners at 4.15pm), longsword with Trevor Stone, North West with Horwich Prize Medal Morris, rapper sword, beginners' clog, advanced clog, and, for the first

time, Appalachian Clog led by an English group – Broken Ankles from Sussex. Clann na Gael leader Barbara Slater also led some choreography workshops, which formed part of a greater emphasis on the presentation of traditional dance.

Most of the workshops for individual instruments were one-off events (daily sessions on Northumbrian pipes, handbells and guitar were the exception) and these included hammer dulcimer, bodhran (finally, after nine years of unofficial events and many requests in the *Festival News*), bones, pipes, banjo, drumming styles of the Pacific (given by the American dance group Dances of the Pacific), English fiddle, harp and ocarina. There was also the opportunity for musicians to develop their skills by playing with fellow musicians: Dave Townsend led a concertina band workshop and the Sidmouth Festival Folkestra made its debut under Guy Crayford. Dave Townsend also led the Festival's first West Gallery Music workshop: playing the music of the church bands of the nineteenth century that Rollo Woods had trailed over ten years previously.

Workshops for singing were not as developed as the dance workshops. Frankie Armstrong had led the way with a different type of song workshop: 'Finding your Voice', and at Sidmouth for a few years, Bill Long from Hampshire led a 'Voice Technique' workshop. There were also workshops on harmony, song

Dave Townsend's workshop

John Lagden

Rokoto

Filarfolket

writing (from Leon Rosselson), the songs collected by Baring-Gould and Balkan vocal techniques. Keith Summers brought his eclectic tastes and record collection to Sidmouth, delivering a five-part history of country and western music, and also introducing speakers on a variety of topics, from travellers' songs from Cornwall, to North-West Morris dancing, to American ballads, to English dance music.

Then there were community folk theatre workshops, storytelling workshops, discussions about giants, origami (from regular festival-goer Dennis Byers who was a fixture on the Esplanade displaying his paper-folding skills) and 'Running along the Cliffs' workshop for joggers, led by Les Barker.

All of this activity was aimed at the adults. Workshops were also an important part of the Children's Festival, although there was less of a distinction between the workshops and the other activities. Margaret Hordley had taken over as Children's Producer, and amongst the activities available to the children were

longsword, clog, North-West Morris, garland, broom, and maypole dancing, as well as Morris Minors. There were also workshops for musicians, for singers (including a harmony workshop), and for making corn dollies and musical instruments. After many years, the Hobby Horse Club disappeared from the Children's Festival programme, to be replaced by the Blackmore Gardens Club and other events. The children also had the opportunity to go on nature trails and to listen to stories told by Taffy Thomas and Duncan Williamson. There were games, puppets, the playgroup and a crèche.

The children's workshop programme again culminated in the Showcase Ceilidh on Thursday evening in the Blackmore Gardens, preceded by a fancy dress procession. This was sponsored by J.Sainsbury plc. The Children's Arena Show on Friday afternoon now disappeared from the programme.

Building on earlier successes, Eddie Upton scheduled themes for four of the evening shows. Monday was African Night with The African Experience from Gambia and Abdul

Tee-Jay's Rokoto. The group from The Gambia was based at an authentically reconstructed village, established in the wake of Alex Haley's book and television series, *Roots*. The group's dancers were accompanied on the distinctive kora and balafon. Whilst the Gambian group stuck to a traditional repertoire, Rokoto brought the sounds of modern African music: hi-life, hip, jazz, soca and soukous combined with an instrumental line-up that included keyboards, brass, guitars and drums. They soon had the audience up on their feet and dancing around the Arena site.

Tuesday was South Asian Dance Night, with the Pulasthi Art Circle from Sri Lanka yet again, and Mallika Sarabhai, a solo Indian dancer. On Wednesday, it was the turn of the Americas, with French-Canadian group Les Danseurs d'la Vallée St Jean, the Dances of the Pacific – a California-based group whose background and repertoire were drawn from Hawaii, Tonga, Samoa (including the Fire Knife

Marta Sebestyen

Only the Lonely – Chris, Keith and Kevin

Dance), the Cook Islands and Fiji, and old friends, Los Jairas from Bolivia. Nistreni from Moldavia in the USSR gave an extended one-hour performance on Thursday evening.

Ever since the Silver Jubilee, the Monday afternoon Arena Show had been for all the overseas groups, with the English dancers performing in the Connaught Gardens. The lack of a hard floor for the clog and other percussive dancers was a factor in bringing about a further change in 1989. The overseas groups kept their Monday afternoon, but Tuesday afternoon was billed as 'The Yetties Introduce the Dancers of Britain', which featured all the invited British dance groups – The Shropshire Bedlams and Martha Rhoden's Tuppenny Dish, Horwich Prize Medal Morris Dancers from Lancashire, Sheffield's Lizzie Dripping, the children's group Fosbrooks from Stockport, the Beacon Wheelchair Dancers, clog dancers Jane Vipond and Jane Lloyd and Clann na Gael. The growth in the number of Morris dance groups in England had been mirrored by a similar interest in the USA, and for the first time an American Morris dance group performed at the Festival – Berkeley Morris and The Swords of Gridlock – and they were also included in this

Dances of the Pacific

Horwich Prize Medal Morris Dancers

show. Some of the British dance groups were also included in the Meet the Team series of events.

The programming of international music and song bands continued, with the return of Sweden's Filarfolket, plus Baraban from Italy and Ti Jaz from Brittany. Blindman's Holiday was an Australian, all-female a capella quartet who specialised in vocal music from around the world. But the two bands that caused the greatest stir were The Davy Spillane Band from Ireland and Vujicsics with Marta Sebestyen from Hungary. The music of Hungary was having a great impact on the growing roots music scene, particularly through the band Muzsicas and the remarkable singer Marta Sebestyen. The repertoire of Vujicsics was drawn from Southern Hungary rather than the more familiar Transylvanian music, but they filled the Arena Marquee on Thursday lunchtime. Davy Spillane had been a member of the legendary Irish band Moving Hearts, and he also filled the Arena Marquee, this time on Wednesday.

Martin Carthy came to the Festival, together with Norma Waterson and their thirteen-year-old daughter Eliza. June Tabor appeared in concerts with Andrew Cronshaw, plus Huw Warren, Jim Sutherland, Ian Blake and Bernard O'Neill, and ceilidh band Tickled Pink made their Festival debut. Tickled Pink band member Simon Care had previously appeared at the Festival with Aunt Thelma's Candlelight Orchestra. Zumzeaux, Spring Chickens, Sisters Unlimited and the Black Spot Champions were amongst the other guests.

Les Barker had been a popular visitor to the Festival for several years. Originally, he used to perform his poems whilst his dog, Mrs Ackroyd, lazily sat on the stage. Sadly, Mrs Ackroyd had passed away, but her name lived on in the name of The Mrs Ackroyd Band (who played at Thursday's Late Night Extra). At the 1989 Festival, Les premiered his folk opera, 'The Stones of Callanish', with a cast which included Martin Carthy, June Tabor and Dan Quinn. There were two performances, afternoon and evening, in the Manor Pavilion on Wednesday. Another themed concert was 'The Liberty Tree: The Story of Tom Paine', presented by Roy Bailey and Leon Rosselson.

Keith Rusby had, by this time, left The Fabulous Salami Brothers, and he joined the team of comperes at several venues, in particular at Carinas. Keith always looks for the humour in any situation, and that included the compering. Keith, Chris Pitt and Kevin Sheils had a series of running jokes, some of which transferred to the *Festival News*. One of the jokes was 'Things they Never Said', for example, June Tabor – 'This one will put a smile on your face'. With the introduction of radio microphones Keith and Chris once tried to compere Carinas from The Dove next door.

- *Hillsborough Stadium disaster: 95 Liverpool fans die*
- *House of Commons televised live*
- *Sky TV – first satellite service*
- *Tiananmen Square protests in China*
- *Berlin Wall demolished*
- *Communism overthrown in Eastern Europe*
- *New Kids on the Block and Jive Bunny and the Mastermixers at No 1*

The three men also sang on occasions, but not too seriously. Keith remembers that Martin Carthy and Norma Waterson recognised that silly element at the Festival and, in 1989, they busked the queue outside Carinas, as did the ceilidh band Gas Mark V. 1989 was also the first year that Chris, Keith and Kevin were involved with the Folk Quiz. Fancy dress events continued and instead of the traditional cocktail party, Windsor Morris and others organised a Titanic Party on the Esplanade. Great Western Morris dressed in white and impersonated an iceberg which came along the Esplanade and tried to sink the party. Les Barker called in and read a poem about an iceberg as well.

The new management had been running the Festival for three years and it was time for some changes. The Festival Office had been operating from a couple of rooms in the East Devon District Council offices at The Knowle, but the council needed the space, and offered the Festival a property in East Street, which was small, damp and dingy. There were fears that the Council was less committed to the Festival, and rumours that the Festival would move to Bournemouth. Steve Heap was reported in the press as saying that the council's spending on the Festival was 'a pin prick' compared with the total tourist promotion budget. The Council, however, did renew its commitment, which allowed Steve Heap and John Heydon to press ahead.

It was decided to appoint a Festival President to present the Festival's 'public face' both during the week and throughout the rest of the year, and the natural choice was David Slater. Michael McGahey, Chairman both of Devon County Council and the West Country Tourist Board, became the new President of the Friends of the Festival.

Alan Bearman had spent two years as Song Producer on a voluntary basis, but by now he had been contracted by Steve Heap's Mrs Casey Music to run several folk music events and festivals. At the end of the

... rumours that the Festival would move to Bournemouth

1989 Festival, he became Artistic Director (Dance and Song), and Bob Mallandine was not replaced as Dance Producer. Eddie Upton continued with a new title, Display Director, whilst Margaret Hordley continued as Children's Festival Producer. In the event, personal reasons forced Margaret Hordley to withdraw from this role several months before the 1990 Festival, and Alan became involved with the programme, and David Slater co-ordinated the events during the week.

John Dowell's fifteen years of working full time with the Festival ended, and he continued as the part-time Publicity and Marketing Officer, whilst developing his own design business, now called Rockford Graphics. He has continued to handle much of the Festival's publicity design, and has also designed this book.

The wider folk, and now roots, music scene was coming out of several years of the doldrums, which had been exacerbated by the economic situation in the early to mid-eighties. Sidmouth Festival had suffered alongside other activities, and the financial position resulting from the bad weather had almost ended the event altogether. After several years worrying that fewer younger people were interested in the music, events such as the BBC Young Tradition Award, the role model of Kathryn Tickell and the activities of the first folk development agency, Folkworks, in the north of England, were helping to contribute to a new interest. The 1989 Festival had its own Young Tradition Concert with Becky Taylor, Simon Thoumire, Paul Higgs, Becky Palmer, Lee Collinson and The Old Rope String Band: there was hope for the future.

It must have been clear to Steve Heap in particular that the Festival was now poised to reap the advantages of its established and committed audience, and the expanding and exciting developments in the wider folk scene. 'We aim to keep Sidmouth at the forefront of the movement, encompassing whatever we think fits – but without losing our commitment to where we all started – in the traditional songs, music and dances of the British Isles.' And so the Festival moved into the nineties.

Martin & Norma busking the queue at Carinas

The Titanic Party on the Esplanade

Putting on the Style

Lonnie Donegan

1990 Alan Bearman now had responsibility for social dance as well as for the song and music events. In order to programme events that would appeal to the experienced dancers, Alan relied on Sheila Mainwaring who became the Dance Adviser, and Sheila also had the role of overseeing this aspect of the Festival during the week itself.

The exclusive label 'Dances for Experienced Dancers Only' of the early 1980s had already been replaced with Connoisseurs' Dances, but even that label disappeared in 1990: instead there was diversity of dance styles and more descriptive labels. The events still appealed to the dancer whose background was likely to be the folk dance club, and there was an interest amongst these dancers for complex pattern making in the dances. The Playford repertoire had already been augmented by the dances of Pat Shaw,

and in the previous few years newer 'dancing masters' writing dances in the same style came to the fore – Charles Bolton, Colin Hume and Mark Elvins for example. The bands tended to be quieter than for the ceilidhs, often piano accordion led and the musicians usually played from written music. Although there were still a large number of such dancers coming to the Festival, they were, in comparison with the ceilidhs, failing to bring younger people into the fold. Sheila called them, affectionately, the 'posh dancers'.

Just prior to the 1990 Festival, it was found that East Devon District Council had carpeted the Council Chamber, so the dance events programmed in the venue had to be moved to St Teresa's Church Hall at the last minute. The other two main evening venues for the 'posh dancers' were the Bowd Marquee and Sidford Village Hall: there were three American Dances, two Scottish, a Playford Ball and a Playford Plus dance. Bill and Barbara Kinsman called separately and together, and one of the events was billed as 'Mistress Kinsman's Assembly'. Other titles included 'Dances with a Difference' (the title of Colin Hume's books of dances), 'A Serious Dance' and the ambiguous yet enduring, 'Dance for Dancers'. The other callers during the week were Charles

Bolton, Colin Hume, Andrew Kellett and John Harris, whilst the bands included Alterations, Dargason, The Craigellachie Band and John Patrick's Festival Reunion Band.

The ceilidh dancers had the well-established Anchor Gardens Ceilidhs at lunchtime, as well as the Drill Hall and Ham Marquee Ceilidhs in the evening and the Late Night Extra at the Bowd Marquee. The bands in 1990 included Cock and Bull Band, The Electropathics, The Bursledon Village Band and Tickled Pink plus the new band Token Women. A one-off special was The John Kirkpatrick All-Stars at Tuesday's Ham Ceilidh – Sue Harris, Martin Carthy, Chris Wood, Martin Brinsford and Michael Gregory, as well as John himself. Callers included Dave Hunt, Mick Brooks, Bob Mallindine and Taffy Thomas.

It was shortly after this time that the design of the marquees changed, which meant that the poles in the middle of the dance floor disappeared.

The Drill Hall had been the venue for some imaginative ceilidhs over the years, but with the Ham Marquee now hosting a ceilidh most evenings, the Drill Hall events needed to be revitalised. Martin Nail, along with Gordon Potts, Diane Moody and others, was involved with the Knees Up Cecil Sharp Ceilidhs at Cecil

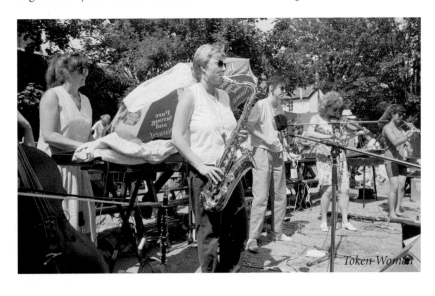

Token Women

Bampton Morris

Danny & Rod Stradling, Peta Webb and Mel Dean at the 'Scan Tester Tribute'

Sharp House in London, which were attracting a new and young audience with the residents, The Committee Band and regular callers Gordon Potts and Nick Walden. Alan Bearman took up Martin's suggestion that some of the Drill Hall events could be labelled 'Knees Ups'. These ceilidhs were instrumental in changing The Committee Band from a scratch band at Cecil Sharp House into one of the established bands on the national ceilidh circuit. One of the bands at the Festival in 1990 was fronted by Dan Quinn: on Sunday at the Drill Hall it was The Dan Quinn Trio, but by Wednesday in the Ham Marquee it had become The Dan Quintet. John and Katie Howson again brought The Old Hat Dance Band, plus some of the traditional singers and musicians from Suffolk to make The Old Hat Concert Party.

The Thursday ceilidh in the Drill Hall was billed as 'A Seaside Fancy Dress Ball' with The Old Hat Dance Band. The Drill Hall was renamed 'Honson's Holiday Camp', and the event billed as a 'Gala Night Out'.

Amongst the items during the evening was a knobbly knees competition (won by Old Hat Concert Party singer Hubert Freeman who said, 'I always win that one'), a game of bingo (contrived so that all the contestants shouted 'House!' at the same time) and occasional

> ... on Sunday it was the Dan Quinn Trio, but by Wednesday it had become the Dan Quintet

announcements for the Redcoats. There was also a Mr Muscles competition with every available saxophone player in Sidmouth – about five of them – playing the tune 'Wheels' as the contestants displayed their bodies! Dan Quinn joined John Howson as co-compere of the 'In the Tradition' events in the Volunteer: the two men have performed similar roles ever since.

On the last night, the Drill Hall band was Folkestra, made up of all the musicians who had been playing in the musicians' workshop led by Guy Crayford, and the callers were drawn from the Calling for Beginners workshop. Blowzabella disbanded in 1990, but Paul James was the Festival's Press Officer during the week and he and Nigel Eaton performed as Ancient Beatbox.

Then there was the silent ceilidh in The Dove. Some people's social life at the Festival revolved around the pub, and the *Festival News* carried 'The Dove Working Programme' which was a spoof on the actual programme. The following year a separate document was devised with such events as 'The Times Crossword' workshop, the 'Experienced Hangover' workshop, and 'Eat the Band' with a variety of guests – the Kippers and the Oysters. As the pub was music-free, the 'Dove Garden Ceilidh' had to be silent, so the *Festival News* announced that the band would include buttonless accordion, didgery don't, cream horn and so on. Eddie Upton and Sheila Mainwaring were the silent callers and the dance took place on the footpath by the side of the pub. The licensing laws had been changed in the previous twelve months, which meant that pubs could now open all day.

The overseas dance groups were due to include the carnival dancers from Ponte Caffaro again, but a family tragedy caused them to cancel their visit. Fortunately, Eddie Upton, the Display Director, was able to find a replacement, the O'Shea Irish Dancers, who were one of the great successes of the Festival. For the

Liam O'Flynn

The Waterdaughters

Pol'ana from Czechoslovakia

Honson's Holiday Camp

second year in a row, dancers from Sri Lanka visited the Festival, this time the Kotte Sama Folk Dance Ensemble. The National Minority Art Ensemble of Beijing, the first group from China to visit the Festival, and the Sri Lankans took centre stage at the Arena on Tuesday evening for an 'Asian Night'. It was now rare for groups to use taped music, so it was disappointing that the Chinese group had to reply on recordings for some of their items. Wednesday was 'Eastern European Night' with Pol'ana from Czechoslovakia and Celjska Folklorna Skupina from Yugoslavia who were joined by the Hungarian band Makvirag.

Until 1987, one overseas group each night had performed at the Late Night Extra, but the problems of transporting large groups up to the Bowd Marquee had put an end to this practice. Their absence was regretted by many and, although in later years some of the smaller groups were programmed to appear, it removed a link between the general season-ticket holders and the overseas dancers. Some of the foreign dancers managed to get up to the Bowd Marquee to soak up the late-night atmosphere and join in the English dancing.

The main opportunity for the festival-goers to enjoy the overseas dancers close up were the Meet the Team events, generally introduced by Keith Wyncoll. At these events, the dancers performed some of their dances, the leader or interpreter explained something about the dances, instruments and costumes,

and the audience was usually given the opportunity to join in. With the wider interest in world music, there was an increasing demand for learning the dances, but not yet the opportunity to include this in the programming.

The British dancers included Bampton Morris (led by Francis Shergold), Corryvrechan Scottish Dancers from Bath, Carlisle Sword and Morris, Sheffield City Morris, Rumworth Morris of Bolton (led by Geoff Hughes), and Broken Ankles from Sussex.

Dick Stanger had been coming to the Festival for many years and he also organised the Chippenham Folk Festival. He and his wife Janet had been Hostel Managers (a role taken by their daughter Jo in 1990), family camp-site wardens and, in recent years, he had compered 'Stanger's Stand'. This was an opportunity for visiting dance groups, musicians and others to perform to an audience at Port Royal. The event continued the earlier 'Slater's Slot' run by David Slater. In 1990, Dick and Janet had a larger role in encouraging and co-ordinating the busking throughout the town. It was felt that there was a need to encourage more street performance and, of course, all the money collected came to the Festival. This was not an easy task. Since the 1987 Festival, dance displays had not been programmed into the Market Square in the evenings, apart from at the weekends, but now there was more pedestrianisation in the Old Fore Street area, and Dick and Janet set about encouraging groups to

perform in both Old Fore Street and the Market Square.

The Esplanade had become a dangerous place for buskers. During the previous winter storms, large quantities of the pebbles had disappeared from the beach and the drop from the Esplanade to the beach was eight feet. This was in the days before the railings had been erected, and there was great concern that someone would fall off the edge, especially whilst watching the dance displays. The Festival quite rightly believed that safety was the responsibility of the council, but the council felt that crash barriers were unnecessary.

The entertainment along the Esplanade did not just come from the dancers. The *Festival News* reported that the West Dorset Accordion Band were already 'Festival regulars' on the Esplanade, and there was some surprise in both the *Festival News* and the *Sidmouth Herald* that one of the busking musicians was a didgeridoo player! The Esplanade had already become the place for musicians to play, solo or in small groups, and it was not unusual to see children, teenagers and adults practising the tunes that they had learnt in the workshops.

The Rugby Club had been used as a song venue for a couple of years earlier in the eighties, but it was now used once again for singarounds in 1990, as an alternative to the established Theatre Bar. The whole Manor Pavilion complex was now being used very extensively and the caretaker, Ken Morton, was a considerable help to the Festival. Although the SWEB building had been used for Festival Information and Sales for a couple of years, the singers filled the venue on Thursday evening in a last farewell, before the building was pulled down in the Autumn. By now, Festival Sales were being handled by Projection Records.

The Watersons (Mike, Lal and Norma Waterson, Martin Carthy, Lal's daughter Maria Knight and Eliza Carthy), appeared at one of the lunchtime concerts in the Arena Marquee, and there was also a concert performance by The Waterdaughters (all the above, minus the men). The Watersons appeared at a Radway Cinema concert which also featured traditional singers appearing at the Festival, including Sheila Stewart and Roisin White. Another of their appearances was a contribution to Vic Gammon's 'Brute Creation', an exploration of the ways in which animals have been used, abused, written and sung about over the centuries. Martin Carthy also performed on the Radway stage with John Kirkpatrick, and solo at

Carinas, whilst John also sang in concerts with Sue Harris.

Other Arena Marquee concerts included Liam O'Flynn, the uillean piper who had been a member of Planxty and countless other combinations since, and Bolivian band Awatinas. Special events included Chris Harris's show 'Kemp's Jig' and Dave Hill's tribute to Irish harpist Turlough O'Carolan. There were memorable performances from The Barely Works and Alias Ron Kavana in Carinas.

The Esplanade had become a dangerous place for buskers

The Barely Works and Alias Ron Kavana also appeared at the 'Late Night Extra Bop' on Tuesday night and Ron was accompanied by Len Davies, who was an accomplished player of the bones. Len joined the band again at Carinas on Wednesday, and then he invited the band up to The Balfour Arms where a pub full of people took part in his bones workshop. Later, Len was a mainstay of the music sessions in The Bedford Hotel until 1997 – he sadly died in 2000.

One of the best selling albums at the Festival was Topic's double album of Scan Tester, the Sussex anglo-concertina player who had visited the Festival in 1967 but died in 1972. Compiler of the album, Reg Hall, joined Rod and Danny Stradling, Mel Dean, Will Duke,

Peta Webb and Vic Gammon in a musical tribute to Scan Tester.

The *Festival News* was dramatically different in 1990. It had improved each year, but in 1990 it was produced as a proper newspaper, published by *The Express and Echo*.

For many years, East Devon District Council had invited the overseas and British dancers to the Knowle council offices on the final Friday morning, to thank them for their attendance and exchange gifts. Some years earlier, the council had provided a barrel of cider and during the proceedings, it fell off its stand and rolled down the hill, with the cider gushing from the tap. Ever since, the event had been known as the 'Barrel Rolling'.

But the performer who attracted the most publicity and attention at the Festival was the Monday evening guest, Lonnie Donegan. His recording of 'Rock Island Line' had been in the charts three times in the year between the first and second Sidmouth Festivals, and this had heralded the skiffle boom which gave a massive impetus to the folk revival at the time. Performing songs such as 'Cumberland Gap' and 'Putting on the Style', as well as several blues songs and his novelty items 'Does your Chewing Gum Lose its Flavour on the Bedpost Overnight?' and 'My Old Man's a Dustman', he was guaranteed to attract a large and ecstatic audience. This 'blast from the past' paved the way for some other big name guests, although the request from Liz Lister – 'Eddie, that was marvellous, can we have Cliff Richard next year?' – has yet to be accomplished!

The Barrel Rolling

Birth of the Bulverton

1991 It was Steve Heap's idea to introduce a new venue in 1991 – the Bulverton Marquee. This was on the top of the hill, opposite the main camp-site, and was on the same site as today's Festival Dance House. The main events that were programmed in the Bulverton were a series of evening Roots Parties. With little car parking space (although there was a footpath from the main Festival car park, now on its present site off Broadway) and a steep walk up from the camp-site, the target audience was mainly the younger festival-goers, although the events attracted a wide age range.

All the evening roots parties were hosted by former Cooking Vinyl Records owner Pete Lawrence who was the DJ. The first band to play up there was Edward II who had just dropped the 'Red Hot Polkas' part of their title, followed by Festival favourites The Oyster Band, German band Jams making only their second appearance in England, Rory McLeod, a Cajun Night with The Crayfish Five and The Boat Band, The Barely Works, and finally Abdul Tee-Jay's Rokoto.

The Roots Parties broadened the audience and also attracted more one-off visitors who just wanted to see a particular band. Describing Pete Lawrence as a 'DJ' rather than

simply as an MC, was also a move to attract a different audience to a different style of event. Pete Lawrence wrote about the Festival in his regular *Folk Roots* column the following October, 'The atmosphere and sense of belonging that was evident was extremely powerful. … For me, the Bulverton is all about presenting the more dance-based side of modern roots music in the 90s – a slick, high energy fast moving show which gets the adrenalin pumping, the successful marriage of live music with DJ links.' The atmosphere was helped by careful use of interior and exterior lighting and good design.

Rees Wesson was a member of Edward II and remembers that, 'The marquee was packed from the word go and there was a real sense of expectancy about the place. The audience loved it and we had a great night with several encores. Dividing the audience into roughly three parts, those nearest the front were young people ogling Glen Latouche who had just joined the band. Behind them were the serious dancers of mixed age and right at the back were the slightly curious older folks and the drinkers. Mind you, most of our audiences looked like that. I loved that old Bulverton, it had a vibe all of its own.'

To give the Bulverton a distinct identity, some of the day-time dance workshops in the marquee also tended to be 'rootsy'. After the Beginners' Ceilidh Dance workshops in the morning, there were Appalachian Clog workshops from American guests the Cripple Creek Cloggers, followed by a series of European dance workshops – one led by Mara!, two Finnish dance sessions with JPP, plus two Cajun and Zydeco workshops. One of these workshops was with The Crayfish Five and dance teachers Peter Levin and Frances Sullivan from London, and the other was with The Boat Band and their occasional American rub-board player, J.C. Gallow, with the dancing taught by Barbara Coppock and Phil Hodson from Cheshire. J.C. Gallow also taught the Zydeco two-step and waltz. This was a boom time for Cajun and Zydeco music and dance, with dances, workshops and clubs opening up all over the country. A couple of years later, the Festival put on some Cajun music workshops, which were swamped by dancers who wanted to take every opportunity to dance!

Appalachian clogging was also enjoying a massive increase in popularity and the *Festival News* carried information about groups up and down the country. The American dance group at the Festival, The Rutherford County Square Dancers

Edward II in 1998

Glen Latouche

American dancers

Borneo

Jugnu Bhangra Dancers

and Cripple Creek Cloggers described their style as 'more freewheeling, less constricted', compared with the set patterns and formations of the Green Grass Cloggers in the USA, which was the preferred style in England. Nevertheless, group leader Steve Cates now remembers that the workshop experience was 'overwhelming' and that their style was greatly appreciated. Steve ran his own festival in Tennessee so he understood the work that went into organising the Festival in Sidmouth. He remembers that visit with great affection, 'the abundant and brilliant flowers, bright sunlight and delicious scones'. On the day the group arrived, a skittle contest was arranged in the Balfour Arms between the Americans and the Russian group Roon, and the landlord provided buckets of beer.

The political situation in Eastern Europe had been changing dramatically over the previous few years. First there was glasnost and perestroika in Russia, then the Berlin Wall came tumbling down and all over Eastern Europe the political climate was changing. The Soviet Union was dismantled, with independent countries being established in each of the republics. As far as the Festival was concerned, the old system frequently meant that culture ministries decided whether and which dance groups could visit Britain, and they were always accompanied by their 'minders'. Now there was more choice and freedom, although the groups had problems

funding their visits. But the groups were keen to visit the west, and dance and music allowed them to express their independence and their national and cultural identities.

Romania was a country that had never before been represented at the Festival. Eddie Upton had seen a Romanian group at a European festival the previous year and wanted to book them. Instead, the Romanian contact brought a different group, Plaiul Romanesc, because they were even better.

> '... the abundant and brilliant flowers, bright sunlight and delicious scones'

'Festival magic, superb, step-perfect dancing,' was the verdict of the *Sidmouth Herald*. The Arena had long been the setting for the Sunday morning Interdenominational Service organised by the Festival and the Sidmouth Council of Churches with David Slater playing a key role. Each year a collection benefited a worthy cause, and over £1,000 was raised for Romanian Orphanages. Nicholas Hill from North Devon exchanged addresses with one of the Romanian musicians and later in the year, in spite of political unrest in the country and riots in the streets of Bucharest, he travelled to Romania where he was made very welcome, given accommodation and taken out

to a remote village – the first foreigner to visit the community since the Second World War.

Another dance group came from the island of Borneo: Rungus and Kadazan Papar. The name came from two villages in the province of Sabah in the northern area of Borneo, which was part of Malaysia.

There was no separate British show at the Arena, although A Concert of English Traditional Dance in the Ham Marquee on Thursday featured Kirtlington Morris Men, Poynton Jemmers, Green Ginger Clog Dancers and, from New York, Half Moon Sword Dancers, who won the newly-titled Ceremonial Dance Competition.

Tuesday evening's Arena Show, compered by Jim Lloyd and recorded for BBC *Folk on Two*, featured dance groups, plus The Boat Band, Chris Wood and Andy Cutting and Fred Jordan. One innovation at the Arena was a New Circus Night on Wednesday. Children's Festival favourite Albert the Idiot introduced an array of new circus performers, headlined by Nick Janson, a spectacular aerial escapologist. Jugglers, fire eaters, acrobats plus the Jugnu Bhangra Dancers from Gravesend in Kent completed the show.

Monday night at the Arena featured Irish band The Fureys and Davey Arthur. Finbar and Eddie Furey on uillean pipes and guitar had been well-known performers in the English folk clubs in the sixties

Romanian dancers

Half Moon

and seventies. In the eighties, they had enjoyed chart success with the song 'When You Were Sweet Sixteen'. Brothers George and Paul Furey were now members of the family band. Monday was truly filled with Irish music because earlier in the day, button accordion player Mairtin O'Connor plus friends performed at the lunch-time Arena Marquee concert. Tuesday saw Maddy Prior and the Rick Kemp Band playing at the same venue. Maddy was still heavily committed with Steeleye Span, but she also performed with The Carnival Band and Silly Sisters, so this was a rare opportunity to see her in a different collaboration.

On Wednesday, the Arena Marquee concert was one of two major performances by The Kipper Family – 'We're Norfolk and Good'. Their 'Trunch Village Variety Show' had two houses, at 6.00 and 8.30pm on Thursday in the Manor Pavilion. This was the Kipper Family's swan song, as Henry Kipper had decided to retire, leaving Sid Kipper to pursue a solo career.

The lunch-time concerts had not yet been extended to every day of the week, but there was still a need for a larger concert venue. The Kathryn Tickell Band, for example, played to a capacity audience at the Radway Cinema on Wednesday evening, with

many disappointed people failing to get in. But where could a larger concert venue be located, could it be filled a couple of times a day, and could the Festival afford the bigger-name guests? These were really questions for the future, but in the meantime the Radway Cinema, Carinas and the Manor Pavilion provided the main concert venues.

Alistair Anderson visited the Festival with his new band, Syncopace, and Roy Bailey appeared both solo and with American songwriter Si Kahn. There was a strong emphasis on fiddle music both in the workshops and the concerts, with a 'Focus on Fiddles' concert in Carinas on Tuesday with JPP from Finland, and Trevor Hunter and Jack Robertson from the Shetlands.

Dave Townsend returned with The Mellstock Band to present their celebration of village band music entitled 'From the Threshing Floor to Church Gallery'. There were also two West Gallery workshop series a day with many of the leading figures in the movement – Mike Bailey and Rollo Woods who were both in the Madding Crowd group, Gordon Ashman, Bob and Jacquie Patten, as well as Dave himself. The musicians and singers also participated in Evensong in the Parish Church on Thursday, and on Friday afternoon there was a concert in the Manor Pavilion to showcase the results of the workshops.

Lucie and Roddy Skeaping, from television's *Playschool* and other programmes, brought their 'Musical

Mystery Tour' to the Radway Cinema. Five members of the Copper family, led by Bob, came to the Festival to headline 'A Sussex Teatime' with Ron Spicer and Bob Lewis. Bob Cann had sadly died the previous year, but his grandson Mark Bazeley, and fellow Dartmoor Pixie Band member Robert Murch, joined Tim Lyons and Fintan Vallely for the In the Tradition events. Another themed concert was entitled 'In the Company of Storytellers'.

Storytelling had become extremely popular: in London there was an International Storytelling Festival and also the renowned Crick-Crack Club. Sidmouth had been promoting storytelling since the 1960s with the annual storytelling competition, which continued with sponsorship from British Telecom. Packie Byrne had become a regular and much-loved visitor to the Festival and he always championed the competition and encouraged storytelling at other events. By now, daily Story Time events were being held in The Volunteer Inn at tea time, with Storyswop sessions in the Theatre Bar earlier in the day. Sidmouth Library joined these established venues in 1991 to provide an event for children. Northern Ireland's top storyteller Liz Weir from County Antrim, and Stanley Robertson, Aberdeen storyteller and ballad singer and nephew of the great Scottish singer Jeannie Robertson, joined Festival regulars Taffy Thomas and Patrick Ryan at the storytelling events. Taffy had been developing his storytelling skills since his stroke, and he remembers being taken to visit Ruth Tongue, the great Somerset storyteller, by Geoff and Bessie Rye many years before. Taffy and Tim Laycock brought their Tall Tales show to the Festival. The Company of Storytellers comprised Hugh Lupton, Ben Haggerty and Pomme Clayton, and they presented a storytelling concert in the Manor Pavlion. The following year, a group of storytellers (including Grace Hallworth, Pat Ryan and Ben Haggarty) gathered in the garden of The Volunteer Inn and founded The Society for Storytelling, which now publishes a magazine and promotes events.

The Knees Up Ceilidhs continued in the Drill Hall. On Thursday, the fancy dress ceilidh was 'Out of the Time Warp Into the Dungeon', with the theme of spacemen and cave-dwellers. Gas Mark V and Whizzard Wheeze (a band led by Gordon Potts and Diane Moody and containing musicians from the Hammersmith and Esperance Morris sides) joined forces to provide the music.

Chris Wood and Andy Cutting made their debut at the Festival as a duo, and for their dances they were joined by Barry Coope on keyboards. A significant influence on their repertoire was the Quebecois fiddle and accordion-based music of French-speaking Canada, and they ran a Quebecois workshop during the week.

The *Festival News* was again published in newspaper format, this time by the *Sidmouth Herald*. Over the first couple of days, the workshops were strongly featured in the *Festival News*, with a paragraph or two on each workshop, or workshop series, describing what was planned.

Martin O'Connor

Maddy Prior

There was an increased number of workshops offering a massive array of choice. The Council Chamber hosted afternoon craft workshops, including lace-making, spinning and weaving, whilst the Jugnu Bhangra Dancers

> ... *the Festival is now an intricate part of the town's fabric* ...

from Gravesend in Kent ran a bhangra disco workshop during the week. Apart from the fiddle, twelve individual instruments were featured in the workshops.

The working programme itself had improved year on year, with each event having its own number, with workshops printed in italics and an easy-on-the-eye layout – which was useful, as there were now over 520 separate events.

The BBC Young Tradition Award was now well-established and in both 1990 and 1991, the BBC arranged to record audition tapes

for young people entering the competition, whilst they were at the Festival. A series of Young Musicians' Workshops was cancelled at the last minute due to the unavailability of the leader, but Sandra Kerr ran a discussion and workshop on the last morning of the Festival, and this was followed by a Young Musicians' Concert with Frances O'Rourke (a former Young Tradition finalist), Sandra's sixteen-year-old daughter Nancy Kerr and other musicians.

'Police praise "nice" folkies' was a headline in the *Sidmouth Herald*, whilst the Editorial in the same newspaper stated, 'This year there have been no complaining letters and the Festival itself seems to be better organised… The Festival is on a more professional footing and has evolved as it has grown to fit in better with the ordinary life of Sidmouth. The conflict is gone and the Festival is now an intricate part of the town's fabric, and this is good.'

Chris Wood, Andy Cutting and Barry Coope

The Kipper Family

A Poor Man's House

1992 In 1992, the Festival staged an elaborate musical play which brought together the local Sidmouth community and festival-goers. 'A Poor Man's House' was based on Stephen Reynolds's 1907 account of the lives of the Sidmouth fishing community. Reynolds's book was turned into a play by Tim Laycock who co-directed it with Martin Bloomer. Rehearsals started amongst Sidmouth residents several weeks before the Festival, and these continued during the week with festival-goers. The music was co-ordinated by Paul Wilson and Marilyn Tucker of The Wren Trust. Four performances were given in the Manor Pavilion on Wednesday and Thursday.

There had been some theatre events before 'A Poor Man's House'. The music halls had included sketches which continued to feature as the event became more of a variety show. There were the shows by the Kipper Family, Les Barker's 'The Stones of Callanish', Vic Gammon's 'Brute Creation', two shows from Chris Harris, and 'A Tolpuddle Man' presented by Endangered Species in 1990. But 'A Poor Man's House' was different – a full-blown play with music and song, which also involved the local community.

Stephen Reynolds was an educated man who turned his back on his middle-class wealth to live and work amongst the fishing community in Sidmouth, lodging and working with the Woolley family, and later working as an Inspector of Fisheries to improve the lot of fishermen in the South-West. He argued that much could be learned from the lives of ordinary working people, 'one's superiors' he called them. He died in 1919 and is buried in Sidmouth churchyard. Tim Laycock took the part of Reynolds in the play. Scenes on the fishing boat searching for herring and mackerel,

in the Woolley home and in the town were interspersed with songs, some of them from a book owned by the Woolley family. Almost a hundred people were involved on stage. 'A brilliant success' was Kingsley Squire's assessment in the *Sidmouth Herald*, and the play did much to help town-festival relations.

Tim Laycock feels that there has always been encouragement to do something experimental at the Festival, and that 'A Poor Man's House' was an excellent example of that opportunity. Tim thought that the way the local and Festival communities came together was 'fantastic'. He remembers borrowing an old fishing boat and some nets from Bagwell's for a scene in which they had a big catch of fish after months with nothing. They had the nets up both aisles, hung with fish

> *... there has always been encouragement to do something experimental at the Festival ...*

made out of silver foil. The nets were raised up so that the audience appeared to be inside the nets.

Such a performance could not have been mounted without a great deal of preparation. Barry Lister and Martin Bloomer were involved in both folk music and the theatre in the local area, and they provided essential local contacts. More than that, for several years there had been a series of theatre workshops at the Festival involving Martin as well as Mick Jones and one of these had culminated in a performance of *Morris on the Somme*, a play which was later broadcast on BBC Radio Four.

This was not the only theatrical performance during the week. Endangered Species from Dorset

returned to present 'The Last of England', the story of what happened to the Tolpuddle Martyrs after they had been transported. The local community arts group The Wren Trust performed 'The Ballad of Newtown' based on an area of Exeter, and Jo Freya presented her new work, 'Perjuring Little Whore?' based on the folk song 'Fanny Blair'. Not to be outdone, Sid Kipper presented his take on *The Secret Diary of an Edwardian Countrywoman*, entitled 'Mrs Prewd's Secrets Explained'.

Eddie Upton's period in charge of the Arena had come to an end, and by the 1992 Festival he and Wendy Lutley were about to launch the folk development agency in the area, Folk South West. After four years as an Arena compere, I became Arena Director, a position I held until 1996. Whereas Eddie had dealt with all the bookings of the overseas dance groups, Alan Bearman now took over that role, and he and I worked together closely to find the right mix of overseas and British dance groups, and further develop the Arena as the Festival's major venue.

Existing venues were generally near capacity, so that the Arena provided the greatest potential for growth. With

- *Yugoslavia split into separate states*
- *War in Bosnia, siege of Sarajevo*
- *Bill Clinton elected US President*
- *Czechoslovakia splits into two countries*
- *Right Said Fred and Whitney Houston at No 1*

Sunduza

more and more people taking foreign holidays to ever more exotic locations, and as many countries in the world had already been represented at the Festival, it became ever more difficult to find groups that would excite the audiences. In addition, it was becoming less and less realistic to programme fifteen Arena shows with the same overseas and British groups: audiences were becoming more discerning. The themed Arena shows continued, but the expanding interest in world music and dance meant that more performers were touring in the UK, and there was the opportunity to bring in small groups for one or two days.

Sunduza was a group on tour in Britain from Zimbabwe. Their style of singing had been popularised by Paul Simon on his *Gracelands* album and by Ladysmith Black Mambazo, but this was the first time that the style had been heard in Sidmouth. The group performed for a couple of minutes at the 'Raising of National Flags' event on Saturday morning and created such an impression that by the time their one-hour show in the Arena Marquee was due to start at 5.30pm, word had got around, and the queue to get in spiralled round and round the marquee. A quick decision to move the performance onto the Arena stage meant that several hundred more people were able to see the group. They headlined the Saturday evening Arena Show where their repertoire of mbube songs and

traditional dances, including the gumboot dance, left the audience cheering for more.

From Ecuador came Huellas, a group of musicians who had

> *... word had got around, and the queue to get in spiralled round and round the marquee*

performed at WOMAD in 1991. They visited the Festival on Tuesday and played at the Arena Marquee in the early evening and then in the Arena Show.

Halychyna from Ukraine had a sensational impact on the Festival all week, and headlined the Thursday evening Arena Show. Another group

that won the hearts of the audience was Cham, a group of Buddhist monks originally from Tibet but in exile in India. Dressed in maroon-coloured robes with piercing music played on horns, their yak and snow-lion dances were very popular, especially when they invited two Rivington Morris dancers to wear the snow-lion costume during their 'A Chance to Meet' event on Sunday (the new title for the event formerly known as Meet the Team).

The desire to be able to learn the dances of the various overseas groups in a workshop environment at last came to fruition with the introduction of the Dance Roots series of events, which continues to the present day.

The music and dance of Europe were very important at the Festival in 1992. The UK held the Presidency of the European Community during the year and to mark the occasion there was a nationwide European Arts Festival. Sidmouth's contribution at the Arena was an evening show 'The Music and Dances of Europe' which featured Sbandieratori Leone San Marco – flag-throwers from Italy – and the return of Lous de Bazats, the French stilt dancers who had first visited the Festival in 1984.

There was a re-assessment of British display dance for the 1992 Festival. It was several years since there had been a display of English social dance at the Arena, and there appeared to be no appropriate groups

Halychyna

The Bearcat Cajun Playboys with Phil Hodson and Barbara Coppock

to invite. The Morris dance scene was diversifying: The Shropshire Bedlams had stimulated an interest in Border Morris and Seven Champions had had a similar impact on Molly dancing. There was a growing interest in 'invented traditions' in a variety of styles, especially the black-faced, anarchic street dancing derived from Border and Molly.

Over the previous few years, the number of Morris teams that wanted to dance informally in the streets and along the Esplanade appeared to have diminished although now that the Market Place and Old Fore Street were pedestrianised, there was more scope for this sort of informal performance. Indeed, Dick and Janet Stanger had proved that there was still a desire by teams to dance in the streets, and that audiences wanted to watch them. It was decided to offer reduced-price tickets to selected Morris teams who would then be programmed into the Market Square, the Esplanade at the York Steps and processions. In addition, the overseas dance groups appeared in the Market Square each evening, generally with one of the British Arena groups. Strong Arena teams were invited – Handsworth Traditional Longsword from Sheffield, Newcastle Cloggies, Bantam Cocks from London, Lancashire's Rivington Morris, Seven Champions Molly Dancers and the Festival's second home-grown Appalachian dance group, Roughshod from Gloucestershire.

There was also a revitalisation of the Morris dance workshops. In the same way that Sheila Mainwaring became dance adviser to Alan Bearman, Sue Swift and Sally Wearing, who were both involved with the Morris Federation, took on

> ... 'has a distinctive vocal style. One to look out for!'

an advisory role for Morris dance. There was a demand for workshops for experienced Cotswold and North-West Morris, but also a need for introductory sessions, so Cotswold, Molly, North-West, Border and longsword each had one introductory morning workshop through the week. The rapper sword workshop was an established part of the programme, with displays from the participants at the end of the week. Increasingly there was an emphasis on the style, speed and presentation of Morris dancing, rather than merely learning the arm and leg movements. At the end of the week Sue and Sally held a discussion session which helped to determine the future direction of Morris at the Festival.

The Boys of the Lough celebrated their twenty-fifth anniversary with an appearance at the Arena on Monday evening: fiddle player Aly Bain had presented several series of music programmes such as *Down Home* on the television. Wednesday

was the World Wide Fund for Nature Gala Night, with the six winning entries in a Song for Nature competition, run in conjunction with the Festival, being performed by Roy Bailey and Martin Carthy.

The Festival also played host, for the second time, to the European Broadcasting Union, and concerts at the Radway Cinema were recorded for future broadcasting throughout Europe. The participating countries were more numerous than last time: apart from Britain, ten countries sent performers, including Hungary and Poland. There was also a Hungarian dance group, Bartina, and a group of dancers from Turkey, The Gürsoy Ensemble, at the Festival.

By 1992 The Watersons had stopped touring, but Norma, Martin and Eliza came to the Festival and appeared at the lunchtime Arena Marquee concert on Wednesday. Eliza Carthy also performed at various events in a duo with Nancy Kerr, including a brief spot at an afternoon Arena Show. Nancy also appeared with her mother, Sandra Kerr, and solo. Another young female singer, who appeared at the Festival for the first time, was Kate Rusby. The souvenir programme said of her, 'has a distinctive vocal style. One to look out for!' Indeed. Kate, Eliza and Nancy, plus Steafan Hannigan and Fiona Larcombe all appeared at a Young Musicians Concert on Tuesday.

Arena Marquee concerts featured guitar maestros John Renbourn and Isaac Guillory; a re-formed Home Service, Bill Caddick's Urban Legend; American singer-songwriter John McCutcheon; and John Tams and The Questionnaires. Two of the Questionnaires were Lester Simpson and Barry Coope who, with Jim Boyes, had just formed Coope, Boyes and Simpson, and they were also guests at the Festival – the first of many visits.

Elsewhere, The Chipolatas appeared – it was at about this time that Tristan Glover joined Sam Thomas (Taffy and Chrissie's son) and Jasper King to continue the tradition of street theatre performance at the Festival, started by Taffy. Andy Irvine appeared solo, Steve Riley and the Mamou Playboys brought Cajun music from Louisiana to the Bulverton Marquee, and The Poozies and Caravanserai appeared in concerts. Derbyshire's Bearcat Cajun Playboys played during one of the Arena shows and Phil Hodson and Barbara Coppock demonstrated the nuances of Cajun dance to the afternoon Arena audience.

In 1992, the Festival lost one of its main concert venues, Carinas, when the owner decided to keep it open as a disco and night club during the Festival. The main replacement was The Bedford Hotel on the Esplanade. Although this was one of the hotels that would not have accommodated the Festival in earlier years, the owners, the Pyne family, welcomed the Festival. The front lounge was already being used for informal music and song, and now the Festival was offered the use of the dining room. The hotel needed to use the room for breakfasts for their residents (increasingly festival-goers and artists) so the chairs and tables had to be set out and cleared every day. This arrangement continues, and when the weather is hot, the open windows attract casual listeners from the Esplanade.

The Balfour Arms also became a concert venue, with mummers' and guitar workshops in the morning giving way to a storytelling session, and then concerts in the middle of the afternoon and evening.

The *Festival News* was still produced in a newspaper format by the *Sidmouth Herald*, but there were only two issues, on Saturday and Thursday, although a 'Do it Yourself' joke issue appeared during the week. The *Festival News* had been attempting to play a number of roles. For the Festival organisation, it was a means of communication, with changes to the programme and running orders for Arena and other concerts – but increasingly it was also a marketing tool. Festival-goers also regarded it as a means of communication – everyone read it for the information, but some people also used it to contact friends, advertise their own events, and send messages to each other. There had been an increasing number of imaginative and amusing stories, but the overall impression was that the *Festival News* was strictly for the in-crowd, and was sometimes incomprehensible to the outsider. A year without it allowed a re-launch in 1993.

Rod Stradling had left Edward II and the Red Hot Polkas over two years previously, and his new band, Feckless, played at the Festival, alongside another newcomer, Florida. Katie Howson played in both The Old Hat Dance Band and Katie's Quartet, and Chris Wood and Andy Cutting played in concerts, at Saturday night's LNE ceilidh and with Nigel Eaton in Waltzer. Scottish music and dance came from Sound Company and their caller Andrew Kellett.

Now pursuing his solo career, Sid Kipper devised 'The Haddiscoe May Do'. The Drill Hall was decorated like the inner area of a maypole, with ribbons from the centre of the

Bill Caddick with Urban Legend

ceiling to the wall – fortunately there was no actual pole, but at the end of the ceilidh, everyone instinctively grabbed a ribbon and performed an impromptu maypole dance. 'The Norfolk Very Long Dance' stretched from the stage, through the door and onto the Esplanade across the road.

'In the Tradition' guests included the three Northumbrian shepherds, Will Atkinson, Willy Taylor and Joe Hutton.

Long-time Festival supporter Frank Lock was the Chairman of East Devon District Council and he welcomed the festival-goers, saying that there was 'a common purpose of singing and dancing together to learn each other's cultures and to create new friendships and make pleasure for the many thousands who come to watch and share.'

Nancy Kerr and Eliza Carthy

Alistair Anderson and the Shepherds in the Volunteer

Little People

39th International Festival of Folk Arts
Sidmouth
30th July–6th August 1993

Children's Festival
Programme 50p

1993 was Ray and Bev Langton's third year as Producers of the Children's Festival. Before 1991, they had not had any experience of running children's events at festivals, although their two children had both enjoyed the events at Sidmouth. They were asked prior to the 1990 Festival to take over in 1991, and they spent the whole Festival observing and taking notes, but also helping David Slater who was the stand-in producer that year. Ray and Bev had a clear philosophy from the very start – they believed the Children's Festival should be about entertainment, education and enjoyment, and that everything should be of the highest quality. They continued with an annual theme – in 1993 it was 'People' – and for more than a dozen years, Ray and Bev have been responsible for a huge growth in this area of the Festival, which has become a significant event for children and their families.

In the early 1990s, the Children's Festival presented a wide array of workshops and fun activities for children, and the focus continued to be the Blackmore Gardens. Although there had been a marquee on the Blackmore Gardens from 1987, it was a dance marquee and was only used by the children once a day. Since 1991 there had been a 'Hospital Marquee' (between Blackmore Gardens and the Hospital) which was used exclusively for children's events. The programme in the Gardens started at 9.30am and continued throughout the day until the late afternoon.

The Morris Minors workshop had continued for many years and although opportunities to learn Morris dancing continued, the format and name had run its course by 1993, the last year of the event. Abigail Reid remembers that in previous years Nick Walden, Rob Fiddler, Matthew Green and Jeff

> *'It was being part of the Festival – you saw the teams on the Esplanade and in the Arena, and you were doing it too!'*

Dando would patiently organise hundreds of children by size and ability for the Morris Minors workshop. 'It was being part of the Festival – you saw the teams on the Esplanade and in the Arena, and *you* were doing it too! The streets rang with bells attached to the children's legs', Abigail now remembers. Both

Laurel and Douglas Swift took part in the children's Morris workshops, and there they met up with Cat and Mikey Radford, and the four of them have remained firm friends ever since. Mikey remembers that in spite of teasing Nick Walden all week (Mikey still calls him Nicky Woo), the children learnt dance after dance in preparation for the Children's Arena Show. 'One of my happiest memories was walking on stage and looking out onto the hill where I had spent so much time watching in the past', Mikey remembers

Morris Minors was followed by the Blackmore Gardens Club with a band, caller and some singers or a dance group. This event could be traced through the Hobby Horse Club, back to the first year of children's events in 1965. Dance displays in the Gardens at lunchtime, with rapper and step-dancing workshops in the marquee, gave way to juggling workshops or story-telling events and 'Dances from Around the World' which featured some of the overseas dance guests. Performances from entertainers such as Colonel Custard or Professor Optical came later in the afternoon.

Over in the Hospital Marquee, Dave Williams led a workshop on 'Making Things'. He had been involved with the Children's Festival for several years and his ability to make all sorts of items, but especially musical instruments, out of junk was legendary. His overflow fife, made

Morris Minors 1985 – Abigail Reid in red shoes

from a piece of plastic overflow piping, caught on to such an extent that Hobgoblin produced and marketed them for several years. Dave also led 'The "C" Team', a workshop based around pocket-sized instruments such as mouth-organs, spoons, kazoos and whistles. Dave himself was able to play more than half a dozen instruments. A natural entertainer, Dave also sang, called dances, compered events, played the melodeon and told stories.

'Making Things' was followed by kite making and a theatre workshop led by Breakout Theatre Company, a highly innovative 'theatre in education' company. As now, the Blackmore Gardens was a place where – on a sunny day – families would meet up, sit on the grass, have their lunch and enjoy the music and dancing.

For several years Ian Carter had run very successful children's singalong sessions, and now Junior Folk Club gave children the opportunity to sing. Over the years, many Festival guests have visited or led the Club: Keith Kendrick, Pippa Reid, Mike Jones and Joan Barr, Tim Laycock and, for the first time in 1992, Mike Jackson from Australia who was often accompanied by Ian Blake, formerly of Pyewackett. And of course there was Dr Sunshine's Pavement Show, who continued to lead the children in many funny and interactive songs: in 1993, they also led the children's shanties workshop. Rachel Reid remembers that in 1986, at the age of five, she had not learned concepts such as inhibition, and she happily sang a whole verse of 'The Farmer's Boy' in front of a full Arena audience. Rachel hopes that the song events 'will go on and on, shantying in the face of *Pop Idol*'.

The playgroup for three to six year olds was another long-established event, led for several years by Alan Rawlinson, but then by his sister Adele Rawlinson and friends from Shropshire. Every day, one of the guests at the Children's Festival would visit and entertain the children. The Rainbow Bunch catered for the slightly older children, aged five to eight, and met in the

Lower Methodist Hall. The Chapel Street Hall had become another regular venue for 'Junior Band' led by Joyce Ingledew of Bursledon Village Band, 'Round Britain in Music' for more advanced players and storytelling with another Festival regular Derek Reid. Richard 'Mogsy' Walker was another storyteller who encouraged Amy Douglas to tell stories at the Festival: Amy is now a professional storyteller.

Elsewhere there was 'Small Bones Small People' led by Greg Smallbone, making masks and costumes for the procession, singing and making music. Greg and Kay Smallbone and their four children were already regular festival-goers – as with so many others, the Festival was *the* annual family holiday. Foreign holiday resorts may have been tempting at other times of the year, but during the first week in August, there was only one place to be. Maypole dancing, more storytelling

(in the town library and at the story tree at the Arena), performance skills, pottery … there was such a wide range of choice. Whenever Ray and Bev included a craft workshop in the programme, there were queues of children, and on one occasion seventy-five children had to be turned away. It was a few years before Ray and Bev could develop The Craft Carousel to enable more youngsters to access craft activities.

Jane Oates continued to help with the Children's Festival long after her children became too old to attend the events. Although her two children were musicians – Jackie Oates and Doug Oates, who is now better known as Jim Moray – Jane felt that the activities that appealed to the non-musical children were very important as well.

The programme also included special shows – for example, from Peter Cutts who was a performer and broadcaster of contemporary

Clog dance workshop in Blackmore Gardens

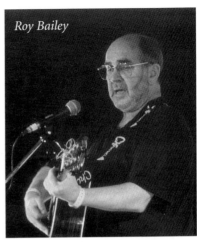
Roy Bailey

children's poetry: his two shows 'Animal Allspice' and 'Blue Hair' were performed in the Manor Pavilion on Sunday. Each evening, 7.30 to 9.30pm, there was a Family Ceilidh at St Francis's Hall with one of the main bands and callers at the Festival, plus entertainment, often from some of the overseas dancers who were encouraged to give their display and then involve the children in one of their dances. They invariably stayed for the rest of the evening. There were further opportunities to see the dance groups at the International Evening on Sunday in the Council Chamber – in 1993 the groups were the Noceu group from Spain, the Royal Jordanian Folklore Ensemble, as well as High Spen Blue Diamonds Rapper and Hellath Wen North-West Morris team from Nantwich in Cheshire. The Grand Family Ceilidh on Thursday evening in the Ham Marquee was a full evening with band, caller, and a couple of dance groups and other entertainers. Formerly a fancy-dress

event, many of the children now dressed up in their best party clothes for this special occasion.

Another special event in 1993 was Roy Bailey's show 'Why Does it Have to be Me?' named after one of his

> ### *... on one occasion seventy-five children had to be turned away*

popular songs. Another of his songs, 'Everything Possible' by Fred Small, was printed in the Children's Festival programme. Its chorus, which starts 'You can be anybody you want to be …' seemed to symbolise the whole approach of the Children's Festival events. Julie Williams with her son Matthew remembers Roy Bailey singing at a children's event as 'magical'. 'I was absolutely in love with this man's voice and his charisma and the messages he was conveying with his songs', Julie recalls.

The end of the week saw the showcase events, when the children were able to perform the songs, tunes, dances, stories and theatre that they had learned during the week. This continues to be an important opportunity for the children to display their talents, and many parents have commented on the boost to their children's confidence given by the workshops and the final showcase. And of course, the showcases are a delight for parents (and often grandparents) and many of them must, like Ray and Bev, have a tear in their eye as the children perform.

Kathryn Tickell was becoming a regular visitor to the Festival, and appeared at Tuesday lunchtime's Arena Marquee concert with her band. Another of the Arena Marquee concerts was entitled 'Hell Bent, Heaven Bound 2 – Money: The Final Frontier', a show on the theme of money conceived by Barb Jungr, and also featuring Michael Parker, Helen Watson and Christine

Dave Williams

Fred Small at the Junior Folk Club

I Tre Martelli

Collister. Tarika Sammy with their music of many Malagasy traditions appeared at the Arena Marquee on Wednesday, with a preview on Tuesday afternoon's Arena show. Ian Anderson, editor of *Folk Roots*, was mixing the sound at a volume level above normal when an irate member of the audience threatened Ian that he would write to the folk press. 'I am the folk press!' retorted Ian.

After several years of high-profile interest in world music in the wider folk scene, collaborations between musicians from different cultures were now emerging. Roger Watson, himself a former Song Producer and a performer at the Festival in several different guises over the years, was by this time Director of TAPS (Traditional Arts Projects), the folk development agency in the south of England. Alianza was a group of musicians and singers from Chile and England brought together by TAPS and they performed at the Radway Cinema on Monday. The Chilean musicians were members of Quimantu whilst their English colleagues were Show of Hands and Dave Townsend. I Tre Martelli performed their Italian music and song from Piemonte during the Arena Show on Wednesday afternoon and later appeared at a

- *Maastricht Treaty*
- *First World Trade Centre Bombing in New York*
- *UN troops killed in Somalia*
- *Take That and Mr Blobby at No 1*

993

Euro-Concert at the Radway Cinema alongside France's bagpipe band, Le Quintette de Cornemuses.

Top Zydeco band John Delafose and the Eunice Playboys came over from Louisiana to perform at the Bulverton and at the Arena – the Thursday Marquee concert moved to the main stage to allow the dancers some space on the grass. Altan performed at the Friday lunch-time Arena Marquee concert: one of the band members arrived half way through the concert after missing his flight and persuading the airline to let him on another flight – he told them he had a gig with rock band U2.

At last a daily workshop was devoted to the small but growing group of young musicians coming to the Festival. 'Young Musicians Meet and Play' was the title of the workshop led by Sandra Kerr: the title suggested that there was a need to provide a focus for young people to do more than play some tunes. Some

of the younger musicians were featured in a South West Folk Showcase Concert in the Bedford Hotel. The guests included the Burgess Brothers (actually Sue and Jane Burgess who are not sisters!) and the Lakeman Brothers (Sean, Sam and Seth who are brothers). The Lakemans also performed in the annual Young Musicians Concert with the Wrigley sisters and Luke Daniels.

Sunduza from Zimbabwe had been so popular on their brief visit in 1992, that they were booked again in 1993 to feature in the Tuesday evening Arena Show. The Yunnan Ensemble from China joined the Festival for the last two days – they headlined Thursday evening's Arena show, and also performed on Friday. Other overseas dance groups came from Jordan, Bulgaria and Columbia (first visits by groups from those three countries), the Asturias region in Northern Spain, Mexico and Russia (The Voronezh Ensemble). The Royal Jordanian Folklore Troupe was sponsored by their state airline and alongside their Arabic dances, their musical instruments also included the Scottish bagpipes. The Bulgarian group was the Pleven Authentic Folklore Ensemble, which aimed to recreate as accurately as possible the folklore, dances, songs and rituals of village life. The rituals included what looked like a mummers' play – with a fight, death, resurrection by a doctor and a hobby-horse. The distinctive sounds and rhythms of Bulgarian music had been heard in Western Europe through the recordings of

Steve Heap surveys the Arena

Jordan

China

Le Mystere des Voix Bulgares and the Trio Bulgarka, so here again was the proof of Imogen Holst's phrase 'dancing is music made visible'.

The British dancers also included several groups that were new to the Arena stage: the clog-dancing Walker Family, Leyland Morris Dancers from Lancashire, and Feet First Appalachian Dancers from Derbyshire, who filled the stage with their expansive routines. Windsor Morris, who had danced informally at the Festival for many years, were finally invited to dance on the Arena stage. Shropshire's Ironmen and Severn Gilders and High Spen made return visits to the Festival.

The Monday evening event at the Arena – 'Forward with Scotland's Past' – proved to be a particularly successful blend of music and dance. After processing from Port Royal, the City of Exeter Pipe Band paraded on the stage, followed by Orkney twins Jennifer and Hazel Wrigley on fiddle and guitar and the Corryvrechan Scottish Dancers. Headliners were Battlefield Band, making their first visit since the 1970s, now with the young and very talented John McCusker.

After concern in 1992 that illegal traders were creaming off income that could otherwise be earned by local shops, a combination of the two councils, the Festival and the police managed to keep the so-called 'hippy traders' off the streets in 1993. They had been causing an obstruction by

selling in front of shop doorways, but within a few years the traders were back on the Esplanade, and the councils and police later seemed unwilling to move them on.

> ### 'Sidmouth Festival is an institution: far greater than the sum of its parts'

The *Festival News* returned, but was geared much more to the marketing of the Festival and its events on a daily basis. Gone were all the esoteric messages and funny stories and quizzes. Some people obviously regretted the absence of the old style publication, and Tony Day went so

far as to produce his own newsletter, *Sid's Mouth: The Alternative Organ*. The opening editorial seemed serious enough: 'A Festival Newspaper produced by festival-goers for festival-goers', but continued, 'And with absolutely no news in it at all!' To emphasise the point, the first issue was largely quotes from previous editions of *Festival News*, but the other two editions contained sufficient new esoteric items to keep the target audience (generally the Middle Bar Singers, and festival-goers in The Dove and The Swan) amused.

Folk Roots published a three-page spread of photographs taken by Dave Peabody, and introduced the feature with the words, 'Sidmouth Festival is an institution: far greater than the sum of its parts'.

Colombia

Ruby Tuesday ... Monday

1994 The fortieth Festival was celebrated in great style. Tuesday was the day selected for the celebrations – Ruby Tuesday. This also happened to be the title of one of the chart successes of Monday night's Arena guest, Melanie, and so the Festival had a Ruby Monday as well!

Melanie was one of the stars of the legendary Woodstock Festival in the USA in 1969. The twenty-fifth anniversary of Woodstock promised considerable media interest as well as a world-wide tour by one of its stars. Alas, that interest failed to materialise and Sidmouth was her only British appearance. Nevertheless, for the audience, including fans who had travelled hundreds of miles, her performance of her chart successes – 'Brand New Key', 'Look What They've Done to My Song, Ma!' as well as 'Ruby Tuesday' – and new songs performed with her daughter, was a great thrill.

Ruby Tuesday itself – the day, not the song – was dogged by rain. The afternoon Arena show featured the firm favourites, The Yetties alongside some of the dance groups, but the whole show was affected by rain, with The Yetties performing from the bandstand. The rain got worse as the afternoon continued and by the end

of the show there were real worries about the evening performance. The Caribbean Carnival Extravaganza was to be the climax of the show, featuring The Trinidad Carnival Dancers and Trinidad Steelband. The elaborate and fragile costumes were not built to withstand the rain, and at tea-time there were frantic discussions about how the show could be saved. In the event, the rain suddenly stopped at about 7.00pm and although the ground was still wet, the audience was able to otherwise enjoy the show and remain dry. Until about 9.30pm. Then the rain re-started and the Caribbean Extravaganza had to be curtailed much to the disappointment of the audience. The souvenir

> ## The elaborate and fragile costumes were not built to withstand the rain

programme promise of 'all the excitement and atmosphere of the Carnival in Trinidad brought to sunny Sidmouth!' was a little optimistic.

The two shows could not be moved to the Arena Marquee because 1994 saw a major change round in accommodation. The Radway

Melanie

Cinema had become too expensive to hire and there was a need for a larger concert venue. The lunchtime concerts at the Arena Marquee had become so popular that people were being turned away, but the venue was unavailable in the afternoons and evenings because of the Arena Shows. The only solution was another marquee but there were two problems – the Festival could not afford an additional marquee, and there was no suitable location. So, the Arena Marquee was dispensed with, and two sites were considered – the camp-site and the top of the Arena car-park – and the council gave permission for the latter.

The Concert Marquee was a 950-seater venue which was used for daily concerts at 3.30pm and 8.00pm, with additional noon concerts on most days. The main event in the new

Brass Monkey

Broken Ankles

marquee was the Brass Monkey concert on Wednesday evening. Brass Monkey had been a major band in the 1980s, featuring Martin Carthy, John Kirkpatrick and Martin Brinsford, plus a brass section from Howard Evans and Richard Cheetham. Topic had re-released their seminal recordings on CD in 1993, but it was seven years since they had last performed live, so the marquee was full to capacity. They also added to the Ruby Tuesday celebrations by playing for the evening ceilidh at the Bowd Marquee. The monkey theme included a spot by the rapper sword team Stone Monkey. This one-off reunion of the Brass Monkey line-up led to further CDs and live performances but, as in the 1980s, performances have been very occasional because of the other commitments of the individual members.

Martin Carthy also appeared at the Concert Marquee in several other guises. Sunday saw Martin, Norma Waterson, Eliza Carthy, Mike Waterson and Jill Pidd in a lunchtime concert, and on Monday, Martin, Norma and Eliza appeared as a trio, supported by Karen Tweed and Ian Carr, and Pete Morton. Finally, Martin appeared solo on Thursday afternoon. With four separate appearances in the Marquee, he was almost the resident singer.

Eliza Carthy and Nancy Kerr sang and played in the Concert Marquee as support to Sid Kipper, who presented his own special anniversary concert – 'Sing-a-long-a-Sid' – on Ruby Tuesday. And on the final day, Sid and Dave Burland appeared as

Partners in Crime. Other concert guests during the week included Liam O'Flynn and Artie McGlynn, June Tabor, Dervish, Chris Wood and Andy Cutting, Show of Hands and The Poozies. Rory McLeod appeared in both the Concert Marquee and at one of the Roots Parties in the Bulverton Marquee.

> *The fact that it was too small and uncomfortable was beside the point – it was a favourite venue*

The Concert Marquee was warmly welcomed, but the location was not so convenient, especially as the Festival was endeavouring to be 'access friendly'. It was only intended to be temporary and 1995 brought something different.

The Manor Pavilion was used for special concerts and workshops, including the very popular 'Harvest Home' harmony workshop, led by Coope, Boyes and Simpson, which culminated in a performance on Friday. Georgina Boyes researched the songs and spoken linking passages: they expected about thirty participants but 140 turned up. The evenings included Magpie Lane's concert of Oxfordshire tunes and songs, 'The Oxford Ramble'; the 'In the Tradition' concert (with a large gathering of Irish musicians from Liverpool); a concert by America's Northern Harmony; 'Really Beautiful Company' with Tim Laycock and Puzzlejug, telling the story of Percy Grainger's folk song collecting in 1907; and 'Take these Chains…' written by Jim Woodland and featuring Taffy Thomas and Janet Russell. This moving and, at times humorous, show included songs and stories about Taffy's recovery from his stroke.

A regular feature at this time was a Manor Pavilion concert involving percussive dance on Monday evening. 'Steps and Stories' featured Taffy Thomas with Clann na Gael, Lizzie Dripping from Sheffield and Dan Keding, an American storyteller and singer from Illinois making his first visit to Sidmouth.

Catriona Macdonald was described in the souvenir programme as a 'charismatic young Shetland fiddler'. She had won the BBC Radio 2 Young Tradition Award in 1991, and was accompanied by Ian Lowthian in the

Coope Boyes & Simpson

concerts. Catriona led the Young Musicians Workshop each lunchtime, and her presence greatly encouraged the aspiring musicians.

King Ligger and the Bathing Boys was a 'monster busking street band' according to Tristan Glover. The musicians were the three members of The Chipolatas (Sam Thomas, Tristan Glover and Jasper King), Eliza Carthy, Barnaby Stradling and Jock Tyldersley, plus other occasional musicians such as Simon Care and Kathryn Tickell. As can be guessed from the surnames, several of these came from families that had long been associated with the Festival. They were all young and energetic and formed another strand of the emerging youth involvement in the Festival. By 1995, Barnaby and Jock had joined The Chipolatas to form The Chipolatas 5 and as such, started playing for ceilidhs and broadening their range.

The Festival in the Church events had now become an established part of the Festival. One of the regular events was President's Night, at which David Slater introduced performers from across the Festival. An extra event was a commemoration of the life of Peter 'The Red' Irving who had died during the previous year, and whose storytelling and filming of the Festival were remembered.

The ceilidhs moved up to the Bowd Marquee in the evenings, and the Ham Marquee became the venue for the country dances. Yankee Ingenuity from New England with American caller Tony Parkes and their repertoire of square and contra dances gave an early taste of the contra craze which did not hit England properly for another eight years. The ceilidh bands included Jackie Rawlinson's new band The Kitchen Girls, which specialised in American tunes, and The John Kirkpatrick Allstars, which now featured John's two sons Benji and

Great Western Morris

Jobie. Peeping Tom celebrated their own anniversary – twenty-one years as a top ceilidh band. In spite of their name, La Toque Bleu came from North-East England and they specialised in tunes from Quebec, Cape Breton and New England. A European dance night featured Mara! from Australia

But one familiar venue disappeared from the programme. The Drill Hall had been used since 1966 for dances, workshops, the late night event, ceilidhs, music halls and concerts. But in 1994 the venue's music and dance licence was withdrawn. This fact was not made very clear to the festival-goers, who were puzzled at the loss of this popular venue. The fact that it was too small and uncomfortable was beside the point – it was a favourite venue for many established festival-goers, who organised a Drill Hall Memorial Ceilidh during the week.

The Drill Hall remained as the Festival headquarters for marketing, stewards and storage for another ten years. Dave Hunt was the Festival's 'lunatic fringe' co-ordinator with the task of encouraging crazy stunts and 'general silliness', and although several took place, including a 'Make a Pig Fly' competition, it seems that most festival-goers were taking their music and dance a lot more seriously.

The group from Georgia was unable to come to the Festival when their sponsor in their home country withdrew financial support at the last moment. Fortunately, and amazingly, a replacement group – Kolos Ensemble from Ukraine – was found at short notice and travelled overland by bus. An American dance group pulled out after a road traffic accident involving the group in the States, and their absence somewhat dented the Sunday night Arena Show 'From New England to New Orleans'. The event featured Northern Harmony from

Sweden

Taiwan

Kolos

Vermont with their shape-note choral singing; singer-songwriter Si Kahn, also from Vermont; and Yankee Ingenuity who played not only reels and jigs but also Tex-Mex polkas and Latin American waltzes. The dance element came from two British dance groups that specialised in Appalachian clogging: Broken Ankles, and local group Alive and Kicking. The impact of the Phoenix New Orleans Parade Band was lost when the leader insisted on walking to the front microphone and announcing the next set of tunes – in a broad Yorkshire accent. But their music was excellent.

An unusual and distinctive group came from Taiwan. The repertoire of the Formosa Aboriginal Singing and Dance Troupe was very different to the dance groups that had visited the Festival from the Chinese mainland. The group members linked arms in a line and danced and sang in harmony in a truly hypnotic style. For the first time for several years, dancers from Sweden – The Viking Dancers – visited the Festival. The Chamber Dance Group and Zengo Music Ensemble from Hungary appeared at the Arena and also ran a Hungarian Dance House evening at St Francis Hall: the Hungarian version of a ceilidh. The dancers and musicians came from the Baranya region of Hungary, which had a Friendship Agreement with Devon.

One opportunity to see the dance groups at close quarters came each year in the Special Display for disabled people and senior citizens, held in the Blackmore Gardens. Clive Morgan was the regular compere for this event.

Roy Dommett gave a talk on 'Forty Years of Morris Change', whilst North American Morris scholar Tony Barrand (a member of Northern Harmony) used the title of his book *Six Fools and a Dancer* as the basis for a talk. Eynsham Morris from Oxfordshire and Mayflower Morris from Surrey were guests throughout the week, as were Great Western Morris, who performed a one-hour show, 'Great Western Bares All' – one of them almost did – in the Ham Marquee.

The fortieth Festival was accompanied by a full feature article in *Folk Roots,* and a summary of forty years of the Festival was published in the souvenir programme, both written by me. The research for these pieces was good preparation for the present book!

The Arena Finale

The Grandaddy of all Folk Festivals

1995

The Sidmouth Festival's status was recognised in *The Rough Guide to World Music*, published late in 1994. There, the Festival was described as 'the grandaddy of all folk festivals'.

The combination of the rain and no Arena Marquee in 1994 had meant that both performers and audience ended up getting wet. But having a marquee standing empty in the afternoons and evenings just in case it rained could not be justified financially. Steve Heap had sat on the Arena bank one afternoon to consider the options, and decided that the solution was to cover the Arena stage, and therefore keep the performers dry and, although it was impossible to cover the whole audience, the covered side stands could accommodate almost as many people as the old marquee. Year after year, the Arena stage, sound system, lighting and back-stage operation had been improved and, although in that first year of the cover, the stage and back-stage were largely unchanged, the improvements continued, taking the whole Arena operation to a new level of professionalism.

It was not only the staging of the shows that had improved – the whole Arena site had been developed. In 1988 the Craft Marquee had been open from noon until 8.00pm with almost sixty stalls, and there had also been a small number of trade stands. The number of craft stalls had steadily declined, but the number of trade stands had grown to almost fifty by 1995: since 1990 there had also been a Music Fair. In 1993, the whole site had been re-labelled 'Arena Showground' and A Living Craft Village had been added, giving the opportunity to watch craftspeople at work. A variety of food and drink outlets against the railings north of the stage and a café area south of the stage had been in place for several years: each year the provision had gradually been extended.

For a number of years there had been children's entertainment during the afternoon, but this had been extended from 1993 to include

> ### Festival-goers were promised that clowns and jugglers would 'mingle with the crowd'

some street theatre such as Original Mixture. Festival-goers were promised that clowns and jugglers would 'mingle with the crowd'. 1994 had seen an even more extensive programme, with two new stages presenting dance displays and other entertainment. The Real Macaws, The Peace Artistes, King Ligger and the Bathing Boys, Avanti

The Chipolatas

Display, Professor Optical, Pete White's Suitcase Circus and Albert all performed on the Arena Showground.

In 1995 even more entertainment was programmed into the Arena Showground site. The Café Stage featured dance groups in the morning, early afternoon and tea-time, there was entertainment on the Bar Stage just after the end of the afternoon Arena Shows, and an even greater variety of entertainers performed around the site during the day. Musicians, street theatre performers, children's entertainers, roaming clowns, stiltwalkers, jugglers … they all appeared around the site during the day. The Pierrotters, The Jelly Rollers, Jongleur, Stroud Street Band, the popular Pete White's Suitcase Circus, the superb Chipolatas, the ever-present Dr Sunshine's Pavement Show, Strawberry the Clown and Ticklish Allsorts. Some of the performers provided entertainment for families at the far south of the site during the afternoon Arena Shows.

The main Arena stage was used for lunchtime events during the week: a couple of 'A Chance to Meet' events, 'Lunchtime Laughter' with The Old Rope String Band and The Chipolatas, and two concert and dance events from The Kitchen Girls, and Bayou Seco and The Delta Sisters. One of the target audiences

Setting up the Arena

Kathryn Roberts and Kate Rusby

Ralph McTell

for these events was families: there was no charge for adults and a nominal £1 for children.

The afternoon and evening Arena Shows were still the centre-piece, but the aim was to attract visitors to the site throughout the day.

All of this entertainment cost money – for the staging and publicity, not to mention payment to the professional artists. An entrance fee of £1 to the Showground site did not appear to be unreasonable, especially in view of the variety and quality of entertainment on offer, although there was some criticism within the town. Perhaps the residents had not even visited the Arena Showground and therefore did not appreciate what was on offer. The charges had started in 1994, £1 a visit, but in 1995 a single payment of £1 lasted the full week, and the amount was deducted from the cost of Arena Show tickets. A plan in 1994 to charge children £2 to enter the Blackmore Gardens had been hurriedly withdrawn just as the Festival was due to start after a deputation of Sidmouth parents. But the issue was just the same: quality entertainment costs money, and that cost had to be covered.

The Craft Fair Marquee was moved in 1995 to the south of the Arena, onto the site of the former Arena Marquee. On the former Craft Fair site, a new marquee was erected – the Arena Dance Marquee – which hosted dance workshops during the day, the afternoon tea dance, tea-time 'A Chance to Meet' events with the overseas dance groups, and an evening country dance. The positioning of the marquee and the new, covered Arena stage ensured that there was very little sound overlap, although the music from the marquee could sometimes be heard if the Arena item was quiet, and vice versa.

The Concert Marquee at the top of the Arena car park had not been very accessible, so the Ham Marquee became the concert venue in 1995. The country dancers had an extra venue – the new Blackmore Gardens Marquee – which they shared with the children (children until 3.00pm, adults after that), and St Nicholas

School Hall continued to be used for dance workshops and an evening country dance. The village hall dances had ended in 1991: audiences had dwindled because fewer people wanted to drive out of town. The Church House Lawn Marquee was also new: this was used throughout the day by the Children's Festival, but was unprogrammed in the evening.

The ceilidh dancers had already moved up to the Bowd Marquee in the evenings – there was the evening ceilidh followed by LNE, whilst St Teresa's Hall in the town centre had replaced the Drill Hall as a smaller venue for ceilidhs. The lunchtime ceilidhs in the Anchor Garden continued to be a great meeting place for dancers, musicians, families and people who just wanted to meet up with friends and enjoy some music.

This was all quite a major change round in venues, but with some significant improvements for the concert-goers as well as for the dancers.

- O.J.Simpson acquitted of murder
- War in Bosnia ends
- Israeli Prime Minister Yitzhak Rabin assassinated
- Oasis, Blur and Robson and Jerome at No 1

1995

The Arena Showground

Meanwhile, this increased activity at the Arena Showground did not mean that the town was neglected. The Market Square and the Esplanade at the York Steps were still programmed with dance groups. The Anchor, The Bedford Hotel, The Volunteer, The Balfour and the Manor Pavilion complex were all centres of Festival activity in the town. The Ham had the new concert marquee and was the main sales point for CDs and musical instruments. The Swan and The Radway were overflowing with informal music sessions.

The Ham Marquee held 850 people, and was able to host three concerts a day, at noon, 3.30pm and 8.00pm. Irish singers and musicians were well to the fore – Kevin Burke's Open House, the young band Deiseal, The Sean Keane Band and The Sean Tyrrell Band. Festival regular Kathryn Tickell brought her trio – the other musicians were Ian Carr and Neil Harland. Ian also dueted with Karen Tweed, and they shared a concert with Kate Rusby, now teamed up with fellow Barnsley girl Kathryn Roberts, winner of the 1994 Young Tradition Award. Kate and Kathryn played support for The Ralph McTell Band at the Arena on Monday. Karen Tweed also appeared with The Poozies, alongside Patsy Seddon, Sally Barker and Mary Macmaster. Some of these performers led a couple of Youth Masterclass events, one with Karen Tweed and Ian Carr for instrumentalists, and the other, for singers, with Kate Rusby and Kathryn Roberts. Programming them all must have been a minefield.

Shooting Roots Showcase in the Bedford

There was an American concert featuring Bayou Seco who popped up all over the Festival – playing for dances, running workshops and performing in concerts. John Renbourn had visited the Festival a couple of years previously, and now it was the turn of fellow former Pentangle member, Bert Jansch. Barry Dransfield sang and played on one of his rare appearances. Coope, Boyes and Simpson collaborated with Flemish musicians to produce the first British performance of their acclaimed show 'We're Here Because We're Here: Concert Party Passchendaele', devised by Piet Chielens. The interval in the performance in the Ham Marquee coincided with the annual two minutes' silence for Hiroshima, which had been marked at the Festival for many years.

Coope, Boyes and Simpson led the Harmony Workshop again, and this time Georgina Boyes drew inspiration from the early days of the folk revival for 'In Search of England'. Ian Russell took time off from playing for the Winster Morris Dancers to lead the 'Carols in August' workshops which gave an opportunity to sing some of the Christmas repertoire from the Sheffield traditions. Shape Note singing had been available from Northern Harmony in a 1994 workshop, and now fellow Americans Village Harmony made a brief visit to sing and lead a workshop. Festival regular Julie McNamara led a workshop 'for women with hidden talents' called 'From a Whisper to a Song', and there was also a workshop series 'Singing for the Nervous'.

On most days, there were two concerts (in the Ham Marquee and The Bedford) at lunchtime, in the afternoon and the evening, plus other song and music events in the Arts Centre and the Manor Pavilion as well as singarounds in the Theatre Bar and the Rugby Club.

Bayou Seco and the Delta Sisters

Bert Jansch

The Bulverton Marquee events continued with the Latin rhythms of Salsa Y Aché, the high-energy Celtic rhythms of Shooglenifty, South African dance rhythms from Zila, and the eclectic rhythms of Dr Didg.

One event which had been running for almost three decades was the entertainment provided by Festival musicians at the Day Centre on Coburg Road, for an audience of local senior citizens. Hundreds of musicians must have played at the Day Centre over the years, quietly and without fuss, bringing entertainment to the residents of the town. In addition dance teams have, over the years, visited residential care homes when their busy schedules have allowed.

In order to take full advantage of the new-look Arena, some spectacular groups were invited. Headlining the Arena shows was Siverko, the group from Arkhangelsk in Northern Russia whose return had often been requested. Thanks to the Festival's friend in Moscow, Irena Novikova, the group was able to repeat the amazing effect they had in 1987. On Tuesday evening, the whole Arena show was devoted to Siverko. 'The performance was faultless, their energy never flagging from beginning to end', reported the *Sidmouth Herald*, and they richly deserved their standing ovation.

The slick, highly choreographed performances of Siverko contrasted with the simplicity of the group from the island of Rodrigues in Mauritius. Groupement des Artistes Rodriguais was a group of friends and family members whose 'performance' resembled a Saturday night party. They gently danced onto the stage performing couple dances such as the kadrille (quadrille) and kotis (scottische) round and round in a circle, although another dance, the sega tambour, was African in origin. The musicians on diatonic accordion and percussion attracted interest and they were invited up to play at a lunchtime session in the Volunteer Inn. Afterwards everyone in the pub session went out into the garden and danced with the Rodrigues islanders.

It was interesting to read some of the later letters from festival-goers:

Rosie Stewart dancing in the Volunteer Garden

some people loved Siverko, but could not understand the dancers from Rodrigues. Others felt that the Russians were over-choreographed, but they loved the relaxed authentic style of the islanders.

Another group made a return journey to the Festival: Canterini della Riviera Jonica from Sicily with their jug thrower. Gymnik from the new republic of Slovakia were warmly welcomed and their 'A Chance to

Sidmouth from the air during the Festicval

Meet' event was full to capacity. By this stage, I had become the UK Delegate and Secretary for CIOFF, and the contacts made at the annual Assembly meetings led to several groups coming to the Festival, including Ma-Wai Hakona Maori Association from New Zealand, whose haka war dance and gentle poi (ball on a string) dance delighted the audiences. Demb Ak Tay from Senegal and Special Edition from the USA completed the overseas teams. The Festival office was then located in Aylesbury in Buckinghamshire which was somewhat confusing for one of the Senegalese dancers who arrived in the country late. The dancer's taxi driver telephoned the Festival – all he had was a PO Box number and yes, he was driving round Aylesbury!

The events for young musicians had grown steadily, and in 1995 a most

> ### 'using the microphones in The Bedford was very exciting and I felt really grown-up'

significant change occurred in this area of the Festival. Acoustic Youth in the South-West and Youthquake in the North-West were developing separate yet similar activities for young people, and Acoustic Youth was due to run the youth events at Sidmouth. But when several people dropped out, Tim van Eyken from Acoustic Youth contacted Jenny Shotliff from Youthquake, and they joined forces with Tanya Rider, David Bowen and Mark Valentine, and they called themselves Shooting Roots. These musicians covered a mix of instruments – strings, melodeon, percussion and wind – and the format was for the workshop participants to work all together as well as in small groups depending upon ability and instrument, and to keep varying the membership of the small groups. Tanya was studying at Birmingham Conservatoire so her technical skills were very useful when arranging music for the variety of instruments that were played by the participants. Jenny herself was a third generation

Maoris

folk music enthusiast, although this was her first visit to Sidmouth: the family were confirmed Whitby-goers.

Kirsty Cotter had been coming to the Festival since 1993 when she was thirteen. She had been most impressed with Catriona Macdonald in 1994, leading to her love of Scottish fiddle music, and was initially disappointed in 1995 that no-one equally as famous had been booked to lead the workshops. Her disappointment quickly disappeared – the atmosphere was 'really good' and the events attracted more people of a higher standard than ever before. At the end of the week Kirsty and her elder brother Colin Cotter played in the 'Music for Youth Showcase' ('using the microphones in The Bedford was very exciting and I felt really grown up', Kirsty remembers) and then joined Shooting Roots for the Arena overture on the last night. Alan Bearman remembers the showcase as very significant in the development of the youth events.

Kirsty and Colin both attended

Farlingaye High School in Woodbridge, Suffolk, where Kirsty was in the same year as Jon Brenner and Laurence Neal. Unlike Kirsty and Colin, Jon's parents were not folk enthusiasts, but his grandparents lived in Sidmouth, and he had been coming to the Festival for several years. Jon had been at primary school with members of another folk enthusiast family, the Pooleys, who also came to Sidmouth. Jon had had no idea that they liked folk music until he had bumped into them at the children's events in the Blackmore Gardens several years before. Laurence's father is Rob Neal who played in several bands, including Katie's Quartet. After the 1995 Festival, Kirsty, Jon and Laurence talked about nothing else except Sidmouth for the following two months, and their school friends thought they had better find out what the fuss was about. The following year, a crowd of them came to the Festival. 'They weren't folkies', Kirsty recalls, 'but they are now!'

Siverko

Frost and Fire

Loudon Wainwright

1996 Frost and Fire was a celebration of the calendar customs of England, combining dance, music, song, theatre and spectacle. The original idea came from Waterson:Carthy, and Mike Bettison was brought in to direct the show with Val Carman as the designer. There was no attempt to re-enact customs and celebrations, but rather to create a performance in which tradition and contemporary interpretation were blended to convey the excitement and celebration of England's changing year. Customs celebrated by many people in their homes combined with elements of the special ceremonies found in particular communities. When the idea was first mooted, Steve Heap floated it past the Festival's insurers, and reported back, 'They're fine about the Frost bit …'

Following in the footsteps of 'A Poor Man's House' in 1992, this was the Festival's largest ever project in which festival-goers performed alongside some of the guests.

In preparation for the Wednesday evening Arena Theatre Show, workshops and rehearsals started in earnest on Sunday, based in a small marquee next to the Bulverton Marquee. In the mornings, there were workshops making a variety of props and costumes – decorations, a maypole, fire baskets and barrels,

lanterns and masks. This was followed by movement and dance workshops for specific scenes – a drum workshop for a massed drum band, led by the Chipolatas; jugglers, acrobats and stilt walkers for the fairground scene; long and short-rope skipping led by Rosie Cross; mock hobby-horse dancing and clog dancing. Mikey Radford arrived at the first juggling workshop an hour early to make sure he could get in.

The Festival guests who took part in the show were Waterson:Carthy,

> **This was one of the shows that Sidmouth Festival could stage so magnificently**

The Kings of Calicutt, The Chipolatas, as well as the American dance group Vanaver Caravan. The name Frost and Fire, was taken from the title of The Watersons' first solo album back in the sixties.

Frost and Fire was linked by verses of Dave Goulder's song 'The January Man', sung by Martin Carthy. It started with the New Year and longsword dancers, followed by clog dancers and an umbrella sequence led by the Chipolatas. Shrovetide skipping (England's genteel alternative to Mardi Gras) and pancake races,

gave way to a pace-egging song, and a drum procession across the stage represented the awakening of the summer at Padstow. Morris dancing was an obvious item to include, but this was overshadowed by the Whitsuntide cheese rolling of Gloucestershire. A giant cheese-shaped structure was made in the workshops, and this was rolled slowly down the Arena bank towards the stage. The big cheese then opened out with rays of sunshine as Mike Waterson's song 'Bright Phoebus' was sung to welcome the summer. The harvest sequence was performed by Vanaver Caravan, a youth dance group who combined modern choreography, drama and a full use of the stage, and this had an impact on future Arena shows. The Goose Fair sequence was represented by an array of jugglers, gymnasts and stilt walkers.

The second half used the darkened Arena to great effect with a pyramid lantern procession, a souling song for late October and a Guy in a wheelbarrow. Christmas included trees and a mummers' play with the members of Waterson:Carthy reciting

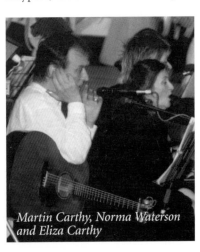

Martin Carthy, Norma Waterson and Eliza Carthy

Frost and Fire

Dave Swarbrick and Martin Carthy

Ali Bain and Phil Cunningham

the lines into the microphones whilst the action took place in front of them on the stage. A raucous rendition of 'The Twelve Days of Christmas' was followed by a solo torch dancer and burning barrel bearers. The year came full circle with the longsword dancers again. Waterson:Carthy and The Kings of Calicutt punctuated the show with songs and tunes.

This was one of the shows that the Sidmouth Festival could stage so magnificently. The open-air Arena with its fully equipped and professional stage; the week-long Festival which gave the opportunity for such a performance to be prepared, rehearsed and staged; the ability to call upon the very best performers; and the commitment of a dedicated and enthusiastic audience who also wanted to take part could not be matched by any other Festival in the country. The origins of the show could be traced back to Taffy Thomas's Fire Show – back even further to Peter Dashwood's Nautical Night in the sixties in the Connaught Gardens. And it led to future shows up to and beyond the Millennium. Simon Pipe was inspired to form The Outside Capering Crew dance group which has taken part in some of the shows since, and nineteen-year-old Laurel Swift omitted to tell her parents in advance that she would be carrying a blazing fire barrel on her head!

The success of the new covered stage in 1995 allowed the further development of the Arena Theatre (its new title) as a concert, as well as a dance display venue. The audiences

for concerts had grown to such an extent that, in addition to the Ham concerts, the Arena hosted three major lunchtime events – Tuesday with Aly Bain and Phil Cunningham, Thursday with The Ballad of Sid Kipper and, in advance of a major tour, Martin Carthy and Dave Swarbrick on Friday, making their first return to the Festival as a duo since 1969.

Monday was Irish night with Stockton's Wing plus the Yetminster Irish Dancers, the Mendip Set Dancers and *Riverdance* singer Aine Ui Cheallaigh. The worldwide phenomenon of *Riverdance* gave a tremendous boost not only to Irish music and dance (groups like the Yetminster dancers had a large influx of new dancers), but also to other folk dance traditions, which were included in *Riverdance* spin-offs such as *Lord of the Dance* and *The Spirit of the Dance*. Irish set dancing had grown in popularity on both sides of the Irish Sea, and Val Knight in Somerset was a nationally-recognised teacher. Although it was very much a participatory dance form, Val put together a group of dancers for a display in this Arena show. By this time, her workshops at the Festival had become very popular, and one of the Bowd Marquee ceilidhs was an Irish Set Dance Ceili.

On Saturday night Loudon Wainwright III sang at the Arena. The *Sidmouth Herald* carried two reviews of the concert: John Dalton, who reviewed the Festival year after year but never seemed to enjoy what he saw, considered Wainwright to be 'boring, coarse and puerile', whereas

the other reviewer, Terence Larkin, described the event as 'magnificent' and Wainwright's songs as 'hilarious and poignant'.

'The Spirit of Tibet' was the name of two groups – The Gangjong Doeghar Folk Group and The Gyume Monks, whose tour of the UK coincided with a visit to this country by His Holiness the Dalai Lama, and they headlined the Sunday night Arena show. Other dance groups came from Armenia (they were based in France), Poland, Portugal and Canada – their French-Canadian dancing and music were very popular, and their young accordion player was welcomed to the music sessions in the pubs.

But the Freetong Players Theatre Group from Sierra Leone was taken to the hearts of the Sidmouth audiences. As Arena Director, I made a point of welcoming each group individually on their arrival. In the dining room at Sidmouth College, the members of the group gathered round to hear my welcome, and then responded with their own greeting – a song:

Chris Ridley and Vic Legg in the Volunteer

Freetong Players

Sidmouth Festival
Hello from Africa
Hello from Sierra Leone
Sidmouth Festival.

The words may have been simple, but the infectious tune still goes round and round my head:

The forty-second time
The world is gathering here
In this beautiful valley
For Sidmouth Festival.

It was difficult not to be moved by the gentle singing and they were quickly added to the performers in the Market Square for the Thursday evening Informal Display.

From very small beginnings
Sidmouth Festival
Is now a famous name
In every continent.

By the time of the Saturday morning Raising of National Flags, the tune was being hummed by the audience:

In this day and age
When peace is hard to find
There's lots of friendship and peace
At Sidmouth Festival.

An adapted version of the song was the centrepiece of the Finale involving all the overseas and British dance groups on the last night. The memory of that song, and the singers and dancers who performed it, is made more poignant when one remembers that within a year Sierra

Leone had been plunged into civil war, and the arts centre where the Freetong Players were based had been destroyed. Fortunately, the group has survived to take their music and dance to other countries as well as to their own communities.

> **By the Saturday morning Raising of National Flags, the tune was being hummed by the audience**

The Ham Concert Marquee was further improved and the guests included Dick Gaughan, Show of Hands, former Incredible String Band member Robin Williamson and Cosmotheka. Monday had two special concerts: one with Freyja European Women's Band, a pan-European folk band with musicians from Spain, Germany, Hungary, France and England, and 'Mothers and Daughters' featuring Norma Waterson and Eliza Carthy, plus Sandra Kerr and Nancy Kerr. Jo Freya (formerly Fraser – the change was necessary to comply with Musicians' Union rules) was a member of Freyja, and also performed as the English representative in the 'Songs of Three Nations' concert with Ray Fisher and Siwsann George – all three women had recorded albums of songs from their countries for Saydisc Records. Two young musicians appeared as a duo – Tim van Eyken and Colin

Cotter. Rock, Salt and Nails performed at the Bulverton and the Ham Marquee and were described as 'at the cutting edge of Shetland boogie'.

One of the discoveries of the Festival was the oddly-named but deeply hilarious Australian band The Sensitive New Age Cowpersons. They were recommended by The Chipolatas, and played excellent bluegrass and country music as well as very familiar songs with spoof introductions. Alan Bearman remembers that they built an audience in the 'classic Sidmouth manner, being billed with familiar names and quickly establishing their own following'. The speed of the buzz around the Festival about the band was the quickest since The Kippers.

The tradition of storytelling at the Festival inspired an East Devon Storytelling Project, with pupils at six schools creating new stories with storyteller Mike Dunstan, and these were performed prior to the Festival. The East Devon Storytelling Chair was used for the project and was then sited at the Arena Showground during the Festival. The guests in 1996 included Caribbean storyteller Alex Pascall and Scottish traveller Duncan Williamson. Amy Douglas reminded the audiences that years of experience were not necessary to be a good storyteller – she was then aged twenty-one – and she was one of the guests at a special Children's Story Swap on Sunday.

Duncan Williamson is also a well-respected singer and musician, and he was included in the 'In the Tradition' events at the Volunteer Inn, Manor Pavilion and the Arts Centre. Veteran had recently released a CD of Sussex singers, *When the May is all in Bloom* and a concert with the same title featured five of the CD singers: Bob and John Copper as solo singers, Bob Lewis, Louie Fuller and Ron Spicer. Vic Legg, accompanied by Chris Ridley on melodeon and Kevin Mitchell, were other 'In the Tradition' performers.

Traditional dance was represented by the Britannia Coco-nut Dancers from Bacup in Lancashire, complete with their silver band

• *Prince Charles and Princess Diana divorce*
• *Mad Cow Disease*
• *Peace treaty in Chechnya signed*
• *Spice Girls have three No 1 hits*

1996

accompaniment. Bill Rutter had tried to get the dancers to come to the Festival back in the 1970s, so their appearance had been long awaited. They even managed a performance in The Volunteer – in the crowded pub, the dancers managed to clear a space in the public bar, whilst the band played from behind the bar. As the various dance groups arrived for the opening Friday evening procession, the 'Nutters' appeared in their normal costume of blacked-up faces, and red and white striped 'kilts', and immediately met up with the dancers from Sierra Leone who had also decided to dress in red and white. They greeted each other like long-lost friends and they lined up for photographs. Sid Kipper promised a performance by the 'Back-Up Walnut Dancers' at his Arena Theatre show.

Tim Laycock could always be guaranteed to present something a bit special at the Festival. Tim and his New Scorpion Band carried on the tradition of village bands, and they presented one of the 'Festival in the Church' events – an evening of sea songs, maritime music and poetry entitled 'Beside the Sea'.

There was even more diversification in the workshop programme, and in addition to most types of English folk dance, there were workshops in Irish, Welsh and Scottish dance, plus salsa, Zydeco, French, jive, Breton, Klezmer, French-Canadian stepping, Arab-Egyptian, Cajun, country and western line dance and Tibetan line dance! Sandra Kerr led the Folk Choir everyday in the Manor Pavilion with a repertoire of songs from Britain, Europe, Africa and the USA, whilst Peter Wilton led a Gregorian Chant workshop which was amazingly popular. Dave Townsend led the Mega-Band workshops, as well as West Gallery events.

In the seventies and eighties, there had been three camp-sites: the main site at Bulverton, the Family Site at Fortescue and the Third Site. The Third Site had been closed in the eighties, and now, in 1996, the Family Site was closed and the camp-site at Bulverton was extended. It was not at first a universally popular move – there was a friendly and communal atmosphere at Fortescue, but it did not make much financial sense to duplicate facilities and there was a need for greater security. A separate family enclosure on the main camp-site continues to the present day.

The 'Music for the Youth Movement' workshops were presented by Shooting Roots again, and some of the musicians from 1995 were involved as tutors. A number of the young people attending the Festival also took part in Frost and Fire, which gave them the opportunity to work together in a project that was more diverse than the existing music-based youth workshops.

The Storytelling Chair

'... after Sidmouth, I invariably go into a deep depression ...'

Although John Heydon was still a director and shareholder of Sidmouth International Festival, he was far less involved in the year-round operational management of the event than Steve Heap. Before the 1996 Festival, John relinquished his shareholding and directorship, but continues to attend and support the Festival each year. Richard Carver had attended the Festival in the seventies as a musician with Pendragon and Woodfidley: his business interests include management consultancy and, it was in that capacity that David Slater had recommended him to Steve and John. Richard's observations and analysis of the Festival's management in the early nineties resulted in him leading an annual Festival management conference from 1992, and becoming a third shareholder. Richard and Steve are now the two shareholders of the non-profit distributing company Sidmouth International Festival Limited, which contracts Mrs Casey Music to organise the Festival.

George Frampton celebrated his twentieth consecutive Festival attendance by writing an article for *The Living Tradition* magazine. Entitled 'Why I Love Sidmouth' George described the Festival as 'the cutting edge of the revival'. He wrote, 'The week after Sidmouth, I invariably go into a deep depression reminiscing about what I was doing seven days previously. It has maintained its position as sole choice for my annual holiday.'

Sensitive New Age Cowpersons at the Bedford

Singing and Dancing in the Rain

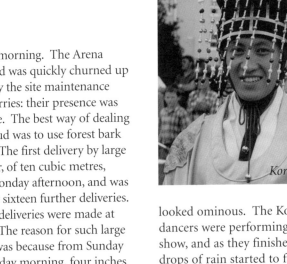
Korean Dancer

1997 Frost and Fire in 1996. Rain and Mud in 1997. The run-up to the Festival (known as build-up week) and the first couple of days of the Festival were generally dry. But Sunday was a different matter. The effect of the rain on Sunday can be judged by a *Festival News* item from the Morris Advisors Sue Swift and Sally Wearing. Commenting on the Morris dance displays on the Esplanade, they wrote, 'A very big thank you to all the soaking wet Morris teams who were fantastic in providing a wonderful display of dedication, fortitude and bloody mindedness.' A photograph in the *Sidmouth Herald* taken on Sunday shows a virtually deserted, and very wet Esplanade.

George Stuart continued in his role as the Festival's chief maintenance person and remembers that Task Force had had an incident-free build-up week, and that all the Festival venues and sites were running smoothly. But then the rain started on Sunday morning. The Arena Showground was quickly churned up into mud by the site maintenance vans and lorries: their presence was unavoidable. The best way of dealing with the mud was to use forest bark chippings. The first delivery by large silage trailer, of ten cubic metres, came on Monday afternoon, and was followed by sixteen further deliveries. Additional deliveries were made at the Bowd. The reason for such large quantities was because from Sunday until Thursday morning, four inches of rain fell in Sidmouth.

> ## ... a wonderful display of dedication, fortitude and bloody mindedness

Viv Smith was at the Blackmore Gardens Special Display with the group from Korea, for which she was team guide, late on Thursday afternoon. She watched the sky turn darker, and the grey clouds looked ominous. The Korean dancers were performing last in the show, and as they finished, the first drops of rain started to fall so she rushed them out of the Gardens and onto the bus. By the time they had arrived back at Sidmouth College, the rain was torrential and there was a power cut in the school because of lightning. Four inches over five days was bad enough, but a further two inches fell over the next few hours.

At the Arena, the already saturated ground could not absorb any more rain, and the water cascaded down the bank, under the stage and flooded the backstage area. The water also flowed out of the Arena gate calf deep, taking with it large quantities of the forest bark chippings, a good deal of which ended up on the Esplanade. This water flowed off the site so quickly because of earlier work to clear the rain water: John Hill had dug a trench two feet wide and one foot deep from the Craft Marquee, running behind the stage up to the middle gate. The Craft Marquee had been returned to its former position on the Showground site, and on Thursday teatime the stall holders were complaining that the water flowing off the car park was an inch deep in the marquee. John Hill went up to clear out the drains on the car park, but what none of the Task Force knew was that the end of the drain was under the marquee. One inch quickly became six inches, and the stall holders were not happy!

Motorists were prevented from leaving the town on Thursday

evening because of the floodwater. Upstream in Sidbury, the River Sid was a raging torrent, and at the Ford, it rose from its customary three inches to over six feet in a couple of hours. At the Ham, the river was rising quickly and there was concern that it might even come over the wall and flood the whole area including the Concert Marquee. Had this happened, it would have been necessary to have evacuated that whole area of the town. Every time there was a quiet moment during the concert, the sound of rushing water could be heard.

Meanwhile, East Devon District Council had activated its emergency plan to provide accommodation at the Knowle council offices as well as at the Sports Centre and rugby and cricket clubs, for campers and householders who might be flooded out. The emergency accommodation was not needed, although the situation in Sidbury was desperate. Houses were flooded and a camp-site in the village accommodating festival-goers was evacuated and the campers moved into homes nearby.

Elsewhere in Devon, there were flood warnings on the River Otter, the Honiton Agricultural Show was cancelled when the showground became a quagmire, 1,000 campers at Campus 97 music festival at Escot Country Park near Honiton were evacuated and the event cancelled, and Ottery St Mary town centre was flooded with cars being washed away by the water. The atrocious weather was largely confined to the South West and festival-goers returning home were amazed to discover that elsewhere the weather had been normal.

Korea in Blackmore Gardens before the Rain

The rain affected all areas of the Festival, but some more than others. The camp-site was badly hit, and cars were only allowed off the site if they were not returning – sadly, a number of people packed up and went home before the end of the week. After a few days, cars were banned from going up to the Bowd Marquee, and determined dancers had to walk. There was mud around the edges of the dance floor, which was decked with sheets of wood, although the mud oozed through the gaps in between. By the end of the week the smell was overpowering.

Open-air events in the Blackmore Gardens and ceilidhs in the Anchor Garden were severely affected and, more than once, the band and dancers sat in the Anchor bar sadly looking out on the rain.

At the Arena Theatre, there was a new Arena Theatre Director, John Kirkpatrick, who certainly had a spectacular 'baptism'. The Arena Theatre stage was, of course, covered but not the audience. A shower or two during a performance could be borne with fortitude, but very few people were prepared to sit in the pouring rain on soaking wet grass. Audiences plummeted, but not one single performance was cancelled, not even on Thursday evening, when the small but determined audience was invited to sit under cover on the actual stage.

Elsewhere on the Arena site, several areas were under water, and one wit placed a sign in the flooded and muddy area near the Craft Marquee: 'Do not feed the hippopotamus' Needless to say, the entertainment around the site and the level of sales by the traders were both adversely affected.

The weather severely tested the Festival organisation's ability to cope. Volunteer stewards, particularly at the front-line at Festival Information and on the camp-site were placed under enormous strain when irate festival-goers found their tents had leaked, or their cars could not be moved. Some people's holidays had

The River Sid as a raging torrent

Appropriate street theatre at the Arena

The Fagans with Roy Bailey

Step-dancing seagull

been ruined, yet the situation was beyond the control of the organisers, never mind the volunteers. In the circumstances, the organisers and volunteers worked amazingly hard to deal with the effects of the weather.

Task Force always spent the weekend packing everything away. George Stuart remembers that every stretch of mud was searched for the duck boards which had to be levered out of the thick mud and hosed down.

The volume of water in the River Sid had a dramatic effect, and surveying the beach on the Saturday morning, it looked as if the 'Help Sid Reach the Sea' workshop of 1975 had finally achieved its aim.

As if the weather was not enough, there were also some difficulties with the international dance groups. As with almost all international festivals, the groups that come to Sidmouth pay their own travel expenses to England, and then the Festival pays for internal travel, accommodation and meals with a contribution towards 'pocket money'. The cost of travel involves the groups in sponsorship, state funding or their own fund raising. But it was a problem with visas that prevented the group from Togo in West Africa coming to the Festival, and Albert Ssempeke and the Master Musicians of Uganda extended their visit from one to three days to cover some of the events.

The Festival recognised that the overseas dancers' accommodation on camp beds in Sidmouth College was below the standard that the groups expected and below what the Festival would have liked to have provided. But there was no alternative in Sidmouth itself. In normal years, the groups would put aside their disappointment as soon as they had seen the Arena Theatre setting and felt the warmth of the audiences. The bad weather prevented this happening and kept the groups indoors at the school for more hours than was ideal. It was not surprising that a couple of the groups complained, stretching the patience of the organisation still further. In addition, the arrangements for the group from Korea had been made by an agent, and the group members themselves were not aware of what had been agreed, and it was not what they had expected. The problems can be illustrated from a musician's comment, 'We do not play in tents'. The fact that there were eighty people in the group did not make it easy to transport them around the town.

The Dasom Dance Company from Korea had another concern. A major air crash in Korea led to several hours of worry as the dancers phoned home – fortunately, none of the group had family members involved in the tragedy. Their Tuesday evening Arena Theatre Show performance was preceded by a minute's silence.

The Ham Concert Marquee was water-proof even if the grass around the edges was sodden. One of the highlights of 1996, Australia's The Sensitive New Age Cowpersons made a welcome return: paired with Chipolata 5, their Wednesday afternoon concert was an hilarious

Martin Hayes and Dennis Cahill

All Blacked Up in The Bedford

Black Umfolosi in the Ham

occasion. The two superb Irish musicians, Martin Hayes and Dennis Cahill, played on Wednesday evening and included their amazing twenty-eight minute medley of tunes which they later recorded on their *Live in Seattle* album. Welsh music was also well represented with Fernhill, whilst from Scotland young Edinburgh band Seelyhoo appeared in concert alongside Gaelic singer Ishbel MacAskill from the Isle of Lewis.

Roy Bailey had sung at festivals and concerts in Australia for several years, and there he met The Fagan Family, whom he recommended to the Festival. James Fagan had already visited Britain and he and Nancy Kerr had formed a duo, but this was the first time that the whole family – parents Bob and Margaret and his sister Kate – had performed in this country. Roy shared his Sunday concert with The Fagans, who were overwhelmed by Sidmouth. Margaret and Bob remember the welcome they received from the organisers and audience alike as 'wonderful: The first sight of the cliffs, the sea front, the dance teams and the flowers have remained long in our memory.' Their abiding memory of the Ham Marquee Concert was the size of the seagulls' feet visible through the marquee roof!

Black Umfolosi from Zimbabwe made their Sidmouth debut at the Arena Theatre on Sunday evening and they performed again in the Ham Concert Marquee on Monday. The style of singing and dancing was reminiscent of Sunduza in 1992, and Black Umfolosi had a similar affect. Their encore song was 'Wimoweh', also known as 'The Lion Sleeps Tonight'. The song reminded older audience members of Karl Denver's 1962 hit record, their children of Tight Fit's 1982 chart-topping version and their grandchildren of the version in the Disney film *The Lion King*. Years earlier, even Martin Carthy had recorded the song! 'Wimoweh's' original title was 'Mbube' which had become so well known in South Africa in the 1940s that this name became the general description of Zulu choral music, mbube.

Martin Carthy teamed up with Chris Wood and Roger Wilson for a Ham Marquee concert. Shooglenifty had first appeared at Sidmouth in 1995 at the start of their festival career, and they returned by popular request to perform at the Bulverton Marquee as well as at a lunchtime Arena Theatre concert. Ceilidh bands such as All Blacked Up played in the lunchtime 'Meet the Band' concerts at The Bedford Hotel

A band that had almost never performed at a British folk festival, The hKippers, was bound to attract a great deal of attention at Sidmouth because it was fronted by popular actor Paul Bradley, who had played the part of Nigel Bates in BBC Television's soap opera, *EastEnders*. 'Wacky, weird and wonderful' was the souvenir programme's description of the band, which just about summed them up. The media interest also drew attention to another *EastEnders'* actor, Victoria Gould who played the newspaper reporter Polly, and who

was a Sidmouth Festival regular. But unlike her previous visits, she could no longer walk around the town unrecognised. Elsewhere in the world of television, Jo Whilley, the television presenter and Radio One DJ, has been a frequent visitor to the town during the Festival and was spotted along the Esplanade during the 2003 event.

Folk South West had become involved in a number of initiatives in the region, but their first major traditional song project centred on the River Parrett in Somerset. 'Songs from a Somerset River' was a concert based on the project, featuring the Stanchester and Bridgwater Quires. Perhaps encouraged by the interest in West Gallery singing and by the wider enthusiasm for community choirs, folk choirs were becoming popular within the folk music movement. Coope, Boyes and Simpson led the harmony workshop, which culminated in a performance 'The Turn of the Tale' which was described as 'a words and music production about storytelling in English songs and tales'.

The hKippers

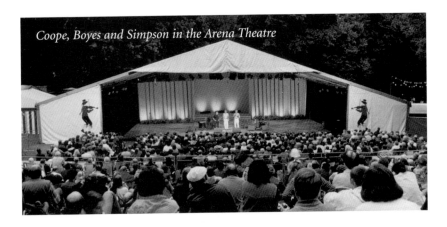
Coope, Boyes and Simpson in the Arena Theatre

Following the success of 'The Poor Man's House', another musical drama was presented at the Manor Pavilion at the start of the week. Tim Laycock was amongst the cast of 'The Widow's Uniform', which was built around Rudyard Kipling's soldiers' poems, as set to music by the late Peter Bellamy. Other cast members included Dave Webber, Anni Fentiman, Johnny Collins, Nancy Kerr and Fi Fraser. Although there was no community involvement, there were some follow-up workshops

1997 was the first year that the name Shooting Roots was used to describe the range of activities, rather than a group of people. At the start of the week, there was a Young Musicians Mini Concert featuring the Shooting Roots workshop leaders, Jenny Shotliff and Tanya Manci (formerly Rider), plus Ben Farmer, Oliver Bootle, The Hedgerows (featuring Benji Kirkpatrick) and Lucy Adams (later a member of the Eliza Carthy Band and daughter of John Adams and Chris Coe). The emphasis on instrumental music was balanced by a song workshop led by Belinda Jones and Laurel Swift. The two young women had met at the Folkworks Adult Summer School in 1996 and then Belinda had joined the Swift family and friends on the campsite at Sidmouth a week later. They went to the youth music workshops

- *Tony Blair becomes Prime Minister*
- *Princess Diana dies*
- *J.K.Rowling's Harry Potter and the Philosopher's Stone published*
- *Mother Theresa dies*
- *Hong Kong reverts to Chinese rule*
- *Aqua's Barbie Girl and Teletubbies at No 1*

but also the Folk Choir which Belinda thought was 'fantastic' and they were inspired to run something similar, but aimed at the younger generation. Laurel remembers that a key reason in offering to run the song workshop was to 'meet more people our own

> *The Festival had successfully avoided telling young people what to do, and instead had given them the opportunity to express it themselves*

age' and go to workshops that were relevant to them as young people at the Festival. In the working programme, the Shooting Roots events suggested the target age range – instrumental workshops for ten to twenty year olds, and the song events for twelve to twenty-five year olds. The song workshop attracted about thirty people, some of whom later became Shooting Roots tutors.

After three years of the Shooting Roots events, it was clear that they were attracting not only the young people who were already coming to the Festival, but also young folk enthusiasts who were new to Sidmouth and, significantly, young people who were new to folk music. The Festival had successfully avoided telling young people what to do, and instead had given them the opportunity to express it themselves: this was obviously an approach that worked.

In the couple of years prior to 1997, there had been concern about the large size of the audiences at the Bowd Marquee for the LNE, as well as the lack of an alternative event. For several years, the positioning of the security fencing at the Bowd had allowed many people to sit on the grass outside the marquee, and the bar and catering area was separate from the main dance area. But there was still a need for something different. After considerable negotiation to obtain the necessary licence, Steve Heap introduced a Late Acoustic Café at the Bulverton Marquee as a chill-out alternative to LNE and owing to the difficulty in accessing the Bowd because of the weather, the new event and venue grew in popularity during the week.

But the over-riding memories of 1997 centre on the rain and the mud. The Festival organisation was sufficiently robust to cope with the extreme conditions occurring during the week. The Festival finances in previous years had allowed the accumulation of a contingency fund, which was wiped out by the severe losses of 1997. It is a matter for concern that the Festival has not been able to build up similar reserves in the years since then.

By Friday afternoon, the rain had stopped and up at the Bowd, the sun was shining whilst the town was enveloped in mist. Arena Theatre Director John Kirkpatrick had already asked Festival President David Slater and his wife Kirsten to start the Friday evening Finale with a waltz, and David and Kirsten had the brilliant idea of dancing on in anoraks with an umbrella, then stopping to put down the umbrella. As John now remembers, it was 'a masterstroke'.

Over the weekend, Sidmouth enjoyed glorious sunshine and high temperatures. The rain had ended, but so had the 1997 Festival.

The BBC Concert Stage

1998 With the bank balances empty, there might have been the temptation to scale down the Festival, and therefore the risk, in 1998. But that was not the way that the Festival, or Steve Heap, had ever operated. Whilst there was certainly financial prudence, the high quality of the Festival had to be maintained. As far as Steve Heap was concerned, the Festival was back where it had been in 1987, with no money in the kitty and, though dispiriting, it was certainly a challenge. It was not easy, however, especially as some of the Festival suppliers in Sidmouth itself, including the churches which rented halls to the Festival, completely ignored the Festival's financial difficulties and hiked up the charges.

As presenter of the BBC *Folk on Two* radio programme, Jim Lloyd had been a great supporter of the Festival, but he had retired at the end of 1997 and the Radio Two folk music programme was regenerated with independent producers, Smooth Operations, led by singer and radio producer John Leonard. Mike Harding was recruited to present the programme which was able to push up the listener numbers to the satisfaction of the BBC. One of the new programme's first 'outside broadcasts' was from Sidmouth, where events at the Ham Concert Marquee were recorded. The new partnership between the Festival and the BBC was marked by the re-naming of the marquee – the Radio Two Concert Stage Ham Marquee. Mike Harding

joined the regular comperes, Sid Long, Kevin Sheils and Keith Rusby, to introduce the concerts, as did Dave Burland, Jo Freya and Christine Collister. The professional approach of the Festival extended to the look of the venues, and the Ham Concert Marquee in particular had already been given a really smart stage with black back-drop and large banner with the Festival name and logo. The same policy extended to the other large venues.

> *... high energy, dance-based music, often fusing more than one musical style*

Concert performers from Ireland included ex-Planxty and Patrick Street member Andy Irvine, songwriter Colum Sands, Jimmy Crowley and two young bands: Anam and Irish-Americans Solas featuring Karen Casey. From Scotland came Dougie MacLean and Ian Bruce. The Poozies now included Kate Rusby, who also performed solo at the Festival. Young talent could also be seen in the music and dance quartet, 6 Foot 3, which united three excellent dancers from the Fosbrooks stable, Tamsin Austin, Carys Reckless and Jane Pollitt, and concertina player Robert Harbron.

Other performers in the concerts included Jez Lowe and the Bad Pennies, bluesman Eric Bibb, The

Fraser Sisters (Jo Freya and Fi Fraser), the Christine Collister Trio, Newfoundland's Great Big Sea and Festival favourites The Kathryn Tickell Band and Black Umfolosi.

After The Fagan Family's visit to the Festival in 1997, James Fagan returned in 1998 to appear in concerts with Nancy Kerr who also dueted with her mother, Sandra. Nancy Kerr and James Fagan continue to perform in both Britain and Australia, and in 2000 were the first winners of the BBC Radio Two Horizon Award for the best newcomers of the year. Sandra Kerr also led the Folk Choir again after an absence in 1997, and the daily workshop was so popular – 225 people turned up on the first day – that the end-of-the-week performance had to be moved from the Manor Pavilion to the Arena Theatre.

The Roots Parties had increased in popularity, especially with younger audiences whom the Festival was keen to encourage. After several years at the Bulverton Marquee, they were switched to the larger Bowd Marquee, and the ceilidhs were re-located to the Bulverton. The Roots Parties continued with high energy, dance-based music, often fusing more than one musical style. Daily Planet, for example, combined bluegrass, Irish and Gypsy jazz and were described as 'deconstructed techno turf bop'. Merengada specialised in the Merengue dance rhythms of the Dominican Republic – hot, fiery, passionate music and dance. Edward II made a return to the

The Poozies

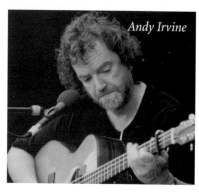

Andy Irvine

Kathryn Tickell

Jez Lowe

Eric Bibb

Festival with their blend of English country dance and reggae roots.

In 1997, the ceilidh programme had been extended to include 4.00pm as well as noon ceilidhs in the Anchor Gardens, but the weather had curtailed the events. The much better weather of 1998 allowed the full programme of two ceilidhs a day to be realised. Some of the newer bands were being featured at these ceilidhs – Whapweasel, The Posh Band, Bedlam and The Bismarcks for example. Up at the Bulverton Marquee, the bands included Florida, Stocai and The English Country Dance Band (featuring Rod Stradling, Paul Burgess, Flos Headford, Jane Burgess and Martin Brinsford), whilst newcomers Jabadaw from Manchester combined English and French tunes and dances. The new and established bands presented a wide variety of styles, from the acoustic and traditional sound of The Bismarcks through to the heavier, up-tempo style of Whapweasel. The callers at the various ceilidhs included some of the best in the country, and they had become firm Sidmouth favourites: Nick Walden, Gordon Potts, Mick Brooks and the ubiquitous Dave

- *Operation Desert Storm: USA and UK bomb Iraq*
- *President Clinton denies Monica Lewinsky charges*
- *Viagra*
- *Good Friday Agreement on Northern Ireland*
- *Frank Sinatra dies*
- *Cher and Billie at No 1*

1998

Hunt. Once again, there was an Irish set dance night with Show the Lady and caller Val Knight.

The Arena Dance Marquee had been moved off the Arena Showground site in 1997, and there had been a new marquee in the Blackmore Gardens, which was again a venue for the country dancers in 1998. The Church House Lawn Marquee and St Teresa's Hall were also used, giving the dancers a choice of three dances most evenings. At about this time, there was increasing attention to improving the quality of all the marquee dance floors, and increasingly better and better sound systems were provided in marquees. There was an American emphasis to the music and dance, with The Boys of Oakhill, The Grumbling Old Men and Keeping Thyme all playing American as well as English tunes. The American dance style, contra dance was beginning to have an impact in England and one of the most sought after bands, Wild Asparagus, came over from Massachusetts for the Festival. English dance music also came from The Little Tinkers (based in The Netherlands). George Marshall was Wild Asparagus's caller, whilst other callers included Bob Archer, Sidmouth enthusiast Mike Courthold, Charles Bolton, newcomer Frances Richardson and the new Dance Advisor, Ray Goodswen from Cornwall who took over from Sheila Mainwaring. The ceilidhs may have attracted more attention, but there was no reduction in the quality of the country dance events, workshops and

dances, and there was more choice and a better quality than at any time in the Festival's history.

The storytelling events welcomed back Taffy Thomas who sported his brand-new Tale Coat. Taffy and Tim Laycock presented one of the concerts in the Parish Church – 'Salty Tales', a programme of stories, legends, songs and music relating to the sea. American storyteller Dan Keding had already visited the Festival from his home in Illinois, and his return was eagerly anticipated.

Another of the Parish Church concerts featured The Tredegar Orpheus Male Voice Choir. The concert was dedicated to the memory of Hazel Morgan who, with her husband Clive, had worked amazingly hard over the years with transport, and in caring for disabled people and parents and babies at the Arena. Hazel was, alas, one of four Festival supporters who had passed away over the previous year. Stuart Ball had first visited the Festival as a student with the folk dancers from Reading University back in the sixties and in recent years had been the Festival's treasurer during the week. Frank Lock was one of the senior councillors in Sidmouth: a member of the former Sidmouth Urban District Council, later serving on both the Town and East Devon Councils. He was a great champion, not only of the Festival, but also of Sidmouth itself, and his widow Monica, whom he met at the Festival, is still a great supporter of the event.

Children's Street Theatre

Jo Freya and Pete Coe try to find the kipper!

And finally, Dave Williams had died soon after the 1997 Festival. He was one of the most popular performers at the Children's Festival, and his 'making things' workshops were legendary. He had a rare knack of bringing forward latent talent, and his presence was much missed. The Sunday afternoon Blackmore Gardens Club became 'Time to Remember' to celebrate Dave's unforgettable contribution to the Festival.

The theme for the Children's Festival was 'Time and Space' and for the second year, the Craft Carousel gave children the opportunity to choose from a whole range of craft activities. There were two or three sessions per day, each session lasted ninety minutes, and there were six activities to choose from with twelve places per activity. It was an important addition to the variety of activities, and added an alternative to the music and dance events. Since the expansion of the Arena Showground, there had been more and more entertainment for children around the site. But in 1998, an extra dimension was added: the Children's Glade which provided a largely separate area for children's activities. In a small marquee in the Glade, the children helped Dr Sunshine build and operate a time machine for the children's procession on Friday. There was also juggling, stories, dance displays, Punch and Judy and other entertainment. The Glade has developed as an additional feature of the Children's Festival, but with

the Blackmore Gardens remaining very much the centre of activity.

Laurel Swift and Belinda Jones repeated their Youth Song workshops, and StaircaseE (Jon Brenner, Allie Beresford, Sam Dolan and Jennie Hawes) ran the music equivalent, with a joint showcase concert on Thursday. Allie and Sam were both from Woodbridge, although neither of them came from a folk music background: they were attracted by the atmosphere and the social life. Since then, Sam's younger sister Rose has been to the Festival along with her parents. Children bringing their parents to the Festival was something of a reversal of roles!

Children bringing their parents to the Festival was something of a reversal of roles!

The large concerts in the Ham Marquee and the Arena Theatre contrasted with the more intimate surroundings of The Bedford Hotel which was used for evening concerts, lunchtime Meet the Band events, afternoon concerts usually with a theme, and tea-time events with a single artist, billed as 'An Hour or So with …'. Over the years, countless performers have praised Oliver Knight for his excellent work on the sound desk in The Bedford. The Arts Centre, Theatre Bar, Rugby Club, Balfour Arms and

Volunteer Inn were also used for a variety of workshops and informal events: singarounds, ballad sessions, storytelling and music sessions. The variety of events, performers and venues could not be surpassed and, as with the dance events, there had never been so much choice.

One of the fairly regular features at The Bedford Hotel (and before that Carinas) was the Festival Quiz, which was devised by Chris Pitt and Keith Rusby, with Kevin Sheils as a permanent team captain ('at least one contestant had to understand what was going on', according to Kevin) and over the years a number of performers have been on the teams. Most of the ideas for the quiz were borrowed from Radio Four programmes, such as *I'm Sorry I Haven't a Clue* and *Just a Minute* and, in more recent years, television's *They Think It's All Over*. There was a round called 'Feel a Folkie' and one year the blindfolded Martin Carthy and Norma Waterson had to feel and try to recognise their daughter Eliza. Sid Kipper was represented by a kipper on the end of an improvised fishing rod – unfortunately it had been left in direct sunlight in Keith Rusby's hotel room, which was unpleasant for him and the quiz team – it took a long time for Pete Coe and Jo Freya to find it, never mind feel it. The whole of Windsor Morris were felt one year by John Kirkpatrick. Some years earlier, the teams, with bags over their heads, had to guess the identity of the mystery guest by asking questions with the quizmaster

Show of Hands and friends

Oysterband Acoustic

interpreting the nods and shakes of the head. Keith remembers other memorable occasions such as Lester Simpson singing 'Wunderbar' in the style of Bob Davenport and Pete Coe singing 'Falling in Love Again' in the style of Marlene Dietrich. Barry Coope had to sing 'The White Cockade' to the tune of 'Nessun Dorma', and in later years Norma Waterson sang Oasis's 'Don't Look Back in Anger', whilst Martin Carthy tried his hand at Ian Dury's 'Sex and Drugs and Rock 'n' Roll'.

One of the two Morris Advisors, Sue Swift, devised, wrote and produced a play 'The Forgotten Mary Neal – The True Spirit of Morris Dance' which looked at the life of the woman who first arranged for Morris dances to be taught outside the Cotswold villages, to young working class London women. This event, in the Manor Pavilion, was a strong inspiration for the Morris shows in the Arena Theatre over the following few years.

Four strong international dance groups visited the Festival for the full week. I continued to advise Alan Bearman and John Kirkpatrick on the selection of overseas dance groups, and as the UK Delegate for CIOFF, I was able to visit several countries for the organisation's annual Congress. On a trip to Puerto Rico, I saw over half a dozen different groups, and was able to persuade the best, Areyto Ballet Folklorico, to visit Sidmouth in 1998. After the rain of 1997, they brought the sun of the Caribbean to Sidmouth. Yatran from Ukraine and Kurumu from Turkey delighted the audiences, as did the Academic Folk Ensemble from Sofia in Bulgaria, a late replacement for the

group from India when their sponsorship deal fell through.

Jaleo Flamenco from Spain was the main guest on Sunday evening in the Arena Theatre, having given a workshop earlier in the day in the Dance Roots series. Most of the groups who ran these Dance Roots events were surprised by the ability and enthusiasm of the participants.

> **the same tune that Pat Shaw had written for Margaret Grant back in the early days of the Festival**

They have provided a unique opportunity to learn directly from dancers from many parts of the world.

British dance groups came from the Greek community in London, the Lyra group, as well as from Gloucestershire (Roughshod Appalachian Dancers and Stroud Morris), London (Hammersmith Morris), Cornwall (Tan Ha Dowr) and Wales (Cwmni Dawns Werin Caerdydd). The sword dancers, Half Moon, came from New York – their second visit to the Festival.

Dervish and Show of Hands each had their own daytime concerts at the Arena Theatre. This was just two years since the Show of Hands solo concert at the Royal Albert Hall: Phil Beer and Steve Knightley grew up in Exeter, and Steve described Sidmouth as his 'musical spiritual home', and recalled sneaking into the Beach Store to see Martin Carthy and Dave Swarbrick back in 1969 when he was only fourteen.

The evening shows at the Arena Theatre included a Saturday 'late night' concert with Oysterband Acoustic (9.00 pm start instead of the usual 8.00pm), a concert of 'Rockney' (Cockney rock 'n' roll) from Chas and Dave on Monday and a Steps and Strings concert on Wednesday. The steps came from 6 Foot 3 and Ira Bernstein, the sensational American step dancer, whilst the strings (and a few more steps) were supplied by Natalie MacMaster and her band. This sensational Cape Breton fiddle player came from a family steeped in musical tradition. Amongst the tunes she played was 'Margaret's Waltz' – the same tune that Pat Shaw had written for Margaret Grant back in the early days of the Festival – a tune which had travelled across the Atlantic and back again. Fiddle players had an even bigger treat when Natalie also led a workshop session during her visit.

At the end of the week, Steve Heap was able to breathe a sigh of relief – it hadn't rained, although ticket sales were down and the Festival made a loss.

Natalie MacMaster

Vin Garbutt

The Best Band in the World

1999 For several years Artistic Director Alan Bearman had been trying without success to book the Quebecois band La Bottine Souriante and, finally, as the old century drew to a close, the band agreed a date. Described as 'The best band in the world', La Bottine Souriante had added a brass section to the already exciting instrumental line-up led by the accordion and fiddle. The nine-piece band now had flavours of jazz, salsa and cajun mixed with the celtic and French-based music. Led by the charismatic accordion player Yves Lambert, and featuring foot percussionist Michel Bordeleau, the band had the Arena Theatre audience members on their feet and dancing from the very first tune.

The biggest challenge for Alan Bearman was arranging all the other Festival events on the same evening because so many of the other performers wanted to be at the Arena Theatre to hear the band.

1998 had been a momentous year for Eliza Carthy. Her new Topic album – the double CD *Red Rice* – had been enthusiastically received and reviewed and earned her a short-listing for the Mercury Music Prize. Neither The Spice Girls nor All Saints had even been nominated for the Mercury, so this was indeed a new brand of 'girl power'. Saturday evening at the Arena Theatre saw Eliza in three separate guises – in a duo with Saul Rose, with parents Martin Carthy and Norma Waterson, plus Saul, in Waterson:Carthy and finally with her own band. As Eliza said

when she walked on stage, 'You're in trouble if you don't like me because I'm in every group tonight: it's your last chance to leave!' Needless to say, no-one moved. It is difficult to imagine any other English festival being able to stage such an event.

If La Bottine Souriante is the 'best band in the world', then the best known folk band in Britain must surely be Steeleye Span. Amazingly, they had reached their thirtieth anniversary year without having previously performed at the Sidmouth Festival. 'All Around my Hat' and 'Gaudete' are known far beyond the folk festival circuit and, not surprisingly, they were the final songs in the band's Sunday evening

> ### 'You're in trouble if you don't like me because I'm in every group tonight'

concert in the Arena Theatre. The membership of the band had of course changed many times over the thirty years, but founder member Gay Woods had recently rejoined, and the title track of their most recent album, *Horkstow Grange*, had featured a character who gave the band their name, John 'Steeleye' Span.

It was thirty years since Vin Garbutt had first performed at the Festival, and fifteen years since his last appearance. Sidmouth was part of his 'Take it Easy After Thirty Years on the Road' tour, which had started at Middlesbrough's Riverside stadium before a Middlesbrough versus Liverpool football match. Performing before a crowd of 35,000 was hardly 'taking it easy'! His appearance was eagerly awaited and the queue for his Ham Concert circled the marquee and drew a capacity audience.

Two thirty-year anniversaries were joined by two twenty-five-year celebrations. Battlefield Band performed under the banner used for their concert at the 1993 Festival 'Forward with Scotland's Past', and The Old Swan Band, who appeared at the festival when only a few months old, came back for their twenty-fifth birthday in a celebration ceilidh at the Bulverton Marquee.

But the oldest anniversary of them all was reserved for Cecil Sharp and William Kimber. 1999 was the centenary of their first meeting, on Boxing Day in Headington outside Oxford when the local Morris dancers, performing out of season with Kimber as their musician, were seen by music teacher Cecil Sharp. At this first meeting Sharp simply noted the tunes, but the event led indirectly to, firstly, the revival of Morris

Flashback – Sharp, Kimber and Headington Quarry Morris Men

Les Barker

dancing, and then to the whole folk dance and song movement. This was indeed an anniversary worth celebrating. After the success of the Mary Neal play the previous year, the Festival commissioned 'Flashback' – an altogether more ambitious show. Written by Jim Woodland, based on a scenario by Sue Swift, and directed by Mike Bettison, 'Flashback' was a full Monday evening show at the Arena Theatre. The part of Cecil Sharp was played by Jim Woodland whilst Dave Plimmer played William Kimber.

The first half included a reconstruction of the historic meeting, with performances by the present-day Headington Quarry Morris Dancers, and seasonal additions including the Handsworth Traditional Sword Dancers, Bampton Morris Dancers and songs by Magpie Lane. The second half included a dance journey through the twentieth century with Kimber enthusiastically explaining the changes in Morris dancing to a more reluctant Sharp.

The show was greeted with enthusiasm by the audience and is still recalled by people as one of the memorable Festival events. 'Flashback' has only ever been performed once, illustrating yet again the ability of the Sidmouth Festival to present something unique.

It was not all landmark anniversaries. Shooting Roots now added a third strand – theatre – to the previous successes in song and music. The Unitarian Hall was used as the base for these youth activities. StaircaseE led the music workshop again, with a quartet of young women, Jessica Pooley, Karen Mair (another Woodbridge folk enthusiast), Anna Perkins and Sophie Holloway-Hintzen in charge of the singing workshop. Laurel Swift moved from song to theatre, laying the foundations for a show for the following year, featuring fiddlers, dancers and storytellers. Jenny Shotliff, then in her mid-twenties and too old for the youth events, compered 'Young Musicians in Concert' in the Bedford Hotel featuring Feis Dhun Eideann, a Gaelic music project based in Edinburgh; Bill Jones and Steve Moffat; and Kirsty Cotter and Rosie Morton.

The three traditional dance groups, Headington Quarry and Bampton Morris Dancers, and the Handsworth Sword Dancers, complemented the song and music-based 'In the Tradition' events. Alan Bearman's main advisor for these events continued to be John Howson. 1999 had the superb Irish concertina player Mary MacNamara from County Clare, The Four Star Trio from County Cork, as well as Somerset's George Withers and Northumberland's Brian Watson.

From Yorkshire, there was the welcome return of Will Noble and John Cocking, who sang alongside Roger Hinchliffe, Stanley Marsden and Billy Mills from the west of Sheffield. This was an area which has its own local pub-based carol-singing tradition and Ian Russell returned with another series of his 'Carols in August' workshop, culminating in a grand carol singing session in The Balfour Arms: the locals did not know what had hit them!

The carols workshop illustrated a feature of the Festival, and the wider scene, that had been developing for several years – the desire to participate in collective singing. The massive popularity of the Folk Choir under Sandra Kerr's direction in 1998 led to a further series in 1999, and the Friday performance was programmed for the Arena Theatre. The event was recorded by Seamus Heffernan and a CD and cassette produced, with proceeds going to the Friends of the Festival.

There was also a great desire by some musicians to play in large groupings. Nick and Mary Barber presented a Big Band workshop, which continued the earlier Folkestra and 'Join the Band' events, but with many more musicians. Jenny Shotliff led a series of fiddle orchestra workshops called 'Big Fiddle', and the Big Band and Big Fiddle workshops had a joint showcase concert in the Manor Pavilion. As if that was not enough, the Massif Village Orchestra workshop remained true to their name, and a large number of musicians came together to play French music in a couple of workshops and a performance.

Dance Roots – China

Kakatsitsi Master Drummers, Ghana

The Orchestra also played for several French dances.

It had long been a dream of Steve Heap to have a folk dance group from China. A couple of previous groups from the country had relied too heavily on taped music, but a trip to China for a CIOFF meeting gave me an excellent opportunity to find a good group. The Kaustinen Festival in Finland is a similar event to the Sidmouth Festival, and the Kaustinen Director, Jyrki Heiskenan, and I both wanted to invite the same group to the two festivals. After much persuasion the Chinese authorities agreed and the Anhui Festive Drum-Lantern Folk Art Troupe came to Sidmouth in 1999. Within a couple of days of their arrival they were being described in the *Festival News* as 'stunning'. They made an immediate impact at the Flag-raising event on Saturday morning when the Chinese flag refused to

> ### ... the cloudy sky could not detract from an amazing experience

unfurl. One of the Chinese dancers climbed up the slender flagpole to loosen the flag and was greeted with a great cheer and a round of applause.

An eagerly-awaited group from the new republic of Uzbekistan was unfortunately not able to travel, and was replaced by the Kakatsitsi Master Drummers of Ghana. Kresala from the Basque Country and Tessedik from Hungary were the other dance groups to attend the Festival all week. Dance and music groups were brought in for a few days each, or for single performances. Kabudu were based in Devon, and included one of the dancers with the Freetong Players from Sierra Leone who visited the Festival in 1996. Musafir was a combination of music, song, dance and circus from Rajasthan, and

although the performance was stunning – with a fire-eating fakir who also walked on broken glass – the size of the audience was affected by rain. Thursday evening was 'All Star Africa' Night at the Arena Theatre, with acrobatics from The Black Eagles from Tanzania, dance and percussion from Assafo from the Ivory Coast, and South African song and dance from Shikisha. The British dance groups included Rivington Morris from Lancashire, Broken Ankles and Fosbrooks from Stockport in Cheshire.

After two years as Arena Theatre Director, John Kirkpatrick was succeeded by Mike Bettison. Mike had been a founder member of Flowers and Frolics, and then had become very involved with community arts projects and The Fabulous Salami Brothers. He was deeply committed to the Festival, and after his massive contribution to the Frost and Fire show in 1996, he was a natural choice to take the Arena Theatre forwards into a new era.

At its Wednesday evening 'Friends and Favourites' concert, the 'Festival in the Church' paid tribute to Frankie Rudd, who had sadly died during the previous year. With her husband Ron, Frankie had been a tireless volunteer at the Festival, in recent years assisting with the distribution of Festival publicity. The families of two of their daughters, Julie and Claire, were heavily involved in the Festival – Claire and her husband Nick Pilley managed the Showground entertainment, whilst Julie's husband, Ken Williams, was the Arena Site Manager. Claire's son Chris Rudd was a member of the Arena Stage Crew, is a manager for Hobgoblin and a member of Broken Ankles. Now Chris and his partner Louise Rannie have two children, Philip and Isobel, who will be the fourth generation of the family at the Festival in its fiftieth year. Ron is now secretary of the Friends of the Festival.

The Children's Festival theme was 'Around the World in Eight Days'. A series of music and song workshops all had the same format of title: String It, Blow It, Hit It, Squeeze It, Sing It and Band It, the latter with the Bursledon Village Band, one of

Kresala Hobby Horses

whose members Joyce Ingledew had been running music workshops for the children for several years.

As the Festival ended, the South West of England prepared for a dramatic natural phenomenon: the total eclipse of the sun. It was thought that some festival-goers would stay on for this once-in-a-lifetime event, and the camp-site was kept open and ceilidhs were arranged in the Anchor Inn. Only a handful of festival-goers took up this opportunity, but for those of us who stayed, plus members of Task Force and some of the Mrs Casey Music staff, the cloudy sky could not detract from an amazing experience.

Onwards, then, to a new Millennium.

Can You Tell What It Is Yet?

2000 The first Festival of the new millennium presented a significant challenge to Festival Director Steve Heap. South West Water needed to undertake essential work to the water treatment unit which is located below the Ham. This involved digging a gigantic hole on the Ham soon after the end of the 1999 Festival and, although the work was largely completed by the time of the 2000 Festival, it was not possible to erect a marquee on the site. As with the last time this happened, in 1961, the Ham could not be used for any Festival events, but this was a much more significant problem than in the sixties. After considering a number of options, including a return to a marquee on the car-park site, an elaborate alteration was made to the Arena Theatre. The stage was brought further forward and the former back-stage area now became an undercover auditorium, seating over 1,000 people. Outdoor performances used the traditional Arena Theatre set up, but the stage could be reversed so that concerts could take place in the new Arena Theatre Marquee. A curtain on a circular rail above part of the stage meant that the stage could face outwards to the amphitheatre or inwards to the marquee, with the curtain being adjusted to provide the necessary backdrop to the performances. The initial concept and design came from Steve Heap and Stage Electrics built it. Stage Electrics has been supplying sound and stage equipment, staff and expertise to the Festival for many years.

But of course, the two 'venues' could not be used at the same time. To meet the expectations of the two audiences – in the Arena Theatre and for the concerts – compromise was needed.

The number of overseas dance groups being invited to the Festival for

> *This involved digging a gigantic hole on the Ham ... it was not possible to erect a marquee on the site*

the week had been reduced over a number of years. As has already been mentioned, audiences were becoming more discerning, and it was no longer feasible to present the same dance groups in different combinations twice a day for the whole week. In addition, the provision of accommodation for the overseas teams had reached a critical state. Camp beds in classrooms at Sidmouth College were no longer acceptable, but there was no alternative in Sidmouth itself. Student halls of residence at Exeter University were already being used by the Festival and, although this involved transporting people backwards and forwards, this accommodation was used for the dance groups. But as the logistics of these new arrangements were untested, the number of week-long groups was reduced still further, some were invited for just a couple of days and the number of dance shows was reduced.

As for the song and music concerts, the new arrangements provided the opportunity to concentrate on some of the bigger-

The Audience for Rolf Harris

Rolf Harris

name guests. Festival marketing explained the new arrangements in terms of ensuring that people were not turned away – as they had been for the Ham concerts featuring The Poozies in 1998 and The John Tams Band in 1999.

The biggest event of the Festival was the appearance of Rolf Harris and his band at the Arena Theatre on Sunday evening. Rolf was in his seventieth birthday year and celebrating fifty years in the business. From his hit records of the sixties – 'Tie Me Kangaroo Down Sport', 'Sun Arise', 'Jake the Peg' and 'Two Little Boys' – through to his work with children's television and his paintings with the famous catchphrase 'Can you tell what it is yet?'; from his chart success with his interpretation of 'Stairway to Heaven', through to his popularity on the student campuses and his television series *Animal Hospital*, Rolf was truly a 'household name'. Even before the Sunday afternoon Arena Theatre dance concert had finished at 5.00pm, the audience had started queuing for the 8.00pm show. The queues snaked round and round the Arena Showground site and when the gates were opened, the amphitheatre was soon packed from edge to edge. And although the sale of tickets had been stopped earlier in the day, the 'house full' sign was not put up (although it was a different story in 2002!).

His backing musicians included several people involved with folk music – Bernard O'Neill (ex-

Boys of the Lough

Zumzeaux), Graeme Taylor (Home Service) and Alan Dunn (John Tams Band) – and they accompanied Rolf as he performed almost all his hit records. As well as the wobble-board, Rolf also played accordion and sang several folk songs, whilst the support act, Shining Bear, played the didgeridoo. Rolf proved to be superbly professional, performing for two hours with tremendous energy in spite of recent surgery on his leg, and afterwards signing autographs until the last person in the queue had been seen, well after midnight.

Another major Arena Theatre performer who was well known outside the folk movement was the 'Bloke from Barking', Billy Bragg. Billy's song-writing had taken him into the pop scene, but the social and political commitment in his lyrics, and his re-working of Woody Guthrie songs, ensured his popularity with the folk audiences. Billy clearly enjoyed the Festival atmosphere and he was seen around the town in several of the venues.

1999 had been an immensely successful year for Kate Rusby. She had been nominated for the Mercury Music Prize, and had won the BBC Radio 2 Folk Awards for Best Singer and for Best Album (*Sleepless*). The Kate Rusby Band drew an enormous audience at the Arena Theatre on Saturday evening: the band members included John McCusker, Mike McGoldrick, Andy Cutting, Ian Carr and Andy Seward.

The Boys of the Lough had just celebrated their thirtieth anniversary year when they returned to the Festival on Wednesday afternoon. Founder members Cathal McConnell and Aly Bain remained the mainstays of the band, providing both brilliant musicianship and traditional integrity.

None of these performers could have been accommodated in the Ham Marquee – too many people would have had to have been turned away – but there was plenty of room in the Arena Theatre.

The Arena Theatre Marquee was used in preference to the outdoor amphitheatre on two evenings: the opening night and on Monday evening when the guest was June Tabor and access was 'season ticket holders only'. Earlier that day, the outdoor Arena Theatre had hosted two separate concerts. 'Whistlestop 2000' was a lunchtime concert of all the British dance groups, and in the

Bash Street Theatre

Billy Bragg

Sheffield City Giants

Susana Seivane

afternoon 'Highlands and Islands' featured the amazing band Blazin' Fiddles as well as the Scottish Stepdance Company.

Most of the lunchtimes had Arena Marquee Concerts, and most of the afternoons, as well as Tuesday, Wednesday and Friday evenings, were 'World of Dance' events. The audiences that did not appreciate the dance events had to look for an alternative on these three evenings, and although the Bowd Marquee still featured the roots events (now called Global Dance Parties), the guests on these evenings (including Chipolata 5 and Shooglenifty) were intended to appeal to the core audience.

Some of the other Arena Marquee concert guests were The Albion Band (which now included young performers Kellie While and Joe Broughton), the ever-popular Sid Kipper, Galician piper Susana Seivane, The Two Duos Quartet (Karen Tweed and Ian Carr, and Chris Wood and Andy Cutting), Martin Simpson and The Sensitive New Age Cowpersons, making a return visit from their native

Australia and supported by the equally strangely-named Diego Brown and the Good Fairy. The queue for the Poozies was very long and the concert was switched to the outdoor Arena.

Dance groups included The Volkovtsi Cossacks, a Russian and Ukrainian ensemble based in Britain; Odra from the Czech Republic; and a Catalan dance group from Spain. Two groups from Southern Africa presented the styles of song and dance that had become popular at the Festival. Imbizo from Zimbabwe performed the choral style of mbube, whilst the dance traditions were presented by Bergville Vuka Zulu Dancers from South Africa. There was a strong British dance presence: High Spen Blue Diamonds rapper sword dancers from Tyneside and the Abingdon Traditional Morris Dancers represented the traditional end of the Morris spectrum. Cotswold Morris was performed by Berkshire Bedlam, and the North Yorkshire dance groups, Ripon City

Morris Dancers and Betty Lupton's Ladle Lakers, danced the North-West Morris style. Clann na Gael made a welcome return to perform Irish dance. The two Sheffield City Giants visited the Festival, making a great spectacle in the processions, the Blackmore Gardens and in the Knowle Arena. They were inspired by Catalonian giants and drew on a tradition that had almost died out in England.

It was not possible to have the Raising of National Flags on the Ham, so instead the event was moved to the roadway at Port Royal and, in the years since, has been renamed 'A Sidmouth Welcome'. The brief dance displays and 'Circassian Circle' for all the dancers and audience members remain, but the flags are already flying before the event starts.

The final night at the Arena Theatre was a little different from previous years, mainly because of the reduced number of dancers. Two groups were brought in especially for the last night: Viva Flamenco and, to end the night, The Bollywood Brass Band, an Indian-style street band which performed a blend of Hindi film tunes, bhangra

The Poozies

- A new Millennium and a controversial Dome
- Y2K bug fails to wreck computer systems
- George W.Bush becomes US President after disputed election
- Air France Concorde crashes in Paris
- Eminem at No 1

2000

rhythms and brass arrangements. The Bollywood Brass Band also led the torchlight procession and played at the corner of Ham Lane as the procession continued down onto the beach prior to the dousing of the torches and the fireworks, the latter having become a regular feature since the fortieth anniversary year.

The concerts at The Bedford, the Parish Church and the Manor Pavilion, as well as the events in the Rugby Club and Arts Centre, were all given a higher profile and provided contrast with what was being programmed at the Arena Theatre. Several of these events were for season ticket holders only, which was part of a longer-term strategy to increase the value of the season ticket and encourage sales to the folk enthusiasts who came to Sidmouth for the week but who did not always buy a ticket. BBC Radio 2 made a live broadcast from the Manor Pavilion on Wednesday evening, although most of the performers were in fact not Festival

... a nerve-wracking gamble ...

guests: Ralph McTell, Show of Hands and Chris While and Julie Matthews. Steve Knightley of Show of Hands did, however, give two performances of his 'Earth and Wires' show which had the theme of the darker side of country life.

The Parish Church concert guests included The Port Talbot Cymric Male Voice Choir which had been founded in 1911, and singer Isla St Clair in her 'Tatties 'n' Herrin' show. An annual event in the Parish Church was President's Night with a selection of guests from various parts of the Festival. This was David Slater's retirement year as Festival President, and the 2000 concert was a very full event: ten guests in two hours.

A highlight of the ceilidhs was the re-forming of the original line-up of Flowers and Frolics, twenty-five years after they had first appeared at the Festival. On Saturday night,

Flowers and Frolics

The Festival Choir

Eddie Upton was the caller at the Bulverton Marquee, whilst Dave Hunt called the dances at their Late Night Extra on Sunday. Other ceilidh bands included Geckoes, Old Hat, Token Women, Tickled Pink and Stömp.

The Shooting Roots Youth events in 1999 had included plans for a theatrical performance in 2000, and 'The Tale Old Time Tells' was staged in the Manor Pavilion on Thursday

following a week of workshop rehearsals. In addition to the music and song workshops, there was also The Forum, an informal folk club event for young musicians and singers in the Theatre Bar every tea-time, hosted by Jon Brenner.

The forty-sixth Festival was a nerve-wracking gamble, but the usual superb planning and organisation ensured that the different arrangements were a success.

Imbizo
(Zimbabwe)

A Spirit of Belonging

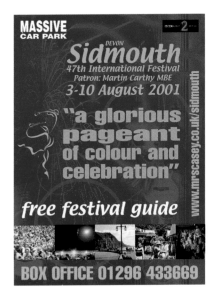

2001 The music journalist Colin Irwin reviewed the 2001 Festival for *Mojo*, an eclectic music magazine that sometimes features folk and roots music. In his enthusiastic review of the Festival Colin wrote, 'The folk scene's steadfast sense of its independence is both its strength and weakness. Yet the Sidmouth Festival, absorbing the entire town for a whole week, shows off its benefits as a musical culture in isolation. … there is irrefutably a spirit of belonging.'

The Ham was available again, and in addition to the concerts in the marquee every day, more use was made of the Arena Theatre as a concert venue. Every evening except Tuesday, Wednesday and Friday was given over to music concerts, although on a couple of evenings, dance was included in the concert programme – for example the Irish dance group Absolutely Legless performed alongside Sharon Shannon and The Woodchoppers on Saturday.

Lonnie Donegan returned to the Arena Theatre stage in his fiftieth anniversary year and stayed on in the town for several days after his Sunday evening concert. Tom Robinson, the musician, broadcaster and political activist, sang on Thursday evening and also dropped into the 'In the Tradition' lunchtime session in the Volunteer Inn to sing a song or two. The prospect of an appearance by The Incredible String Band, one of the legendary bands of the sixties, was intriguing, but the reality was a little different. The band proved to be a great disappointment to many who liked them in the sixties and, in the words of the *Sidmouth Herald*, 'a little haphazard'. The nine-year-old daughter of a friend sat on the bank, shook her head and proclaimed, 'Derek will *have* to put this in the book'.

Blue Murder was a band whose original members were Swan Arcade and The Watersons, but with the demise of Swan Arcade and the sad death of Lal Waterson, it seemed as if the band would not perform again. But Jim Boyes from Swan Arcade was now a member of Coope, Boyes and Simpson, and the trio had joined Norma and Mike Waterson, Martin and Eliza Carthy for a single concert appearance in Yorkshire the previous year. The Sidmouth concert was therefore only the second performance with this line-up; the band went on to record a Topic album the following year.

The 'World of Dance' concerts were mainly in the afternoons. After some teething problems had been ironed out, the new arrangements for accommodating the dance groups in Exeter were repeated, although no overseas dance group attended the Festival for the whole week. Martishor Folk Music and Dance Ensemble from Moldova came from Sunday to Thursday, before travelling on to the Billingham Festival, and there were also groups from Sicily, Zimbabwe (the ever-popular Black Umfolosi, as well as Siyaya Arts), Kenya, the South Pacific (Te Vaka), Japan (U.Stage), as well as taiko drummers and bhangra dancers. Indeed, there were more countries represented than ever before, but audiences no longer had the luxury of deciding when in the week they would choose to see them.

Even though some of the groups were only at the Festival for a couple of days, the 'Dance Roots' and 'A Chance to Meet' events continued, compered by John Braithwaite and Chris Rose respectively. For John, 'Dance Roots' is a unique opportunity to actually learn the dances and sing the songs with the members of the groups themselves, and he notices that the devotees return year after year to learn something new.

The British dance groups were featured in the World of Dance events, as well as in 'The Home Front'

Siyaya Arts

on Friday afternoon: many of the groups had visited the Festival before but they were still amongst the best British dance groups – Great Western Morris, Roughshod Appalachian Dancers, The Shropshire Bedlams and Martha Rhoden's Tuppenny Dish, Chinewrde Morris and Ouse Washes Molly Dancers.

Before 1997 there had been a Sunday morning procession from Port Royal to the Interdenominational Service at the Arena, but since 1997 the service had been held in the Connaught Gardens so the nature of the procession had been changed and its route reversed. Starting from the Knowle Drive above the Arena site, the procession was exclusively for the British dance groups, and was the prelude to the now traditional informal displays along the Esplanade from a great variety of Morris and sword teams. Great Western Morris continued with their great sense of fun by hiring a 'stretch limo' which was part of the procession. Members of the team, dressed as security men with radios and dark glasses, walked alongside the car and frisked by-standers, including Steve Heap and anyone else they recognised. They arranged for a group of adoring, screaming 'fans' to rush the car and lie down in the road. Ordinary by-standers were taken in by all this, and by the time the 'limo' reached the Esplanade the popular view was that Lonnie Donegan was inside. At Port Royal, the truth was revealed when the rest of Great Western Morris emerged from the car ready to dance.

Evidence of the growing number of young, talented singers and musicians could be seen in the Ham Concert Marquee events. Belinda Jones had now shortened her name to Bill and earlier in the year had won the BBC Radio 2 Horizon Award: she headlined the Tuesday afternoon concert alongside 422 who had won the BBC Radio 2 Young Folk Award in 2000. Some of the members of 422 were studying on the first Folk Music degree course in England, at Newcastle University. Some of us had been distracted from our university studies by our enthusiasm for folk

music, so we were somewhat amused to reflect that it was now possible to get a degree in it!

Dr Faustus was another new, young band, whose members were nevertheless already known to Sidmouth audiences – Tim van Eyken, Robert Harbron, Benji Kirkpatrick and Paul Sartin – and they were supported by Commotion, featuring Kirsty Cotter and Young Scottish Traditional Musician of the Year, Gillian Frame.

Young performers were not confined to Britain. Kieron Means sang American songs, some of them learnt from his mother Sara Grey; Slainthe Mhath were a young Canadian band specialising in Celtic music; Danú from Ireland was another BBC Radio 2 award winner (Best Group); and Kevin Rowsome was the grandson of legendary uillean piper Leo Rowsome.

> ... we were somewhat amused to reflect that it was now possible to get a degree in it!

Established performers included The Cock and Bull Band who had been appearing at the Festival since the eighties; another Festival favourite Les Barker; Norma Waterson and Martin Carthy; Artisan; long-time Festival performer Pete Coe; and

Nic Jones and Shirley Collins

Blowzabella, making one of their reunion appearances. Two occasional duos were Roy Bailey and John Kirkpatrick (the two men also appeared solo) and Dick Gaughan and Brian McNeill. Ralph Jordan was another seasoned Sidmouth performer, and he appeared alongside The Fraser Sisters, Jo Freya and Fi Fraser, as well as in the trio Patterson-Jordan-Dipper.

Cretian music duo Ta Perivolia and Gwelloc'h with Katell and Brigitte Kloareg from Brittany appeared at the Festival. From the other side of the Atlantic, New Yorkers Dan Milner and Bob Conroy sang throughout the week, including a 'Crossing the Pond' concert which also featured Walt Michael, a singer and hammered dulcimer player.

Steve Heap and Dave Hunt on the Wingnut seat

Although she had retired from singing, Shirley Collins came to the Festival and gave three talks in the Arts Centre: one was based on her collecting trip to the USA with Alan Lomax ('America over the Water' – now the title of her book on the subject), an 'In Conversation' event with Eddie Upton, and 'In Praise of English Music' about the early days of the folk song revival. It was at the end of this latter event that Nic Jones, who had not appeared at a major folk music event since his car accident twenty years earlier, made a surprise, yet emotional, appearance at the window – unable to get in because the event was full up.

One of the reasons why Nic had come to the Festival was for the Special Benefit Concert for Tony Rose, who had been diagnosed with cancer. Although no longer singing in public, Nic joined the performers (including Norma Waterson and Martin Carthy, John Kirkpatrick, Roy Bailey and Ryburn 3 Step) plus Tony, on the stage for the final song, 'Wild Mountain Thyme'. Tony and Nic reunited on stage again was an emotional high point of the Festival for many. Sadly, Tony died less than a year later.

Dave Hunt's partner in Dr Sunshine, Professor Wingnut, also known as Vic Baker, had died in 1999, and Dave, Steve Heap and Chris Coe decided to have a permanent memorial to Vic in Sidmouth. On Saturday lunchtime a memorial bench, shaped like a wingnut, was opened in the Arena Showground Children's Glade. Friends sang 'Climbing up a Sunshine Mountain' whilst sheltering under umbrellas.

In January 2001, one of the Festival's greatest supporters in the town died at the age of eighty-four. Ted Pinney had been on the former Urban District Council back in 1955

when the Festival first started, and he had continued his support on East Devon District Council and the County Council and was still a member of the Town Council when he died. But he was not just a great supporter of the Festival: his title 'Mr Sidmouth' was recognition that he always wanted what was best for Sidmouth, and whilst he fought to maintain the town's unique character, he was always aware of the need to progress.

Shooting Roots now became the title of the Youth Festival, receiving financial support from South West Arts Regional Arts Lottery Project. On Saturday the Shooting Roots tutors presented 'Ignition' – their concert party, featuring Commotion, Jennie Hawes, Karen Mair, Jon Brenner and others. Commotion was Sam Pirt, Joey Oliver, Kirsty Cotter, Gillian Frame and Rachel Unthank, and they led a mixed song and music workshop. There were also workshops on song, music and theatre, the latter featuring Black Swan Rapper, Cloggin Init, Andy Mussell, Fiona Cole, Laurel Swift (who was now co-ordinating the Youth Festival) and Doug Swift and Mikey Radford. Mikey's love of circus skills had started at Sidmouth and he had studied for a year at one of the few circus schools in the country: he and Doug taught juggling.

On Wednesday, the theatre workshop gave two performances

called 'Uprising': one in the Manor Pavilion and another in the Market Square, both of them also involving music and song, whilst the Shooting Roots Showcase performance took place on Thursday in the Manor Pavilion.

The working programme had now become a substantial document. With almost sixty pages, it not only listed all the events for the week, but also gave venue information (with disabled persons' access details), a separate workshop summary and a list of all artists, the events at which they were performing and brief biographical information. The souvenir programme had become an interesting, yet dispensable publication, taking up a great deal of time to prepare and publish, and it was decided not to produce one in 2001. Festival publicity still started with a leaflet in January, continued with a more up-to-date leaflet in March and now a thirty-page 'Festival Guide' was published in May with a detailed outline programme. The Festival also advertised, naturally, in national and regional folk magazines, and there was an advert in *fRoots* (the new name for *Folk Roots*) almost every month of the year, thanks to media sponsorship from the magazine. The internet was now an additional means of advertising, allowing regular updates of information. This all seemed a long way from the ink-duplicated programme and *Festival News* of the seventies.

Dick Stanger (left) and the Ceilidh in the Ford

The Dragons of Sidmouth

Bev & Ray Langton

2002 They may not have had any experience of running children's events when they started in 1991, but Children's Festival Producers Ray and Bev Langton were nationally recognised for the quality of their work by the time of the 2002 and 2003 Festivals. Sidmouth has the largest children's programme of any British folk festival, and they had been invited to co-ordinate and write the section on 'Children' in the Health and Safety Executive's *The Event Safety Guide*, published in 1999. Subtitled *A Guide to Health, Safety and Welfare at Music and Similar Events*, the book has become essential reading for anyone organising any sort of music event, and their contribution led to Ray and Bev being invited to national conferences. Compared with 1991, never mind 1965 when the first children's event took place at Sidmouth, there are now many more factors to take into account in running this part of the Festival. Child protection issues are paramount: health and safety, allergies to materials being used in craft workshops and the careful vetting of stewards, volunteer helpers and performers are just some of the aspects that have to be considered.

'Waves, Wings and Seaside Things' was the theme of the Children's Festival in 2002. Amongst the highlights in both 2002 and 2003 were the band workshops led by Whapweasel. How could the young musicians resist the 'Whap Pack'? – a tune book, practice tape, t-shirt and 'a few other cool things'.

The members of Whapweasel were apprehensive when they were first asked to run this workshop, and the band's melodeon player Robin Jowett remembers turning up at the hall early on the first morning and

> ## 'Look! There's Dr Sunshine dressed up as a real person!'

finding a queue of children at the door. Robin says, 'The children were a joy to work with and, although we set them some challenging goals, we were amazed at what they had achieved by the end of the week.' Bass player Brian Bell was impressed by the 'unbelievable creativity and open minds of the children'.

The Whapweasel Workshop Band played for the final Blackmore Gardens Club in both years, and the space needed for the band took a great chunk out of the dance floor. 'That was a fantastic event,' remembers Robin. Cittern player Mike Coleman admits to feeling 'very emotional' during the children's performance. 'Any band that is offered the chance to run the workshop should seize it – it's an opportunity not to be missed', says Robin.

Friday morning is still filled with the showcase events – one for music and another for dance. Appalachian clog, circus skills, Morris dancing, Irish dance, recorders, woodwind, drama, rapper sword, longsword, singing, strings, harmonica and crafts were just some of the workshops in 2002 and 2003.

One of the key figures in the Children's Festival events over the years has been Dr Sunshine, also known as Dave Hunt. So many years, in fact, that children who came to the events more than twenty years ago are now bringing their own children, and they still remember the songs, dances and games of their childhood. Andrea Holland remembers that her daughter Molly Evans, when aged about five or six, spotted Dave Hunt calling at a ceilidh. She called her mother over and whispered excitedly, 'Look! There's Dr Sunshine dressed up as a real person!'

Andrea fondly recalls sunny afternoons in the Blackmore Gardens, watching the same parents she has been seeing there for the last twelve years, 'seeing their children growing up, watching children's confidence grow as they learn instruments and perform on the children's open stage'.

Many people have spoken of the start of the school summer holiday, the preparation and anticipation of Sidmouth, the sadness at going home,

Whapweasel workshop band

Open Stage

Children's Showcase

but the joy at recalling all the happy memories from the week's events for the rest of the summer holiday, indeed the rest of the year. For Andrea and Molly, the traditional calendar has been abandoned, and the whole year is on a Sidmouth cycle – how many weeks till Sidmouth? 'I wouldn't miss it for a trip to Disneyland Florida – once suggested, but Sidmouth won!' Molly explains.

Many parents, and their children, have spoken about the importance of the Festival in broadening musical horizons and in introducing them to the music and dance of other cultures in other countries.

The impact of the Children's Festival has been immeasurable. Rachel Reid has attended every Festival since she was born, and is now twenty-two. 'Sidmouth Festival is a collection of sensations and experiences. It is irreplaceable and imprinted to the point where it feels like my second home. There are some experiences in your life without which your personality would be completely different. I am proud to say that Sidmouth's Children's Festival is a very big example of this for me.'

The Smallbone family – Greg and Kay and their four children Josh, Todd, Willow and Zach – have all been deeply involved with the Children's Festival since the early nineties. Greg and Kay have been involved with a variety of workshops, whilst the children have been participants and are now

volunteers themselves. Josh Smallbone, nineteen-years-old in mid-2004, and his brother Todd, seventeen, both helped with Whapweasel's band workshops in 2002 and 2003, and they both played with the band at the Grand Family Ceilidh. Josh and Todd, plus Ian Tilling, were given responsibility for hosting the Children's Festival Open Stage in 2001 and 2002, and in 2003 Josh and Ian passed this on to Todd and Willow, now fourteen. Some of the guests were recent Children's Festival participants. Danny Harmer and Florence Bearman, for example, are now active in Shooting Roots, but they were both booked to perform at the Open Stage. Florence is the daughter of Alan Bearman and Jane Bunting, and now aged fifteen, is an accomplished fiddle player, whilst Danny is a young melodeon player. But the main focus of the Open Stage was on the current children and, as Todd Smallbone says, 'It was great to encourage children to

perform and give them the chances we had had'.

For Willow Smallbone, 'Sidmouth is truly a part of my heart, it has its own place. I love everything about it', whilst Zach, aged twelve, says, 'Sidmouth is a way of life for me – I have been every summer since I was born.'

Looking at the impact on their family of the Festival in general, but the Children's Festival in particular, Kay and Greg Smallbone comment, 'Sidmouth is full of firsts for our family. First musical performance, first walk on their own, first pint, first night out without parents, first still awake at sunrise, first opportunity to run their own workshops, first long drive on a motorway, first opportunity to play in their own right with a great band – Whapweasel. We have made wonderful friends over the years from all over the world. We feel that our children are the wonderful people they are today because of all the opportunities opened up for them by Sidmouth.'

Josh reiterates Rachel Reid's comments: 'Sidmouth Festival has been, is, and hopefully still will be, such a huge part of making me the person I am today'.

Derek Reid, who has been involved with storytelling at the Children's Festival for many years, writes: 'I have watched so many children take traditional song and dance back with them into the world from Sidmouth and they have spun me summers long in sunlight, star nights and spellbinding. I have seen them and still see them growing. They are ageless and now their children tell me so.'

As the children reach their teens, so they gravitate to the Shooting Roots youth events, often returning to the Children's Festival to help and remember, thankful for the confidence, the encouragement and the opportunities.

The workshops are a significant part of the Children's Festival, but they are no less important for the adults' Festival. A glance at the workshop programme in the last few years gives an idea of the variety of different genres of dance, song and music that are being catered for. But just as important is the variety of levels that are available.

In recent years, the fiddle has been the most popular instrument and in 2002 there were workshops for absolute beginners, as well as workshops on fiddle playing for dancing, writing fiddle tunes, old-time fiddle tunes from Bruce Molsky, and Klezmer fiddle music. The melodeon workshops included two sessions for beginners, two intermediate and one advanced, and

Parachute Games with Dr Sunshine

there were also workshops for concertina, guitar, bodhran, banjo, bouzouki, wind instruments and percussion. For musicians who wanted to play alongside the players of other instruments, there was Pete Coe's 'Playing in a Ceilidh Band' workshop and the Big Band workshop. For a few years the latter had been led by Nick and Mary Barber, and it culminated in the Big

> *'You think it's a bit esoteric and there won't be many there, but the house full sign is up: people are hungry for information'*

Band playing for a ceilidh at the end of the week. As with the similar children's event, the huge band with dozens of musicians encroached on the dance floor.

The singing workshops once again gave the opportunity to specialise in a

single style – American shape note, rounds, South African choral singing, gospel, Italian, Georgian, maritime songs – or to come together in the Festival Choir, led in 2002 by Janet Russell. West Gallery music and song have not featured in the workshop programme every year, but the West Gallery enthusiasts now gather each morning of the Festival in the beach shelter at the western end of the Esplanade to chat about the previous day's events, and then to sing, for their own amusement and the entertainment of passers-by.

Over the years there have been talks and lectures of such variety and quality that they could have filled a folklore conference or two. Many of these have analysed singing or playing styles, and have given the opportunity for people to discuss approaches and participate. Sue Burnett has managed the workshop events and venues over several years, and she is always reassured by the interest in the lectures. 'You think it's a bit esoteric and there won't be many there, but the house full sign

Ira Bernstein workshop

The Big Session

is up: people are hungry for information.'

Sue believes that for many of the workshop events, there is no other similar platform anywhere else in the country and that, although there are specialist weekends and events, they are mainly for the people who are already interested. Sidmouth gives the opportunity for people to discover something new. Sue would love to make a video diary of the workshops – she says a montage would show just how much is being learned by so many people.

In 2002, as in other years, there were workshops on most aspects of English folk dance (Morris and sword, clog, percussive, and social), as well as on the dances of several other countries and communities (Irish, Cajun, French, Scandinavian, Dutch, Indian, Portuguese, Indian and Egyptian) and, as the programme pointed out, most of them could be tackled by the relative newcomer to folk dancing. But there was also an 'Absolute Beginners Dance' workshop, led by Kerry Fletcher, one of the countless people who have contributed in so many different ways to the Festival over the years. This workshop covered dancing in time with the music, how to dance with a partner, and the basic social dance

steps. There was also a 'Beginners Ceilidh' workshop and, at the start of the week, a taster or beginners session in Morris dancing followed by workshops in each of the Morris styles – Cotswold, North-West, Molly and Border, as well as rapper and longsword. This inclusive, welcoming approach is a theme which goes back to the sixties and reflects Bill Rutter's approach: 'I don't care about the people who know how to do things. I'm only interested in those who don't'. Of course now, as then, there are many opportunities for people who already 'know how to do things', to hone their skills and do it even better, whether they are musicians, singers or dancers.

There is probably more choice of workshops for the country dancers than for any other group at the Festival. In 2002, from Saturday to Friday, from 9.30am to 2.45pm, there were three workshops a day in the Blackmore Dance Marquee (with fifteen minutes for coffee break and thirty minutes for lunch), or, until 12.30pm, two workshops a day at the Church House Lawn Marquee. Early Playford dances, Scottish country dance, dances with 'modified square figures', contras, American dances, dances with numbers in the title were just some of the workshops. The leaders included Andrew Shaw, Erica Archer, David and Kathryn Wright and Barrie Bullimore, whilst the music came from Fiddlin' Around, Devil Among the Tailors, Momentum, Belshazzar's Feast

(a cross-over band who were applauded by the country dancers and the ceilidh goers) and Stradivarious, whose leader, on accordion, shares the same name as the melodeon player, Rod Stradling.

After the workshops, the country dancers continued dancing through the afternoon at the Tea Dance in the Blackmore Dance Marquee. In the evenings there was a choice between the Church House Lawn and Blackmore Dance Marquees.

2002 saw the return to the Arena Theatre Stage of Rolf Harris. Even more popular than on his previous visit, this was the first time ever that the open-air site had been declared 'House Full' and people were turned away. All the favourite songs were there again, and at the end he led the audience in a version of 'Tie me Kangaroo Down Sport' to the tune of 'Land of Hope and Glory'. Sidmouth had seen nothing like it. Once again, he appealed to every generation, with a group of teenage fans screaming 'We love you Rolf' at the end of the show.

There were some momentous concerts during the week. Song Links was a project dear to Martyn Wyndham-Read's heart, and in it the links between a selection of traditional songs in England and their Australian versions were explored. As well as Martyn, the singers included The Copper Family, John Kirkpatrick, and a young duo from Australia – Ruth Hazleton and Kate Burke. The concert was narrated by Shirley Collins and a double CD of studio recordings of the songs was released the following year.

The idea of The Big Session came from The Oysterband, who wanted to capture the spontaneity of a pub session and put it on the concert stage with a large group of emerging performers: Sidmouth was The Big Session's only performance in 2002. To complement the workshop emphasis on fiddle music, Saturday evening's Arena Theatre Show was 'A Fiddling Feast' with Blazin' Fiddles, the musicians of Compagnia Balari e Sonadur Ponte Caffaro, (making a very welcome return to the Festival), Gina Le Faux, Bruce Molsky, Ira

Bernstein and Brad Leftwich, with Catriona Macdonald as compere.

Martin Carthy was again seen in several different guises – with Brass Monkey (in both a concert and a ceilidh), sharing a stage with Martin Simpson, and there was also a brief appearance in Ashley Hutchings's tribute to Morris dancing, 'Grandson of Morris On'. Since 1999, Martin had been the Festival's Patron.

Another significant change to venues occurred in 2002. It was decided to reduce the Global Roots Parties aspect of the Festival, and the Bowd and Bulverton Marquees were merged into a new Festival Dance House on the Bulverton site. This new arrangement, with a larger marquee, and a separate bar and catering marquee, reduced the amount of traffic on the main road at a stroke, with festival-goers walking up the hill from the camp-

Blazin' Fiddles

> *An ocean of friendly faces from around the world invited to sing, dance and play*

site or catching the bus back to town. The Festival Dance House hosted dance workshops during the day and a ceilidh in the evening before the Late Night Extra from 11.15pm. The dancers were at first cautious about the new arrangements, but enthusiastic by the middle of the week.

In addition to the dancers from Ponte Caffaro in Italy, there was the Yi-tzy Folk Dance Troupe from Taiwan, the Mtiebi Male Ensemble

choir from Georgia, as well as dance groups from France, Portugal and the Netherlands. The Russian Cossack State Song and Dance Ensemble visited the Festival for two days to headline a 'World of Dance Special' on Wednesday evening, and appear at 'A Chance to Meet'. The Britannia Coco-nut Dancers from Bacup returned, this time to concertina accompaniment, and other English dance groups included Windsor Morris and The Witchmen, whilst the longsword dancers, Orion, came from Boston, Massachusetts.

The final evening – 'The Night of Dragons' – was the culmination of a series of workshops during the week. A small team of festival-goers built, painted and operated a dragon, and the Shooting Roots participants also built 'The Lambton Worm' with which they illustrated the song of the same title. There were also children's workshops, the Festival Choir rehearsed a song, musicians learnt some tunes and Windsor Morris ran a workshop for dozens of Morris dancers who filled the stage for a newly-composed

dance and tune. To complete the Friday evening show, The Great Wall Arts Troupe brought their Chinese Dragon and acrobats, and there were bhangra dancers and African masks and drums. The whole project was led by the Wren Trust, although mud on the Arena site from rain earlier in the week, affected the show.

The Chipolatas celebrated their tenth birthday at the Festival Dance House with guests including Eliza Carthy, and the programme promised 'a combination of riotous routines and rhythmic roots'. For Chipolatas' members Tristan Glover and Sam Thomas in particular, the Sidmouth Festival has been part of their childhood, their family and now their careers. They describe the Festival as, 'A true carnival in every sense of the word, normal life is put on standby, as the circus comes to town! This is all a Festival can be, a sense of celebration and altered state, an atmosphere anchored by adrenaline. An ocean of friendly faces from around the world invited to sing, dance and play.'

Louis Killen and Cyril Tawney

Roots and Shoots

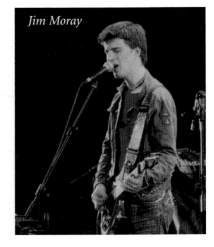
Jim Moray

2003 David Slater's 1986 hope that the 'real' Sidmouth of 2000 and beyond would be guaranteed by nurturing the children of that year was amazingly accurate. The six-year-old in 1986 would have been twenty-three in 2003: perhaps a participant in, or even a tutor at, the Shooting Roots events.

The Shooting Roots generation – festival-goers aged twelve to twenty-five – might, in previous years, have included Mike Waterson, Pete Coe, Beryl Jukes, Jo Freya, Steve Heap and me: all of us were within this age range when we first came to the Festival. But we had continued to grow up with the Festival. The new Shooting Roots generation needed space and opportunities to perform and experiment. The Festival Director, Steve Heap, created both the space and the opportunity, and the young festival-goers themselves have been essential in devising the programme.

Having led this part of the Festival for a few years, Laurel Swift became the Shooting Roots Artistic Director in 2003. Laurel had been coming to the Festival with her parents John and Sue Swift and her brother Doug since she was a child. She had danced in the Blackmore Gardens, joined in the Morris Minors, taken part in the band workshops and performed on the Arena Stage. An excellent musician and dancer, she has worked in folk arts management and performance since graduating in 1999.

In 2003 there were four series of daily workshops: Shooting Roots Ensemble was for instrumentalists and singers, who worked on learning, arranging and harmonising tunes. Shooting Roots Skills examined the techniques required for playing folk music on particular instruments, playing styles and stagecraft. Shooting Roots in Theatre focused on street theatre techniques, performance and teamwork skills, whilst Shooting Roots Dance concentrated on clog, rapper and molly dance. All four series worked towards showcase

> *'Being able to escape the adults, swap instruments and make new, like-minded, musical friends, was fantastic ...'*

events: on Wednesday for the theatre workshop members who performed on the Arena Showground; on Thursday evening for the dance performances; and on Thursday afternoon for the music and song workshop members who performed in the Manor Pavilion. The Forum led by John Brenner and Sam Dolan was a further opportunity for young people to perform in an informal folk club style setting.

The tutors included Mikey and Cat Radford, members of Black Swan Rapper, Doug Swift, Miriam Ayling, Jackie Oates, Sarah Stuart, Debbie Kay, Anna Tabbush, Anthea Beasant, Katy Hayes, Jim Moray, Lauren McCormick and John Dipper. There are plenty of recognisable surnames in that list, but having parents who are regular and well-known festival-goers is not a criterion for involvement and many young participants have had no previous family connections with the Festival. Some of them had never heard of the Festival, and in some cases had no experience of folk music, until school, college or university friends introduced them to the event.

Jennie Hawes came to the Festival as a child, then the family had a few years off, before she persuaded her parents that it was time to return. Jennie was immediately drawn into Shooting Roots, first as a participant. 'You were always encouraged and always made to feel able to join in – if anyone was struggling, there was always someone older or with more experience to offer help. The tutors themselves succeeded in making the music accessible. Being able to escape the adults, swap instruments and make new, like-minded, musical friends, was fantastic', Jennie remembers.

After a few years of participating, Jennie had been asked to help with tutoring and had then become the leader of the music workshops. 'This is one of the greatest things

Shooting Roots Dance

FolkESTRA north!

String Stir

about Shooting Roots: the way it allows young people from within the workshops, who have spent a few years developing their skills, the opportunity to become tutors themselves and help young musicians advance.' Jennie describes her five years as a tutor as 'fantastic: having the chance to teach such a wide variety of folk music to many wonderful and talented young people!' Jennie was sad to stop tutoring, but as she herself says, 'I had reached the age when it was time for someone else to have a go.'

Quite apart from the Shooting Roots events, several of the participants were also being featured in Festival venues including the Parish Church, Bedford Hotel and the Ham Concert Marquee, where they joined an increasing number of young performers. FolkESTRA north! is The Sage Gateshead's youth folk ensemble. Aged between fourteen and nineteen, these highly talented young musicians from many parts of

Northern England appeared alongside the Kathryn Tickell Band at the Ham Concert Marquee on Thursday evening. Kathryn is FolkESTRA north!'s artistic director and, of course, having made her own Festival debut at the age of sixteen, she was another of the people who might have been in Shooting Roots had it existed back then. Her band and FolkESTRA north! all played together on stage at a concert which was the talking point of the Festival the next day. The previous evening, FolkESTRA north! had been joined by Kathryn when they played in the Volunteer Inn Garden Marquee, a new informal venue. Also from the North-East were sisters Rachel and Becky Unthank who sang, played and clog danced.

Then there was Kerfuffle from the East Midlands; The Witches of Elswick; the winners of the BBC Radio 2 Young Folk Award, Uiscedwr; and two bands featuring Kirsty Cotter, String Stir and Watson-Cotter. String Stir was a mainly female band featuring young

fiddle players, singers and dancers: the other members included Laurel Swift, Lori Watson and Miranda Rutter. Watson-Cotter were Lori and Kirsty again, plus Gordon Middler on keyboards. Seasoned festival-goer Jim Moray spent most of the week as a Shooting Roots tutor but he also appeared in the Ham Concert Marquee. His debut album, *Sweet England*, had been enthusiastically received and in 2004 he won two BBC Radio 2 Folk Awards – Horizon and Best Album.

A combination of music and dance was presented by Fosbrooks – The Front Line. Fosbrooks dance groups, who had been to the Festival several times, were originally based in the school where the leader, Liza Austin-Strange, taught. Liza had since established the Fosbrook Folk Education Trust to run classes and workshops for young people in the Stockport area to spectacular effect. Two duos in Fosbrooks also performed in their own right: Murray Grainger and Amy Thatcher

Shooting Roots Ensemble

Shooting Roots Showcase

John Kirkpatrick

who appeared in the Arts Centre, and Nicola Lyons and Jamie Schofield (no relation!) who performed at a 'Roots and Shoots' concert in the Parish Church on Tuesday evening.

With several FolkESTRA north! and Fosbrooks members also taking part in Shooting Roots, and as several of the musicians and singers were involved in more than one band, the programming was complex.

But for the more mature festival-goers who had been coming to Sidmouth for many years, the whole effect of the young bands, musicians, dancers and singers was extremely reassuring. The artistic future of the Festival and the wider folk movement looked more secure than for many years.

La Bottine Souriante returned to the Arena Theatre stage on Saturday evening and whilst they may not have had the same impact as their last appearance – they were now without the charismatic accordion player Yves Lambert – they still drew a large audience. Lindisfarne, Altan and Eliza Carthy all featured in their own concerts at the Arena Theatre. Altan were supported by John Spiers and Jon Boden.

The Festival was now more confident with the Exeter

• *England wins Rugby World Cup*
• *Second Gulf War – USA and UK invade Iraq*
• *Saddam Hussein overthrown as Iraqi leader*
• *Bob Hope dies aged 100*
• *Concorde makes its last commercial flight*
• *Beyonce and Black-Eyed Peas at No 1*

2003

---

accommodation arrangements for the international dance groups and, during the week, there were groups from Russia, Spain, Ghana, Korea and Poland. English dance groups included the Grenoside Traditional Sword Dancers (renewing the Festival's long-standing association with Sheffield), Gog Magog Molly, Slubbing Billy's, Chiltern Hundreds, Berkshire Bedlam and Hexham Morris.

During the week, the Festival Choir and Orchestra each rehearsed the music for 'A Fanfare for the South West', a tribute to Cecil Sharp to mark the centenary of his first folk song collecting in Somerset. Specially commissioned by Folk South West, the piece comprised traditional songs with linking music by Gina Le Faux, arranged and orchestrated by John Kirkpatrick. The performance was on Thursday evening in the Arena Theatre, when the audience included civic heads from all over Devon and beyond –

> *... Civic heads from all over Devon and beyond gave the Fanfare and its performers a standing ovation*

they gave the Fanfare and its performers a standing ovation.

There were further allusions to Cecil Sharp in Magpie Lane's Saturday concert in the Manor Pavilion, which had as its title the first song that Sharp collected, 'The Seeds of Love'. Other Manor Pavilion concerts included The Mellstock Band's 'Ghosts and Lovers: Songs and Tales of the Erotic and the Supernatural', and an 'In the Tradition' concert featuring Vic Legg from Cornwall, Sheena Blackhall (singer, poet and storyteller from Aberdeen), Billy Teare from Northern Ireland, Bob Lewis from Sussex and the Linane Family and friends from London's Irish music community. Later in the week, the Millen Family from Kent sang their family songs in the Arts Centre and at the Volunteer Inn.

As if running the Children's Festival band workshop was not enough, Whapweasel also played for several ceilidhs, including Saturday's LNE and Monday evening's Festival Dance House Ceilidh, plus an Anchor Garden Ceilidh. In the sweltering heat of LNE, their Whap fans (the ones used to cool you down) were a stroke of genius. The band launched their new album, *Relentless*, during the week and their popularity at Sidmouth was one of the contributing factors to them being nominated for the BBC Folk Awards Horizon Award – the first ceilidh band to be nominated for any of the awards.

Peeping Tom brought their Big Band line-up to Saturday's Festival Dance House Ceilidh. Grand Union, Chalktown, Bedlam, Random and Token Women also appeared during the week and there was so much buzz about the resurgence of English Ceilidh (or e-ceilidh as it is sometimes known) amongst the younger festival-goers that Sidmouth was heavily featured in a major article on the ceilidh scene in *fRoots* early in 2004. Bridging the country dance and ceilidh divide was Rodney Miller's Airdance, the leading American contradance band, led by one of the very best New England style fiddlers. The band played for dance workshops, contradances for the country dancers, and high energy dances for the ceilidh-goers at LNE.

Several of the dance and music elements across the generations came together in the Monday evening Arena Theatre Show 'Flame!'

Directed by Sue Swift, and with support from Arts Council England and the PRS Foundation, this was a spectacular dance and music performance which traced English dances from the reign of Elizabeth I. Narrated by Tim Laycock and Sonia Ritter, the first half music was from the Mellstock Band and the dances included a galliard from Renaissance historical dance group, members of The Outside Capering Crew with their hobby horses, Berkshire Bedlam performing a matachin dance with clashing swords, and the Grenoside Traditional Sword Dancers. Will Kemp's 'Nine Daies Wonder' dance in 1600 from London to Norwich was represented, not by Will himself, but by the maid (Laurel Swift) he met on his travels, who 'danced a jig for more than an hour'.

Part two, with music from The English Acoustic Collective, took the audience to the future and, according to the narrator, to 'the creative freedom of the dance'. Morris Offspring, mostly in their twenties, took traditional Morris steps and figures and turned them into a new dance format, complete with unicorn and boar's heads. In the darkness, Black Swan Rapper came onto the stage with blazing swords, which remained alight through the intricacies of the figures, culminating in a fiery sword lock. And then, in the stillness, the Thaxted Morris Men performed their Horn Dance (derived from the Abbots Bromley tradition), which they normally only perform in their own village. The Arena was silent as the fiddle could

be heard in the distance, and the dancers gently weaved their way towards the stage, escorted by members of Morris Offspring holding flaming torches. And then they retreated, back into the night.

The links between 'Flame!' and the earlier 'Flashback' and 'Frost and Fire' were clear: Sidmouth had achieved another unique success.

Janet Dowling, reviewing Flame! on the internet and in the magazine *Morris Matters* called the show 'gobsmackingly good'. Her comment about the show and Morris Offspring – 'while they are developing the Morris and interpreting it in new ways, they will still respect and protect the old ways' – could also be a comment on the whole Festival.

When Janet Dowling first came to the Sidmouth Festival in the seventies, she kept bumping into people who told her that they had

'gobsmackingly good!'

been coming for two, five, seven years, and she remembers thinking 'with the arrogance of youth, how boring to keep going back to the same place year after year. I don't think I quite understood part of the spirit of Sidmouth. Now, twenty-seven years later, I no longer make the decision about whether or not to attend. I just go. It's a community that is spread out across the country, it grows and develops.'

Lynne Render summarised the views of many people, 'There's a feeling of coming home every year'.

Alan Bearman

As with many others, Lynne has particular images and sounds to cherish: 'Going to bed and listening to the sound of the sea and music drifting in through the window from the lone musician, who can't resist one more tune.' Pamela Gold and her husband Albert came to Sidmouth in the mid-nineties specifically for the Festival, even though they had no experience of folk music and dance – 'an acquaintance had told us a little about it'. She says, 'The title of this amazing week doesn't begin to do it justice: it has a completely universal appeal. The title fails to conjure up the colour, excitement, spectacle, verve and vitality that abound. It's as if a benign deity had sprinkled magic dust over the whole town, and I wish I knew how to sprinkle it over the rest of the world.'

John 'Maca' McDonald had a good story which reflected the conflicting attitudes to the Festival in the town. 'I was stood at a bus stop in Sidmouth and the streets

A Fanfare for the South West

Sidmouth Steppers

Whapweasel

were full of colourfully dressed people with music all around. An old chap came up to me and said, "We retire down here to die," and then with a glint in his eye and a smile, he continued, "Then you buggers come down here and remind us what life is all about".

Frances Watt first came to the Festival in 1994 and could not believe the queue of people to get into the Brass Monkey concert: 'It was the first time I had seen so many people as enthusiastic and excited about the music I was into'. By 1999 Frances was working for Mrs Casey Music where she is part of the eight person office team who focus on the event all year round. 'Watching it all come together with the mighty Task Force, and then working with the 500 or more volunteer stewards and helpers and being part of a bigger team that actually makes it all happen – there's nothing else like it.'

The volunteer stewards are part of the spirit of Sidmouth: the desire to be involved and make a

contribution. Alan Bearman recognises that there is less of a distinction between performers and audience: everyone sees themselves as an active participant in the event. Artist liaison, headed by Gill Brice and Andy Dixson-Smith, assist the smooth running of the whole week.

> **'We retire down here to die... then you buggers come down here and remind us what life is all about'**

Richard Carver did not have a view about the Festival's value during the time he and his family were involved with Woodfidley in the seventies. 'Then I looked back and realised how valuable and formative it had been for us as a family and for our children, and for me musically. The children in contact with many other children, new acquaintances and

friendships, a significantly wider age range than at school. New activities, new situations, lots of supportive adults, lots of family groups being happy together and happy apart. All of that has an important effect on your values and how you want to live your life. It is not just about the event, it's also about the people who are here. That's all about support and friendship. It *is* about international peace, goodwill and understanding. It *is* about co-operation for mutual benefit. It *is* about understanding and appreciating other cultures. I don't know anything else that does that other than Sidmouth.'

Fifty years ago, the music and the dancing may not have been so loud and energetic, but the dancers in 1955 had been the same age – younger in some cases – as the ceilidh dancers of 2003 and the Shooting Roots participants. Their motives and their sense of fun were the same. The spirit of 1955 lives on amongst the Shooting Roots generation.

Music in the Bedford Hotel

West Dorset Accordion Group

Golden Jubilation

2004

As Bill Rutter wrote at the time of the Silver Jubilee in 1979, 'We are celebrating with a mixture of nostalgia and the current scene. Expect nothing. Create everything anew.'

This chapter is being written on May Day, three months before the 2004 Festival actually takes place, and is therefore a preview rather than a review.

As far as nostalgia is concerned, the international dance groups will hopefully include Halychyna from Ukraine who visited the Festival in 1992; The Wild Goose Chase Cloggers who came in 1988; Kasava from the Czech Republic from 1981; and Esbart Dansaire de Rubi from Catalonia in Spain, who first visited the Festival in 1970 and returned in 1972 and 1979 – we think they will notice a few changes! Black Umfolosi 5 have been firm favourites in the last few years.

From Britain, Hammersmith Morris Men first visited in 1967, whilst Albion Morris came in 1974, Seven Champions' first appearance was in Silver Jubilee year, and the Britannia Coco-nut Dancers, although making their third appearance, are more recent visitors.

The anniversary has generated several reunions. The Songwainers have reformed and look set to delight those who remember their memorable appearances in the sixties and seventies. Flowers and Frolics will play for a Golden Jubilee Ceilidh, the world-music influenced Tiger Moth have reformed for the summer, whilst Oysterband are bringing back several former members to give us The Oyster Ceilidh Band. For the first time since 1992, 'A Poor Man's House' returns to the stage of the Manor Pavilion, directed by Tim Laycock and Barry Lister.

Several guests are sharing anniversaries with us: The Old Swan Band (thirty years), Steeleye Span (thirty-five years) and Ralph McTell (in his sixtieth birthday year). It is also the tenth anniversary of Shooting Roots.

And then there are the guests who have appeared over and over again, and who have helped make Sidmouth the Festival it has become: The Yetties; John Kirkpatrick; Tim Laycock; Taffy Thomas; Coope, Boyes and Simpson; Roy Bailey; The Old Hat Concert Party; Patrick Ryan; Gordon Potts; Dave Hunt; Roisin White; Rosie Stewart; Jim Coleman and Denis Smith; the Weston Country Dance Band; Alan Bell; Pete Coe; Strawberry; and Sid Kipper (after all the Festival is named after his mouth).

There is a Generations theme running right through the Festival: John Kirpatrick and his son Benji; Sara Grey and her son Kieron Means; Carolyn Robson and her daughters The Tabbush Sisters; John Adams and Chris Coe and their daughter Lucy Adams; and Scalene (Nancy Kerr and her mother Sandra plus James Fagan); and James's family band, The Fagan Family. There is a Waterson Family Special with Martin Carthy and Norma Waterson with their daughter Eliza Carthy; Mike Waterson and his daughter Eleanor Waterson; Oliver Knight and Maria Knight (Lal Waterson's son and daughter) plus Saul Rose and Tim van Eyken. Taffy Thomas and his son Sam Thomas with the rest of the Chipolatas and special guests will present a special show 'Alive, Alive O', which promises to be full of retrospectives, tributes,

music, stories, comedy and street theatre. The Generations theme will also extend to all aspects of the Festival and up to four generations of some families will be involved.

As for 'the current scene', there are some performers making their Sidmouth debut including Tony Benn (with Roy Bailey), BELLOWhead (the Spiers and Boden Big Band), Kepa Junkera Band from the Basque Country, Tibetan Monks from Tashi Lhunpo Monastery and Banditaliana from Italy. They join John Tams and Barry Coope; bands such as Whapweasel, Hekety and Jabadaw; and American callers Gene Morrow and Cis Hinkle; as well as the town's own Sidmouth Steppers.

The special events (as if the rest of the Festival is not special!) will include 'On English Ground' with Morris Offspring and Chris Wood; an Arena Theatre concert with Kate Rusby and John McCusker and guests including Eddi Reader and Dave Burland; Song Links 2 (this time, English songs and their American counterparts); and 'Leap!' (a 'jaunty journey' through fifty years of Morris dancing at the Festival, narrated by Sid Kipper). Shooting Roots have a party with John Spiers and Jon Boden.

But some people will be coming to the Festival for the first time: for them it will be new, and we look forward to introducing them to the delights that are The Sidmouth International Festival!

Three Directors: John Dowell and Steve Heap on Bill Rutter's seat

2005 and Beyond

David Slater

It is tempting to write that the Festival has now settled on the right combination of venues and events. Certainly the current programme is very well received by festival-goers, whether they are visitors to the town or local residents. But the Sidmouth Festival has never, and probably will never, stand still. Improvements will always be considered and changing tastes will always be taken into account.

What is less settled is the financial structure on which the Festival is built. In recent years the Festival has had a budget of approximately three-quarters of a million pounds, of which two-thirds is guaranteed as long as advance ticket sales are maintained, along with other revenue sources, before the Festival begins. That leaves almost a quarter of a million pounds to be raised during the week itself. As most of that income needs to come from the Arena Theatre shows, where the audience sits in the open air, and given the unpredictability of the English weather, the nature of the risk is only too apparent.

That risk is being borne, not by arts organisations, local councils, central government or businesses through sponsorship, but by the two company shareholders: Steve Heap and Richard Carver. Getting people to recognise their personal commitment has become a cause that is very dear to David Slater's heart. President of the Festival in Golden Jubilee Year, David says, 'To allow these two men to run up that sort of personal financial risk is totally unacceptable. I take my hat off to them. They are men of courage and conviction.' David's message is clearly aimed at the local councils and businesses in Sidmouth: 'I think the town of Sidmouth should be proud, pleased and highly collaborative in putting on the Festival'.

The current Festival is sometimes described as 'too commercial', perhaps by people who do not readily realise the nature of the financial structure of the event. My dictionary defines 'commercial' as 'interested in financial return rather than artistry', and nothing could be further from the truth as far as the Sidmouth Festival is concerned. Sidmouth International Festival is a non-profit distributing company and the contract payment to Steve Heap's business, Mrs Casey Music, for running the Festival is so low that Mrs Casey Music's other activities actually subsidise the Sidmouth event. When the Festival has not been able to pay the contract charge in full, Mrs Casey Music has waived part of the payment. The ticket prices compare most favourably with many other arts and leisure activities, which are often publicly subsidised, and the growth in the number of sales outlets on the Arena Showground is a legitimate and

> 'I think the town of Sidmouth should be proud, pleased and highly collaborative in putting on the Festival'

honest way of generating more Festival income in order to guarantee the financial stability of the whole event.

Over the years the Festival has enjoyed good relations with many friendly local businesses and organisations, and some of them have recognised the financial and artistic value of the Festival to the town by providing some financial support for the event. Their support, though welcome, has never been enough to provide the financial stability that is necessary to reduce the personal risk to the organisers. Other businesses have prospered from the Festival without offering any support. The owners of many businesses admit, in private if not in public, that if it were not for the Festival, they would not be able to survive.

Clearly, the financial basis has to be changed if the event is to continue after the Fiftieth Festival.

But David Slater wants the town of Sidmouth to recognise the value of the Festival over and above the purely financial benefits.

David says, 'In a world that is staggeringly divided in so many different ways – even the society in which we belong – the Festival is saying that people are very different, and that is what makes them attractive and worth our attention.

'I think there are two reasons why the Sidmouth Festival should be treasured. Firstly, Sidmouth has remembered and brought our traditional folk culture into the present and made it valuable for the future. It has allowed us to be proud and knowledgeable about our roots, made us able to rejoice, join in and go forward. And secondly, it has invited all of us to look at other traditions and other cultures, some of which we may find genuinely difficult to understand, but to do so with an open heart and mind. I can't imagine two things more valuable to say to everybody – be proud of your own country, but be friends with the world.'

Whatever the future, there is no doubt that the Sidmouth International Festival has made a significant contribution to enriching the lives of many thousands of people, and is a vital chapter in the history of the British folk music and dance movement.

Directors and Producers

Over the years, different titles have been given to the individuals who have directed the various parts of the Festival. To simplify matters, the following terms are used: Dance Producer (DP), Song Producer (SP), Music Producer (MP), Arena Producer (AP) and Children's Producer (CP).

In the 1950s, Margaret Grant was Co-Director, in charge of organisation.
From 1961 to 1979 Bill Rutter was Festival Director.
From 1979 to 1989 John Dowell was Festival Director.
From 1990 to the present day Steve Heap has been Festival Director.

1955-1960: Nibs Matthews (DP), Jean Forsyth (Matthews) (MP), Margaret Grant (Co-Director)
1961   Tony Foxworthy (DP), Beryl Marriott (MP).
1962   Tony Foxworthy (DP), Beryl Marriott (MP), John Burgess (SP).
1963   Jack Hamilton (DP), Denis Smith (MP), John Burgess (SP).
1964   Jack Hamilton (DP), John Burgess (SP).
1965-1966 Ron Smedley (DP), Tony Foxworthy (SP).
1967-1968 Peter Dashwood (DP), Denis Manners (SP).
1969   Peter Dashwood (DP), Dave Wood (SP).
1970   Brian Heaton (DP), Tony Rose (SP).
1971   Peter Dashwood (DP), Roger Watson (SP).
1972   Jan Willcocks (DP), Mike Price (SP).
1973   Jan Willcocks (DP), Colin Cater (SP).
1974   John Brock (DP), Colin Cater (SP).
1975   John Brock (DP), Keith Glover (SP).

1976   Brian Jones (AP), John Brock (DP), Keith Glover (SP).
1977   Brian Jones (AP), John Brock (DP), Barry Lister (SP), Paul Weir (CP).
1978   Les Willcox (AP), Barry Lewis (DP), Barry Lister (SP), Paul Weir (CP).
1979   Les Willcox (AP), Barry Lewis (DP), Rod Ferguson (SP), Jim Reynolds (CP).
1980   David Slater (AP), Tom Brown (DP), Rod Ferguson (SP), Jim Reynolds (CP).
1981   David Slater (AP), Tom Brown (DP), John Heydon (SP), John Middleton (CP).
1982   Cathy Lesurf (AP), Eddie Upton (DP), John Heydon (SP), John Middleton (CP).
1983   Cathy Lesurf (AP), Eddie Upton (DP), Barry Coope (SP), Ian Carter (CP).
1984   Barry Lister (AP), Hugh Rippon (DP), Barry Coope (SP), Ian Carter (CP).
1985   Barry Lister (AP), Hugh Rippon (DP), Pat Ryan (SP), David Slater (CP).
1986   Eddie Upton (AP), Gordon Potts (DP), Pat Ryan (SP), David Slater (CP).
1987   Eddie Upton (AP), Gordon Potts (DP), Alan Bearman (SP), Nigel Barrell (CP).
1988   Eddie Upton (AP), Bob Mallindine (DP), Alan Bearman (SP), Nigel Barrell (CP).
1989   Eddie Upton (AP), Bob Mallindine (DP), Alan Bearman (SP), Margaret Hordley (CP).
1990   Alan Bearman (Artistic Director), Eddie Upton (AP), David Slater (CP).
1991   Alan Bearman (Artistic Director), Eddie Upton (AP), Ray and Bev Langton (CP).
1992-1996 Alan Bearman (Artistic Director), Derek Schofield (AP), Ray and Bev Langton (CP).
1997-1998 Alan Bearman (Artistic Director), John Kirkpatrick (AP), Ray and Bev Langton (CP).
1999-2004 Alan Bearman (Artistic Director), Mike Bettison (AP), Ray and Bev Langton (CP).

Freedom of the Festival

From time to time, the Freedom of the Festival has been awarded for outstanding service. The recipients of this award are:

Mr and Mrs J.G. Alford
Mrs Eileen Allen and Mr E Allen
Mr Stuart Ball
Mrs Alice Brooks
Mr John and Mrs Ivy Brunt
Mr Antony Brunt
Mr Packie Byrne
Mr and Mrs Tom Chambers

Mr John and Mrs Mandy Dowell
Mr and Mrs Tony Eacock
Mr Alan and Mrs Vera Gibberd
Mr John R.Gilling
Miss Olive Gooding
Mrs and Mrs Doug Holsgrove
Mr and Mrs Eric Howarth
Mr Frank and Mrs Monica Lock
Mr Clive and Mrs Hazel Morgan
Mr Stan and Mrs Eileen Nicholls
The Rory O'Connor Dancers
Mr and Mrs F.A.C. (Ted) Pinney
Mr Bill and Mrs Terry Rutter
Mr and Mrs Bob Seldon
Rev Canon David and Mrs Kirsten Slater
Mr Dick Stanger
Mr Alan White
Mr Dave Williams

Festival Map of Sidmouth

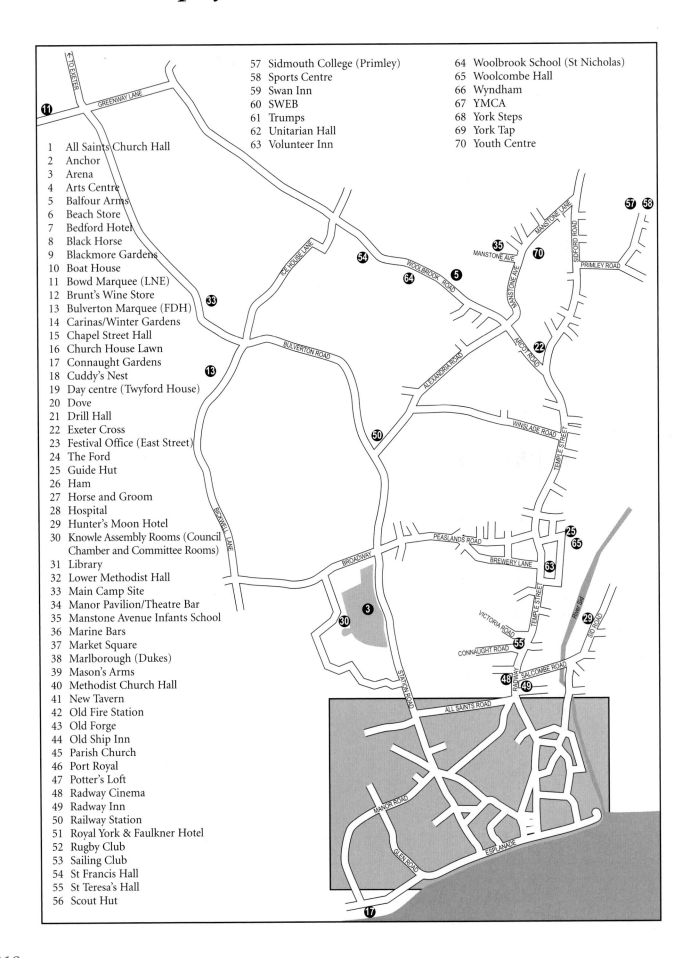

57 Sidmouth College (Primley)
58 Sports Centre
59 Swan Inn
60 SWEB
61 Trumps
62 Unitarian Hall
63 Volunteer Inn

64 Woolbrook School (St Nicholas)
65 Woolcombe Hall
66 Wyndham
67 YMCA
68 York Steps
69 York Tap
70 Youth Centre

1 All Saints Church Hall
2 Anchor
3 Arena
4 Arts Centre
5 Balfour Arms
6 Beach Store
7 Bedford Hotel
8 Black Horse
9 Blackmore Gardens
10 Boat House
11 Bowd Marquee (LNE)
12 Brunt's Wine Store
13 Bulverton Marquee (FDH)
14 Carinas/Winter Gardens
15 Chapel Street Hall
16 Church House Lawn
17 Connaught Gardens
18 Cuddy's Nest
19 Day centre (Twyford House)
20 Dove
21 Drill Hall
22 Exeter Cross
23 Festival Office (East Street)
24 The Ford
25 Guide Hut
26 Ham
27 Horse and Groom
28 Hospital
29 Hunter's Moon Hotel
30 Knowle Assembly Rooms (Council
   Chamber and Committee Rooms)
31 Library
32 Lower Methodist Hall
33 Main Camp Site
34 Manor Pavilion/Theatre Bar
35 Manstone Avenue Infants School
36 Marine Bars
37 Market Square
38 Marlborough (Dukes)
39 Mason's Arms
40 Methodist Church Hall
41 New Tavern
42 Old Fire Station
43 Old Forge
44 Old Ship Inn
45 Parish Church
46 Port Royal
47 Potter's Loft
48 Radway Cinema
49 Radway Inn
50 Railway Station
51 Royal York & Faulkner Hotel
52 Rugby Club
53 Sailing Club
54 St Francis Hall
55 St Teresa's Hall
56 Scout Hut

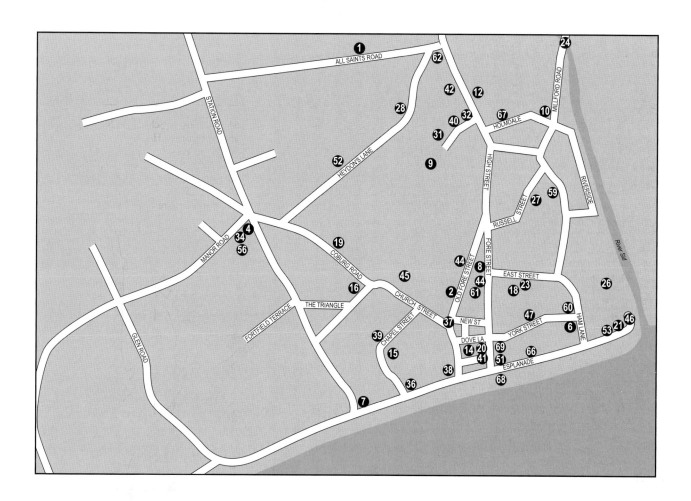

Photographic Credits

All photographs in the year-by-year chapters were taken at the Festival. In many cases, they were taken by festival-goers rather than by professional photographers. In spite of my best efforts, not all the photographers have been identified. 'Festival Archives' means that there is no indication who the photographer was. Some of the early photographs may have come from Miss Poyton of Sidmouth, and some from the early 1980s onwards from Doc Rowe or Derek Brooks. Thanks to Malcolm Taylor of the Vaughan Williams Memorial Library (VWML); to Ian Anderson of *fRoots;* to Emma Silverthorne (Editor) and Simon Horn (Photographic Editor) of the *Sidmouth Herald* for giving me access to their photographic archives, and for use of their photographs; and to all the people listed below.

The following abbreviations are used:
T (top), M (middle), B (bottom), L (left) and R (right).

ABC Television: 26T, Ian Anderson (*fRoots*): 124TR, 149T, 179BL, 208, 212, 214TR, Ian Anderson (Taunton): 113, Alvin Barrett: 117TR, 117B, Gerry Bates: 37, 42, John Brock: 77B, 80, 81T, 81B, 82T, 89T, Neil Brookes: 203T, Duncan Broomhead: 186T, Derek Brooks: 116BR, 135BR, 137, 142B, 144, 154B, 165B, 172TR, 172B, 173BL, 176TL, 176TR, Sue Burgess: 134TR, Iain Burns: 147TR, Simon Care: 122B, Val Carman: 121TL, 121BL, 121BR, Alan Casey: 9, Shirley Collins: 25T, John Crane: 75T, 91T, Janet Dashwood: 55T, Tony Day: 122T, John Dowell: 119TR, Mick Duff: 207T, 207BR, 210B, 211BL, Festival Archives: 15, 16T, 78, 82B,

87BL, 88B, 104TL, 106, 115T, 118T, 123B, 124TL, 124TM, 125TL, 125TR, 125BR, 126BL, 128T, 130T, 130B, 131T, 134B, 135TR, 135BL, 141BR, 142T, 147TL, 167T, 177B, 178B, 180B, 182BL, 182BR, 185B, 186B, 187BR, 190, 200TL, 201B, Harold Fish: 64T, George Frampton: 117TM, Alan Gentle: 41-70 (*except* 42, 54, 55T, 56B, 57T, 61, 62, 63B, 64, 66, 68T, 68M, 69B), Great Western Morris: 109T, Shirley Harry: 138, 139, 140BR, Bob Hawkes: 104B, Bernadette Hayes: 179T, Ron Hill: 160, 170TR, 173T, 178TL, 178TR, 179BR, 182T, 183TL, 183TR, 184T, 185T, 187BL, 188BL, 189, 191, 192, 193TL, 194, 195TL, 196T, 197B, 198BR, 199, 200TR, 200B, 201M, 202B, 209T, 210T, Andrea Holland: 206TL, Tom Howard 7, Maggie Hunt: 158TR, 180T, 183B, Paul Hutchinson: 105B, Roger Jackson: 119TL, 120T, Kasava: 120B, Yolande Kortlever: 145, 146T, 146BL, 155BR, 188TR, 211TL, 211TR, Jason Locke: 181B, Roger Marriott: 14, 28B, Mel McClellan: 141BL, 146BR, Lisa McDermott: 173BR, 174, 175, 176B, 181T, Mary Meeks: 61T, Sheila Miller: 133TL, 151T, 153BR, 155BL, 167BR, Bob Naylor: 75M, 75B, 79B, 100T, 103B, Anny Northcote: 136, Paddy O'Biernes: 72T, 73T, 83T, 83B, 85B, 92BR, Bergen O'Brien: 188TL , Dave Peabody: 171B, Miss Poyton: 62T, 76, 77T, 84T, 90T, 114B, Gordon Read: 12, 16B - 40 (*except* 23T, 25, 26, 28B, 37), Derek Reid: 168B, 170BR, Mike Roberts: 177T, Megan Rose: 64B, Doc Rowe: 126BR, 128M, 128B, 132, 167BL, Peter Rushby: 56B, Terry Rutter: 23T, 54T, 71, 74L, 92BL, 107BL, 112B, Derek Schofield: 68T, 68M, 86T, 87BR, 88T, 90B, 105T, 108B, 110B, 111, 115B, 116T, 116BL, 129B, 143, 148TR, 149BR, 150, 151B, 152, 153TL, 153TR, 153BL, 154T, 156T, 156BL, 157, 158TL, 159, 161TL, 161TR, 162, 163, 165T, 166T, 171T, 172TL, 187T, 188BR, 195B, 196BL, 196BR, 197T, 198BL, 201T, 203B, 204B, 206TR, 206B, 207BL, 209BL, 211BR, 213, 214TL, 214BL, 214BR, 215, 216, Kevin Sheils: 193TR, Sidmouth Herald: 61B, 62B, 63B, 74R, 78BL, 84B, 85T, 89B, 90M, 91B, 92T, 93, 94, 95, 96, 97, 98, 99, 100B, 102, 104TR, 107BR, 108T, 109B, 110T, 112T, 118B, 125BL, 127, 129T, 135TL, 140T, 140BL, 148TL, 148B, 156BR, 161TM, Greg Smallbone: 205T, Bryan Smith: 66, Rosemary Sowden: 54B, Dick Stanger: 78BR, 121TR, Jenny Stephenson: 57T, 73B, Sue Swift: 86B, 87T, 169, 170TL, Eddis Thomas (VWML): 25B, Peter Thomas: 69B, 72B, 79T, 101, Taffy Thomas: 133TL, Pippa Todd: 114T, Jean Turner: 134TL, Vaughan Williams Memorial Library of the EFDSS: 11, 13, Barbara Wearne: 209BR, Whapweasel: 205B, Christine Williams: 170BL, Aileen Wills: 14, Eric Winter archive (*fRoots*) 26BL, 26BR.

Index

220